1983

N

# DIRKSEN:
## Portrait of a Public Man

Books by Neil MacNeil

*Forge of Democracy: The House of Representatives*

*Dirksen: Portrait of a Public Man*

Neil MacNeil

# DIRKSEN:
## Portrait of a Public Man

The World Publishing Company

New York and Cleveland

Published by The World Publishing Company
2231 West 110th Street, Cleveland, Ohio 44102
Published simultaneously in Canada
by Nelson, Foster & Scott Ltd.
First Printing—1970
Copyright © 1970 by Neil MacNeil
Library of Congress Catalog Card Number: 79-112432
Printed in the United States of America

WORLD PUBLISHING
TIMES MIRROR

For Laurie

# Contents

Illustrations following page 178

# Preface

There is an ancient and kindly custom among publishers to allow an author a few words to explain, if he can, why he wrote his book and to thank those who helped him in the task. Thus at the start an author is offered the chance to have his say and to repay in small measure his benefactors. In this kindliness by the publishers, there is at least a subtle suggestion that the author show the good grace thereafter to intrude as little as possible on the reader's attention. I have tried to stay out of sight in the pages that follow these. Wherever possible, I have tried to let Senator Dirksen speak for himself, never forgetting, however, the conscientious writer's responsibility to act as an impartial judge between fact and fiction, between reality and rationale.

As a Congressional correspondent I had the opportunity to watch at first hand Everett Dirksen's career in the Senate from its start to its close. I met him first in 1951, shortly after he had first taken the oath as a senator. In his early years in the Senate I had only occasional professional dealings with him. Later, as he rose in the Senate's hierarchy, those dealings necessarily became more frequent, and for the final ten years of his life, when he operated as a commanding figure in the Senate, my professional interests in him were constant and uninterrupted. It was not possible in those years to write intelligently about the Senate without an intimate knowledge of Dirksen's daily activities. In those years I enjoyed a confidential relationship with Senator Dirksen that provided whatever insights into his mind, motives, and methods are reflected in this biography of his political and legislative life.

For several years I considered writing this biography. Dirksen seemed an obvious subject for such a work. Not only was he a man of great national importance, but he was as well a man of fascinating, even intriguing, personality. I had known him well for many years, and I had collected in my own files substantial amounts of material about him and the Senate. In 1966 I resolved to undertake this work, and I so informed Dirksen, asking him then to take time when he could to answer my questions about himself and his career. He agreed to do so, without conditions; and in the years that followed, he often did take time from his always crowded schedule to answer those questions. These private meetings were, of course, in addition to the frequent interviews that, as a working journalist, I had with him on questions and controversies of the moment. In our private meetings Dirksen consistently followed a totally correct professional course. He never once in any way inquired about this book nor about its thrust or direction. He seemed, indeed, to have a genuine desire to have the story of his life told whole—warts and all. On numerous occasions he volunteered information otherwise unavailable about himself and his maneuvers that plainly could be used against him. He did so in the knowledge that I would print this information, but also, I assume, with the presumption that this information would be part of a larger whole. To a striking degree, Dirksen knew his own virtues and faults, his strengths and his weaknesses; and in these final years of his life he had reached a point of inner repose that allowed him to discuss them with candor and almost clinical detachment. He wanted to be shown as he really was.

For a biographer, then, Senator Dirksen proved an almost ideal subject. His very willingness to be interrogated and to respond as meaningfully as he could, inside his own understanding of himself, offered an opportunity rarely available to a writer to describe a fellow man, especially one so engaged in the great events of contemporary history. Whatever failures there are to portray him adequately in this book properly belong to me. When he died, he left me with no substantial question unanswered.

Beyond my debt to Senator Dirksen for his cooperation, I am indebted to Mrs. Dirksen, to Senator Dirksen's daughter, Joy Dirksen Baker, to his brother, Thomas Reed Dirksen, and to his son-in-law, Senator Howard Baker, Jr., of Tennessee, all of whom helped me in many ways. To Mrs. Glee Gomien, Senator Dirksen's personal secretary, I owe a special debt, for it was she who time after time so arranged the senator's schedule that I might spend uninterrupted time with him.

Many senators contributed to my understanding of Dirksen, none more than Mike Mansfield of Montana, the Democratic leader of the Senate. Other senators who were especially helpful included Thomas Kuchel of California, Thruston Morton of Kentucky, Roman Hruska of Nebraska, Paul H. Douglas of Illinois, Hugh Scott of Pennsylvania, Barry Goldwater of Arizona, Lyndon B. Johnson of Texas, Joseph Clark of Pennsylvania, Charles Mathias of Maryland, Philip Hart of Michigan, Robert Griffin of Michigan, and George Aiken of Vermont. Among the members of the House of Representatives who were especially helpful were Gerald R. Ford of Michigan, Leslie C. Arends, Sidney Yates, and Robert Michel of Illinois, Melvin Laird and John Byrnes of Wisconsin, Charles Halleck of Indiana, and Silvio Conte of Massachusetts. Others to whom I am grateful for help are Lawrence F. O'Brien, former Governor William

Scranton of Pennsylvania, Ray Bliss, and Mike Manatos. I have a special debt to Richard Hupman, Librarian of the Senate, who extended to me many courtesies.

I am indebted as well to Charles Ferris, Andrew Glass, Charles Clapp, Max Kampelman, William Perry, Frances Kelley, Albert Abrahams, D. B. Hardeman, Sayre Sheldon, Steven Horn, William Bates, Robert G. Baker, Duff Reed, Bernard Norwich, Oliver Dompierre, Bernard Yudain, Roger Mudd, Peter Lisagor, Keith Wheeler, Samuel Shaffer, Richard Clurman, Murray Gart, Hugh Sidey, Edwin Goodpaster, Hays Gorey, Frank Mason, Raymond Lahr, Leslie C. Whitten, John Steele, Clarence Mitchell, Jesse Birnbaum, Andrew Biemiller, and Audrey Kellison. For suggestions and advice I am particularly grateful to Robert Gutwillig and John Hawkins.

This book would not have been written without the encouragement and help of my wife.

NEIL MACNEIL

# DIRKSEN:
## Portrait of a Public Man

# Chapter 1

# The Professional

*I am not a moralist. I am a legislator.*

In off moments, Everett McKinley Dirksen of Illinois, for eleven years the Republican leader in the United States Senate, liked to claim that his finest achievements in Congress were the bills he prevented from being enacted into law. "One thing that will endure," he said in 1965 of his own career, "is that I have stopped unsound things from getting on the statute books." At his last news conference, on August 12, 1969, he made a similar argument in defending the slack legislative performance of Congress that year. "We haven't hurt the country one bit," Senator Dirksen said with a smile. He went on to cite what he called one of his favorite maxims of Edward Gibbon, the English historian: "Progress is made not by what goes on the statute books, but by what comes off."

If such an epigram were an adequate criterion by which to judge Dirksen's Congressional career, he would have to be put down as a failure in his chosen profession. What is more, throughout his long career in Congress he proved himself a deliberate delinquent to the spirit of that negative philosophy of legislative inaction. His years in Congress, sixteen in the House of Representatives and nineteen in the Senate, spanned the most creative legislative period in the history of the United States. Indeed, his legislative career began with the fabled "One Hundred Days" of the Seventy-third Congress in President Franklin Roosevelt's first administration, and before its close, his career included the extraordinary accomplishments of the Eighty-ninth Congress, which under the goading of President Lyndon Johnson all but wiped clean the Democratic legislative agenda. Only the laws enacted by the First Congress, in 1789 and 1790, which started the American government on its course, had a more profound effect on resolving what life would be in the United States. Through the extended period he served as a member of Congress, from 1933 to 1969, Dirksen did not confine himself to voting "no." Instinctively, he was not a "nay-sayer." He was not inherently an obstructionist.

Dirksen could not be understood without the realization that above all else he was a political activist. He had cold contempt for politicians who did not work. "You get an idea that you put a hundred dollars in the campaign hat during the election," he told one group, "and then there's nothing to be done but sit at the club, turn on the TV, and wait for the results." Dirksen could not be content with winning public office and then sitting back to enjoy its perquisites. He wanted action, and it was not just action for its own sake that he craved. He wanted important action, the stuff of history. He wanted nothing less than to run the American government, and it was the national government alone that attracted him. He had no desire for state or local office, and he never bothered to try to build a political machine of his own in his home state of Illinois.

As a politician, Dirksen ironically was fated to spend all but four brief years of his Congressional career as a member of the minority party. That automatically cast him into the ranks of the opposition. As such he was associated with men and a political party committed to blocking the legislation and programs of the majority party, the Democrats. Dirksen never treated the matter quite that neatly or simply, and it was not alone his activist impulses that encouraged him to take a different view. The Republican Party when Dirksen formally joined it was not what it was to become. In the 1920's it was the majority party, and it had been so with but few interruptions since the Civil War. Of the two major parties, the Republican was the party committed historically to centralized government, to federal action. The historic reversal of party roles, under way even as Dirksen first arrived in Washington, had its roots in the tremendous convulsions then shaking the American economy, the repudiation of the Republicans by the voters, and the altered sense of responsibility by the Democrats in this national crisis. These extraordinary events affected Dirksen intellectually and psychologically, as they did all American politicians, but they did not dampen his bent for action nor turn him away from the view that the legislative process was a strenuous and dynamic function of the federal government. "You can enact anything if you want to," he once said, "if there's a will and a determination." That was his real view, his instinctive view. All his life, Dirksen was an enthusiast. He took a buoyant, sanguine, optimistic view of life and politics, and he misspoke himself whenever he classed himself among those whose primary aim was to keep legislation off the statute books. His stated theory conflicted with his actual practice, and there could be no doubt how he would have acted had he ever led the Senate with a majority at his back.

Fated, as he was, to belong to the minority party, and therefore the opposition party, Dirksen all the same insisted upon taking a creative and activist's role in the legislative process. Unlike many of his Republican colleagues, he did not oppose President Roosevelt's New Deal program in the 1930's. On the contrary, he spoke and voted for many of those landmark bills. More than that, he early devised tactical ways to bring forward his own ideas on legislation and to force them on the attention of the majority party. Over all those long years of his minority status, no other member of the Republican Party could match Dirksen's astonishing list of legislative triumphs. By the very nature of partisan politics, no majority party ever willingly gave consideration to legislation introduced by members of the minority and opposition party. To suggest enacting such legislation, laboring under such sponsorship, would amount to a form of political heresy. As an instinctive legislative activist, however, Dirksen would not be denied by these traditional rules of the game. In his years in the House of Representatives, he perfected the technique of forcing votes on his own legislative proposals through the device of offering them as amendments to pending bills. Later, as a senator, he reached a political stature in Congress so great that he could command some of the most consequential legislation of his time. The civil-rights acts of the 1960's were his acts. He did more than sponsor them. He did more even than produce the necessary votes to enact them. He also did what few of his colleagues were capable of doing: he played the principal role in drafting their language, and thus he determined their exact legislative thrust and intent. Dirksen prided himself on his legislative craftsmanship. He was a professional legislator, and his business was writing laws.

His legislative prowess and parliamentary skills, however, were but one phase of the talents that produced his remarkable career. They were the result, in part, of his willingness to work beyond the point of physical exhaustion. A compulsive worker, he was normally at his legislative chores before dawn. He never seemed to tire of the tedium of studying committee hearings and reports. Even in his old age he worked without let, despite his failing health and vigor. "I guess I've got everything any seventy-year-old man has," he said in 1966, "except floating kidney and housemaid's knee, but you know it was Teddy Roosevelt who said most of the world's work is done by men who don't feel well." As a congressman, he early mastered the rules of the House of Representatives, and later, when he moved on to the Senate, he mastered the rules of that chamber too. He had the capacity in all his work to take infinite pains with details. He developed, for example, the professional politician's disarming knack of re-membering people's names, and he could startle a seeming stranger by greeting him cordially, calling him by his first name, and then reminding him where and when they had met years before. Even as the Senate's minority leader, Dirksen took the trouble each year to learn the names of the new group of Senate pages. His intimacy with the precedents and practices of Con-gress and his knowledge of the inmost details of pending ques-tions were tools to Dirksen, the professional legislator and poli-tician. He devised other tools also for his use, and these were such as to set him apart from all other politicians of his time.

By a variety of devices peculiarly his own, Dirksen contrived to look and act differently than other men. Part of this, plainly, was his inner yearning to be distinguishable from his fellows; part also was the calculated decision of a politician to make himself readily remembered by those who met him, saw him, or heard him. Many politicians have sought distinction with expensive, tailored clothes; Dirksen sought distinction by delib-erately cultivating a rumpled appearance. He liked to look like "just folks." He did not try to stand on his dignity. Rather, he made himself a cartoonist's delight by himself offering the sug-gestion that he be sketched as a ragamuffin or a melancholy, bedraggled clown. It was part of the image he wanted of himself. It amused him, for the real man behind that image was an earnest student and practitioner of government. The image he created for himself made him hard to forget. Even more distinctive than his baggy clothes, however, was his hair and the way he deliber-ately kept it. Dirksen every day made sure that his hair was not neatly combed. He kept it mussed. With quick fingering, he made sure that his hair stood awry, on end, and this tousled hair he regarded as his personal identification, a special badge of his own devising. It was once described by Richard Strout in *The*

*Christian Science Monitor* as resembling "the kelp of the Sargasso Sea." There was no question that it made Dirksen look unlike other men.

"Dirksen, just turned 71," *Newsweek* magazine reported in 1967, "is a rather noble old ruin—a Victorian relic with misty blue eyes, a tiara of gray-gold ringlets run amok, and the melancholy mien of a homeless basset hound."

For Dirksen, however, the real triumph of his uniqueness was his oratory. He practiced and perfected his rhetorical techniques as few before him. In his early years, he normally bellowed his speeches in a mongrel mix of grand opera and hog-calling. Over the years, however, he made refinements and improvements that gave him an extraordinary capacity to fascinate and delight his audiences. His voice became one of those most readily identifiable in the country, and he was asked periodically whether he used his high-blown rhetoric of the public stage in all conversation. "That would be a pretty pompous way to live," he once conceded. "You'd feel like every day you were reciting George Washington's farewell address." He developed what American audiences have always loved in their orators—not only a striking personality but also a gift for picturesque and striking language. He had quaint and even bizarre ways of pronouncing common words. For example, he pronounced "missile" as "mizz-el" and "Vietnam" as "Veet-nam." His studied mannerisms and eccentric vocabulary prompted one critic to describe him as "the last of the Fourth of July picnic orators" and another to say that "he was born with a golden thesaurus on his larynx." He liked to play games with verbal circumlocutions. He would not merely say that he would scold an erring colleague: "I shall invoke upon him every condign imprecation." He delighted in such unusual words as "baleful" and "felicitous." He was a natural talker who did his best on his feet, speaking free-style. His written speeches, like his other writing, tended to be drab, without the flair he usually gave his spoken word. "As senators know," he once said in debate, "I do not read a manuscript very well." He needed an audience before him to do his best, and he disliked the confining strictures of a written text. "I always temporize," he once said. "I love the diversions, the detours. Without notes you may digress. You may dart. And after you've taken an interrupter, you don't have to flounder around the piece of paper trying to find where the hell you were." His speeches were rambling and crowded with irrelevancies. "It is somewhat difficult," Senator Paul Douglas once said in responding to a Dirksen speech, "to reply to such a speech, which covers everything and touches nothing." Dirksen used to joke about his verbal meanderings. "I have a surprise for you," he told his Senate colleagues one day. "I shall depart from my usual custom and talk about the bill that is up for discussion today." His speeches did not usually read well, certainly not as well as when he spoke them, for his charm lay more in how he said things than in what he said. It was a point of pride with him that he kept neither a ghost writer nor a personal publicity agent on his staff. He had no use for either. On occasion, in an impassioned speech, he was known to persuade fellow senators to change their minds and their votes on a pending measure. This was the ultimate achievement. "I learned long ago," he once said, "that no souls are saved after the first twenty minutes." Normally, however, he was not trying to change minds and votes; he spoke for the sheer pleasure of beguiling an audience. He laced his speeches with jokes and anecdotes, and he had a special penchant for quoting Abraham Lincoln—"the distilled wisdom of Lincoln," he called these quotations—and familiar passages from the Bible. He had no qualms at all about repeating what he had already said in earlier speeches.

"He just loves to talk," his wife once said. "I don't pay any attention because I've heard it all before."

"Now, Toots," Dirksen said, in mock chagrin, "you *know* that's not true."

In the history of the Senate, many great orators have graced its chamber, none with greater reputations than Daniel Webster, John C. Calhoun, and Henry Clay. Their era has been called the Senate's Golden Age. For generations their names have been revered in the Senate: Webster, thundering his eloquence to save the Union; Calhoun, brilliant and humorless; Clay, charming and always engaging. Dirksen was indifferent to them; he studied their careers not at all for his own benefit. He took models closer at hand. One evening in Dirksen's backroom hideaway in the Capitol, over drinks, Dirksen was asked which senator, in the long reach of the Senate's history, did he admire most. "Pat Harrison," Dirksen replied instantly, referring to a now but dimly remembered senator from Mississippi who died in 1941. "I had great admiration of his ability to handle about anything." He paused a moment. "I had great admiration for Alben Barkley," he said, referring to the senator from Kentucky who became Vice-President in 1949. "He was well grounded. Bob Taft. . . . Harrison had a lot on the ball." Dirksen was pensive now, letting his memory roam. "Jay Ham Lewis," he said, naming a senator from Illinois who had died in 1939. "He had a facility with words. He was a good student. When the time came, on a dramatic subject, Jay could charm the Senate and the galleries, but when it came to the mechanics, he was completely lost." Again he paused. "I admired Bob La Follette," he started again. "I admired him for his guts and sometimes for the scornful way he looked at senators." Unconsciously, Dirksen was describing more of himself than he knew. He admired eloquence, but it was not enough, plainly, for a senator to be merely eloquent. He gave the palm to those senators who could get things done. More than this, each of the senators he named, he had himself known in their lives. He had reacted to them, indeed learned from them, because he had known them. The great senators of earlier American history, Webster, Clay, and Calhoun among them, were but impersonal names he knew from the pages of books. He might borrow their names or their eloquence, as the need of the moment arose, but in personal terms they and their struggles were largely meaningless to him. They were of the past, the distant past, and they had no immediate relevance to Dirksen's career in the Senate. Dirksen did have a sense of history, but it was the history every day unfolding in his own hands, the history in whose making he had a share.

Dirksen drew from the men he had known, and from far more senators and congressmen than those he then named, but he fashioned for himself from what he learned from them his own special style and methods as a legislator and politician. Those methods he devised were heavy with technical competence for the immediate business at hand, whether charming an audience or cajoling a colleague for a vote on a pending question. With his unique appearance and style, and with the flair he gave his words and acts, Dirksen in time made himself a rival in public notoriety even to the President. He was "a political original," as Peter Lisagor described him in *The Chicago Daily News*. There were no others like him. He was, indeed, totally distinct from other politicians. At one time there circulated around the Senate an apocryphal story that amusingly differentiated Dirksen's special style from that of two of his most prominent colleagues in the Senate. The story purported to give their reactions on learning that the mother of one of their colleagues had fallen and broken her hip: "Everett Dirksen grasped the senator's elbow and whispered that he would offer a prayer for her. Lyndon Johnson held both the senator's hands and offered to pay the hospital bill. Hubert Humphrey put his head on the man's shoulder and cried."

Dirksen had emotions like other men, but he liked to think that in public he could turn them on and off at will, that he could use them as rhetorical foils. A special feature in his repertoire, for example, was his contrived anger, which, on occasion, he would loose for purposes of his own. "I can glower at the Senate," he once said privately, describing this technique, "and then issue a broad grin or smile and let the incandescent anger go up in smoke. These mannerisms are just tools that you apply. Here you are discussing a given subject. You warm up to it. You brandish your fists in the air. You raise your voice to a high level. Somebody suddenly asks you to yield and throws a little barbed question at you. You brandish your arms. You give him a rugged answer. Then you smile." He was a master of such floor tactics. His control of his anger, however, was sometimes like the control of his tongue. "I dislike to speak ill of people," he once said, but sometimes he could not stop himself. He had a long and vindictive antagonism with his Illinois colleague in the Senate, Paul Douglas, and more than once their mutual taunts on the Senate floor brought real anger to the surface. "I know my facts," Dirksen snarled at Douglas in one such instance in Senate debate. "I do not have to sit at the feet of the learned professor from the University of Chicago in order to marshal my logic and my argument." Dirksen disliked revealing real anger in public. It was unprofessional. It was the telltale mark of an amateur.

He did manage to control his emotions to a remarkable degree. His face was as pliable to his purpose as his oratory. Now and again, however, his eyes would betray his studied control. He could not always hide his inner feelings, much as he tried, and his eyes then showed a sensitive nerve had been touched. Once, in a troubled time for him, when he was under assault even from his fellow Republican senators, he was asked at a news conference about a report that another senator, Roman Hruska of Nebraska, might challenge him for the party leadership. "I haven't heard anything about it," Dirksen answered quickly. From his initial surprise at the question, he recovered swiftly and smilingly with an easy, offhand reply. "We've got lots of good men," he said. "The woods are full of them. Whenever you get afraid of the competition, you have no business in this." He had not liked the question; the telltale excitement in his eyes showed that, but he controlled his words and his face with his best professional's skill so as not to acknowledge that he had been bothered by it.

Even in his storytelling, Dirksen took a somewhat mechanistic approach, and he told stories, as he often conceded, because of the calculated effect they had on his audiences. "There are few good storytellers, you know," he told one interviewer. "Most storytellers are too verbose. They're dabblers. They lose their audiences. A good story has a genuine biological effect. If you can get a good, sound belly laugh, it starts a blood surge. Your audience might have been tired; its attention was wandering. You come up with a good story, and they are back with you. You have to keep stimulating the audience." From his own experience he had found that audiences, normally looking up at the speaker, tended to get drowsy as a result. He interjected anecdotes and jokes into his speeches to keep them awake and attentive.

Dirksen was a student of audiences, of their moods, of their biases, of their reactions. Each audience was different and had to be dealt with in a different way, and Dirksen took considerable pride in his ability to handle any crowd. Standing before a crowd, he groped to find the way to reach that audience, to capture and hold their attention, and it was this need more than any inability to write out a speech in advance that made him ill at ease reading a prepared text.

"What do you do when you face ten thousand people in a hall for one minute?" he once asked, by way of explaining this technique. "They're boisterous. They're noisy. Most chairmen don't know which way is up. They just rap the gavel, and the first thing you know you're on your feet looking at this mob. What are you going to do? Start in when they can't hear you? There's a strange psychology to it. It may take two minutes. What you are actually doing is staring down the audience. Suppose someone lets out a guffaw, and others join in. You've lost them."

Dirksen loved to tell of an incident when he was in Town Hall in New York City for a debate, and he peeked out from behind the stage curtain to take a look at the audience. He found the audience packed with maritime-union workers, and they were hostile to Dirksen's side of the debate. The union members spotted Dirksen, and they let out a roar of disapproval at him, taunting him with catcalls and boos. Dirksen stepped out on the stage, walked over to the microphone through the din of heckling, and tapped it to see if it was turned on. "I'm going to take care of you guys a little later on," he snarled into the microphone. Dirksen's crack and his brazenness in facing the jeering caught the fancy of the union workers. They burst into laughter and applause, and Dirksen had no further trouble that night.

"What does this all add up to if it isn't *command*?" Dirksen asked. "Is the audience running you, or are you running them? If you are going to be the master of the situation, first you've got to make them listen. Second, you've got to tell them what's on your heart—and make them listen. You have to command that audience, or they'll command you."

Like every man who has made Congress a career, Dirksen was tempered by the living of that life in Congress. He entered the House of Representatives young enough and resilient enough to adjust quickly to Congress and its ways. In time he was shaped and moulded by the traditions and manners and accommodations of Congress, by the common understanding and sense of things that Congressmen tend to share. Dirksen learned early that "compromise" was a word respected by his Congressional associates, and had been from the earliest days of the American republic. "If there were no compromise," Dirksen once said, "there might not have been a Constitution of the United States." Dirksen never changed that view. "The longer one is identified with public life, especially at the national level," he said, "the more one is persuaded, as an ancient philosopher said, that politics is the art of the possible."

Dirksen brought with him to Washington a primitive pragmatism that made his adjustment to Congress that much easier, and from the start he had as well a nondoctrinaire view of public affairs that was equally helpful. Many of the members of Congress have always been lawyers, and Congressmen have long tended to take a lawyer's view of controversy: they act on behalf of their clients, the constituents who elected them, but they do not regard their political opponents as their personal enemies. Dirksen had in his papers a letter he received from former President Harry S Truman, of which he was proud. "I may have thrown a couple of political bricks at you since you came to the Senate," Truman wrote to him, "but, fortunately, we can disagree on policy and still always be personal friends." Dirksen had no difficulty adopting himself to this professional's attitude, for he was a big, friendly, gregarious man with an open manner that he never lost. He accepted readily enough the live-and-let-live philosophy that motivated most Congressmen in their relationships with each other. There was something more to this than merely an amoral indifference to ethical considerations. Rather, this was, at its best, a tolerance for the other fellow's views and a willingness to let those views be voiced and voted. It was, in fact, a recognition of the basic right of disagreement which lies at the core of a free society. To the outsider viewing Dirksen in his maturity, however, there was in this same Congressional attitude a tendency to softness and an urge to pliableness, in moralistic terms, that was not commendable. This was an age-old problem for Congressmen. Dirksen from his earliest years as a working politician had an intuition for the flexible response. Congress enhanced that tendency, and Dirksen in his age found himself denounced because of it. It was taken as a demonstration that he lacked principles and a proper sense of political morality. "They say I am a chameleon," he himself said. It was true that he normally eschewed the doctrinaire, but he regarded this as a virtue, not a vice. His operating principle, other than his flexibility, was his pragmatism. He did not believe in trying to make the facts fit a theory. "You just can't rebut a fact," he once said.

His pragmatism took many forms. "I always think of the practical terms and the practical frame in which you have got to work," he said. Sometimes he liked to boast that he was indeed prepared to die for an idea: "I will die in the cause, if need be." Then, perhaps on second thought, he would concede: "I never feel so deeply about a thing that I am unable to be persuaded to change course." He was, in fact, far more committed to the idea of compromise as a good in itself than to any other basic political principle; it was the principle that made Congress a viable political institution. "You always try," he said. "Out of reasonable discussion by reasonable people, there might be worked out something that would be acceptable to reasonable people."

He could be intractable, as he was in the struggle to undo the decisions of the Supreme Court on apportionment and in filibustering the proposed repeal of the "right-to-work" section of the Taft-Hartley labor law. "I am just going to put up my dukes and fight," he said. These, however, were special exceptions to his normal operating rule of trying to work inside the system to arrange middle-ground solutions where possible. As a party leader, he was willing to fight if necessary, especially on the important partisan issues, and in any parliamentary struggle Dirksen could be a resourceful and dangerous opponent. "The problem always is to marshal your forces," he once explained. In matters of protecting the prerogatives of his home state of Illinois, he could be harsh and abrasive. Once there was an effort afoot in the Senate to deny funds for a 375-million-dollar Atomic Energy Commission installation in Illinois unless Illinois changed its housing laws. "Is that the kind of blackmail we're going to have around here?" Dirksen asked. "Well, we'll find out." He threatened to cut off all similar funds to the other states. "What other retaliatory course is open to you?" Dirksen asked. "This fight is looming now. If that's the way it's got to be, that's the way it's got to be. If they don't put the money in the bill, that's where the fight begins." The Senate voted the funds for that Illinois project. Dirksen did not believe, however, in merely fighting for the sake of fighting. "I don't go around throwing rocks," he once said, "that may cause me difficulty later." He preferred to negotiate terms, if he could, and he was skillful at it. He was a rough negotiator, if one willing to compromise. "Suppose you forfeit all your leverage before you get what you have to get," he once argued. "You don't eat your cake till last." One reluctant admirer of his negotiating talents believed that Dirksen required "an element of deception" to make such political trading interesting and that he could not enjoy a negotiated deal unless he had "swindled someone in its production." Actually, in off-the-floor negotiations Dirksen tended to be so bluntly frank in stating his terms as to approach the brazen. Negotiations, of course, were a parliamentary necessity for any party leader; there was not time or energy to muster a party fight on every question that arose. "You don't resist everything," Dirksen said; "you have to be selective about it." Occasionally, he miscalculated. In one such instance in 1963, Dirksen decided to attack a minor but seemingly susceptible bill sponsored by the Kennedy administration. Belatedly Dirksen discovered that he had no chance of defeating it. He hastily backed away and let the bill pass without challenge. "I'd have been licked on it," he said at the time. "The prudent thing to do was not to have a vote." Normally, before he acted, Dirksen liked to scout the legislative terrain carefully to get the lie of the land. "You do not march down the road alone," he said. He had learned and relearned the familiar Congressional adage that no one ever won by losing. "That's the way you play around here," Dirksen said on the eve of one Senate struggle. "You try to assess the enemy's strength and tactics." Then he acted accordingly.

Dirksen's pragmatism was not of itself a form of cynicism, but he had in his makeup all the same a cynicism that often belied the sentimental chauvinisms of his public speech-making. In his years in politics, he had seen much, and not all of it was spiritually elevating. He had no illusions about realities. He knew the difference between public protestation and private motives. He tended to take a harsh view of his fellow man. This, for example, was his privately expressed opinion on how the United States should handle Latin America: "You'll never run it without an iron fist. There isn't any other way. You've got to find a guy who won't be too much of a burglar. Let him steal a little and share the rest with the people. That makes sense to me." Like other politicians, Dirksen was not given to self-analysis, not even in its less virulent forms. He was not tortured by self-doubt. He had, however, a rough working knowledge of the mechanics of psychology, and he used that knowledge like the other tools of his politician's trade. "I know," he said, "that you can attract flies if you put a little sugar on." He studied men. He appraised their motives. He examined their backgrounds, and he calculated their ambitions and goals. By so doing, he knew what moved them and how they could be reached. He wanted to get beneath the outward veneer they presented to the world. He wanted to get behind the masks they wore. He made mistakes in this, as in other things, but his skill in this delicate art was the secret of his persuasive powers in the cloakrooms and private offices of the Senate.

Once, at a committee meeting, Senator Thomas Dodd of Connecticut voted the opposite way he had pledged in advance to Dirksen that he would vote. Dirksen suspected the reason, that President Johnson had telephoned Dodd. "You're a fine guy!" Dirksen taunted Dodd as they left the committee room together. "What do you do?" Dodd replied. "You're working a long time to get your law partner on the federal bench, and then you get a call: 'You better get in line or that partner of yours is never going on the federal bench.'" Dirksen was amused, not annoyed. It was all part of the game of politics, and he had had such patronage struggles himself. He was himself not the least abashed at approaching a fellow senator and asking him to change his vote. "I do not get conscience-stricken then," he once said, "if I ask whether it would be possible for him to change his vote, but I try to be circumspect about it and never offensive." All the same, he could be quite blunt, and occasionally this crept into even his public statements. "Maybe I can find comfort," he said at a news conference, "in the fact that you have to be a pretty strong bastard to take the slings and arrows." He thought a moment. "Strike the word 'bastard,'" he said. In private negotiation and confrontation, he preferred straightforward candor to pretense. "There's no guile about that fellow," he once said of a fellow senator, Wayne Morse of Oregon, in genuine admiration. At the time, he and Morse were locked in a struggle over a bill on the Senate floor, and neither was sure of winning. Both sides were delaying the vote, trying to bring in the absentees. Morse approached Dirksen. "You know what we're doing," he said to Dirksen.

"Sure I know," Dirksen laughed. "You're on the telephone. Open confession in open places is good for the soul. We're stalling a little too. It's a double stall."

Dirksen approached the crises and confrontations of his own political career in much the same pragmatic manner that he used on less immediate questions, and his pragmatism in this was not unmixed with cynicism. There were times in his political career, as when he first maneuvered to win a seat in the Senate, that he compromised himself to an extent that went beyond even the usual Congressional tolerance. He was marked then, for that, by some of his colleagues as a self-serving politician overanxious for public office. He lost the respect of men who had earlier admired him. Such political expedience, however, was hardly unknown among politicians; indeed, it was commonplace. John F. Kennedy radically changed course on farm policy when his ambition moved from the Senate to the White House. Lyndon Johnson had a wildly inconsistent record on civil rights. Richard Nixon reversed himself utterly on the Vietnam War. None of these men, however, had a reputation at large for political fickleness comparable to that of Dirksen. Dirksen changed course more often, more publicly, and on more questions by far than they. More than once he seemed to follow the rule that the politician's first

responsibility was self-survival. Yet Dirksen did not yield automatically to public or private pressures. Notably in the field of
foreign affairs, but in other areas also, Dirksen at times openly
and courageously defied his Illinois constituents, risking their
retaliation for the stands he took. There were times when his
pragmatism, his cynicism, his flexibility, made him appear a
rank opportunist, but there were other times when he willingly
sacrificed himself for a greater cause than his own political
fortune. President Eisenhower was genuinely grateful to Dirksen
for his courageous help. President Kennedy found Dirksen difficult at times, but at others immensely useful. President Johnson
regarded Dirksen as nothing less than a patriot. President Nixon
knew that he could count on Dirksen's support for every one of
his domestic and foreign policies. Under the Democratic Presidents, Dirksen endured bitter criticism from his own rank-and-file
rather than let foreign policy become partisan and his own loyal
opposition degenerate into something blind, obstructionist, and
truculent. "I go on the theory that I must do what is good for the
country," he said. There were times when he did this at unques-
tioned political cost to himself.

Despite his instinct for pragmatism and the cynicism that went
with it, Dirksen often saw himself in the role of hero and patriot.
One of his favorite stories was about the Baron Rothschild, and
he told it from time to time as a way to explain himself and his
motives. "One man cannot save England," Rothschild was told
in the midst of an English crisis, by Dirksen's account. "No,"
said the baron, "but one man can try." Dirksen felt the emotionalism of that gallantry.

By his willingness to let himself be persuaded into new positions, by his flexibility, Dirksen constantly found himself explaining himself. Repeatedly, over the years, and often amusingly, he
tried to make clear why he was willing to change. Needless to say,
he eschewed the explanation of simple expediency. He argued
rather a philosophical thesis that the one primordial law of life

is change. He had a favorite story to illustrate his meaning. "Years ago," he said, "a professor who thought he had developed an uncontrovertible scientific premise submitted it to his faculty associates. Quickly they picked it apart. In agony he cried out, 'Is nothing eternal?' To this one of his associates replied, 'Nothing is eternal except change.' " That had nothing to do with Dirksen's reason for changing his views on a given piece of legislation, but that did not bother him. He argued the same theme more frequently this way: "Life is not a static thing. The only people who do not change their minds are incompetents in asylums, who can't, and those in cemeteries." There were other versions, too. "I'm a mortal person who makes a mistake, and then, when I discover my mistake, I freely confess that I have fallen into the path of error. . . . Open confession is good for the soul." At another time, he put it this way: "Pray God the time will never come when, under given circumstances, I won't change my mind, for otherwise I'd have to confess to you that I'm a chained stand-patter and that nothing can get me off the rock." His flexibility and his explanations for it became in time a cause for considerable merriment among his Senate colleagues. Once in the course of a Senate debate, Senator Richard Russell of Georgia yielded the floor to Dirksen to concede an error. "Yes," Dirksen said, "I am mistaken. I will confess my sins in public any old time." Senator Russell interrupted him. "Mr. President," Russell said, "I refuse to yield for that long a time, at any time." In Senate circles, Russell's retort was regarded as a witticism of unusual merit.

Dirksen liked to speak in terms of simplicities and truisms, but he was a subtle, complex, and sophisticated man difficult to fathom. When he first arrived in Congress, he was naïvely and intensely ambitious to be President. He saw no real reason why he, by dint of hard work and persistence, should not attain that ultimate and obvious goal. Later, as his experience deepened, and as he learned the complexities and inequities of American political life, he saw other routes to notoriety and power, although he abandoned his quest for national office only reluctantly and with bitterness. At the end, with power won and ambition slaked, he played the game of politics for the zest of the game itself, for its fascination, for its exhilaration, for the sense it gave him of being intensely alive and active in the decision-making processes of history itself. He had become by then so consummate an actor, so much of him was so carefully contrived, that there were doubts even among those who knew him intimately about what of him was real and what artificial. The stage he acted on, no doubt, was reality itself, and he had the remarkable experience of playing on that stage a role of his own composition. For him, in his years of power and national influence, each day was sufficient unto itself. There was an immediacy to his mind and thinking that dismissed the past and let tomorrow take care of itself. He did not bother to doctor his Senate speeches before they appeared in the permanent version of the *Congressional Record*, and his indifference to those past performances revealed more of his mind than confidence in his capacity to parse a sentence on his feet. In this, he had a cool contempt for those of his Senate colleagues who could not speak extemporaneously without committing clumsy verbal gaucheries and who therefore rewrote their spoken words for the *Congressional Record*. "Congress," he said once in debate, "is really the home of the split infinitive, where it finds its finest fruition. This is the place where the dangling participle is certainly nourished. This is the home of the broken sentence." He let his own speeches stand as he spoke them; they were of yesterday. He accepted life as he found it, and like most American politicians, he had no one to bequeath him a political legacy. He wrenched from the system what he got, and because of that he believed that the system itself was sound. He lived by his wits and his nerve. Like a troubadour out of the Middle Ages, he sang for his supper or he got none.

Dirksen loved the theatrics of politics—the speech-making, the ceremonials, the formalities—and he clowned or pranced or strode through them as the mood struck him. As he rose to his feet on the Senate floor, his chin stuck out, and assumed his characteristic half-slouch to address the chair, there was to him satisfaction in the knowledge that above, in the press gallery, an aide was shouting to the reporters: "Dirksen's up!" As he perched on a table in that press gallery, bumming cigarettes from the reporters and fielding their questions with jokes and political confidences, there was satisfaction too. More than the theatrics, however, Dirksen loved the collisions of politics: the showdowns on the Senate floor, the deadlocks in committee, the back-room negotiations with the cigarette and cigar smoke thick and the whiskey pouring. He loved the wheeling and dealing, the bargaining and bluffing, out of which the decisions were made. There was a breezy, whimsical informality to Dirksen. His friends called him "Ev" spontaneously, and it never seemed amiss. His telephone, number 3135 on the Capitol switchboard, was constantly jangling, and Dirksen liked it that way, especially when the call came from the President or a member of the President's cabinet anxious for negotiation. "Can I come see you?" Attorney General Nicholas Katzenbach said in one such call. "I want to drink a little of your whiskey and talk to you." That was what Dirksen really loved.

He came to Washington first with a genuine and generous desire to serve his country, and he never lost that feeling for the place. He said it many times and in many ways. "I am just a humble citizen trying to do my duty," he put it once, in his best mock-humility. "I am prepared," he said another time, this in heroic fustian, "to stay at my post and discharge my duty as a United States senator." He wanted to be part of it; he wanted to have "some impact," as he said, "on the destiny of my country." He wanted to help shape the time in which he lived, and this he did. From the start, however, he was never free from criticism. "I saw no one bow down to the shrine of Dirksen," he once said. He was censured and condemned from many quarters.

"I don't care," he said. "I do what I have to do."

# Chapter 2

# Out of These Roots

*As a child, I learned not to put my hand on a hot stove.*

When Everett McKinley Dirksen first came to Washington in 1933 and took up residence in a downtown hotel, he was, at thirty-seven, one of the youngest members of Congress. He was a man tempered by his own experience and background, by his family and his schooling, by his home in downstate Illinois and the kind of life that the people there lived. He had been born on January 4, 1896, at Pekin, a town on the east bank of the Illinois River, and he lived there still. The town had been a haven for immigrants in the decades after the Civil War; Dirksen's parents had come there with a colony of their German countrymen in the 1870's. Steamboats had long plied the river, and they brought a more diverse economy and society to Pekin than other heartland America towns would know. There was small industry in Pekin, a few coal mines, a distillery, a wagon factory, and the waterfront shops that catered to the river traffic. Yet Pekin at heart was a farming town, with frame houses along streets lined with maple trees. The corn crop and the price of hogs had more bearing on the well-being and happiness of the townspeople than anything the steamboats might bring. The people were frugal, industrious, intensely patriotic, and Republican.

The town of Pekin, curiously, had a mock tradition of Oriental-ism, contrived from the way the town got its name. Originally the settlers called it Townsite, for no better reason than that was where they decided to build the town. Some years later, according to the local folklore, the inhabitants decided they needed a more appropriate name for their town, but they quarrelled over what the name should be. Unable to resolve the controversy amicably, they agreed to let the town be named by the wife of an Army major then stationed there. The major's wife took a map of the world, calculated that the town was located between the 40th and 41st parallels, and then followed that line around the world until she struck the name of Peking, China, on the map. She named the town Pekin, and its Oriental origin had an effect ever after, for the townspeople liked to give an artificial Chinese cast to their ceremonials and community affairs. They called the town on such occasions "Pekin, the celestial city," and in later years the members of the high-school football team were nicknamed "The Chinks." In town parades, the flamboyant effigy of a Chinese dragon normally received a place of honor.

The synthetic Orientalism of the town's ceremonials scarcely disguised the reality of life in Pekin in the years when Dirksen was growing to manhood. The people were Midwest Republicans, but there was a special temper to the town's Republicanism, for this was Lincoln country. Pekin was the seat of Tazewell County, and as such the site of the county courthouse. It was a town known to Abraham Lincoln for just about all the years of his adult life. He had stopped overnight at Pekin as early as 1832 on his way home to New Salem from the Black Hawk War. Year after year, spring and fall, Lincoln had come back to Pekin as a lawyer for the sessions of the Tazewell circuit court, staying a week or two on each visit. As a delegate in the Illinois state legislature Lincoln had sponsored the bill that built the state road from Peoria to Pekin. When Lincoln became a member of Congress in 1847, this town was part of his Congressional district. Indeed, it was at a party convention in Pekin that Lincoln struck the bargain with his political rivals, the so-called "Pekin agreement," that gave him the nomination to Congress. A decade after his single term in Congress, when Lincoln debated Stephen A. Douglas for a seat in the United States Senate, he made one of his principal campaign speeches in Pekin. This was a place where Lincoln had had many friends, and when Dirksen was a boy there were men and women in this town who had known Lincoln in his life, and known him well.

That fact pervaded life in Pekin. It was as much a part of the tradition of Pekin as the reading of the Declaration of Independence on the Fourth of July, and Dirksen grew up with it. Throughout his life Dirksen would carry an enduring image of Lincoln in his mind and emotions: Lincoln, the Emancipator; Lincoln, the Storyteller; Lincoln, the Martyr. Growing up here little more than thirty years after Lincoln's death, Dirksen had inbred in him the idea that Lincoln was the great man of American history, the man who saved the Union and freed the slaves. There was in this a reverential quality of almost religious intensity, a compelling emotion that at times could reach sentimental heights of cloying proportions. Dirksen was inflamed to personal ambition by the knowledge of Lincoln's humble origins in nearby New Salem. He was haunted by Lincoln's career of greatness and by Lincoln's melancholy words. For years Dirksen nursed the belief that he might well parallel Lincoln's career, even to the Presidency, and he liked as a man to describe his youth in the words that Lincoln used to describe his own: "the short and simple annals of the poor."

That the Dirksen family was as poor as the Lincoln family was a Dirksen sentimentality, although making ends meet in the Dirksen household was often a struggle. For young Dirksen, however, there was no log-cabin home, no studying by the light of an open fire. Dirksen's father, Johann Frederick Dirksen, was by trade a decorator of carriages and buggies at a local factory in Pekin, Smith's Wagon Works, and for his time he was moderately prosperous. He was a man of some standing in the community; at one time he was elected trustee of the Pekin school. With his long beard and full mustache, he had the distinction of looking remarkably like Charles Dickens, the English novelist then at the height of his popularity. Dirksen's father, who was born in 1842, had come to the United States from Ostfriesland in northern Germany. The Dirksen surname, however, was Danish, and the family took some pride that one of their name had been a general in the Danish Army. Dirksen's mother had also come from Ostfriesland, but she did not marry Johann Dirksen until some years later, when she was a widow with two young sons. She was forty-two years old when Dirksen was born; his father was not quite fifty-four. Dirksen's parents, of course, spoke English with a German accent, and at home they normally conversed in German of the unique dialect of Ostfriese. "You get it with your mother's milk," Dirksen said of this dialect, "or you don't get it." His mother was self-reliant and intensely religious. With her hands she had helped build the Calvinist church at Pekin.

Dirksen's father, like his neighbors, was an unadorned Republican, instinctively, inherently, unquestioningly, and he demonstrated his party affiliation with the names he gave his three sons. Dirksen he gave the middle name McKinley, for the Republican Governor of Ohio soon to be elected President. Dirksen's twin he named for the Republican Speaker of the United States House of Representatives, Thomas Reed. Their brother, two years older than the twins, he named for the last Republican President, Benjamin Harrison. The three brothers were labeled for life as Republicans. Theirs was a Republican home, and for Dirksen, his commitment to Republicanism was emotional, sentimental, irrational, like his sense of the meaningfulness of Lincoln; it was not predicated on intellectual postures or reasoned logic.

The Dirksens lived in an old farmhouse at the edge of town on a plot of land that measured about an acre and a half. The house was pleasant in summer, but in the winter it was not proof against the cold. There was, of course, no central heating, and always there was need for caulking somewhere against the chill. What light they had was by kerosene lamp. They kept four cows, a half-dozen hogs, chickens, a few ducks and geese, and fifteen stands of bees. They had a berry patch and a truck garden where they grew such vegetables and greens as lettuce, onions, and turnips. With the father working, they made out comfortably enough, but when Dirksen was five, his father suffered a paralyzing stroke. He lived on for another four years, needing to be dressed and fed. He died April 15, 1905. Dirksen's mother had to become the family provider. She took in washing and sewing, and she put her young sons to work to help out too. They did the chores. "We had to do more work than other boys did," Thomas Dirksen said, "because Dad died." Dirksen got up before dawn; all his life he was to be an early riser. He milked the cows and delivered the milk to neighbor customers before he went to school. He was paid five cents a quart. He hoed the weeds and tended the chickens. He sold eggs and vegetables to the neighbors too. He and his brothers went to school in overalls. "We could not afford anything better." Later, in high school, he clerked in a grocery store after school and on Saturdays.

"There was a certain ruggedness about life," Dirksen recalled of his youth, "and a certain ruggedness in living that life."

Like the houses of their neighbors, the Dirksens' home had its parlor, and, like theirs, it was used only on Sunday. On the parlor floor lay a Brussels rug, then the height of mid-America fashion, and there were kept the pictures of the relatives. Against the wall stood a horsehair sofa, and in the middle of the room was a marble-top table.

"And on top of that table," Dirksen recalled, years later, "was The Big Book, and you opened The Big Book in those days."

Indeed, in the Dirksen household religion was a major preoccupation. Dirksen was an unusually devout boy, tutored thus by his mother. Sundays he spent almost entirely in religious activities. In the morning he attended church services. In the afternoon there was Sunday school, in the early evening the young people's Christian Endeavor, and finally, at night, another church service. Dirksen sang in the choir. In later years he credited this hymn-singing for providing him with the voice training (it was all the real training he felt he ever got) on which he based his oratorical powers. The secret, he discovered, was to sing or speak off the diaphragm, not the vocal cords, and it was in the church that Dirksen learned the trick. For several years Dirksen was elected president of the Christian Endeavor. This was a post the other youngsters shunned. "They had difficulty getting someone to take it," Dirksen said in later years. Dirksen had deep religious sensibilities as a youth, and the minister of his church even had hopes for a while that eventually Dirksen might enter the clergy.

Dirksen was a somewhat prim, bookish boy who liked to stay around home near his widowed mother. At her pleadings, he did not swear like the other boys, and he minded his mother's scruples against reading such wicked books as *Dead-eye Dick* and the adventures of Jesse James.

Of course, it was not all praying and hymn-singing for Dirksen as a boy. He and his brothers played games like "Stink base," "Run, sheep, run," and "Duck on the stump." They played marbles, too, and they had special fun in climbing trees. "You could climb up one tree," Dirksen's brother Thomas recalled, "and go all the way around the block without touching the ground, climbing from tree to tree." Dirksen liked to go fishing in the river for crappies and perch, using a willow pole and a store-bought hook. He was not a hunter, for he disliked the idea of killing birds or animals. He was a husky boy, heavy-boned and strong. On the track team at high school Dirksen was a long-distance runner, and he played center on the high-school football team. The team's usual play from scrimmage was "the center rush," which Dirksen normally led. "It took rough shoulders," he said, "and a hard skull." Dirksen liked school, and he did well in his studies. He seemed to have a special aptitude for mathematics and chemistry, and he decided he would like to be a chemical engineer. In his class, he graduated first among the boys. That brought him selection as class salutatorian, and he delivered in high-blown language the class's greeting to the faculty. Even then Dirksen had a local reputation for "big-wordities," as his class book noted. He had been a member of the debating team, and he had argued such burning questions of the hour as: "Resolved: that the Philippines should be given their independence forthwith." He loved to read, and he would read whenever he had the chance. "There was Ev," one of his half-brothers said, "at five o'clock on a cold morning, in his nightshirt, just out of bed, in his bare feet, standing by the table reading his darn book. First he would hoist one foot up, to warm it against the other leg. Then he'd put that leg down, and hoist the other one up. Just like a rooster in the snow." Dirksen particularly liked the grandiloquent passages of Shakespeare and Sir Walter Scott. On rainy days Dirksen liked nothing better than to go out to the barn, hammer together a crude platform, and practice speech-making. "Preaching to himself," his brother Thomas said, "that's what he did."

Dirksen was the only one of his brothers to finish high school. His older brother, Ben, dropped out after the seventh grade; his twin brother, Tom, after the sixth. "We foolishly thought it was more important to smoke corncob pipes and carry dinner buckets," Ben said. Dirksen thought of going to the University of Illinois, but he had no way to pay his way. So, at seventeen, he went to work at a corn-refining company in Pekin, one that produced starch, glucose, and feed. He worked an average of twelve hours a day, six days a week, and he was paid fifty-five dollars a month. "I felt I was in clover," he said. His salary he gave to his mother, and she gave him an allowance. At first he picked out samples for quality-control tests; later, under the exaggerated title of "assistant chemist," he worked in the laboratory, washing the test tubes and conducting a few of the simpler tests. "What I knew about chem-

istry," he said years later, "you could put in your eye." At the end
of a year Dirksen was entitled to a two-week vacation, without pay,
and he went to visit a half-brother in Minneapolis. There he
discovered the University of Minnesota, and he found that he could
afford to go there, for the city had many job opportunities.

Dirksen's mother approved his idea, and he matriculated at the
university in the fall of 1914. He paid his way at first with a night
job at *The Minneapolis Tribune*, taking classified ads. He was
paid thirty dollars a month. Later he worked as a rate adjuster for
a shipping firm. He tried selling magazine subscriptions. In the
summer of 1915 he canvassed the farmlands of South Dakota,
sleeping at night in the haylofts of barns and by day trying to
peddle a home-remedy book for farmers and their animals. Among
other benefits, the book had sure cures for lumpjaw, scabies, and
stringhalt, by Dirksen's telling, but the farmers were wary. Another
salesman had preceded him through this territory, ostensibly selling maps, but the farmers who signed with him belatedly discovered that they had bought rather expensive lightning rods. That did
not improve Dirksen's chances with his home-remedy book.

At the University of Minnesota Dirksen turned to law. He had
had enough of chemistry at the corn-refining plant at Pekin. He
joined the literary society, and he joined the cadet corps. "Maybe,"
he said, "I liked to strut around in a uniform." At the university
he discovered politics. There was a political organization on
campus, and he got active as well in party affairs in the city,
making speeches at their meetings. In 1916 he threw himself into
the local effort by the Republicans to elect Charles Evans Hughes
as President. At one rally Dirksen was the chief speaker, and he
was proud to see his name printed on the handbills for the event.
His budding political career did not impress one particular law
professor. "Make up your mind," the professor warned him,
"whether you want to be a lawyer or a politician."

When the United States went to war in April, 1917, Dirksen
enlisted. He was sent for basic training to an Army camp in Battle

Creek, Michigan, and then in January, 1918, he was shipped to France. There he spent several months at the artillery school at Saumur, where he received a commission as a second lieutenant. Later he was assigned to the balloon service, a branch of the artillery, and he undertook further training. It was a ticklish job. He manned a tethered balloon some 3,500 feet over the ground, and from that perch he spotted targets for the artillery, observed and then corrected the firing. The balloons were tempting targets for the enemy; German fighter pilots fired tracer bullets at them in hopes of setting them ablaze. Dirksen had only a crude parachute and rudimentary instructions on how to fly the balloon should it cut loose from its mooring. Dirksen was lucky to escape unscathed after six weeks over the lines at St. Mihiel. After the armistice, Dirksen was assigned inside Germany with the censor's office. For almost a year he traveled around Europe on this assignment, visiting Italy, Belgium, Great Britain, Ireland, and Holland. Not until October, 1919, did he return to Pekin.

He was twenty-three years old and uncertain what to do. In the Army he had saved some thirty-five hundred dollars, but he decided against going back to college. His two brothers had opened a grocery store, and for a while Dirksen worked there, but waiting on customers and delivering the groceries offered him little incentive. Then he joined up with a local friend who had an idea that he could make and sell an electric washing machine. Dirksen invested what money he had in the venture. From the start there were problems. At first they could not obtain the component parts. Then hard times came to the farmers and there was little ready cash around Tazewell County to buy the newfangled washing machines. Dirksen sold out at a loss. Next he joined a dredging company, and he directed its operations for about four years. But that company was doomed: its equipment was wearing out and the company did not have adequate funds or financing to buy new machinery. Dirksen's brothers meanwhile had abandoned the grocery business and bought a wholesale bakery, and Dirksen went back to work with them. It was a family business, with everyone helping out. Dirksen took his turn baking the pies and kneading the bread, and he also drove the delivery truck to their retail outlets. He had to be at work every morning except Sunday by four o'clock. When he entered politics, the newspapers labeled him "The Baker Boy of Pekin." Dirksen did not mind a bit.

In these same years, when he was struggling to find success in business, Dirksen was also trying his hand at creative writing and theatrics. He had hopes, but he was less successful with his writing than in business. He wrote five full-length novels. He wrote short story after short story, perhaps one hundred in all. "I sent them out," he said, "and got back the rejection slips." His literary efforts were not, of course, a total loss. For one thing, he was learning how to handle language, how to create effects with words, how to manipulate an audience. In the literary world of the 1920's, it was a time of tough, lean, earthy prose, but Dirksen doggedly wrote what he knew and felt: heart-rending sentimentalities in highly stilted jargon. With one work he was successful. This was a play, written in collaboration with an old schoolmate, Hubert Ropp, for the local amateur theatrical group. It was called *Chinese Love*, inspired by Pekin's mock Oriental heritage. A Chicago publisher liked it well enough to print it and pay the young playwrights three hundred dollars for it.

The play, inevitably, told a melodramatic tale, that of a Chinese lover named Sing Loo finding, losing, and then finding again his true love, Pan Toy. The play was filled with such histrionic morsels as this from the mouth of Sing Loo: "My Cherry Blossom, look you yonder. The sun rises like a fiery ball to bathe the world in splendor. But one rival has he for splendor, and that is my Pan Toy." At Pekin, where it was played, it was a hit.

Dirksen wrote other plays for the Pekin players, but none of them found a publisher. Indeed, Dirksen was a leading figure in Pekin theatrical circles. He not only wrote some of the plays, he acted in more, and some he directed. Frequently Dirksen played the lead, and in one such role, in *The Slave with Two Faces*, Dirksen fairly shocked the staid and parochial town. He pranced on stage, mostly nude, wearing only socks and abbreviated shorts; his body was painted blue and gold. Dirksen later gave up any thoughts of a theatrical career at his mother's urgent pleading. He assumed she objected because of her religious scruples against the theater, but she may have been using other criteria.

Like other veterans of the war in Europe, Dirksen had joined the American Legion, and, as in so many things, he played an active role in its affairs. It was a natural habitat for him—the fellowship, the meetings, the sense of remembered patriotism. The Legion for him was his initial introduction to real politics. He rose quickly in the local hierarchy, and in time he was elected commander of his Legion district. He attended all the local functions and the ceremonies on Memorial Day, the Fourth of July, and Armistice Day. At some, he was the orator of the day.

In 1926 Dirksen made his first try at elective office. He ran in a nonpartisan election for membership on Pekin's Town Commission. There were forty-four candidates in the field, and the primary thinned them down to eight. In the general election in November, four of these were chosen to serve, and Dirksen led the field with the largest vote. He became Commissioner of Finance. He was a familiar man in town, known to all, of course, and he had won friends in all his various activities. Dirksen and his fellow commissioners had big plans for Pekin. "We set out to run that town," he said years later. "We were an aggressive council." The automobile was a reality now, and they wanted to pave the streets and enact zoning laws. That caused controversy, for the town's citizens at first were hostile to paying the additional taxes necessary for these luxuries. One case was carried all the way to the state supreme court. Dirksen and the other commissioners were aggressive and militant in carrying out what they felt were their duties. He had a zest for action. He saw no purpose to sitting idly in the job.

As a city commissioner and as a rising figure among the Legionnaires, Dirksen had ample opportunity to make speeches to his
townspeople at civic meetings. He cultivated them. He sought
them. He made speech-making a major concern. "The more I got
around," he said, "the more I was in demand." He would drive as
much as seventy-five or eighty miles to make a speech, even if it
meant he would not return home before midnight. Some years
before, Dirksen chanced to meet William Jennings Bryan, the
famed "Boy Orator of the Platte." Dirksen had won a local oratorical contest conducted by a national prohibition society, and he
had been sent to Lexington, Kentucky, for the national finals. There
he spotted Bryan, and he went up to him and asked him for advice
on making speeches. "Always speak to the folks in the back rows,
my boy," Bryan had told him, "and the rest will be sure to hear
you." Thus counselled, Dirksen developed a strident, booming outdoor voice, but he knew that there was more to oratory than that.
He tutored himself to think topically about his subjects and thereby
to discipline himself to speak without notes, relying on memory
and nerve. He made special preparations for his speeches, and he
tried to offer his listeners interesting information. Once, in a speech
long remembered, he addressed a hardware dealers' convention on
the history of tools. He taught himself Lincoln's trick of telling jokes
and anecdotes to make a point and to give life to his speeches.
Unlike Lincoln, who off the stump told earthy stories, Dirksen had
a natural distaste for off-color stories. He took pains to note down
those anecdotes he heard that were worth repeating. At times he
was making speeches as often as once a week, and all the time he
was perfecting his techniques. "These were the trial years," he said
years later. "I went around studying my techniques, I'd make a
sally and see what kind of a response it received. Then I'd try
another. I particularly watched the audiences. I learned how to
appraise an audience—whether it was hostile, friendly, or indifferent. The indifferent ones, they're the worst. I learned to make contact with an audience—because if you don't make contact, only a

little will be remembered and even less understood. I made a study of people, their attributes, and their foibles, what registered with them and what didn't." He had no desire to run for reelection to the Pekin city council, and to him state office had no appeal either. "I wanted to serve at the federal level," he said years later, "which I felt was the big show." He wanted to run for Congress.

What manner of man was this who at thirty-four set his goal at Congress? He was, of course, like every man a product of his own time and place, and in most aspects of his being he went with that grain, not against it. These made him, automatically, a Republican of the Midwest agrarian breed, with an unspecified romantic attachment to the idea of Abraham Lincoln and what he stood for, and with an instinct as well for the conservative side of things. He had spent the better part of two years in Europe, but that had been nothing more to him than an interlude, more akin through his soldiering to the patriotism of the American Legion brand than to any vague commitment to internationalism. He had come back to Pekin to live, and Pekin was isolated from the great world and its convulsions and crises. Dirksen liked it because of that, and in later years he gloried in its seclusion and presumed wholesomeness.

Indeed, with a nostalgia that went over the line of mawkishness, Dirksen in time came to romanticize these formative years of his, these years of his shaping and tempering. In memory, this was to him a kind of bucolic paradise. There was to him in this place something special, something inspiriting. He had the idea that Pekin and nearby Peoria and the rural world that encompassed them had to themselves an essential goodness and salubriousness hardly to be found elsewhere. The very lack of sophistication Dirksen idealized into what he took to be an almost uniquely beneficent way of life, untrammelled by cosmopolitan meanness and vulgarities. Time and again in his later years Dirksen harked back to that life and the people who lived it, and he found that life idealized perfectly in the

pastoral poem "The Deserted Village" by the Irish poet Oliver
Goldsmith. He never tired of reciting the opening lines of that
paean to rustic simplicity:

Sweet Auburn! loveliest village of the plain,
Where health and plenty cheer'd the labouring swain.

Dirksen felt a glow within him from these words. "I tasted of
that atmosphere," he said, "at a time when we knew no wickedness. . . ." He had been bred to the homely virtues by his family and
his neighbors: trustworthy, loyal, helpful, friendly, courteous, kind,
obedient, cheerful, thrifty, brave, clean, and reverent. That he lived
to these specifications in all their particulars, not even he would
claim, but they were the ideal, and they formed the basis for his
idealizing the life he and his friends lived in that river town. They
knew not wickedness in their memories of the place, but that such
was the reality of life in Pekin could hardly be believed. It was,
after all, a port of call for all the steamboats on the river, and their
rough crews frequented the bars and gambling dens of the waterfront. The county courthouse had a different clientele, not always
more elevated. They suggested a more worldly view of life creeping
tiptoe into the thinking of the young boys growing up in Pekin.

Dirksen himself could recall quite vividly many years later that at
least some of their neighbors were less than exemplars of his bucolic
ideals. There was a routine among the coal miners, for example,
when the brutalizing week's work was done. "They came home
Saturday night," Dirksen remembered, "and they'd get drunk as a
lord." Once in a while, in that condition, one or another of them
would run wild, seize a kitchen knife or other weapon, and send his
family scurrying for safety from his threats.

"I've seen mother go up to them," Dirksen recalled, "and say,
'Give me that knife and take yourself inside and go to bed.' She
had a way with her, and they would respond. She was a very
courageous woman. She had to be."

These were intrusions on the romantic wholesomeness of his

memories of the place, recalled only because they illustrated other virtues of his bringing-up, the quiet and undoubted courage of his widowed mother. Dirksen idealized his mother. "If ever there was a saint on earth," he said of her, "it was my mother." She had come to America on her own in 1874, speaking only German, and with a note pinned to her clothes to send her to Pekin. She buried two husbands, and she lost six children at birth or in early infancy. She raised her surviving sons with a fortitude that those sons had to cherish. She shaped and moulded Dirksen in many ways. "She was just so intensely practical in all things," he said. A devoutly religious woman, she tutored him to respect religion and its works. She encouraged and fostered his bent for education and study. An immensely practical woman, she taught him to make do with what was available to him. "She had a natural talent," Dirksen said, "for knowing the right thing to do in any circumstances." It was from her that Dirksen drew his first intimations of pragmatism, not in philosophic terms, but in terms of everyday living. "She was one of the hardest workers I've ever known, and the best manager," he said. "She left nothing undone." "She brought us through the lean years," Dirksen's brother Thomas said. Dirksen's mother it was who chose the family home, selected because its acreage offered them the chance to earn money by raising and selling vegetables and other foods. She bought a second house from savings and rented it to supplement their income. It was from his mother as well that Dirksen developed his own methodical ways. She was a methodical woman in her daily chores. "It gives you a certain stability of mind," Dirksen said of the methodical approach. "Don't dart into the middle of a thing; start at the beginning." A friendly, gregarious woman, she was among the first to come to the aid of a neighbor in trouble. An activist and doer, she taught her son the buoyant self-confidence he had from his earliest years. She taught him to save against the rainy day. "We are a rather frugal family," Dirksen said, "and we learned a long time ago to live within the family income. That's been the rule in our family as long as I can remember. It's been an instinct in the Dirksen family—to be thrifty. You always had a nest egg behind you." She symbolized for Dirksen always an American ideal: Mother. She died in 1923, when Dirksen was 27 years old.

Dirksen's attitudes toward much of the modern world stemmed from this idealization of his mother and of the family life he knew in Pekin. In his seventies, he still recalled with affection his grammar-school teachers, and one, his first-grade teacher, Miss Amelia Weimer, he remembered with special tenderness for her "sweetness, serenity, and patience." He had an abiding distaste for the salacious. Love in the Dirksen household was an embodiment of something noble, not a mere sexual impulse or craving as described so often in the outer world in song, novel, motion picture, and psychiatrist's text. For religious reasons, dancing had been proscribed in the Dirksen household, and Dirksen did not learn to dance until he was in college. His father, however, had been a robust bass, and he loved to sing the popular songs of his day, the lilting melodies with the saccharine rhymes. They set for Dirksen a pattern; he always preferred such romantic ballads as "After the Ball," and "My Reverie." The words of these tunes, rendered feelingly, plighted eternal troths and quickened the pulse with their unabashed sentimentalities. They were a far cry, as was Pekin itself, from the sophisticated outer world into which Dirksen was to move and act. Dirksen never quite attuned to the discord of that outer world. He lived to regret "the acceleration of today," as he put it, a clear contradiction to "the contemplation and the deliberation" of his youth and the time of his youth. To him the jarring tempo and jangling phrasing of modern jazz were as the braying of "a laughing jackass." The suggestiveness of sexuality in their lyrics was as foreign and tasteless.

For Dirksen, his youth and early manhood were often times of gangling awkwardness, with him reduced to timidity and confusion. "It may sound funny," he recalled many years later, "but I was a pretty shy fellow in those days. I was frightened to death to ask a girl for a date. You had to walk around the block a couple of times to get up the nerve." Later, as a working politician, and a brazen one at that, Dirksen liked to josh about the bashful courting of the country gallants. One of his favorite stories, which he retold endlessly over the years, was about a farmboy wooing his lady friend. They sat at opposite ends of the sofa in the parlor. "They sat there in silence for perhaps an hour," Dirksen would relate, "and finally he turned to her in mental desperation and said, 'Mary, how is your ma? Not that I give a dern, but just to make talk.' " It was the kind of story that country folk love, because they had lived it. Dirksen himself had lived it; as a young swell about Pekin, he was hardly a sophisticate. His mother had bred in him, with her strong religious feelings, a horror of the evils of alcohol. "In those days," he once said, "I thought the Demon Rum was deadlier than a gun." He met the girl he was to marry, Louella Carver, somewhat by chance. He and his fellow playwright, Hubert Ropp, spotted her on a downtown street in Pekin and decided instantly that she must play the lead in one of their plays. Before she could agree, however, they had to persuade her mother. Dirksen used to walk Louella home after rehearsals. He courted her at the soda fountain, plying her with banana splits and sarsaparilla. They were married in 1927 and they had one daughter, Danice Joy.

Dirksen's wife had clerked in a Pekin department store, and she had doubts about her husband's ambitions to make a career in politics. "I was the practical one," she recalled. "He was sure what he was going to do and how he was going to get there. I must confess I did not have enough faith. I'd seen a lot of people in politics come and go, so I kept prodding him to go on and get his law degree." She believed that was a more practical course than to depend on the whims of the voters. She kept the family books. "I'll try to make the money," Dirksen told her early in their marriage, "and I'll turn it over to you. If you want to save, fine, but if you want to spend, I'll go out and help you spend it."

Dirksen grew up in a world of neighborliness, Fourth of July patriotism, and good fellowship. The county fair was an annual event of more than passing interest. Preaching and political oratory were art forms that carried more than a message: they brought diversion and entertainment to the quiet lives of the citizenry. Dirksen was a joiner, and in time he belonged to many fraternal and civic organizations besides the American Legion. Among them were the Elks, the Loyal Order of Moose, the Veterans of Foreign Wars, the Eagles, the Masons, and the Eastern Star. Membership in such organizations provided the credentials of respectability and acceptance essential to a practicing politician in the Midwest. Off the social mores of his neighbors, Dirksen naturally was an optimist and a booster. He believed with unaffected confidence in the America he knew—free enterprise, capitalism, and individualism. His was not a philosophy that he consciously chose; it was simply a way of life he lived. He assumed that hard work and diligence would bring any man success, and he never shrank throughout his life from the drudgery of painstaking labor to achieve what he wanted. He accepted without question the distinctly American idea that every man was bounded only by the limits of his own energy and ambition. He and his fellows might flinch when they thought of the crabbed and stunted lives of the mass of men who lived in the crowded cities, but they were far off from Tazewell County.

Without embarrassment Dirksen voiced the idealism he found in the way of life he lived, but all the same he had a staunch commitment to hardheaded realism. The people he lived among were practical people who presupposed that a man had to earn his keep and be worth his hire. Dirksen as well had learned enough of the ways of the world in Pekin not to bark his shins unnecessarily in futile gestures and purposeless posing. He saw no essential contradiction in being both a realist and idealist. There were other logical incompatibilities in his mind that he held with equal impunity. All his life, for example, he would treat religion in one sense as though it were akin to, or even a branch of, American capitalism, as though Jesus Christ in the twentieth century might well have been a successful businessman with a talented sales staff in his employ. Dirksen mixed more than metaphor when he described the Apostle Paul this way: "Well, I thought he was the greatest sales manager that ever lived. No greater salesman ever was, because he sold the gospel. . . ."

To the intellectual or agnostic in Chicago or the East, Dirksen's approach to life might smack of a bumptious Babbitt. His ideas would offend the inner sensibilities of that outer world. He and his kind were foreign to cosmopolitan life, and proud of it. It was otherwise in Pekin and Tazewell County. There Dirksen was part of the way of living and believing, and he and his neighbors saw themselves as uniquely American, uncorrupted by those hostile ideologies festering in the alien cities. Dirksen had valid credentials for these people in downstate Illinois. He was one of them, and he did not forget that Abraham Lincoln had showed the way.

# Chapter 3

# The Apprentice

*When I got my first taste of Congress in 1933
and I was called Honorable, and invited to dinners
without having to pay for them, and people came saluting
me in my office, I thought, "This is for me."*

Dirksen himself admitted that when he first talked about running for Congress, his friends laughed at him. He laughed a bit himself, although he had the idea as early as his years at the University of Minnesota. "We used to sit around and swap yarns in the men's union," he said years later. "It was a general feeling; namely, if you want to go in for a political career, it certainly would not be state or local. It would be national." Dirksen confronted formidable obstacles. The Congressional district in which he lived, the Sixteenth Illinois, comprised six rural counties that had scarcely changed since the 1890's. Since World War I, the district had been comfortably Republican, returning party stalwarts to Congress year after year. The incumbent Congressman, William E. Hull of Peoria, had no desire to retire. Dirksen would have to defeat him in the party primary, not an easy task, but not impossible. Hull himself had won the Congressional seat eight years before, in 1922, by defeating the then incumbent, Clifford Ireland, for the Republican nomination. In the years since, Hull had worked hard to entrench himself in his Congressional district, and by Dirksen's calculations Hull had done that work well. Hull controlled the Republican party organization in the district, and he had the full support of the local newspapers. Hull was a businessman from Peoria and very rich; estimates of his wealth ran as high as thirty-four million dollars. He was president of a chemical company, and he had made a fortune as well with a company bottling rye whiskey. The report was that he was willing to spend his money to keep his seat in Congress. Dirksen had heard that at least one editor on a Peoria newspaper was on Hull's payroll. "The only weapons I had," Dirksen said, "were my voice and my energy. I went any place I could get a hearing." To finance his campaign, Dirksen borrowed eight hundred dollars. In all, Dirksen spent more than three thousand dollars on his campaign; he was told that Hull spent ninety thousand dollars.

Hull had vulnerable points. His record in Congress had been undistinguished. His main argument for reelection was his thus far abortive efforts to bring the Congressional district a federally funded deep waterway, an argument that Dirksen ridiculed on the grounds that downstate Illinois towns on the Illinois River could hardly be turned into ocean ports. In the House of Representatives, Hull had voted for the so-called "Life-for-a-pint" bill, a measure designed at harsh enforcement of the Eighteenth Amendment and Prohibition. Among Hull's whiskey-producing and whiskey-drinking constituents, his claim that he voted for it only as a device to compel the repeal of Prohibition did not scour. Dirksen was to make the most of it. There was another sensitive point for Hull, his age. In 1926, when he turned sixty, he discreetly stopped listing his birthday in the *Congressional Directory*. When Dirksen entered the party primary in 1930, he was thirty-four, a full generation younger than Congressman Hull.

If Hull had great wealth, control of the local party, and the favor of the newspaper publishers and editors, Dirksen had the American Legion, a growing political force in Illinois and the nation. At first, just back from Europe, Dirksen had been reluctant to join the American Legion. The Pekin unit was organized by men who used it, in effect, to hustle local merchants into buying tickets to their too frequent social affairs. "The wrong guys were in charge," Dirksen said. "They were running a sandbag operation. They were making money on a patriotic appeal." Later, however, Dirksen did join,* and he rose quickly in the Legion hierarchy. He joined the campaign to rid the local unit of the officers who were using the organization for their dubious money-raising schemes and neglecting to render any accounting of this money. "We just horsed those guys out," Dirksen said. Dirksen was chosen Legion commander for Tazewell County in 1924 and district commander in 1926. The Legion district was made up of the identical territory as the Sixteenth Congressional district; it comprised the same six counties. In the Legion district there were thirty-six separate local posts, potentially a formidable political base for an aspiring politician. Dirksen attended every Legion meeting that he could, paying special attention to the large post in the city of Peoria. "I naturally gravitated to the gang up in Peoria," Dirksen said. In a sense, as district commander, Dirksen had a constituency of his own, identical in its territorial boundaries to that of Congressman Hull. Indeed, Dirksen exploited a district-wide meeting of the Legion at Bloomington, Illinois, in late 1929 to announce his candidacy for Congress. He made the gesture the more dramatic by resigning his Legion office, as he was required to do under Legion rules. It was a clever tactic by Dirksen to get himself publicity from the hostile press, and the story even made page one in both newspapers in Peoria, despite their commitments to Hull.

Hull personally ignored Dirksen's campaign, although Dirksen time after time challenged him to come home from Washington and debate with him. He did not reply to Dirksen's telegrams.

* Ironically, Dirksen was persuaded to join the American Legion in 1922 by his friend Scott Lucas, a Democratic lawyer in Havana, Illinois. Later Lucas served in the U.S. House of Representatives, 1935–1939, and then in the U.S. Senate, 1939–1951. Dirksen entered the Senate by defeating Lucas in the 1950 election.

Hull knew better than to give his upstart challenger that kind of recognition. Hull, however, had his own advocates in the district, and one of these, a prominent Peoria attorney, made a canvass of the district, speaking on behalf of Hull. Dirksen drove himself relentlessly, speaking and hand-shaking wherever he could find voters. "He made every little mothers' club and church meeting," Mrs. Dirksen said. He had his own campaign slogan, the only one he ever used in his political career: "Hull, Hoey, and Horse Feathers!" In four months Dirksen estimated he lost thirty pounds. He bellowed his speeches, as Bryan had suggested, and he told amusing anecdotes and stories, mimicking Lincoln, every time he got the chance. They were homey things, these anecdotes, meant to tickle and flatter the audience and sometimes to underscore a point at issue. One of these stories Dirksen used to illustrate a confused and tangled situation. "It is a good deal," Dirksen said, "like the old fellow who asked his son if he was married, and the son said, 'What if I is and what if I ain't!' And the old gentleman said, 'I ain't asking you is you ain't. I'm asking you ain't you is?' " It was the sort of story that went over with "the folks."

Another story he told that amused his audiences was about "a Swedish friend of mine" attending a funeral. When the minister completed the eulogy, he asked whether anybody else would like to speak. There was an awkward pause. "My Swedish friend stood up," Dirksen related, "and said, 'If nobody has anything more to say about the deceased, I will say a few words about the income tax.' "

Dirksen's stories began to give effect to his campaigning, enough to cause some concern by Hull's supporters, and before one audience Hull's stand-in spokesman berated Dirksen as a mere storyteller, not fit to send to Congress. This was a mistake, and Dirksen quickly seized the opportunity it offered. He reminded the same crowd that this Congressional district had sent a storyteller to Congress once before, a fellow named Abraham Lincoln.

Dirksen's campaigning and his oratory, which he himself

described at the time as "a display of political pyrotechnics such as characterized the campaigns of other years," brought him into prominence throughout the district, but he lost the primary to Hull by 1,155 votes. At the last moment, Hull's supporters played a trick on Dirksen that he regarded as a "vile slander." The eastern portion of Bureau County, one of the six counties in the Congressional district, had a substantial number of Italian-American voters, and the night before election day Hull's people circulated there hand-bills purporting that Dirksen was a member of the Ku Klux Klan. "My friends saved copies for me," Dirksen said. "I had the evidence." He had no chance to deny the accusation, however, before the balloting, and he always figured that that hoax on the voters in Bureau County cost him that primary defeat. Dirksen was not discouraged. The morning after election day he was out early campaigning. He encountered a newspaperman who asked him what he was doing. "Campaigning," Dirksen said. "But the election is over," the newspaperman said. "And another campaign is just beginning," Dirksen said. He had resolved to go to Congress, come what may. "This time," he recounted, "I solemnly warned the voters that if they failed to nominate me this time, it would become necessary for me to reappear two years hence with the same request." He kept right on campaigning for the next party primary two years away. He went back to his job at the dough bench and driving the delivery truck of the family bakery. He had campaign debts to pay and a livelihood to earn for himself and his wife and daughter. He had come close, and Congressman Hull seemed in trouble. The national economy had been felled by the Great Depression, and Hull defeated his Democratic opponent in November, 1930, by fewer than four thousand votes. "Day in and day out," Dirksen described his renewed efforts, "I continued to meet the voters and address meetings." He continued to speak any place where he could get himself invited: luncheon clubs, Farm Bureau meetings, women's clubs, schools, fraternal lodges, churches. In the primary of 1932 he defeated Hull by 2,570 votes. He had made the first major step toward Congress, but by then the nomination seemed almost worthless. Well before the April primary, just about everyone had concluded that 1932 would be a year for a national Democratic landslide. "I set myself resolutely to the task of fashioning a political philosophy that would stand fire under the trying circumstances of the November campaign," he said. This Congressional district had not always been safely Republican. Back before World War I the district had been for a time Democratic. It would test Dirksen's ingenuity to get himself elected there as a Republican in 1932.

Surveying the delicately awkward political landscape, Dirksen realized that extraordinary methods would be needed to win. In later years Dirksen was to earn a reputation for political dexterity and flexibility almost unmatched in modern American politics, and in this 1932 campaign he demonstrated convincingly his suppleness and pliableness under pressure. With shrewd calculation Dirksen devised a campaign strategy to meet the unprecedented political situation. It was a strategy that raised in his own mind some doubts, as he noted at the time, "as to whether it was a sound and ethical course." He would not be bound, he decided, by the formalized strictures of party doctrine. He resolved to do or say nothing that might offend Democrats individually or collectively. He saw that he needed Democratic votes. He knew that he would only hurt himself by trying to defend the Republican Party and President Hoover. "What," he wrote shortly thereafter in an extraordinarily candid analysis of his own campaign, "could one say in behalf of Herbert Hoover and against Franklin D. Roosevelt that would have made any appreciable political effect? How could one successfully apologize for Republican leadership when the nation was bleeding from the wounds of the Depression?" Dirksen did not try. "I had no stomach for hurling real or fancied charges against the Democrats." With his Republican Party in desperate straits, this was no time for him to emphasize partisanship. Instead, he deliberately praised Democrats. He had only kind words for the Democratic candidate for governor of Illinois, a man Dirksen described in his speeches as

sional district, and Dirksen knew what that meant. The Republicans in November had managed to elect only 117 of the 435 members of the House of Representatives; they made up less than one-third of the House's membership. Dirksen understood, even as a freshman member, what that massive Democratic majority meant to him and his Republican colleagues. "Any member of the minority," he said at the time, "who essays to speak on any administration measure must feel a great deal like the fellow who was in jail and who, as he saw a buddy going along, called and said, 'Hey, partner, what time is it?' He said, 'What do you care? You are not going anywhere.' So we of the minority know that we are not going anywhere. . . ." Dirksen believed, however, that there was a role for him, and that hard work and persistence would find its reward. "What can a young, inexperienced Republican Congressman, divested of all patronage, do for his country and his district in the midst of a three-to-one Democratic majority?" he asked rhetorically. His role would be difficult, he knew, but not hopeless. Indeed, he had a sense that the hand of Providence might well be upon him. "The function of the minority party is, after all, in the salutary influence which it can exercise in resolutely opposing things which are fundamentally wrong and supporting these measures which are right," he wrote even before he took the oath of office. "Under such circumstances, opportunities for service are certain to arise. In 1846 when Polk was President, Illinois was represented in the House of Representatives by seven Democrats and one Republican. That lone Republican served only one term in Congress and yet that term produced an opportunity which elevated him to high station. He was Abraham Lincoln."*

Dirksen distorted the political events that swept Lincoln into the White House in a moment of national peril; Lincoln's election as President had little to do with his brief and almost unnoticed term in Congress. Dirksen, however, felt obsessed by the phenomenon

* Lincoln actually served in the House of Representatives from December, 1847, to March, 1849.

of Lincoln and his own parallel with Lincoln's career. Dirksen was in Congress now, as Lincoln had been, and he held personal ambitions at least as high as any of the 148 other freshmen members who entered the House of Representatives with him. Those ambitions gave him a perspective on his career in Congress that transcended the drudgery of the daily routine and any blind adherence to party doctrine. He sensed the necessity for compromise to survive politically in this tidal wave of the Democrats. He felt the compelling force of the electorate behind President Roosevelt and his New Deal, and he had no intention of obstructing it. "The belief is still extant," he wrote at this time, "that a loyal party man will oppose everything which the other party proposes, right or wrong. This is the doctrine of regularity carried to a vicious extreme. I do not believe that such political gospel appeals to the citizenry of this country." He had already been accused of expediency and equivocation in his election campaign, and there was a danger now, in grabbing at these opportunities he saw, of seeming opportunistic as well. Dirksen did not oppose the New Deal, not the way it was opposed by his party leader, Bertrand Snell. Dirksen could see the farms foreclosed, the banks bankrupt, the millions unemployed, and the moral desperation of the country. He sensed the mandate for Roosevelt. Dirksen was pliable. "Now," he wrote, "is the time for a new political credo." He saw in the New Deal, as he said at the time, the possibility of fulfilling "a glorious promise."

Dirksen intended to serve as a legislator in fact, not merely as a hanger-on in the legislative process. For this reason he came to Washington in late February, 1933, to attend the final days of the "lame-duck" session of the outgoing Seventy-second Congress. He sat in the gallery of the House of Representatives to listen to the debates, to study the motions and maneuvers, and to watch the floor leaders and members in action. He wanted to learn what he could in advance of the techniques and procedures of the House's parliamentary life. Then, as a freshman member of the Seventy-third Congress, he spent his time on the House floor at every session in those first weeks to familiarize himself still further with the House's ways. He was not an awed country rube, abashed at his new and splendid surroundings. He had come to learn, but he was not a bit backward or shy. When he submitted his formal request for committee assignment, he listed his preferences as three of the most powerful and prestigious committees of the House. Appropriations, Ways and Means, and Interstate and Foreign Commerce, in that order. He was taken aback when he was summarily relegated by his party elders to three minor committees. They were the Committee on Territories, the Committee on Immigration and Naturalization, and the District of Columbia Committee.

Dirksen had been studying his own party leaders. Bertrand Snell, the floor leader, was a doctrinaire Republican conservative without the flexibility that Dirksen himself was anxious to perfect. Snell represented New York's sparsely populated Thirty-first Congressional District that bordered on Canada, a traditionally safe Republican stronghold. Joseph Martin of Massachusetts, an assistant party leader, was a politician more to Dirksen's taste. Representing a mixed constituency of farmers and factory workers, Martin was easygoing and pliant, a conservative but not unduly dogmatic about it.

"Bert Snell was a hard-nosed Republican," Dirksen said, "and he was at an age when he thought in terms of rugged Republican gospel. Snell was of the old school, extremely prim, impeccably dressed. You didn't regard Snell as one of the boys. Joe Martin was. He was very knowledgeable, a clever political operator. Joe was a likable person, and he got along extremely well with his party associates, and with the Democrats in the House, by his consummate patience and an inordinate amount of common sense, and a little more flexibility than Bert Snell."

Dirksen called on Martin for advice. Snell was sixty-two years old; Martin was forty-eight. Snell would not have many more years in the House; Martin had his House career before him. "I did the wise thing," Dirksen said, "by cultivating Joe Martin." Dirksen latched his career to the rising leader in the party, and Martin gave him advice then that has served for every young member anxious to make a mark in the House.

"Take the assignments you can get," Martin told him, "and work at them. Perfect yourself in committee work, and in due course you'll start up the ladder. Study the rules. Those who know the rules know how to operate in the House, because you operate under the rules."

Dirksen followed that advice. It was no great burden for him, for he was by nature a tireless worker. Always an early riser, since his days milking the family cows, Dirksen rose every day by five-thirty and started his legislative chores. He was normally at his desk by eight in the morning, frequently an hour earlier, and he took an armful of work home with him every evening for study before he went to bed. In these early days in Congress Dirksen set the work pattern he was to follow in all his years in Congress. He pored over the House's book of rules and Asher Hinds's *Precedents of the House of Representatives*, and he mastered their intricacies. In time he became one of the most skillful of parliamentarians in the chamber, an invaluable asset to the ambitious legislator.

His approach to his work suggested the careful scholar, but Dirksen had no hesitation jumping into debate as soon as he found the chance. There was in him none of that diffidence and modesty that the House's elders traditionally have found so becoming in freshman members. He had been a member of the House less than two weeks when he seized an opportune moment to announce his presence in that chamber. "Mr. Speaker and gentlemen of the House," he bellowed at his colleagues, "I represent the Sixteenth Illinois District, the district that sent Abraham Lincoln to Congress in 1846." That wrung applause, and he quickly rattled off four comic stories as if in evidence of his right to borrow Lincoln's name. He first recounted the plight of two Army chaplains lost on a battlefield. "They were wandering around in mud and shell holes," Dirksen said, "when they heard a voice from a trench saying, 'Who in hell led that ace?' The chaplains got up and embraced each other and said, 'Thank Goodness we are among Christians.' " That brought laughter from the members of the House, and Dirksen plunged on.

The bill at hand, Dirksen said, was confusing many members. "I realize it is not up to expectations. I think it is a good deal like the stockings that the Negro lady bought down here in Washington. They did not fit, and she took them back. The clerk said, 'What's the matter? Do they not come up to expectations?' She replied, 'Lawsy, boss, they do not even come up to my knees.' "

Then Dirksen told an Irish joke. An Irishman had fallen down the steps of the House Office Building a few nights before, Dirksen told his colleagues. "He had a bottle of that good old Maryland rye in his hip pocket. He fell down, and as he got up he felt something trickling down his leg, and he said, 'Begorra! And I hope it's blood.' "

The very next day, when the House was considering a bill affecting the sale of beer in Washington, Dirksen was on his feet again. "I assume, of course," he said, "that if Hamlet could come in here from Denmark with a New York accent he might say, 'To *beer* or not to *beer*, that is the question.' " This time his colleagues greeted him with pained silence.

A few days later, on March 29, Dirksen again took the floor, this time on the reciprocal-trade bill. "We have heard so much speculation as to what is wrong," Dirksen said. "Some say overproduction. Others say underconsumption. I incline to the latter view. I am like the little colored boy who sat among a pile of watermelons with distended stomach, unable to eat any more. Some kindly gentleman came along and asked, 'What's the matter, too much melon?' The little boy said, 'Nope, too little nigger.' That is it," Dirksen concluded, "too little consuming capacity."

From then on Dirksen was known as a storyteller, and he scarcely took the House floor to speak without rattling off at least one anecdote. To Dirksen, however, the anecdotes and jokes were merely a way to catch the attention of his colleagues. He used them to make his arguments more telling, to make them more persuasive than they otherwise might be. In essence, Dirksen was not a jokester or a comic. He was at heart an earnest legislator, and he injected humor into his speeches to make them more palatable. His diligence on legislation hardly flagged. He took the bills home, and with them the hearings and reports, and he mastered the details of all the measures that he handled. He made himself into a legislative technician of formidable skill. He ignored Washington's social life, preferring by the quirk of his ambition the burden of his self-imposed homework. Yet he was labeled from the start as a funnyman, and it seems he could not at times resist any chance for comedy.

Dirksen had more in mind in his intensive study of pending legislation than a perverse desire merely to understand the bills and resolutions. Out of these studies, he was devising the means to give himself and his Republican colleagues a way to put their stamp on the legislation despite their minority status in Congress. Under the committee system and by the vicissitudes of serving in that minority, Dirksen was cut off from the normal and casual methods of affecting legislation. Under the House rules, however, any member could offer amendments. "What else is left for minority members?" Dirksen once asked, when questioned about this tactic of offering amendments. For almost his entire career in Congress Dirksen was fated to serve in the minority party, but from his earliest years in the House he knew how to claim the floor and change a bill. Indeed, he perfected to an art the technique of offering amendments.

"Go over the bill carefully," Dirksen explained. "See if there are any weaknesses or omissions and how they could be cured. Most bills aren't read by the members. You take them home. You study them. Things begin to suggest themselves."

Over the years Dirksen found many weaknesses and omissions, by his own account anyway, in the legislation brought before Congress. He offered amendment after amendment. One student of the

Congressional process, in a book published in 1950, reported: "Rep. Dirksen . . . introduced more amendments to wreck price control than any other Member of Congress." That was just one area of Dirksen's never flagging zeal to play a principal role himself in the legislative process, in the writing of national law. He offered amendments—the inevitable Dirksen amendment—whenever and wherever he saw a viable opening, and more than one was accepted by the House. In so doing, he marked himself as an activist legislator and an imaginative, inventive politician. He won publicity and notoriety for himself, a matter of major concern for a politician with ambitions. More than this, he emerged as an identifiable Congressman out of the amorphous, faceless rank-and-file of his party in the House of Representatives, and in time he took on the aura of a nascent party leader.

Dirksen quit college before completing the study of law, and, of course, he had not qualified as a lawyer. Partially to make himself a better legislator, and at his wife's continued urging, Dirksen in 1935 resolved to complete his law training, and quickly. He took a cram course from an attorney in downtown Washington who specialized in getting his students past the bar examination. To Dirksen's chagrin, he flunked the examination when he took it. Some months later, as a member of Congress, not as an aspiring law student, Dirksen met one of the members of the board of law examiners, and he inquired not too discreetly about what had gone wrong. The examiner's reply suggested to Dirksen that there was a world of reality he had not imagined behind the formality of the bar examination. Dirksen, the examiner suggested, had made two basic mistakes: he had handwritten his answers instead of typing them, and he had written long answers. The examiners simply had no patience with either type of examination paper. Thus counseled, Dirksen took the bar examination again in 1936, and he passed it without further difficulty.

Dirksen had no intention of practicing law, and he made no attempt to join a law firm. He devoted his full attentions to his work in Congress. His status as lawyer, of course, enhanced his standing in Congress, where the essential business was the writing of law. An even more important consideration for Dirksen was the protection financially and professionally that his acceptance at the bar gave him. If the voters of his Congressional district turned him out of office, he would not have to return to his old job at the dough bench in the bakery.

So intent was Dirksen on his Congressional work that he shaped his family life to its demands. "Our family life was quite broken up," Mrs. Dirksen said. During the sessions of Congress, Dirksen and his wife lived in a Washington hotel, normally the Mayflower, and their daughter, Joy, lived with her maternal grandmother in the Carver home in Pekin. Joy went to school in Pekin, and her mother visited her whenever she could. In Washington Mrs. Dirksen worked with her husband, helping him with his Congressional chores. Despite the difficulties, they had a close family life, and Dirksen had a special affection for his only daughter, perhaps made stronger by his absences. "She thinks her father hung the moon," her mother said.

From his earliest days in Congress, Dirksen had an instinctive flair for the provocative. Sometimes his antics got him into trouble. Such an incident took place the very first time Dirksen was invited to the White House, in January, 1934, for the President's annual reception for Congress. It was a full-dress affair, and Dirksen, fresh from the country, had no such paraphernalia. He had difficulty renting a dress suit, and he made the most of it when he recounted his troubles to a Washington correspondent.

"Everywhere I went," Dirksen told the reporter, "the tailors told me they had rented everything in the house to senators and representatives already. I thought all these fellows had dress suits already. Nobody ever said anything about renting one. Finally I found a shop which had one left, and it fit me.

"As I was going out, I saw another member of the House duck into an anteroom. I just yelled: 'Hello, Congressman!' But he didn't answer me. Looked like he was embarrassed. I don't see any reason to be ashamed of renting one. Why, we corn-huskers from the Middle West don't get a chance to step out like this very often."

The reporter's story, carried nationwide on the wires of the Associated Press, touched off a series of stories about the incident. It was good journalistic sport for half a week. Dirksen's colleagues in the House, however, were not amused. They did not enjoy the laugh on them. A widow wrote to Dirksen, offering him her late husband's wardrobe for ten dollars, cash. Out in his Congressional district, some of Dirksen's constituents started collecting money to buy him a dress suit of his own; they collected far more than expected, twenty-eight hundred dollars. Dirksen abruptly found himself in an awkward position; he was embarrassed. "This is my undoing," he thought, by his recollection of the now painful affair. He asked that the money already collected go to charity. "I'm down here to legislate, not to go about wearing dress suits," he announced rather stiffly in a statement to the press. "I can afford to buy one of those things, and when I decide to go in for full dress in a big way, I'll do so." He wanted the matter closed. Years later, looking back at the incident, Dirksen could laugh at it. "Shall we call these the naïve stumblings of a country Congressman?" he asked.

Later in 1934, Dirksen found himself engaged in an even more painful matter, this one involving the impeachment of three federal judges in Chicago on charges of "almost criminal negligence." The judges were Republicans, appointed by Republican Presidents, but that did not deter Dirksen from playing an activist's role, however distasteful, in trying to bring them to book. He felt a responsibility to do so, but he did not enjoy the effort. "One of the most squeamish situations in which one can find oneself," he stated at the time, "is to be compelled to pass judgment on public officials who are members of one's own party, on the basis of a record which is none too glorious." It was not only that the judges were Republicans and that his Republican colleagues in Congress took a jaded view of his acting to punish them that troubled Dirksen. He flinched from the role of prosecutor. A compassionate man all his life, Dirksen shrank from the anguish he was inflicting on the accused. As it turned out, the House subcommittee that investigated the charges did not recommend removing the judges from the bench, but the case soured Dirksen permanently on the Constitution's impeachment processes. He did not believe they should be used in such cases. The matter remained for Dirksen a cheerless memory, and in later years he refused to talk about his role in it.

That same year, and with his eye on the press-gallery reporters, Dirksen made a deliberate play for a headline. He had discovered that the glue used on United States postage stamps was made from flour imported from the East Indies, and duty-free flour at that. American farmers could not sell their crops, and Dirksen received some slight attention in the press by his announced horror at this evil. "If our farmers only knew what they are licking," he exclaimed, "when they lick a postage stamp!"

Friendly and gregarious, Dirksen had a way about him that his colleagues found engaging. His neighborliness normally dispelled any offense, and he went often beyond mere courtesy with his seniors in the House to avoid their displeasure. He deliberately cultivated them, knowing that they could as they chose help or hurt his own career in Congress. When he had sketched an amendment to a pending bill, he normally consulted the senior members of his party in advance of offering that amendment. He talked to the ranking Republicans on the appropriate committee. He wanted their advice and judgment. Not only did this help forestall any resentment from these older members, but it helped to enlist them in support of the amendment. It also helped blunt antagonism from the party leaders over the independent course Dirksen frequently followed in these years, a course that often placed Dirksen at odds with his Republican party leaders.

As he had made plain even before taking his seat in the House of Representatives, he was no party-liner. He supported some of the New Deal bills; he opposed others. His first vote on a major bill, the Economy Act of 1933, put him in trouble with his constituents as well as his party leaders. The bill was aimed at cutting the federal budget by reducing the salaries of government workers and the benefits provided veterans. The leaders of the House were so anxious to push this popular bill through Congress that they did not take time to have the bill formally printed. Dirksen voted against it, and he immediately received a deluge of abusive mail from his constituents, threatening to vote against him at the next election. "And when some of those were signed by some of your closest friends," Dirksen said, "it really made you wince. On that one I think I wept a little that first night." Against his party leaders, Dirksen voted for the National Industrial Recovery Act, the Agricultural Adjustment Act, and the Federal Emergency Relief Act. He voted against the Tennessee Valley Act, the Securities Exchange Act, and the Reciprocal Tariff Act. He voted for the Gold Reserve Act, by which the dollar was devalued. Frequently Dirksen could be found in opposition to the party floor leader, Bertrand Snell, on these fundamental questions of the role of the federal government in dealing with the national economy. Even before taking office as a Congressman, Dirksen had stated that he favored action to cure the nation's economic ills. "No one will contend," he said then, "that within this nation we cannot find men with sufficient vision and knowledge to fabricate feasible and practical and constitutional measures for the relief of business, agriculture, banking, transportation, and other enterprises." Dirksen was not a stickler over constitutional niceties, as were his party regulars, and when the Supreme Court in 1935 struck down President Roosevelt's national recovery program, Dirksen voiced angry dissent with the court's decision. "The mind is no match with the heart in persuasiveness," he exclaimed. "Constitutionality is no match with compassion." In 1935 he voted for the Social Security Act and the Soil Conservation Act. In 1937 he voted for the Housing Act and for the National Labor Relations Act, which established the minimum-wage-and-hour law.

"Mr. Speaker," he said, "there will be at least one Republican who, without tongue in cheek or fingers crossed, without fear of gaining or losing industries, without regard to political expediency or tradition, will be recorded in favor of the bill to proscribe maximum hours and minimum wages. That will be me. Too long has our party been identified as the champion of the big, the rich, the powerful, and the entrenched."

Clearly he did not believe in carrying his Republicanism to any "vicious extreme" of blind opposition to the Democratic program. He could, of course, see the clear mandate of the Democrats. The 117 Republicans in the House of Representatives of the Seventy-third Congress shrank to 102 in the Seventy-fourth Congress, and, incredibly, after Roosevelt's reelection landslide in 1936, to only 89 in the Seventy-fifth Congress. Dirksen continued to win his own elections, but by decreasing margins. He did cater to the parochialism of his district by voting isolationist and protectionist on foreign questions, and he never went over to the stance of "rubber stamp" for the Democratic administration on domestic questions. In fact, on lesser measures than the landmark bills, Dirksen built a conservative record. Despite his independent voting record on major legislation, he grew enormously in reputation within Congress in these years. In the complimentary shorthand language of the House, he was a man who did his homework. One Congressional correspondent, in a private memo, wrote this of him in his days in the House of Representatives: "Dirksen is one of the most influential Republicans in Congress, one of the House's best legislation analysts. He's industrious, diligent, hard-worker, well-informed. An able and convincing debater." Another reporter described him in a story in *The Washington Post* as "tolerant, broadminded, and reasonable. When shown that he is wrong, he will change." Nor did his party leaders deny him access to the House's power. In 1937 he won appointment to the Appropriations Committee. From that spot he had a say on every dollar spent by the federal government, and he specialized there on agriculture appropriations, crucial to his constituents in rural Illinois.

Dirksen, whatever position he took on a pending question, normally exacted a hearing from his colleagues. It was said of him that he was one of the few members who actually could change votes with his persuasive arguments, with his command of the legislation before the House. His speeches were not all laced with wit and anecdote. Occasionally they carried bite, a touch of acid. Mockery was one of his specialties. In 1937 he excoriated his fellow Republicans for their laments over the election catastrophe the year before. "You're salvaging your own consciences here this morning," he told them. "We haven't got enough members of Congress to force a roll call, and still we have to listen to rhetorical pap . . . like 'the American way of life.' " He berated the State Department for its ruling that American diplomats could wear knee breeches at the coronation of King George VI. "I hope those silk pants slit down the seams when they genuflect before the King," Dirksen said. "I'm not so much against genuflecting as I am against silk pants. I don't think our American diplomats ought to go native."

In his first years Dirksen usually addressed the House with his outdoor voice—the booming style recommended to him years before by William Jennings Bryan. "In fact," one reporter wrote, "he seemed to subscribe to the theory that the louder he said it, the more effective he was." It was a style not without merit in the years before the House of Representatives installed a loudspeaker system, for in those days it took a major effort to be heard above the general din of the House floor. Indeed, the style was even deliberately cultivated, and it was said of one member of the House, John P. Hale of New Hampshire, who served in the 1840's, that he could stand atop Mount Washington and be heard throughout his entire state. Dirksen was in the Hale tradition, one of the loudest-voiced members of the House. Only later did Dirksen learn that there is another tradition in the House of Representatives, that the loudest voices were not always coupled with the best minds. He began to develop an entirely different oratorical technique. He spoke for effect, and often in whispers. His previous style, as one contemporary commentator noted, was neither polished nor subtle. His new style was more in keeping with his growing prestige and influence in the House, but his changed pace, his whispered speeches, were noted by his colleagues and regarded as an affectation. One colleague, Leon Gavin of Pennsylvania, a leather-lunged Republican noted for his roaring speeches, one day rose in the House and mimicked Dirksen in his new style. Gavin whispered his words so softly as to be almost inaudible. One of his colleagues, seemingly perplexed, questioned Gavin. What had happened to his familiar bellow? There was nothing wrong, Gavin explained. "I am trying to appear as a statesman." No one missed Gavin's barb at Dirksen, and the members of the House burst into laughter.

Dirksen had such ambitions. He had won recognition in the House from his colleagues and the press. He was a member of acknowledged talent and formidable energy. He had mastered his job, and he wanted office above and beyond the House.

# Chapter 4

# Ambition Rampant

*I want to serve my country in national office.*

With his appointment to the Appropriations Committee in 1937 Everett Dirksen had become a part of the ruling apparatus in Congress. Assignment to that committee bestowed on him automatically something of the influence and power inherent in the committee itself. As a member of that committee, if only a junior member, Dirksen acquired status within the House otherwise unobtainable. He was marked, in that moment of his promotion, as a member in the favor of his party leaders. In a real way, membership on this powerful committee took away part of the onus of belonging to the minority party, for in terms of deference receivable, even senior senators acted graciously toward any man with a voice in the allocation and distribution of the government's moneys. Political careers hung on the fateful decisions of this committee and on the ability of working politicians to inveigle federal funds for their projects and purposes. For Dirksen, an instinctive, nimble-witted political activist, this was his introduction to power politics in Washington. Assignment to the Appropriations Committee offered him entrée to the great game of decision-making, and it gave him his first access to the levers of national power.

The committee could prove an ideal base from which to launch his ideas and to press his personal political ambitions. Dirksen had already demonstrated an immense capacity for hard work, an indifference to the toil necessary to acquire legislative competence, and this had always been the key to influence and power in the House of Representatives. Dirksen as well had earned a reputation as a man committed to good government, so much so that his appointment to the Appropriations Committee caused consternation within the city government of Washington. Dirksen had been from the start of his House career a member of the District of Columbia Committee, and unlike most of his committee colleagues he had worked tirelessly on that committee's business, running the local government of the nation's capital. The Democratic-controlled city government formally petitioned that Dirksen be allowed to continue to serve on the District committee, in exception to his party's established rule that members of the "exclusive" Appropriations Committee serve on no other House committees. It was an unusual request, and a remarkable tribute to his talent and energy, and, by special dispensation of his party's elders, it was granted.

In Dirksen's first years in the House, the principal business before Congress was the economic catastrophe of the national depression. Dirksen, as we have seen, responded to the various proposals put forward by the Democratic administration in a totally pragmatic way, divorced from any hard commitment to Republican Party doctrine. Some he favored; some he opposed. He found himself frequently speaking and voting against his party leaders, particularly on bills affecting the state of the union. Dirksen justified his support of these Democratic bills, as he said at the time, on the grounds that the nation faced an unprecedented crisis. He was willing to experiment, to turn to national solutions, and without too close an inspection of the constitutional niceties. Because of his doctrinal flexibility, Dirksen was regarded as a Republican progressive, and he found favor with the Eastern press because of it. Not until later, much later, when he was a senator, did the accusations come that he was a man of no fixed political principles, so flexible that he shifted with the change of every gust of popular opinion. In his years in the House of Representatives, Dirksen found praise for failing to be what was expected of a rural, Midwestern Congressman, a die-hard economic conservative. He was regarded as a Congressman who took a larger view of the political-economic realities than the provincial concerns of his own district. He was seen as a national Congressman, not a parochial Congressman, and, indeed, his views were national. There lay his ambitions, and there his hopes. There lay his constituency.

With millions of Americans unemployed, hungry, and desperate, the primary attention of the American government was concentrated on righting the national economy, but the United States was not the only land prostrated by economic disaster. At first the travails of these other countries were largely ignored in the United States. Then war and the threat of war engulfed Europe and Asia, and their effects reverberated in American politics. The New Deal economic programs began to give way, victims of President Roosevelt's political blunder in trying to pack the Supreme Court, of the election returns of 1938, and of the international tension. The Spanish Civil War, the aggression of Mussolini's Italy against Ethiopia, Hitler's obvious ambitions in Europe, and the Japanese incursions on China deeply divided Americans on the proper course for the United States. The grotesque horrors of trench warfare of World War I were not forgotten, and Americans generally were disillusioned as well about any further efforts to "save" democracy in the outside world.

Through these years Dirksen stood stridently for American isolationism. He shared the common view that the United States by word and deed should stand aloof from the agonizing spasms of these far-off places. To many Americans, including Dirksen, George Washington had but spoken plain wisdom in his farewell advice to his countrymen to avoid insidious entanglements in the broils of foreign lands. "The most refreshing thing we can indulge in at this hysterical hour," Dirksen said in the neutrality debate in 1937, "is the gratifying business of minding our own business. Mothers, wives, and sisters, and other God-fearing women out in my district . . . shudder at the very thought of war."

In 1937 Dirksen voted for the arms embargo to prohibit shipments of American munitions to Spain, although the final version of that act was unsatisfactory to him. "The bill," he said in 1939, "did not go far enough to suit me." In the months that followed, Dirksen voted against any weakening of its strictures. He voted as well against everything that might seem to belligerent countries as untoward hostility by the United States. In February, 1939, Dirksen voted against President Roosevelt's request for five million dollars to fortify the island of Guam in the Pacific, a vote that embarrassed many Congressmen when that outpost was seized by the Japanese less than three years later. When general war broke out in Europe after Germany's invasion of Poland, Dirksen resisted as strongly as he could Roosevelt's efforts to give aid to Great Britain and France. Roosevelt proposed selling to the Allied Powers what military supplies they could pay for and transport.

"Hate will ride the torpedoes," Dirksen said in House debate on repealing the arms embargo in October, 1939, "as they seek to sink the cash-and-carry cargoes of munitions almost as soon as the vessels have slipped their hawsers. Hate will supersede reason, and there will be 'incidents.' There will be notes and explanations. There will be reports and demands. It will be intoxicating. The fever will grow. And then we shall see whether the nation can be kept out of war."

Dirksen voted against that repeal, of course, and less than a year later, on September 7, 1940, he voted against establishing the draft to build up the American Army in those tense times. A few months later, the House was asked to extend credit to Britain, whose financial resources were exhausted, and Dirksen voted no on this change from cash-and-carry to lend-lease. He then voted against the appropriation to carry out lend-lease, one of fifty-five bitter-enders in this struggle in the House. Dirksen voted against legislation to allow seizure of Axis ships immobilized in American ports. In the summer of 1941 the draft law's one-year authority was expiring, and the President asked for an eighteen-month extension. The measure came to a vote in the House on August 12, and Dirksen voted no. The bill was approved, however, 203 to 202, and the U.S. Army was not maimed in the months immediately before the Japanese attack on Pearl Harbor.

By his words and votes, Dirksen followed a consistent line of isolationism all through this period, and that was the stance of his Republican Party in Congress. In 1940 the Republicans nominated Wendell Willkie for President, and he had, in effect, favored Roosevelt's foreign and preparedness policies, a matter of some awkwardness for the Republican Party stalwarts in Congress. As a Republican, Dirksen had supported Willkie's election, if not his internationalism. All the same, there had been a shift in national sentiment from the stark isolationism of the mid-1930's, and, in time, Congress began to reflect it. The people sympathized with Britain but did not want to intervene directly in the war. Dirksen witnessed this change, and he was not immune to the logic of events nor the realities of national politics. It troubled him enough that at last he made what he called at the time a searching inventory of the nation's position and his own and his party's attitude toward it. His conclusions were difficult, especially in terms of his own voting record, but he resolved to abandon his previous isolationism and support the President's foreign policy.

Thus it was that on September 18, 1941, less than six weeks after he had voted against extending the draft, Dirksen took the House floor to make a brief and remarkable speech. In it, he renounced isolationism. He did not propose to silence responsible Republican criticism of administration mistakes, but the time had come, he said, to praise President Roosevelt and Secretary of State Cordell Hull for "their cautious and delicate handling" of the evolving crisis with Japan. He believed, moreover, that now that

Congress had endorsed the policy of helping Britain, "we should provide such funds, supplies, and authority as are needed to make that policy effective." Dirksen himself had voted against the policy and then against implementing it.

Roosevelt had outlined a policy toward the belligerents that was as openly friendly to Britain as it was hostile to Germany and Italy. It was predicated on avoiding direct American participation in the war.

"That policy," Dirksen said, "is now known to all the world. To disavow or oppose that policy now could only weaken the President's position, impair our prestige, and imperil the nation."

From Dirksen, a rising leader in the opposition party, this was a startling and dramatic pronouncement, and it caused a sensation. His Republican colleagues were "amazed," as one reporter described them. The Japanese attack on Pearl Harbor was to strike a blow against American isolationism from which, many believed, it would never recover, but that attack still lay almost three months away in the uncharted future. Dirksen did more than renounce isolationism; he also disassociated himself from his Republican colleagues who bitterly opposed Roosevelt's foreign policies. The shock of war would silence them, and soon, but it would be years before the leaders of Dirksen's party, like Senator Arthur Vandenberg of Michigan, would forswear the isolationism that had always guided their approach to foreign policy. What was truly remarkable about Dirksen's disavowal of isolationism was that it came before Pearl Harbor.

By thus rejecting isolationism and then persisting in the heresy to traditional Midwest Republicanism, Dirksen alienated the most powerful and influential Republicans in Illinois. The party's councils were dominated by Colonel Robert McCormick, publisher of *The Chicago Tribune*, and through the pages of his newspaper McCormick repeatedly fulminated against Dirksen's apostasy. Other leaders of the party in Illinois, like Governor Dwight Green and United States Senator C. Wayland Brooks, reflected McCormick's disposition and stood ready to block Dirksen's presumed ambitions for statewide office. Dirksen's new posture in foreign affairs, as well as his activist role in other Congressional matters, won him applause as one of the ablest members of Congress, but by so acting Dirksen placed at hazard his chances of building a political base in his home state. Dirksen's Congressional colleagues from Illinois, by one contemporary account, had assumed all along that Dirksen aspired to a seat in the United States Senate, but they also supposed that he would wait until 1944 to run against Democratic Senator Scott Lucas. Now, with his dramatic change, the McCormick camp speculated that Dirksen might be calculating to challenge Republican Senator Brooks in the 1942 party primaries. They surmised that he was casting his lot with the Willkie wing of the national party. In fact, in terms of ambition, Dirksen had greater goals than the voters of Illinois alone could bestow: his speech repudiating isolationism was couched in national terms; it was not designed to help him politically in Illinois.

Dirksen's speech supporting President Roosevelt's handling of foreign affairs was but the beginning of his conversion to internationalism, a conversion that lasted throughout his remaining years in the House of Representatives. In May, 1942, with the United States now engaged in the world war, Dirksen made a series of twelve foreign-policy speeches in the House of Representatives. He had no less a purpose than to transform the Republican Party's stance on foreign policy; he intended to convert his party to his own new internationalism. In the words of a confidential memorandum filed by a journalist who conferred privately with Dirksen at this time, Dirksen was "conducting a sort of skull practice for the boneheads in the House." In these speeches Dirksen's principal argument was that the country and its government should start then on planning to solve the postwar problems being created by the war under way. The United States, he argued, would have to share fully in a new world organization to try to preserve future peace, and he suggested that the United States might have to spend its money to rehabilitate those places in the world most devastated by the war. "Organized forces of union, of federation, of world government, of international government, are already at work," he said. "They are symbols of the spirit reaching forth from behind the barriers of frustration to a new hope that cooperation, comity, and understanding can be achieved and that the blight of warfare will be no more. These forces need study. They need direction. They need exploration." Dirksen's thesis, spoken a year before Congress agreed to support even the concept of the United Nations, foretold his support of those postwar programs when they did come before Congress five years later.

By this time Dirksen had perfected his oratorical powers to the point that he was recognized as one of the best, if not the best, speech-makers in the House. There was talk in 1941 of selecting him as Republican National Chairman, the party spokesman. He had a wide range to his rhetoric. He was abrasive and brutal in political harangues, dangerous in cut-and-thrust debate, devastating in ridicule, and yet cordial and engaging in his not forgotten tactic of telling pointed anecdotes to make his case. He had long since become master of himself, at ease and imperturbable on the stump, in the cloakroom, or on the House floor. He had already cultivated his insignia, a head of tousled hair.

On two different occasions in 1940 Dirksen tangled with squads of Democrats to defend Willkie, newly nominated by the Republicans for President, and he gave better than he received in those bruising battles. "I will take my stand with Willkie," he shouted, "whose only sin has been success through diligence and hard work. . . . He is American to the core." On another, he lashed at the Roosevelt administration's preparedness program. "If there be any doubt about confusion, bewilderment, chaos, misdirection, discordance, inefficaciousness, and mysticism which now besets this program," he said, "one need only visit the defense establishments in Washington and get an indelible picture of rampant confusion." With the nation at war, Dirksen did not hesitate to criticize blunders and blunderers as he saw them. At one point he demanded that the Secretary of Agriculture be removed summarily and replaced by a "good tough food czar."

Earlier, Dirksen ridiculed a New Deal program out of existence with a single adroit speech. This was the Federal Theater Project, employing some nine thousand otherwise unemployed actors and artisans. Dirksen struck the project at its weakest point—some of the risqué plays performed. He mocked them, pirouetting on the House floor, and pulled laughter from his colleagues by calling out their titles with all the scorn he could muster: *Up in Mabel's Room, A Boudoir Diplomat, Just a Love Nest, Cheating Husbands, Your Sex Will Find You Out, Lend Me Your Husband*. From hundreds of plays the federal group had performed, Dirksen carefully selected those that would most tell with moralists. "Now," he said to his colleagues in the House, "if you want that kind of salacious tripe, very well, vote for it." The House abolished the federal program instantly by a vote of 192 to 56.

On other occasions Dirksen diverted his audience with a story, in the Lincoln style. One afternoon in 1940, for example, he told this story to make a point, an anecdote that remained one of Dirksen's favorites over the years. It was about a fellow who applied for an insurance policy and was asked at what age each of his parents had died and from what cause. "Unfortunately," Dirksen went on, "his father had been hanged and he did not like to say that in the application. So after some study he wrote: 'My mother was sixty when she passed away and died of pneumonia. My father was fifty-five, and he came to his end while participating in a public function when the platform gave way."

In these years of war, Dirksen applied himself with extraordinary diligence to his job as Congressman, working seventeen and eighteen hours a day with scarcely time taken out to eat and sleep. In April, 1943, *Fortune* magazine printed an extensive, in-depth study of Congressman Dirksen at work. The magazine chose Dirksen to illustrate the travail of Congress in wartime and the perseverance of one unusually diligent Congressman in meeting it. The article described Dirksen as "an extraordinarily able and hardworking Congressman . . . a big, tough, shrewd, and hearty fellow who loves his job and is very good at it." He had myriad problems with officials and constituents, scores of legislative and appropriations decisions to make, and yet he was one of the most prescient in looking down the road for legislative cures to the problems ahead. He was urging Congressional planning on postwar problems and reconstruction, peace preparation, greater governmental efficiency and economy. Most intensively of all he worked to establish a Committee on Congressional Reorganization, and his primary intent here was to try to restore the flagging powers of Congress from the incursions of the Presidency. Dirksen was among the first to advocate that Congress needed competent professional staffing in all fields of its jurisdiction.

"We ought to have men of our own," he said, "that we could send out into the field to actually see what's going on; whether, for instance, some agency is using a hundred men for a job that fifty could do. And when an agency comes into a committee meeting to ask for an appropriation, we ought to have at our elbow a man who had spent a year in that agency and found out all about it. He could be counsel to the committee, cross-examine, analyze the testimony expertly. Then we'd have a chance of finding out what really goes on."

Despite all his varied activities, Dirksen as well kept up a self-imposed chore of his own. Each week he typed out his own news-letter, "The Congressional Front," a chatty report he had been sending to Illinois newspapers during each session of Congress since he first arrived in Washington. The two- or three-page memorandum, which he deliberately kept nonpolitical to assure its widest publication, was printed in 145 newspapers, most of them weeklies.

Dirksen's "constructive statesmanship" in the House, as *Fortune* magazine called it, his growing national reputation, and his obvious talents brought new speculation that he would seek higher office. There were reports in 1943 that he might run the next year for governor of Illinois, bracing the McCormick oligarchy, or for the Senate seat of Scott Lucas. Dirksen, however, had a different goal. By late 1943 it appeared that there was no single, obvious Republican candidate for President. Willkie, the 1940 nominee, was already running, and the governors of New York, Ohio, and California were regarded as Willkie's principal rivals. There was no candidate from Congress for the nomination, and this prompted some of the House Republicans to sound out Dirksen about making himself "available," as the expression is. Dirksen took the suggestion seriously. In a deadlocked convention, which was a possibility, anything might happen. Moreover, if a state governor were chosen, the party might want a skilled politician with Washington experience for the Vice-Presidential nomination. With the help of a staff assistant, Harold Rainville, Dirksen devised a clever tactic: he drafted an appropriate petition and passed it around among his House colleagues for their approval. The petition proposed that Dirksen run for President.

"From intimate and close association with Congressman Everett M. Dirksen of Illinois," the petition read, "we know his diligence in the public welfare, his devotion to sound and balanced government, his broad grasp of federal functions, and his capacity for dealing with national problems."

In all, thirty-six of Dirksen's colleagues signed it, all there was room for on the single sheet of paper. They came from thirteen states; all but four of the signers were from the Middle West. Thus armed, Dirksen called in the press on December 2, 1943, and announced that he was a candidate for President. He offered himself, in effect, as the Middle West farm candidate, intimately familiar with all national problems and committed to what he called "some kind of decent international collaboration." No, he replied to one question, he would not be a "stalking horse" for any other candidate, and, no, he would not be merely "a favorite son." He was a serious candidate. He had adequate financing in hand, he said, but he did not intend to enter any of the party primaries.

Those who talked privately to Dirksen at the time found that he had no illusions that he would win the Presidential nomination. Dirksen gave them the impression that he believed it was conceivable, if unlikely. "I want to serve my country in national office," he told one. Some of his House supporters suggested his real target; they said he had as good a chance as anyone for the Vice-Presidential nomination. Failing that, they added, Dirksen might well put himself in a strong position for a high position in the House leadership if the Republicans won control of Congress in the coming election.

Dirksen was forty-seven years old, a veteran of eleven years in the House of Representatives, when he announced his Presidential campaign. In his House races, he had had the support of both farm organizations and organized labor, an unusual feat. With his stand on foreign affairs, he had the sympathy of the internationalists in and out of the Republican Party. In an article about his candidacy, *The Washington Post* described him as "politically fearless" and cited his defiance of the powerful Republican isolationists in his home state as evidence. Colonel McCormick, who himself was considering running for President, was infuriated at Dirksen's announcement, and he had *The Chicago Tribune* denounce him in its pages. Admittedly, however, Dirksen was only a long-shot candidate, and he ran a low-key campaign, claiming no delegate strength and attacking none of the other party hopefuls. By mid-February Dirksen had canvassed fourteen states, making speeches and conferring with party leaders. He was, he said, running "under no misapprehension," but he was running all the same. By May he and his supporters were candidly admitting that he really sought the Vice-Presidential nomination. On June 6, D day in Europe, thirty-six of Dirksen's Republican colleagues in the House gave him a formal testimonial dinner at the Mayflower Hotel in Washington to endorse him for Vice-President. "We want Dirksen to be our candidate for Vice-President," said Representative Frank Keefe of Wisconsin, one of several speakers who echoed the same theme. In his own response to this, Dirksen showed that he was not entirely unaffected by the flattery. "If in the wisdom of the party leaders," Dirksen said, with more than a trace of the pretentious, "they see fit to accord me the honor of a place on the national ticket, I can only say that I shall bend what light I have to the task of conveying a growing hope into victory."

This, however, was not to be. By the time the Republican National Convention met in Chicago on June 26, Dirksen had carried his campaign to twenty-seven states. By then Governor Thomas E. Dewey of New York had won the support of more than a majority of the party delegates, and he wanted Governor Earl Warren of California as his running mate. Warren demurred, and Dewey turned to Governor John W. Bricker of Ohio. Bricker gratefully accepted. Had he too refused, Dirksen might well have been asked. With his political credentials, Dirksen was an acceptable alternative. He had already shown his friending to the New York governor, and, indeed, before the first ballot, Dirksen went before the convention to endorse Dewey for President. "So, here and now," Dirksen shouted at the applauding delegates, "I want to offer my hand and my heart, my support and my energy to . . . Governor Thomas E. Dewey of New York."

There was no humiliation to Dirksen's failure. On the contrary, he had gained a greater national notoriety than he had ever had before, and he was regarded with enough earnestness by his party leaders to be granted time to address the convention at a crucial moment in its proceedings. There would be other conventions, other offices, and Dirksen had in his political portfolio the prestige and credits of having made a national campaign. One immediate and unusual benefit emerged from his abortive campaign. His political allies and friends in his Congressional district had raised $5,100 for his Presidential campaign. Dirksen had spent little of this fund, and the question rose what to do with the money that was left, some $4,200. One of the fund-raisers, F. M. McNaughton, publisher of The Pekin Times, proposed that the money be used to pay for a world tour for Dirksen, "to make a good Congressman better."

Dirksen fell in with the idea readily enough, and so it was that on February 25, 1945, after his reelection to the House, Dirksen arrived in London on the first stop of his journey. No, he told the correspondents, he was not thinking about the 1948 Presidential race; he was there to see and hear. On March 12 he was in New Delhi, India, inspecting U.S. war agencies there. On March 30 he had reached Jerusalem. On April 19 he was in Cairo, still inspecting battlefronts. On May 5 he had an audience with the Pope at the Vatican. The day before, he had toured the front held by the U.S. Fifth Army. The idea from its inception was unique in Congressman-constituent relations, a privately endowed grand tour to "enlarge the background," as one of the sponsors put it, of their representative in Congress. Dirksen saw not only the far-flung military forces of the United States, but the devastation wrought by the war in many lands. He came back more "world-minded" than before he went, as he and his supporters intended, better equipped to deal with international problems in national office.

With World War II won, Congress turned its attention to the myriad problems at home and abroad. Dirksen, like every activist member of Congress, was caught up in these convulsive efforts to restore the country to peacetime operations, and many of these were painful, like the struggles over full employment, price and rent controls, fair employment practices, and the increasing of minimum wages. More than anything else, Dirksen devoted himself to his long-argued thesis that Congress itself needed basic overhauling. Dirksen almost automatically had been named a member of the special Joint Committee on the Organization of Congress, created in 1945. He had many ideas on how Congress might be improved. In January, 1946, for example, he proposed that both parties in Congress establish policy committees and that these committees serve in part to bring "better understanding" between Congress and the President. He was among the first, and the most adamant, in insisting that the number of Congressional committees be slashed. The House then had forty-eight standing committees and the Senate thirty-three. Dirksen wanted them cut by half, at least, and then to assign the new committees direct oversight of the executive departments and agencies in their jurisdiction. Dirksen played a significant role not only in drafting the Legislative Reorganization Act of 1946, but he was credited at the time as being one of the key men who persuaded Congress to adopt it.

Dirksen's immense energy and the extraordinary dedication he gave to his work in Congress brought him the deepening respect of his colleagues. In its August, 1946, issue, *Pageant* magazine published the findings of a secret poll it had conducted among the members of Congress on how they rated their own colleagues. Dirksen ranked as "the most effective speaker" in the House of Representatives, and he stood among the first four in the House with the "best grasp of domestic affairs." Overall, Dirksen ranked second only to James Wadsworth of New York as "the ablest member" of the House, with Sam Rayburn of Texas, the Democratic Speaker of the House, rated third. Dirksen, with such esteem from his fellow Congressmen, had reason to expect a still greater role in national politics than he had already achieved.

In the 1946 election the Republicans won control of Congress for the first time since 1930, and the party's success triggered a scramble for the leadership posts. The Speakership was conceded to Joseph Martin of Massachusetts, long the Republican leader in the House, but his elevation left vacant the splended position of party floor leader. Dirksen made an effort, somewhat halfhearted, to win it. His candidacy brought commendations, however, from some prominent newspapers. "He is known as a 'moderate' with a flair for effecting compromises among conflicting factions," *The New York Herald Tribune* stated approvingly. *The Washington Star* described Dirksen as "one of the best speakers" in the House with "a progressive record." From the start Dirksen had only a frail and elusive chance, for the real competitors for the post were Charles Halleck of Indiana and Clarence Brown of Ohio. Halleck had been chairman of the Republican Congressional Campaign

Committee for the previous three years; Brown had been director of the 1946 campaign for the Republican National Committee. Dirksen's only hope depended on the unlikely possibility that Halleck and Brown would deadlock the party's caucus, and that hope vanished before Halleck's shrewd maneuvering. Halleck's allies quietly approached Thomas Jenkins, "dean" of the Ohio Republicans in the House, with his twelve terms of seniority. Playing on Jenkins' vanity, they persuaded him that he, not Brown, a mere five-termer, should be the Ohio candidate for floor leader. As a result, Jenkins entered the race for the floor leadership, and that split the Ohio delegation, Brown's political base. In the end, Brown was forced to withdraw as a candidate, and that, in turn, assured Halleck's election by the caucus. Dirksen went to see Halleck. "I've been looking around, Charlie," he said to Halleck, "and you have the votes." Dirksen withdrew.

Dirksen's campaign for the floor leadership thus died aborning, as had his campaign for President, frustrating again his blossoming ambitions. In the new Congress, however, the majority status of the Republican Party brought other emoluments to Dirksen, if not as splendid as those he had sought. Under the seniority system, Dirksen was entitled to hold the chairmanship of both the District of Columbia Committee and the subcommittee on agriculture appropriations. Despite the party rules, the party's leaders agreed to permit Dirksen to retain both chairmanships. Otherwise he would have had to choose between them. Dirksen concentrated such energy and time to his work on both committees that his colleagues felt justified in allowing him to hold both chairmanships. In fact, Dirksen worked so hard at his job as Congressman that he had lost interest in such diversions as golf and swimming that he once enjoyed. As chairman of the District of Columbia Committee, Dirksen in effect acted as the "mayor" of Washington, a job he relished, but it was a far cry from national leadership.

In the fall of 1947, on behalf of two House committees, Dirksen returned to Europe, and he made a detailed, thirty-six-day inspection of occupied Germany. What he learned alarmed him. The year before, Dirksen had caused the staff of the Library of Congress to undertake an objective study of the economic, social, and political fabric of Russia, and the staff's finding on Russia's formidable military potential caused widespread comment. In his own on-the-spot survey, Dirksen found what he believed were unmistakable signs of Russia's hostile intent toward the West. He stated on October 9 in Berlin that the Germans had not enough to eat, and he called for swift and massive economic aid to Germany and the rest of Western Europe. Otherwise, he warned, Europe would fall to Russian communism. On his return to Washington the following month, Dirksen urged President Truman to call a special session of Congress to vote such aid immediately. "Freedom is in jeopardy as it never was before," Dirksen told one audience. On November 18 he made what he called a personal report to the House in which he stated that "the Soviet Union is feverishly preparing for military war" and that the United States must act to save Europe. "To abandon Europe now is to abandon freedom, not only for them but for ourselves," Dirksen said. "It means placing Western culture and Western civilization in peril." Dirksen spelled out his own ten-point program to rescue Europe from its danger, with special emphasis on restoring Germany to economic stability.

Dirksen's thesis, and the insistence with which he argued it, placed him in direct opposition to some of the most powerful Republicans in Congress. Representative John Taber of New York, Chairman of the House Appropriations Committee, on which Dirksen served, had made a hurried trip to Europe and reported that there were no underfed people there. They seemed healthy enough in the hotels where he stayed. Implicit in Taber's finding was that the United States need not be involved. Taber, a long-time fiscal conservative and isolationist, was appalled at the central point in Dirksen's proposition: the United States must appropriate billions of dollars to help Europe. Dirksen's stand made him one of the foremost internationalists in Congress, and he supported with all his vigor and eloquence the implementation of the plan for European recovery outlined by President Truman's Secretary of State, George Marshall. "If we fail in the first year of the European Recovery program," Dirksen said, "we fail for good." Sam Rayburn of Texas, the Democratic leader, credited Dirksen's speech in the House with actually persuading reluctant members to vote for the Marshall Plan.

Dirksen's support for the Marshall Plan was in keeping with his own record on international affairs, going back to his dramatic endorsement of Roosevelt's foreign policy before Pearl Harbor, and in keeping too with the non-Congressional wing of the Republican Party as reflected by its Presidential candidates in 1940 and 1944, Willkie and Dewey. Dirksen took a national view, seeing his constituency as national, and not the parochial isolationism of his Illinois party leaders. His posture lent credence to the idea that he would play an important role in the party's 1948 national convention. Abruptly, however, Dirksen's political career was cut short. In late 1947 he began to notice that he was having difficulty with his eyes. He woke one morning to find "cobwebs" in his eyes. He thought at first that he was merely suffering eyestrain from too much reading, but the trouble persisted. He consulted a doctor, then others. His ailment was finally diagnosed as chorioretinitis, an inflammation of the retina of the right eye. At first the doctors feared cancer; later, with the spread of the disease to his left eye, that was ruled out, but his doctors recommended that the right eye be removed or he would risk blindness in both eyes. Dirksen agonized over the decision. At one point, by his own telling, on a train from Washington to Baltimore, where he was to consult an eye specialist at Johns Hopkins Hospital, Dirksen sought divine guidance. "I got down on my knees," he said, "to ask the Bigger Doctor, and uttered my prayers, whether blindness would be my lot." The eye specialist confirmed the diagnosis that Dirksen's right eye should be removed. "I guess not," Dirksen told him, refusing to allow the operation. "I called on the Big Doctor, the Big Doctor Upstairs, and the answer is no."

Even so, Dirksen could not continue as he had. He needed therapy for his eyes, and above all an extended rest. Under the circumstances, he did not feel he could ask his constituents to reelect him. On January 3, 1948, Dirksen announced that for "compelling personal reasons" he would retire at the end of his current term in Congress. His decision caused genuine regret. Speaker Martin and House Republican Whip Leslie Arends made an effort to draft Dirksen for reelection with the understanding he would not return to his work until he had recovered fully. Dirksen would have none of it. The newspapers eulogized him. *The Washington Star* described him as "an outstanding member" of Congress, deep in the esteem and respect of his colleagues. *The Washington Post* said this: "By dint of hard work, native intelligence, and a commendable flexibility of mind, Mr. Dirksen has become one of the most powerful and highly esteemed leaders of the House of Representatives. . . . His dynamic personality, his skill in debate, and the habit of informing himself on every major public issue have given his influence a contagious quality." Even more striking was the praise he received from some of the Democrats in Congress. "As far as I am concerned," said Sam Rayburn of Texas, the Democratic leader, "I never did want too many Republicans around here, but if they are going to send Republicans to Congress, then let them send Republicans of the Everett Dirksen kind." John McCormack of Massachusetts, Rayburn's lieutenant in the Democratic leadership, expressed his regret too at Dirksen's retirement. Dirksen, he said, "wields a powerful influence upon his colleagues as a result of his sound logic and his gracious, simple, yet effective eloquence."

Dirksen did take a brief vacation to rest his eyes and to apply the treatments recommended by the medical specialists. By springtime, Dirksen's eyes were on the mend. Full sight returned first to his right eye, and vision in his left eye soon followed. Returning to the House of Representatives, Dirksen threw himself back into political affairs. He played a major role in passing the appropriation to fund the Marshall Plan. On his own, he offered an amendment to restore one billion dollars of the funds cut by the Appropriations Committee. Before he left Washington, he asked for an appointment with President Truman. For all Dirksen knew, he was leaving this city forever, and he wished to pay his respects to the President whose foreign affairs program he had so fully supported.

"You should not have quit," Truman told him,* when Dirksen visited the President at the White House.

"I had an eye malady," Dirksen said. "I felt I should quit in the interest of my recovery."

"We need fellows like you," Truman said to him.

"I could not leave Washington," Dirksen said, "until I said good-bye."

Shortly thereafter Dirksen was working furiously for the Presidential nomination of Governor Dewey of New York, and the newspapers described Dirksen as "a bosom friend" of Dewey. Dirksen fought the Republican leaders in his own state, Colonel McCormick and Governor Green, for control of the Illinois delegation at the Republican convention. McCormick and Green favored Senator Robert Taft of Ohio for President. Dirksen expected that Dewey might choose him as his running mate. His eyes were fully recovered by convention time. Later there was an assumption that Dewey, once elected, would name Dirksen to his cabinet as Secretary of Agriculture. There was talk as well in the Dewey camp that Dirksen might be named Republican National Chairman. It was far too late for Dirksen to change his decision on running for reelection to the House that year; the filing deadline had been in late January. Obviously, however, his political career was not over, and he had a target of his own in his sights. By early summer, 1948, he was making plans to run for the United States Senate two years hence.

* Dirksen described this interview with Truman in a Senate speech on April 13, 1959, and Truman read his words in the *Congressional Record*. "I remember meeting at the time you left the House," Truman wrote to Dirksen, "and I felt exactly as you said."

# Chapter 5

# Triumph and Defeat

*We followed you before, and you took us down the path to defeat!*

As Dirksen himself many times told the story, he ran for the Senate at least partially against his own will. Repeatedly in late 1948 and early 1949 he was solicited by Republican politicians and various party delegations to make the race for the Senate in 1950. At that time, Scott Lucas, the Democratic leader of the Senate, would be running for reelection. Dirksen declined to make the decision alone. One night after dinner at the family home in Pekin, he convened a family council. "We've got a question to resolve," he told his wife and twenty-one-year-old daughter, Joy. "I have to say something. Do I run for the Senate or don't I?"

The family conference was conducted under the rules of the House of Representatives; each member was allowed five minutes to make an argument for or against the proposition. Joy began by stating that she had always wanted to work in a senator's office. Mrs. Dirksen took a different tack. "You've been looking wistfully at the Senate," she told her husband, referring to his many years in the House of Representatives. She argued that if he did not at least try now for the Senate, he would live in the frustration that he might have succeeded. Dirksen himself did not offer an argument, and in the family balloting he voted no. His wife and daughter, however, voted that he run.

"Kids," he said to them, "I do not run for the Senate. We run for the Senate. I have to have your help."

Dirksen's homely story of his decision smacked of the sentimental and maudlin. There was a great deal more to his decision than his version of it suggested. He had, of course, fully regained his eyesight, and he had no physical disability to dissuade him or to prevent him from making a vigorous campaign. His record in Congress, however, eloquently proclaimed that he had forsworn building for himself a statewide political base in Illinois. His active leadership in advocating international participation by the United States had alienated the most powerful Republican leaders in the state. He had systematically defied Colonel McCormick, the dominant and domineering Republican in Illinois politics, and McCormick had retaliated by using the pages of his newspaper, *The Chicago Tribune*, to flay Dirksen for his apostasy to Midwest Republicanism. McCormick's chief political henchmen, Governor Green and Senator Brooks, followed the publisher's cues as faithfully as the editors of his newspaper. All had braced themselves over the years to frustrate any incipient ambition by the heretic Dirksen for statewide office. Aiming at national office, Dirksen had never put them to the test. Dirksen's associates believed, however, that only Governor Green's violent objections had prevented Governor Dewey from choosing Dirksen as his Vice-Presidential running mate in 1944. In the 1948 election Green had lost the governorship to Adlai E. Stevenson, and Brooks lost his Senate seat to Paul H. Douglas. These losses, of course, hurt the McCormick oligarchy in Illinois, but they did not deprive the Colonel of his awesome power in party matters.

Dirksen started his campaign early, travelling with his wife and daughter, speaking wherever he could find an audience, and attending those functions where a candidate could make points with voters. By February, 1949, he was well on his way, a full twenty months before election day. In his touring, he had found the farmers unhappy with the incumbent Democrats, a hopeful sign for him. Already some of the state's Republican leaders were launching a boomlet to nominate Dirksen for the Senate. All through the spring and summer Dirksen moved around the state, campaigning at a frenetic pace. "He is campaigning now like a whirling dervish," one political reporter wrote at the time. "In recent months he has made a minimum of four appearances in each county in the state." Dirksen drove himself relentlessly. On retiring from the House of Representatives, he had joined a law firm in Peoria, but he practiced little law. He was too busy campaigning. He financed himself off past savings and some legal fees. "We shook a lot of hands," he said of his campaigning. He was in full physical health. A reporter on *The New York Times* described him in mid-campaign this way: "Mr. Dirksen is a tall, well-built man with a shock of unruly and curly brown hair. He is a master orator, with a deep, ingratiating voice, an excellent command of exposition and of imagery, and a first-rate stock of jokes and anecdotes. He is adept at finding the pitch of his audience, large or small." Not until September 18, 1949, did Dirksen finally announce formally, in Peoria, that he was a candidate for the Republican nomination to the Senate. Through the summer he maintained a discreet silence on his internationalism, with no real hint that he might be reconsidering. Indeed, in midsummer the political analysts at the Republican senatorial campaign headquarters in Washington were gloating that Dirksen would be helped in his campaign by that internationalism. They calculated that it would let him woo successfully the liberal-internationalist Republicans who had defected from the party to support Senator Douglas in the 1948 campaign. They reasoned further that the failure of Colonel McCormick to endorse Dirksen would prove a positive benefit to him.

Dirksen did not assess the political situation in Illinois the same way. He had fought *The Chicago Tribune* for years on international matters and on some domestic concerns as well. He had opposed

McCormick's candidate for President in 1944 and again in 1948, when he fought the McCormick oligarchy for control of the Illinois delegation to the national convention. Dirksen supported Dewey; McCormick supported Senator Robert Taft of Ohio. With such a background of party warring, there would seem no way for Dirksen to placate Colonel McCormick at this late date. As a Congressman Dirksen had been able to maintain a safe independence from the State's party leaders, for his constituents were beyond the reach of the publisher and regularly returned Dirksen to the House of Representatives. Now it was different, and by midsummer Dirksen was talking publicly of the threat of government centralization in Washington and of the danger to individual freedom inherent in the Truman administration's fiscal policies. Dirksen, in fact, was working out an accommodation with Colonel McCormick. Even earlier, according to the political insiders, Senator Taft had conferred privately with McCormick on Dirksen's behalf. By their accounts, Taft told the publisher that it was mandatory to elect Dirksen to the Senate. Dirksen went far beyond belaboring the Truman administration's domestic stance. Even more dramatically, Dirksen denounced the Truman administration's foreign policy, and by so doing he renounced his own internationalism. With swelling rhetoric, Dirksen mocked the Marshall Plan that he had helped enact and fund. "It was a good gamble for the first year," Dirksen said now, "but look at the report for the first year. We haven't gotten our money's worth. . . . It is a bottomless pit."

Dirksen's sudden aberration found its reward in the pages of *The Chicago Tribune*, proof that Colonel McCormick had welcomed him back into the isolationist-conservative fold. Dirksen's picture became a staple in *The Tribune*'s pages; his words were glowingly reported. His catering to McCormick assured him the party nomination without serious opposition, but it prompted a mix of cynicism and shock among those who had admired him and his positions of the past. "But, after all," wrote newspaper columnist Marquis Childs, "the prime necessity of a politician is to win elections, and Dirksen must have concluded that this is the way to get elected to the Senate." Others were not so charitable. "The case of Representative Dirksen is not essentially significant," the Alsop brothers wrote in their syndicated newspaper column, "unless the essential squalor of political human nature happens to excite your morbid interest."

For Dirksen this was the beginning of his savaging by the Eastern press. By his defection to the isolationist-conservative wing of the Republican Party, he brought on himself as well the contumely of the internationalist-liberal wing he abandoned. In his House days he had been admired for his flexibility, his agility and suppleness in debate, his willingness to change position under changed circumstances. His renunciation of internationalism, and for base political motives, savored of treachery to those he now abjured. To them he no longer was a man to be trusted. With his defection began the assumption that he was a politician of convenient opinions and easy principles, an assumption that would haunt his steps for the rest of his life.

Dirksen's sudden change of allegiance to Colonel McCormick and *The Chicago Tribune* reverberated through the power structure and factions of Chicago's political world, exciting intense bitterness from the rivals and enemies of the Colonel and his newspaper. The editors of *The Chicago Sun-Times* were furious at Dirksen for his desertion, and they made plans to punish him. They ordered prepared what they called "a hatchet job" on Dirksen. This took the form of a five-part series of articles excoriating Dirksen's record in the House of Representatives. *The Sun-Times* printed these articles in the first week of October, 1950, to have maximum impact on the election a month later. The burden of the newspaper articles was to demonstrate that in the House of Representatives Dirksen had proved a politician of astonishing fickleness. The first of the series carried the most damaging charge, that as a Congressman Dirksen had changed his position thirty-one times on military preparedness, sixty-two times on foreign policy, and seventy times on farm policy. "Taking a long view of his legislative career," the article summarized, "observers felt that Dirksen not only stood upon both sides of some issues but also sometimes appeared to surround a question entirely." For the rest of Dirksen's political career this damaging account of his record in the House of Representatives would be endlessly repeated, cited in every important article about him and finally in his obituaries. The genuine respect he had earned from his colleagues and the press while in the House was forgotten, and these much-quoted statistics of his alleged voting record became the capsule summary of his House career. The statistics themselves, which were never questioned, suggested that the newspaper had conducted a careful, independent, and painstaking review of Dirksen's sixteen years in the House, even though the articles themselves did not support the statistics in any detail. The articles did not identify the source of the materials used, and it would have been a matter of some embarrassment for the newspaper to have done so, ruining the retaliatory effect intended against Dirksen. The materials had come from the Democratic Congressional campaign committee in Washington, an organization that, like *The Chicago Sun-Times*, had a partisan interest in defeating Dirksen. It was an irony for Dirksen that his distinguished record in the House, where his flexibility had been so much admired, would be thus turned against him. In a real sense, however, Dirksen had brought this upon himself, for in joining the cause of Colonel McCormick and his newspaper he had himself repudiated much of his own House career.

In the campaign, Senator Lucas did his best to exploit Dirksen's desertion of internationalism, and he couched his accusations in words of contempt and scorn. "But I tell you this," Lucas told one crowd, "and I am speaking straight from the shoulder, I have never used the foreign policy of America, which deals directly with the lives of American boys, as a subject for political maneuvering to catch votes. . . . My opponent has flip-flopped from one position to another and back again on foreign policy." Lucas berated Dirksen as a politician whose "masters" at *The Chicago Tribune* called the tune for him. "In his public life," Lucas said, "he has proved his astonishing ability to warble one tune after another while he swings back and forth on the flying trapeze."

Dirksen did not wilt under that attack. Far from it. He retorted as ferociously on the "flip-flops," as he called them, that Lucas himself had made in the Senate. Lucas had voted for the Taft-Hartley labor bill in 1947, and then he had reversed himself to vote to sustain President Truman's veto of that controversial bill. Moreover, as the Democratic leader of the Senate, Lucas had sponsored and supported much of Truman's domestic program. In his campaign, Lucas blandly opposed several of these very measures, including the President's farm plan and his health-insurance bill. The Dirksen counterassault on Lucas thus blunted the damaging effect of his own inconsistency, and he voiced his isolationism with increased vitriol. He branded the Marshall Plan a "mistake" and charged that the Truman administration, with the help of Senator Lucas, was pouring American taxpayers' dollars "down a rathole." With the advent of the Korean War in June, 1950, Dirksen's broad-scale attack on Truman's "blunders" in foreign affairs took on an extra edge. Like many Republicans that year, Dirksen adopted for his own the jingoistic sloganeering of Senator Joseph McCarthy of Wisconsin, then at the start of his demagogic career of hunting Communists in government. Dirksen echoed McCarthy's accusations that President Truman and his Secretary of State, Dean Acheson, were "coddling" Communists in the federal establishment. McCarthy came to Illinois for Dirksen and campaigned in his behalf against Lucas.

Dirksen and Lucas were personal friends. They had known each other from early manhood, when Lucas was a star in the Three-I League of professional baseball. They had grown up in neighboring towns, only thirty miles apart, and they had made their own careers in strikingly similar ways. Both were lawyers. Both were Legionnaires. Lucas had been elected to the House of Representatives two years after Dirksen, and he represented the adjoining Congressional district. They had served together in Congress for many years, often making common cause on legislation. They both agreed at the start of their campaign for the Senate that they would make no personal charges against each other. The pledge did not survive the campaign. Lucas continually mocked Dirksen's subservience to Colonel McCormick and *The Chicago Tribune*. Dirksen called Lucas a "faker" and accused him of "cowardice." It was a bruising, brutal campaign, with Dirksen counting on the Republican downstate majority and Lucas depending on Chicago's Democratic machine for his plurality. The very closeness of their contest raised the temper of the invective.

Dirksen repeatedly challenged Lucas to debate the issues with him. Lucas, the incumbent, naturally declined, suggesting instead that Dirksen debate his own "revolving record." On at least one occasion, in Decatur, a downstate industrial city, Dirksen dramatically debated an empty chair placed beside him on the platform with a placard on it reading: "Reserved for Scott Lucas."

Lucas, as the incumbent and as the acknowledged adviser to the President, had an initial advantage over Dirksen. He had disadvantages, too. For one, he was tied to the Senate by his responsibilities as his party's floor leader there, and he was unable to return to Illinois for serious campaigning while the Senate was in session. Dirksen meanwhile thoroughly canvassed the entire state. By his own estimate, Dirksen traveled 250,000 miles around Illinois, visiting every cross-corner at least once, and making two thousand speeches in the twenty-one months he committed to his campaign. He burned out two automobiles with this constant traveling. In the final months of the campaign Lucas was badly hurt by a political scandal in Chicago. There, it was revealed, the Democratic candidate for sheriff had close and politically embarrassing associations with Chicago's gangsters. To make matters worse for Lucas, Senator Estes Kefauver of Tennessee brought a Senate investigating committee to Chicago three different times in this election year to question the Democratic culprits before television cameras. Lucas never forgave Kefauver, a fellow Democrat but one bent on his own political ambitions.

Despite their similar backgrounds, Dirksen and Lucas stood in striking contrast to each other. Both were large, heavy-boned men, but Lucas was handsomely suave, always impeccably dressed in expensive suits, his hair gracefully combed. He was articulate, if not eloquent, and he adopted to his purposes a manner somewhat stand-offish, the bearing of a statesman burdened with the cares and responsibilities of great office. There was a gentle irony in his voice and the suggestion of the sardonic in his words. Dirksen cultivated a totally different manner, a rumpled "just-folks" approach to the voters. His hair was always unruly. He dressed carelessly. With small groups, he would abandon the microphone and the platform and go down into the crowd. "I like to get closer to the people," he explained to them time after time. He constantly quoted Lincoln and the Bible, and he drew heavily on the pithy jokes and anecdotes that he had been accumulating over the years.

These jokes and anecdotes gave a tone to Dirksen and his campaign that was the converse of Scott Lucas'. They were deliberately unsophisticated stories, calculatedly simplistic, and they were the stock in trade for Dirksen over all the years of his political life. They were his way of ingratiating himself to the ordinary people in the crowds, his technique of preventing any insulation between himself and the voters. Dirksen's professional interests as a politician went to the heart of national policy and the substantive questions before the country, a statesman's interests. In his campaign, however, he carefully shunned the mannerisms of the statesman and even those lesser stylistic gambits of that other aloof creature, the self-satisfied politician. Many of the jokes and anecdotes of this campaign he had used when he first started in politics in the early 1930's. Some of them were still in his repertoire three decades later.

One standby joke of this senatorial campaign Dirksen used to illustrate the burden of the national debt, then calculated at seventeen hundred dollars per capita. A new father visited the maternity ward at a hospital and asked the nurse on duty why so many of the babies were crying. "Mister," said the nurse, as Dirksen told it, "if you were out of a job, and you owed seventeen hundred dollars, and your pants were wet, you'd squall too." It was long a Dirksen favorite. Another he used in this campaign to mock the Washington bureaucracy. A federal official wore an identification badge reading BAIK, and, asked what the initials meant, he replied: "Boy, Am I Confused!" Told that *confused* is not spelled with a K, the bureaucrat answered, "Boy, you don't know how confused I am." On a typical campaign appearance, Dirksen would move swiftly from telling such a joke into the Biblical arena. "I couldn't pass up Sodom and Gomorrah," he told one audience, "destroyed by the Lord because they were lacking in righteous citizens. I believe there were righteous citizens in those cities but they weren't vocal. . . ." That, in turn, reminded him of another story, about an Irishman named Pat who bought a talking bird and sent it home to his wife.

"Mary, did the bird arrive?" Pat asked his wife when he got home.

"Yes, it did."

"Where is it?"

"I got him in the oven."

"But that's a valuable bird. He speaks eight languages."

"Why didn't he speak up?"

In the wave of laughter, Dirksen made his point. "We had better speak up," he told the crowd. "The salvation of America may be decided in 1950. Join the crusade."

This mix of folksiness and jokes, the Bible and the Korean War, and the scandals in the Chicago police was more than Senator Lucas could withstand in this off-year election. On election day Dirksen won, 1,951,984 votes to 1,657,630 for Lucas. Dirksen had won a seat in the United States Senate.

On January 3, 1951, shortly after noon, Dirksen was escorted to the presiding officer's desk in the Senate by his Illinois colleague,

Paul Douglas, and there Vice-President Alben Barkley administered to him the oath as a senator. The Senate Dirksen thus joined was organized by the Democrats; they had only marginal control of the Senate, with forty-nine of the ninety-six members. This Senate was distinctly conservative in political hue, with the Southern Democrats and the Republicans forming a clear voting majority against the liberal-internationalist President, Harry Truman. The Democratic floor leader, just chosen to replace defeated Scott Lucas, was Ernest McFarland of Arizona, an awkward man in debate and without significant party influence. The real power among the Democrats in the Senate lay in the hands of such senior members as Richard Russell of Georgia, Kenneth McKellar of Tennessee, and Pat McCarran of Nevada. A similar arrangement existed on the Republican side of the center aisle. There Kenneth Wherry of Nebraska, a good-natured but inept politician,* was formally designated as the party floor leader, but the real power was held in commission by Robert Taft of Ohio, Eugene Millikin of Colorado, Styles Bridges of New Hampshire, and their lieutenants. Taft, cold and forbidding, was enormously respected; he was clearly first among them. Millikin looked and voted like an austere banker, but he had a robust, ribald sense of humor that enlivened the Senate's cloakroom. Bridges, a creature of the shadows, was cynically amused at the world and human foibles; he had a shrewdness about him that bordered on cunning. Arthur Vandenberg of Michigan had a national reputation comparable to Taft's, but he was failing, and death was not far off. Vandenberg led the small band of Republican internationalists in the Senate. The Taft wing, however, had clear preponderance over the Senate's Republicans and included such conservative stalwarts as Owen Brewster of Maine, William

---

* Wherry had a remarkable penchant for misspeaking himself, and his malapropisms were collected by the reporters covering the Senate's debates as "Wherryisms." He once made an hour's speech in the Senate on "Indigo-China." On another occasion he assured a fellow senator that he would have "opple ampertunity" to make a speech in the chamber that day, and on still another he referred to the nation's highest military officers as "the Chief Joints of Staff."

Knowland of California, and John W. Bricker of Ohio. Dirksen had long since made peace with Taft and the Taft wing of the Republican Party. Senator Taft, in fact, had come to Illinois in the fall campaign to help elect Dirksen. Dirksen readily and easily took his place in the Senate as a staunch Taft man. Forgotten were the years he had spent with the Willkie-Dewey internationalists. Indeed, Taft gave Dirksen unusual recognition on his arrival in the Senate; he arranged Dirksen's appointment as chairman of the Republican Senatorial Campaign Committee, a remarkable honor for a first-year freshman senator.

Dirksen thus was more than welcome, and he plunged headlong into the Senate's affairs. With his zest for legislative chores, with the rich background he had accumulated in his many years in the House of Representatives, Dirksen had an inner knowledge of the workings of the federal establishment that was especially useful in a chamber where few members have the time, energy, or inclination to master details. With no hesitation Dirksen leaped into the Senate's debates, and in the course of his first year—the year most freshman senators modestly choose to be silent—he addressed the Senate on a bewildering array of subjects. He talked about the box-car shortage, British trade with Communist countries, the Bureau of Indian Affairs, the Central Arizona Project, civilian defense, the State Department, the shortage of medical doctors, crop insurance, savings accounts, public housing, peanut acreage allotments, and as many other diverse topics of the hour. On twenty-seven different occasions he spoke about defense production. He was scarcely less active on legislation, offering amendments to a half-dozen of the appropriations bills and to many other measures. He was blatantly hostile to foreign aid. "The hatchet will be very sharp," he said, "and I shall be ready to proceed." He voted for every amendment to cut foreign aid, and he voted for almost every amendment to reduce the other appropriations, even that for agriculture.

The country was at war in Korea, and the fighting was going badly. Dirksen, like other Republicans, excoriated the Truman administration for the presumed blunders. "It is," he said, "the most expensive, costly, and disastrous piece of policing in the history of mankind." On another occasion, he branded the Democrats as the war party and damned them for the mounting casualties. "So when we lift our eyes, like Ishmael did in the wilderness centuries ago," he intoned in one fiery antiadministration speech, "what do we contemplate? Fever, ferment, warfare, and casualties which are now up to sixty thousand." He blamed the Truman administration for indecision and accused the President of failing to explain why he was keeping troops in Korea under such unfavorable conditions. "In heaven's name," Dirksen protested, "let us not slaughter any more youngsters over there when it looks as if they are going to run us out of there anyway." He would take a far different stand from this in the years of the Vietnam War. Dirksen was one of the Republican cabal in the Senate that fulminated against President Truman when he removed General Douglas MacArthur as the commanding officer in Korea. The limitations placed on the fighting bred partisanship, but the Republicans as well had the excruciating frustration of the lost 1948 Presidential election to exacerbate their words. When Senator McCarthy in early 1950 opened what seemed an abortive attack on the State Department for allegedly harboring Communists in its employ, no less a party leader than Senator Taft himself had encouraged McCarthy to press that attack. The Republican ranks in Congress were swept with bitterness and partisanship against the Democratic administration, and Dirksen joined vociferously in the political caterwauling. The scandals that shook the last years of the Truman administration were ready materials also for as skilled an orator and partisan as Dirksen. "There is a spiritual and moral letdown in Washington," he told one audience, "as evidenced by gifts of mink coats and revelations of great abuses of public trusts." No administration action was exempt from Dirksen's verbal wrath. He belabored the Democrats for their "waste, extravagance, and riotous spending," and he accused them of "deceit" in their conduct of foreign affairs. This was a Dirksen that his Congressional colleagues had not known before. In his years in the House of Representatives, he had never flinched from raking the Democrats in public. That was part of the game, but his partisanship then had limits and restraints. He was, in fact, one of the founders of the bipartisan approach in foreign affairs. In the Presidential campaign of 1944 he had shown unusual political courage in one extraordinary incident. He was quoted widely for a speech in Old Orchard, Maine, accusing President Roosevelt of seeking reelection "under false pretenses." The charge excited a brief national controversy. The speech he made had been handed to him by the Republican National Committee and released for publication by the committee. Unknown to the reporters who wrote their stories in Washington from the press release, Dirksen had declined to read the offensive passage, and on his return from Maine he acknowledged publicly that he made no such charge against President Roosevelt. That had been a damaging admission for the Republicans in the midst of the 1944 campaign, but the Dirksen of 1951 did not appear to be so strict in his sensibilities as then.

In one notable instance Dirksen reached a remarkable height of intemperance. This came in May, 1951, when the Senate was considering President Truman's proposal to give two million tons of American wheat to India to relieve widespread famine there. Senator Bridges saw a political opening, and he demanded that as a condition for receiving the wheat the Indian government relax its prohibition on the export of monazite sands, a material Bridges described to the Senate as essential in the construction of jet engines. "In my judgment, Mr. President," Bridges shouted, "a vote against the amendment is a vote against jet airplanes for the defense of the nation." Dirksen quickly joined Bridges, and he made a fiery speech supporting the amendment Bridges had offered. "Always get your fee while the tears are hot," he cried, demanding the concession from the Indian government. There was a callousness in his words that sent a shock through the Senate galleries; the people in

India were starving. The effect Dirksen left was all the worse when Clyde Hoey of North Carolina, the last of the frock-coated senators, quietly told the Senate that his state had an inexhaustible supply of monazite and that most of the monazite mines were closed for the simple reason that the price of monazite was inadequate to keep them open. Ignoring Senator Hoey's telling argument, Dirksen jumped to his feet and demanded a yea-and-nay record vote. Bridges, who saw more clearly, grabbed Dirksen by the coattail and pulled him back into his chair. The amendment was defeated without the embarrassment of a roll-call vote.

With these and other antics, Dirksen lost much of the respect he had once commanded in the press gallery and with his Congressional colleagues of differing political views. Washington correspondents who had not known Dirksen in his House years had difficulty believing that he had once been so universally admired. In December, 1951, the American Federation of Labor published what it called its "All-American team of reactionary senators," and Dirksen was chosen as assistant to "Coach Taft" in the team's operations. Dirksen's decline in general favor in Washington went far beyond the imprecations and gimmickry of an antagonistic labor organization. It went farther even than would have been deserved by a politician who had turned his coat for self-serving political ends. Dirksen's very manner had changed on becoming a senator. This is a delicate point, not always understood by the uninitiated, but the Senate has a way of corroding a politician's inner being that is not admirable. Few senators escape the Senate's wanton blandishments for building self-esteem. The elaborate deference senators traditionally pay each other takes its toll even on unassuming men, as does the slavish catering to their whims by so many of the Senate's hired help. The senatorial system tends to sow arrogance in its members, what Senator John F. Kennedy of Massachusetts once called, quoting Hamlet, "the insolence of office." Rare indeed is the politician who does not provide a fertile field for haughtiness with his own inherently egocentric view of life. Dirksen was not among the exceptions. He drew about himself the senatorial toga, as scores of senators had done before him. When he spoke, there was a suggestion now of unctuousness and pomposity that would have been intolerable in the House of Representatives. He cultivated special pretensions in his enunciation. A familiar word like "liberty" he pronounced as "libartay," and he matched the ostentation of his diction with exaggerated flourishes of his arms and hands. Membership in the Senate was a far cry from the easy camaraderie and fellowship of the House of Representatives, and Dirksen fell victim to the not uncommon senatorial view that the world waited breathlessly on his words. That Dirksen was a man of great intellectual and oratorical talents, none denied, but he was now dismissed in the press gallery as just another "stuffed shirt," however talented. If Dirksen was aware of his altered status, he paid it no mind, for he was already intensely preoccupied with his own political future.

In the late summer of 1951, Dirksen was somewhat taken aback by the decision of his daughter to get married. The Dirksens had rented a cottage on Chesapeake Bay in Maryland where they spent weekends, and there one Sunday morning Joy arrived with Howard Baker, Jr., a young lawyer whom she had been dating. He was the son of Congressman Baker of Tennessee, a close friend of Dirksen. Baker suggested that Dirksen take a walk with him along the beach, and there Baker explained that he and Joy wished to get married. "I didn't ask him," Baker said. "I told him." It was a difficult business for young Baker all the same. "He was the most formidable character I'd ever met," Baker said. "He was pretty deeply moved. I'm sure he knew. He listened. He listened, and I ran out of things to say." Back at the cottage, Dirksen asked Joy if she had chosen a date for the wedding. "December 22," she said instantly. "Well," Dirksen laughed, "you've figured out all the details, haven't you?" He was surprised to discover that his daughter and wife had already made all the necessary arrangements. He himself had been extraordinarily busy in these months with his own political activities.

As chairman of the Republican Senatorial Campaign Committee,

Dirksen had the responsibility of making plans for the 1952 senatorial elections. By July, 1951, he had visited twenty-five states, talking politics, candidates, and campaign funds, and he was confidently predicting that the Republicans would win control of the Senate by defeating no less than four incumbent Democrats. Dirksen, however, had even grander goals than a Republican Senate; he wanted a Republican President. There had been a brief flurry of speculation that Dirksen might again seek the party's Presidential nomination, but he had no such illusions. He was for Senator Taft, and in November, 1951, the Taft forces announced that Dirksen and Taft had formed an alliance. Dirksen would take charge of Taft's campaign for convention delegates in Illinois. The arrangement obviously had greater implications than that. "The announcement raised speculation," the United Press reported, "that Dirksen may have the inside track as Taft's Vice-Presidential running mate, should the Ohioan win the nomination." In fact, Dirksen had become one of Taft's closest advisers, and he entertained precisely that ambition to run for Vice-President with Taft. There was much work to be done. Dirksen did successfully manage Taft's Illinois campaign, lining up fifty-nine of the state's sixty delegates for the Ohio senator. Dirksen, as the leading Republican in office from Illinois, formed a committee of the state's party leaders and officeholders. He had the support of Colonel McCormick and *The Chicago Tribune*, and there was no real contest for the Illinois delegation to the convention. Dirksen, however, took on greater chores for Taft than the Illinois delegation. He toured the Middle West and mountain states for Taft, speaking at such meetings as the Republican state party conventions in Montana and North Dakota. He helped raise funds; at a one-hundred-dollar-a-plate dinner for Dirksen in Chicago some forty-three thousand dollars was contributed. He reported to Taft on his findings and he advised Taft on strategy.

Dirksen as well served as one of Taft's chief spokesmen. Taft's major opponent for the nomination was General Dwight Eisenhower, and Dirksen played an important role in harassing Eisenhower and those sponsoring his candidacy. Taft based his campaign on rejecting both the domestic and foreign policies of the previous Democratic administrations. He and his followers argued that the "me-tooism" of the Republican Presidential candidates since 1940 had cost them the elections. In November, 1951, Dirksen demanded that Eisenhower end his silence on whether he would run for the nomination. "The men going to the Republican convention," Dirksen said, "will be rock-ribbed Republicans. They want a real choice to present to the country." The Taft forces wanted Eisenhower an announced candidate and thereby exposed to political attack. The following April, Dirksen publicly demanded that Eisenhower make an "uniquivocal statement" on where he stood on eight important national issues. Dirksen wanted to force Eisenhower to demonstrate that he would not be "a real choice" for the voters, that instead he reflected the "me-tooism" of Willkie and Dewey.

Taft was not an easy man to run for public office. He lacked political grace and finesse, and no one knew it better than Dirksen. On one occasion, early in 1952, as Taft and Dirksen were walking down a Senate corridor, Dirksen spotted a Republican delegation from West Virginia approaching them. He quickly whispered to Taft who they were: they had invited Taft to come to their meeting in West Virginia and Taft had sent a telegram instead. Dirksen formally introduced Taft to the delegation, and one of them thanked Taft for the telegram. "Oh, that's all right," Taft replied. "We send those telegrams to everybody." Dirksen was aghast at Taft's tactless blunder. "I could have killed him," Dirksen said later with a laugh.

Taft was difficult even with his friends and allies. A deeply introspective man, his very concentration on the affairs of state made him appear rude at times even to intimates. Dirksen, who came to revere Senator Taft, liked to tell of an incident in which Taft seemed to snub him. "At the Congressional Country Club once," Dirksen said, "I passed Taft in the doorway. You'd think I was an absolute stranger. I think it was two days later Taft said to me: 'I'm terribly sorry I didn't say "Hello" Sunday afternoon. I knew it was you. Something was on my mind.' " Dirksen had not taken offense, but Dirksen saw that Taft's intense absorption with his work and his essential humorlessness often gave offense to others.

Well before the July convention, there was continuing speculation that Dirksen might be Taft's choice for Vice-President. Dirksen was fully aware of this, for his friends were talking in party councils about a Taft-Dirksen ticket and the newspapers were printing the fact. Not a shy man, Dirksen took the question up directly with Taft. He told Taft that he had only one interest in the campaign, and that was Taft's nomination and election as President. "If after you are nominated," Dirksen said to him, "I look like a likely . . ." Well, Dirksen went on, that would be entirely up to Taft. He should make the decision on a running mate according to the dictates of his own best political interests, not on the basis of friendship or any sense of debt to Dirksen for services rendered in the campaign. Dirksen did not regard the geographic proximity of his own Illinois to Taft's Ohio as grounds to disqualify him from serious consideration. Dirksen explained that he had been somewhat embarrassed by the talk about the Vice-President nomination, but he wanted Taft to know that he was available if Taft wanted him. Clearly, Dirksen wanted that Vice-Presidential nomination, but he was wary about making too open an attempt to seek it now. "I had my lightning rod up for the Vice-Presidency once before," he said, looking back at the incident. Taft made no commitment to Dirksen on the Vice-Presidency. He did, however, ask Dirksen to present his name in nomination at the national convention. At the time, Dirksen had hopes that Taft might choose him for Vice-President, but years later he came to believe that Taft probably would not have done so. "I got generally the feeling," Dirksen said, "that if Bob picked anyone it would have been Bill Knowland, not me. Illinois is so close to Ohio."

At the convention, which was held in Chicago, Taft's delegate strength came principally from the Middle West, with additional support from the border and mountain states. General Eisenhower had some scattered support in the Middle West, but his main strength came from New England and the Mid-Atlantic states. The real struggle, on which depended control of the convention, hung on the Southern delegations, traditionally a collection of nondescript politicians without influence in the party except at national conventions. From the start these delegations had been the target for both the Taft and Eisenhower managers, and they fought for their allegiance in less than virtuous terms. At one point in the preconvention struggle Taft had shown what he thought of them in a private conversation with Dirksen and Congressman Clarence Brown of Ohio, another of Taft's advisers. "They could be bought," Taft said of the Southern delegations, "if they weren't afraid." In three of the Southern states—Georgia, Louisiana, and Texas—the political infighting was unusually savage, and the competing factions sent rival Taft and Eisenhower delegations to Chicago amid ugly charges of corruption and bribery. The National Republican Committee, controlled by the Taft forces, voted to seat the Taft delegations in each case. It was inevitable that the rejected Eisenhower delegates would appeal to the convention itself for installment, but it was not inevitable that any of the contests would amount to more than the traditional bickering. Senator Henry Cabot Lodge of Massachusetts and Governor Dewey of New York, however, were acting as political managers for Eisenhower at the convention, and they cleverly chose to make of these contested delegates a paramount moral issue. The Eisenhower forces proclaimed their own "honesty" and stated that they would not tolerate this "theft" of their delegates. They rallied to the slogan: "Thou shalt not steal!" It was a bad turn for Senator Taft, and he maneuvered ineffectually to blunt this Eisenhower tactic.

As a preliminary to the main struggle, the Eisenhower forces offered in convention a "fair-play" amendment to deny voting rights to any of the contested delegates until the convention itself could pass on their credentials. Involved were sixty-eight delegates, fifty of them pledged to Taft, and the convention decision on their credentials could determine who would receive the Presidential nomination of the party. The Taft forces were confused and dismayed by the virulence of the charge of moral corruption made against them. They decided not to fight the fair-play amendment directly, but instead to try to exempt only seven of the Louisiana delegates. That motion, made for Taft by Congressman Brown, provided the first real show of strength between the Taft and Eisenhower forces at the convention, and the Taft forces lost it by 548 votes against 658 for the Eisenhower position. Shaken by this defeat, the Taft forces altered their strategy on the credentials fight. They decided to surrender all of the Louisiana delegates and concentrate their efforts on the seating of the Taft factions from Georgia and Texas. This decision precipitated an even more momentous struggle on the convention floor, with the Taft forces plainly at a disadvantage. Taft chose Dirksen to make his side's argument to the convention, to try to save his flagging cause.

For Dirksen this was the most important speech of his life. On it depended Taft's last chance for the Presidential nomination, and Dirksen's hopes as well. Not only were the convention delegates at fever pitch and watching him at the rostrum with intense interest, so also was the nation, watching on television. Dirksen made the most of it, and his speech was recognized universally as the dramatic highlight of the convention. He began with his mellifluous voice in full play, weaving an easy blend of Fourth of July and Biblical oratory. When he quoted sacred parchments, "Come let us reason together," he had the great multitude before him enthralled and enchanted. But his voice changed and his meaning changed as he moved into the thrust of his argument. A political realist, Dirksen could see the inevitable defeat ahead for Taft and himself in the reality of the test vote already taken on the fair-play amendment. He became bitter. He berated the Republican Party for its "habit," as he put it, of winning conventions and losing elections. He told the delegates that he had stood by the party in the past in those convention decisions. He had campaigned for Dewey, he said, in eighteen states in 1944 and in twenty-three states in 1948. From the podium he looked down at Governor Dewey on the convention floor. He shook his finger dramatically in Dewey's face. "We followed you before," Dirksen cried out, "and you took us down the path to defeat!"

Even before Dirksen reached his climax, the delegates had caught his meaning, his bitterness, and some started booing in anticipation of it. The Taft delegates were booing Governor Dewey, and Eisenhower delegates were booing Dirksen. As he hurled the studied insult into Dewey's face, a great howl rose from the delegates on the floor and swept into the packed galleries. Dewey sat smiling grimly among the New York delegates, as the party faithful vented their feelings at his failures. For a while it appeared as though the convention might get out of control, but the temporary chairman gaveled the delegates back to order.

Dirksen was in complete command of himself. He was not rattled by the tremendous emotional outpouring from the convention. He sipped from a glass of water as the crowd howled. "Fellow delegates," he said at last when the uproar quieted, "I assure you that I didn't mean to precipitate a controversy."

For Dirksen that one speech engendered more resentment against him than anything he had ever said or done before. Even those who agreed with him about Governor Dewey and the party's Eastern wing of liberals and internationalists resented his using such a forum for such a speech. The Eastern bloc was furious. For Dirksen and for Taft, the rest of the convention was the ruin of their ambitions. The convention voted to seat the Eisenhower delegates from both Georgia and Texas, and then, on the first ballot, nominated Eisenhower for President. Dirksen made the nominating speech for Taft, but it was a tame performance compared to his assault on Governor Dewey. As the first ballot neared its close, Eisenhower was clearly the winner, and Taft delegations began to switch their votes to the general. There was an attempt within the Illinois delegation to do the same, but Dirksen, as chairman of the delegation, refused to allow it. "Let the record stand," he told the delegation. "It represents our convictions. Bob Taft wouldn't think much of us if we ran for the bandwagon now." Burning within Dirksen were resentments of his own, fed by the fuels of his own crushed ambitions. He was fifty-six years old. There would be no more chances.

There was one final grim note for Dirksen at this convention. The chief supporters of Eisenhower caucused in a hotel room to choose a Vice-Presidential running mate for Eisenhower. Senator Frank Carlson of Kansas was called from the session to answer the telephone. He returned to explain that the call had been from Senator Taft. Taft wanted Dirksen considered for Vice-President. The proposal took the Eisenhower chiefs aback. Finally Governor William Beardsley of Iowa spoke up. "Mr. Chairman," he said, "all I have to say is that after what Dirksen said the other night, the people of Iowa wouldn't use him to wipe their feet on."

"That," wrote Governor Sherman Adams of New Hampshire, who was there, "was the end of Dirksen."

# Chapter 6

# The Black Years

*How bad must be the evil acids eating at the soul
if finally they stir in such a way our passions and our tempers.*

In the aftermath of the Chicago convention, General Eisenhower's
political managers feared that Senator Taft and the Republican
regulars like Dirksen would give little or no help in the Presidential
campaign. When Eisenhower had called on Taft at his headquarters
immediately after winning the nomination from him, the defeated
Senator had uttered the usual congratulations and pledges of help
expected of a good loser. Around him, however, his campaign
workers were weeping. The Old Guard party stalwarts were bitter;
the Eastern liberal-internationalists had wrenched the party away
from them again. Privately Taft tried to persuade his lieutenants
not to engage in recriminations against Eisenhower, but they went
on all the same. In the Republican organization in Illinois especially
the disappointment and resentment over Eisenhower's nomination
were unusually severe. There the party regulars lapsed into sullen
apathy. Colonel McCormick, publisher of *The Chicago Tribune*,
was openly hostile to Eisenhower. He advised all Republicans to
stay home on election day.

Dirksen, whose hopes had been broken with Taft's, had no heart
or zest to campaign for Eisenhower. He was, of course, chairman of

the Republican Senatorial Campaign Committee, and, as such, regarded with special concern by the Eisenhower managers. As early as July 21 Dirksen said he would work to elect Eisenhower, but his main thrust was to concentrate his efforts on helping Republican candidates win election to the Senate.

"I expect," he said, "to be in the thick of the campaign myself and will visit every state where there is a Republican senatorial candidate on the ticket. I feel quite confident that when the Eighty-third Congress meets in 1953, a Republican President will have the full cooperation of a Republican Congress."

Eisenhower invited Dirksen to join him and other party leaders in Denver in early August to help map campaign strategy. Dirksen did not immediately reply, and this caused exaggerated fears within the Eisenhower camp that Dirksen was sulking and would not attend the planned meeting. Not until two days before the meeting did Dirksen send word that he would come. Once there, smilingly he gave assurances that he was "without animus or bile." He accepted a pro-forma appointment to Eisenhower's six-man board of strategy. On paper, Dirksen's visit to Denver looked like the return of the prodigal and was so treated by the press, but there was something less than enthusiasm in Dirksen for the man who had defeated Taft and thus also deprived Dirksen of his fling at national office.

In the campaign Dirksen belabored the Democratic administration in Washington and the Democratic Presidential nominee, Adlai Stevenson. "I want a real change," he said of the Truman administration. "I don't want someone telling me you can have a change by leaving on the soiled diaper and just changing the safety pins." Dirksen in other speeches denounced Stevenson as one of the "worst" governors Illinois had ever had and blamed him for running a state administration rife with scandal. For this, Dirksen found himself in a public shouting match with a Presbyterian minister from Springfield, Illinois, who accused Dirksen of telling "a blatant lie." When Eisenhower's campaign train whistle-stopped through

Illinois, Dirksen was aboard and appeared with him. Repeatedly in his speeches Dirksen predicted the election of Eisenhower.

Dirksen, however, placed his real emphasis on aiding Republican candidates for the Senate, as he said he would. He made two separate tours around the country, visiting twenty-five states, on behalf of these Republican candidates. As chairman of the party's Senatorial Campaign Committee, this was his special assignment, but there was a strong suggestion of coolness toward Eisenhower in Dirksen's manner and words. For example, Dirksen went out of his way in his speeches to compliment Senator Joseph McCarthy as a "great legislator and a great marine." McCarthy, deeply engaged in his controversial attacks on many Americans, was a painful embarrassment to Eisenhower throughout the campaign. McCarthy and his associate, Senator William Jenner of Indiana, who was also running for reelection that year, were members of the Taft wing of the Republican party, not the Eisenhower-Dewey wing, and Dirksen's extravagant praise for them could only cause grief to the Eastern Republicans. That did not deter Dirksen, and he argued in his campaign speeches McCarthy's thesis against the Democrats: they "sold" Poland and China to the Communists. "Joe McCarthy was essentially on good ground," Dirksen told one applauding audience in Chicago, "and don't let anyone kid you about it."

The Eastern wing of the Republican Party did not forgive Dirksen for his convention attack on Governor Dewey. Dirksen himself declined to take back what he had said. "Regrets?" he said. "My goodness, no. How can you have regrets about stating a fact? I simply told the truth about Dewey, that's all." The incident continued to engender resentment against Dirksen. Earlier, for example, Dirksen had been invited as the speaker at a Republican clambake in Rhode Island, but the invitation was cancelled after his rebuke of Dewey. "Prejudices Dirksen has created," said a spokesman for the Rhode Island Republican Club, the sponsoring group, "would hurt the candidates here." Other Eastern Republicans had a similar worry about Dirksen and a similar distaste for him. In his campaign tours, Dirksen swung through the Middle West, the Far West, and the South, largely avoiding the Eastern states, even though there were five contested Senate seats in New England alone. "It is understood," reported *The New York Times*, "that Republican organizations in parts of the East believe their Senate candidates would not be helped by appearances by Mr. Dirksen. . . ."

This was not the ingratiating stuff of party harmony, and, after Eisenhower's election as President, Dirksen found himself, emotionally and practically, a member of a Republican faction at odds with the Republican administration about to assume command of the American government. The Republicans in the same election won marginal control of the House of Representatives and bare control of the Senate. The Republican cabal that controlled the party's councils in the Senate, however, were Taft men through and through, led by Taft himself. They were conservatives, professional politicians, mostly from the Middle West, and they eyed Eisenhower with unadorned skepticism. Only a year before there had been doubt whether Eisenhower in fact was a Republican; now he was the formal chief of the party. There were lingering doubts still on where he stood on many of the critical issues confronting the government and the American people. The Senate Republicans loyal to Taft had an aching sense of loss and thereby an instinctive antipathy toward the man and men who had caused that loss.

All of this made Dirksen and the other Taft Republicans in the Senate less than instantly responsive to the overtures and programs of the new President. There was, however, something more: none of them had ever known the experience of serving in Congress as the majority under a President of their own party. The most senior Republican was Styles Bridges of New Hampshire, elected to the Senate in 1936, a full four years after Franklin Roosevelt had won the White House for the Democrats. Taft had arrived in the Senate two years after Bridges. They and the other Republican senators had been trained to opposition, to the traditional stance of a minority. "The business of the opposition," Taft once said, "is to oppose." They had spent their careers opposing Presidential measures and programs, and it would not be easy, especially for those of the Taft faction, to learn to act otherwise. Some few of the Republican senators were consciously aware of their altered status and tried to act accordingly, men like Homer Capehart of Indiana, new chairman of the Senate Banking Committee. Their efforts were not always successful or even graceful, for they were strange to the posture of acting responsibly and responsively toward any President. Most notable of all of those who made the effort was Senator Taft.

Even as the 1952 Presidential campaign was getting under way, Taft had made terms with Eisenhower. The two met at the general's home at Columbia University, and Taft brought to the meeting a lengthy manifesto he had drafted, detailing orthodox Republican dogma as conservative Midwestern Republicans understood that dogma. In a two-hour meeting Eisenhower had subscribed to Taft's statement in full, and Taft emerged from their conference convinced that Eisenhower was sound on fundamental Republican "principles." Others were shocked that Eisenhower would thus clumsily succumb to Taft's terms, and they described the formal agreement as "The Surrender of Morningside Heights." Taft strongly urged his followers to back Eisenhower in the campaign, and when the new Congress convened Taft himself was ready to do his best to see that the incoming Republican administration proved a success. In the Senate Taft was chairman of the Republican Policy Committee, ranking Republican on the Labor Committee and entitled to its chairmanship, and second-ranking Republican on the influential Finance Committee. He sacrificed all these powerful positions to take on the onerous and usually thankless post of his party's floor leader in the Senate. As such, he would lead the Republican leaders to the White House once each week for their legislative conference with the President. As such, he would have charge of passing the entire Eisenhower program. He intended to guide and shape that program as well as pass it.

For Dirksen, Taft's maneuvers were prompted by unfamiliar instincts. They were cut from different cloth, these two men, however cordial had been their relationship for the past two years. Dirksen's instincts were not self-deprecating; to him there was more to political life than blind service to the party, and he found himself closer to the Senate's conservative old-timers than to the new Republican crowd that had taken over the executive branch of the government. There had been talk, not entirely free from remembrance of his notoriety at the Chicago convention, of creating a new Senate post for Dirksen as assistant party floor leader. That had fallen through, but he was permitted to continue as chairman of the party's Senatorial Campaign Committee. More significantly, he was now awarded assignment to three of the Senate's most influential committees, Appropriations, Judiciary, and Government Operations. It was recognition of his enhanced status within the Republican Party in the Senate. His standing in the national party was something else; among Dewey Republicans his name was still anathema. At the White House there was a desire to placate him, for the President's staff knew his growing influence within the Senate, and he was feared.

Even before Eisenhower took the oath as President, Dirksen engaged Eisenhower's chief political henchmen in an abrasive and bruising quarrel over party patronage. Dirksen's real opponents in this struggle were the Republican politicians in Chicago and downstate Illinois, with the Eisenhower men in Washington trying desperately not to alienate either side. Dirksen blatantly insisted on his rights as the ranking elected Republican in Illinois to dictate who from Illinois received appointments to the judiciary and other important federal posts. Dirksen boldly threatened to use his full power as Illinois' Republican senator to block any nominations he opposed from Senate confirmation.

"Nobody is going to make a patronage football of the federal bench in Chicago," he said at one point. "I am determined that Senate courtesy in such appointments will be followed. Those judges must be the best men available."

That was the parliamentary way of stating that he insisted on the right to name the men, or clear the men named. Otherwise he would declare those named "personally obnoxious" to him, the signal words for all senators to rally around a colleague and protect him from the presumed outrages he was suffering from the President and the outside world. "If necessary," Dirksen threatened, "I'll fight with all that's in me on the Senate floor. . . ."

In late December Eisenhower's special agent in such matters, National Republican Chairman Arthur E. Summerfield, capitulated to Dirksen. He assured Dirksen that he would be the first man consulted on all important appointments to federal office in Illinois. "We'd be crazy," one Republican professional in Washington confided at the time, "to bypass Dirksen on these judicial and other Illinois nominations requiring Senate confirmation." These assurances, however, were not enough, and the struggle between Dirksen and the Eisenhower administration over party patronage dragged on for many weeks, engaging not only Summerfield but also Herbert Brownell, the new Attorney General. The battling, conducted in private offices and laced with bitterness, made relations between the Senator and the new administration strained and difficult. No one questioned Dirksen's willingness to retaliate against the administration, striking in varied ways at those who failed to meet his terms, and some of Dirksen's actions against the administration in these early months of the Eisenhower administration were presumed motivated by his churlish intent to avenge himself for patronage plums not received.

In the new Senate that convened January 3, 1953, the Republicans held a bare one-seat margin over the Democrats. With the antipathy of the Republican Senate leaders to most of the Democratic internationalism of the past two score years, Eisenhower had to depend on help for his foreign policies and programs from the Senate Democrats, who had just elected Lyndon B. Johnson of Texas as their new floor leader. There were a handful of new Democrats in the Senate, including John F. Kennedy of Massachusetts and Mike Mansfield of Montana. On the Republican side, there were also some newcomers, among them Barry Goldwater of Arizona. The real power of the Senate, by that one-vote margin, had shifted to the Republican Party's seniors, led by Taft. Of almost equal influence with Taft in the Senate were Styles Bridges of New Hampshire, now chairman of the Appropriations Committee and President Pro Tempore of the Senate, and Eugene Millikin, now chairman of the Finance Committee. At the next echelon stood William Knowland of California, whom Taft made chairman of the Republican Policy Committee, the influential post Taft himself had held. They were all staunch party partisans; their instincts were insular in international affairs and deeply conservative in domestic matters. They wanted the new government in safe hands, men of their own kind, and they intended to slash federal spending. They wished to repudiate the Democratic programs that had gone before.

Despite his own internationalism and his moderation in domestic policy, Eisenhower resolved from the very start to work with the Republican leadership in Congress, come what may. "My position," he told the new cabinet, "is simply this: our long-term good requires that leadership on the Hill be exercised through the party organization there. This is the key to success. . . ." He had to depend on Taft and on Taft's Senate hierarchy, and it was not easy on either side. When he named his Secretary of Labor, Martin Durkin, a one-time plumber and labor leader, Taft could not control himself. "Incredible!" he exclaimed. Taft was shaken again when Eisenhower named as Secretary of the Treasury George Humphrey, a Taft opponent from Ohio. Taft, however, smothered his sense of chagrin, and he guided both nominations through the Senate. There was greater difficulty, however, when Eisenhower named a new ambassador to Russia, Charles ("Chip") Bohlen, a brilliant career diplomat. Not Senator Taft, but the Taft wing of the Senate mutinied.

President Eisenhower had cleared the appointment of Bohlen in advance with Taft, something he had neglected to do with the nominations of Secretaries Humphrey and Durkin. Taft, however, could not quiet the virulent objections of his isolationist colleagues in the Senate. Senator McCarthy, increasingly reckless, led the Republican attack against Bohlen, blaming him for the "treason" of the Yalta agreement negotiated by President Roosevelt with the Russians. McCarthy as well associated Bohlen with the "traitor" Alger Hiss, and he tried to make Bohlen appear "subservient" to the Russians. McCarthy's venomous assault on Bohlen became so bitter that President Eisenhower finally agreed to permit Senator Taft and a Democratic senator, John Sparkman of Alabama, to examine the alleged "derogatory" information on Bohlen in the files of the Federal Bureau of Investigation.

Dirksen was among the group of senators who joined McCarthy in opposing Bohlen's appointment, although Dirksen shrank from impugning Bohlen's loyalty to the United States as McCarthy had done. Instead Dirksen paraphrased the argument of Senator Bridges that the American people could have no confidence in a man so closely connected with the "discredited" foreign policies of the previous Democratic administrations. "Chip Bohlen was at Yalta," Dirksen said. "If he were my brother, I would take the same attitude I am expressing in the Senate this afternoon. He was associated with the failure. Mr. President, in the language of Missouri, the tail must go with the hide. I reject Yalta. So I reject Yalta men." When the Senate voted approval of Bohlen's appointment as ambassador on March 27, Dirksen was one of the thirteen senators who voted no.

The mutiny within the Senate against the Bohlen nomination was not an isolated incident of hostility toward President Eisenhower and his approach to international affairs. Rather it was symptomatic of a festering unhappiness and frustration among many conservative senators, including Dirksen, with the whole course of American policies at home and abroad. That malaise especially infected the senators of the Taft faction, ill at ease with the internationalist wing of their party in command of the government. From their ranks came an assault not only against the President's internationalism but also against the office of the President and his control of foreign relations.

From the moment Eisenhower had taken office, his administration concentrated on cutting the huge budget submitted in January by outgoing President Truman for the next fiscal year. That budget projected a deficit of almost ten billion dollars, and the Eisenhower men found that they, bearing the responsibility of conducting the government, could not cut that deficit by more than four and one-half billion dollars. The Republican leaders in the Senate were furious. "With a program like this," Taft shouted, when shown the figures of the Eisenhower budget, "we'll never elect a Republican Congress in 1954." Taft and Dirksen and the other Republican conservatives wanted the President to cut enough funds to balance the budget. "I feel most frustrated," Dirksen said. "I could cry." Offended by the administration's failure, Dirksen stated that only Congress could make the economies needed. If his colleagues on the Appropriations Committee would "show a little guts," Dirksen said, the job could be done. Dirksen believed that the way to cut a budget was to cut it. President Eisenhower argued that it would be folly to risk world peace and the nation's security by making deeper cuts than those already made. Dirksen disagreed, and so did his friend and ally Styles Bridges.

On May 16, 1953, as chairman of the Appropriations Committee, Bridges announced that he was sending a two-man special subcommittee to the Far East, and another similar subcommittee to Europe, to study on the spot how much foreign aid was really needed by American allies. He named Dirksen as head of the Asian subcommittee, and Dirksen spent six weeks in the Far East searching for the "deep cuts" that could be made in the foreign-aid program. He toured Japan, Korea, Indochina, the Philippines, and Formosa, where he dined with Chiang Kai-shek. On his return to Washington Dirksen made a detailed report in secret to the Appropriations Committee. Although his findings were never made public, there could be no doubt of his recommendations. In voting on the authorization bill for foreign aid, Dirksen supported an amendment to slash two billion dollars from that program, and when the amendment was defeated, he supported another unsuccessful amendment to cut one billion dollars from foreign aid. With Dirksen's help, the Appropriations Committee cut seven hundred million dollars from the funds Eisenhower had asked for foreign aid. Senator Taft, speaking for the Senate's Republicans, carried that action one step further: he advised the foreign-aid administrator, Harold Stassen, to prepare a "liquidation program" for foreign aid.

Dirksen favored reductions in other of the President's requests for appropriations. On the independent-offices appropriations bill, for example, he himself offered an amendment, which was rejected, to cut a full five percent of all the funds provided in the bill, exempting only the President's salary. On the legislative-appropriations bill, which provided funds for Congress, Dirksen was not so parsimonious. The Appropriations Committee voted extra funds to allow senators to hire additional clerks for their offices. When a senator in debate protested that this went against the grain of economizing and left the senators open to public criticism, Dirksen took the floor. He mocked his colleague's fears. "There is no timidity about me," he stated, "when I am seeking the help I need to handle the office to which I was elected." The funds were approved.

If Dirksen insisted on his own prerogatives over federal patronage and in securing what federal funds he wanted to run his senatorial office, he took a jaundiced view of the men and the money President Eisenhower wanted to operate the federal establishment. In this, his feelings ran deeper than latent hostility toward President Eisenhower. Within himself he harbored an inherent animosity toward the executive branch of government as such, no doubt heightened by his sense of loss and denial at the Chicago convention. Like many senators, Dirksen labored under an institutional sense of antagonism toward the executive branch, built off his long years in the legislative branch and now enhanced by his own deepening sense of the grandeur of the office he held as senator. It was an intensification, this notion of his rank of senator, of the not uncommon feeling among senators that somehow their election by the people gave them an automatic superiority to all members of the executive branch, save only the President, who was elected too. It was an imperious sentiment, the kernel ingredient of arrogance, that allowed senators to dismiss at will any *appointed* members of the executive branch as mere "bureaucrats." Dirksen took consolation in that concept of his office. He knew that as a senator he held power in his own right, and so too did the Senate, of which he was now an influential member.

The attack on foreign aid was not the only such assault from the Republican Senate on the President's internationalism, nor the most serious. There were others, and Dirksen took an activist's role in all of them. Most consequential of all was a proposal by Senator John Bricker of Ohio, Taft's colleague, to so amend the Constitution as to limit the President's freedom in negotiating treaties with other countries. Bricker proposed that treaties no longer rank as "the supreme law of the land" and that they no longer apply as binding domestic law in the United States unless Congress enacts "appropriate legislation" to make them so. Dirksen co-sponsored the Bricker amendment, as did the other influential Republicans in the Senate, including Taft, Knowland, Bridges, and McCarthy. For three months Dirksen sat as a member of a subcommittee of the Judiciary Committee holding hearings on the proposed constitutional amendment, and those hearings provided a forum for all those who wanted to reverse the country's international course. President Eisenhower took alarm; it was plain that there were enough votes in the Senate to approve the Bricker amendment. On March 26 the President protested that the amendment, if adopted, would prevent him from conducting the nation's foreign relations effectively. On April 6 Secretary of State John Foster Dulles objected that the Bricker amendment would endanger the nation's peace and security. All the same, the Judiciary Committee on June 15 approved the proposal on a nine-to-five vote that had Dirksen's support. With Senate approval of the amendment imminent, Eisenhower's Attorney General, Herbert Brownell, started consultations with Senator Knowland. Together they worked out a compromise to blunt the severity of the proposal as it had emerged from the Judiciary Committee, and this compromise Knowland announced on July 22. This maneuver confused the issue and thereby delayed any formal Senate action on the matter. For years after, the question hung over the Senate and the Senate's relationship with President Eisenhower, and throughout the struggle Dirksen stuck with Bricker and his isolationist allies. As late as March, 1956, Dirksen was trying to find a means of passing some constitutional amendment that would carry out Bricker's intent. On March 7 of that year he offered a substitute proposal that had Bricker's "wholehearted support," but that proposal never came to a vote in the Senate. Finally Bricker himself abandoned the struggle.

In the early months of Eisenhower's first year as President, Bricker led another assault on the existing international arrangements of the American government, and in this struggle too he had the full support of Senator Dirksen. Pending before the Senate were three treaties dealing with United States participation in the North Atlantic Treaty Organization. To one of them Bricker proposed a reservation under which the United States would hold exclusive jurisdiction over any crimes committed by American troops stationed in NATO countries. Again Bricker had the backing of the Taft men in the Senate, including Senators Malone of Nevada, Welker of Idaho, and Schoeppel of Kansas. On the day Bricker's reservation came to a vote in the Senate, Dirksen spoke forcefully in its favor. "Mr. President," he said, "I shall not leave our American soldiers who are abroad to the mercies of any country." The Senate, however, rejected the proposal, 27 to 53, and then approved the treaties unencumbered. Dirksen was one of the fifteen senators who voted not to ratify them. That vote, like his vote on the Bohlen nomination, showed plainly where Dirksen stood in the Senate, with the fractious minority of his own party, still angry with the world.

In another tack to impose Congressional leverage on the conduct of U.S. foreign policy, Dirksen this same year acted on his own. In the Appropriations Committee he proposed a rider to a bill that would automatically cut off any further financial support of the United Nations if Communist China were admitted to membership in that international organization. The committee approved it 20 to 3, and again President Eisenhower felt compelled to act. He summoned the Republican leaders of Congress to the White House on June 2, 1953, for a special meeting to deal with the Dirksen rider. There he told them that he regarded the proposal as a grave mistake. The Dirksen proposal was not only an improper way to serve such notice on the United Nations, he said, but the United States could not risk isolating itself this way from the world. Senator Knowland proposed offering a meaningless substitute for the Dirksen amendment, and Senator Bridges agreed to sponsor it. Thus this Dirksen assault was blunted. The Senate unanimously adopted the Bridges language, which merely stated that it was "the sense of Congress" that Communist China should not be admitted to the United Nations.

In mid-spring, even as these struggles were shaping, an event occurred that profoundly affected the Senate, Senator Dirksen, and the President's relations with the Senate. Senator Taft took ill. There were exploratory examinations, and then in late May Taft knew the worst. He had cancer. With considerable gallantry Taft tried to attend to his duties in the Senate, hobbling about on crutches. His illness grew more grave, and more and more he had to absent himself. In these periods he asked Senator Knowland to stand in for him as floor leader in the Senate. Finally, on June 10, Taft recognized that had to step aside as his party's leader, and he appointed Knowland as "acting" majority leader. This was an extraordinary maneuver; normally the party caucus would make such a choice, not Taft. Under the circumstances, however, no one complained, even though in retrospect Taft had thus chosen his successor and blocked the personal ambitions of Senator Dirksen, among others, for advancement. In early July Taft was transferred to New York, where he underwent surgery. He continued to fail, and on July 31 he died.

For President Eisenhower, Taft's death was a stunning blow, for he had depended on Taft above all others to moderate the instinctive antagonism of many Republican senators to the domestic and foreign policies he was trying to implement. Eisenhower counted on Taft to temper the actions of senators like Dirksen and Bridges, especially to draw them away from supporting the growingly hostile antics of Senator McCarthy. With Taft dead, that restraining influence was gone. On August 4, the day Taft was buried, the Republicans in the Senate formally elected Knowland, the man designated by Taft, as their leader. He was to prove an inept parliamentarian, often at odds with the Eisenhower administration. For Dirksen, whatever anguish he felt in seeing the party leadership go to a younger rival, the gradual replacement of Taft by Knowland in the late spring and summer of 1953 had the natural effect of estranging him still further from the Eisenhower administration. Taft had been Dirksen's leader, to whom he would listen. Knowland, at forty-five, twelve years younger than Dirksen, was a much different man. Knowland felt that his responsibility as leader was to speak to the President for the Senate, not to the Senate for the President. The result was to encourage, not lessen, antipathy among Republican senators toward the President and his programs.

At the beginning of the 1953 session of the Senate Dirksen had been named to the Government Operations Committee, and the chairman of that committee, Senator McCarthy, had picked Dirksen to serve on that committee's permanent investigations subcommittee, which McCarthy also chaired. In the previous three years McCarthy had repeatedly and savagely assaulted the Truman administration, charging deep infiltration by Communists into the

State Department and other agencies. Taft had encouraged McCarthy in this work, and Dirksen had been McCarthy's defender. In these years McCarthy gained a national notoriety, unmatched in his time, with his rash and often unsupported accusations. The key to his success, such as it was, was to attack those in public offices of great responsibility, and when the Eisenhower administration took charge of the federal government McCarthy saw no reason to change. Indeed, with his new authority as chairman of a powerful Senate committee, he increased his destructive attack. Now, however, he was libelling Republicans, not Democrats, and that gravely distressed the Eisenhower administration and Senator Taft. McCarthy, however, had many allies among the Senate's Republicans, and President Eisenhower hesitated to confront him directly.

In early 1953, on his own, Senator McCarthy negotiated a "treaty" with a group of Greek shipowners under which they agreed not to engage in trade with Communist countries. It was a mark of McCarthy's brazenness that he would thus seek to usurp the constitutional prerogatives of the President. For the Eisenhower administration, Harold Stassen appeared before McCarthy's committee and testily stated that McCarthy had undermined the President's own negotiations to end this very trade with Communist nations. Dirksen stood with McCarthy. President Eisenhower, fearful of the effect on McCarthy of Stassen's harsh accusation, forced Stassen to retract the word "undermine" and substitute "infringe." This retreat before McCarthy startled the country and the world. The leader of the British Labor Party, Clement Attlee, acidly questioned whether President Eisenhower or Senator McCarthy conducted U.S. foreign policy. The incident was an ill omen for what was to come.

Already McCarthy had shown that he did not intend to stay his investigations and accusations because of the advent of a Republican administration. Within a week after Eisenhower took the oath as President, McCarthy launched an investigation of the government's program of stockpiling strategic materials. Within weeks he had parallel investigations under way of the public-assistance program, the State Department's personnel files, the General Services Administration, the Voice of America, and the Navy. McCarthy repeatedly claimed he had evidence of subversion, communism, and disloyalty within the government now run by Eisenhower. At his side throughout sat Dirksen, and the entire temper of the McCarthy investigations was hostile to the new administration. On February 16 McCarthy warned the Eisenhower administration that he and his colleagues would not tolerate "any reprisals" against any administration witnesses who testified before the subcommittee. As early as March 7 the new President publicly indicated concern at the course of McCarthy's investigations. By midsummer McCarthy charged that Communists had access to the secrets of the Atomic Energy Commission and the Central Intelligence Agency. He attacked the State Department for its use of "Communist" books in its overseas libraries. On August 31 he claimed evidence of Communist infiltration of the military, and six weeks later he opened hearings on alleged Communist espionage at the Army base at Fort Monmouth, New Jersey. This was the start of what proved to be a climactic confrontation between McCarthy and the Eisenhower administration. Dirksen sided with McCarthy.

As other administration leaders had also done, Army Secretary Robert Stevens tried to placate Senator McCarthy. In the first weeks thirty-three Army employees at Fort Monmouth were suspended. McCarthy plunged on. He called the Army's Chief of Intelligence, a major general, "completely incompetent." All through the fall and winter, newspaper headlines daily told of new McCarthy sensations. The attack on the Army was peculiarly sensitive to the administration, for Eisenhower had held the rank of five-star general and had been the Army's Chief of Staff. In February, 1954, McCarthy accused an Army brigadier general, a man of proven gallantry, of being "unfit" to wear the Army's uniform. Under McCarthy's savage assault, the Army's morale was wilting, and Secretary

Stevens could placate no longer. He ordered the general not to appear again before McCarthy's subcommittee. McCarthy blandly suggested that the case might involve treason.

Still Dirksen stayed with McCarthy, supporting him unflaggingly. On February 24, in Dirksen's Senate office, over a lunch of fried chicken, Stevens met privately with McCarthy, Dirksen, and the two other Republican members of the subcommittee. There Stevens agreed to permit Army officers to testify before the subcommittee. McCarthy was triumphant. "Stevens could not have given in more abjectly," McCarthy told reporters, "if he had got down on his knees." It was a disaster to the Eisenhower administration's prestige; the newspapers reported that the Army had "surrendered" to Senator McCarthy. In this extraordinary state of affairs, President Eisenhower tried to salvage the ruin. He invited Dirksen to the White House and asked him to get assurances from the subcommittee that Army witnesses would not be abused. When that maneuver failed, the President's staff prepared a formal statement for Stevens, issued from the White House, that at the meeting in Dirksen's office the subcommittee members had in fact given Stevens just such "assurances."

On March 11 the Army released a report on how McCarthy had made extraordinary attempts to get special treatment for a subcommittee staff member who had been drafted. McCarthy retorted that the Army was trying to "blackmail" him out of uncovering Communists in the Army. In this welter of wild charges, the subcommittee itself opened an investigation of the conflicting claims, with McCarthy stepping aside as chairman. All spring, before television cameras, this investigation raged, and then on into summer, with McCarthy constantly making wild accusations of malfeasance or worse against administration officials. Dirksen proclaimed impartiality for himself, but repeatedly he tried to rescue McCarthy from this madness. In mid-May, when public opinion turned against McCarthy, Dirksen even moved to close down the hearings. When that failed, he tried to arrange for the hearings to be held in secret, hidden from the eyes of the country. In the end, the subcommittee's Republicans, including Dirksen, exonerated McCarthy in their formal report, and Dirksen issued supplemental views of his own that McCarthy had done nothing "improper."

Inside the White House there was deep dismay at the continuing harassment by Senator McCarthy, but the President declined to confront McCarthy himself. At one point Eisenhower conferred with Republican National Chairman Leonard Hall about McCarthy and sent Hall to see the Senator. Hall used less than adamant words in describing his approach to McCarthy. "While Joe is fighting communism," Hall said, "I go along and we all go along. When he begins to attack persons who are fighting communism just as conscientiously as he is, I can't go along with him." Needless to say, Hall did not stay McCarthy's attacks. President Eisenhower had hopes from the very start that he could isolate McCarthy in the Senate; he had special hopes that he could persuade Dirksen to abandon McCarthy. "My hope . . . was that we might eventually be able to split off a number of senators from the 'McCarthy-Malone axis' and thus reduce the remaining splinter group to practical impotence," Eisenhower wrote in his memoirs. The President's hesitation to confront McCarthy directly, which amounted to vacillation in the continuing crisis, demoralized the executive branch of the government. When the effort came to halt McCarthy, it came from within the Senate.

In July Senator Ralph Flanders of Vermont, a Republican, formally proposed to the Senate a resolution to censure Senator McCarthy. Dirksen quickly rose to McCarthy's defense. He charged that Flanders was proposing "a conspiracy to destroy" McCarthy. Senator Knowland, the Republican floor leader, also protested against Flanders' resolution, but the Senate voted to create a special select committee to hold hearings on the proposal. After a two-week study that committee on September 27 recommended that McCarthy be censured by the Senate for his actions. By now McCarthy was in total defiance of the Eisenhower administration, which as an entity he accused of treason. Dirksen became McCarthy's chief defender against the Eisenhower administration and the special Senate committee. He described himself as McCarthy's lawyer in the censure proceedings, and he bent every effort to prevent censure. More than any other senator, Dirksen thrust himself forward as McCarthy's advocate and friend. No longer did he make any pretense of impartiality between McCarthy and the Eisenhower administration that McCarthy attacked. Public opinion had turned against McCarthy, and with it so did the Senate. There was nothing Dirksen could do to stay the Senate's formal rebuke of McCarthy. Still Dirksen would not give up. McCarthy had been confined in the Bethesda, Maryland, naval hospital with an injured elbow and bursitis, and Dirksen went there to see him.

"I went up to Joe's room on the sixteenth floor," Dirksen recalled. "He grinned like a Cheshire cat when he saw me."

Dirksen knew that McCarthy's plight was desperate; the Senate seemed resolved to vote a censure of McCarthy. "This thing was all cooked and ready," Dirksen said. In this extremity, Dirksen had devised a tactic that he thought might yet save McCarthy. He had drafted three letters, each of different intensity, addressed to the chairman of the select committee that had investigated the charges against McCarthy and also addressed to Vice-President Richard Nixon, the president of the Senate. Dirksen went to the hospital to persuade McCarthy to sign at least one of them. The letters, as Dirksen described them, amounted to "an apology without seeming to be an apology." He thought that if McCarthy signed one of them, he might escape censure.

"How about a drink?" McCarthy said to him.

"I don't mind," Dirksen said.

McCarthy got out of his hospital bed and mixed two stiff drinks of bourbon.

"I'm your friend and your lawyer," Dirksen said to McCarthy, "and you ought to pay attention to me. I've got a little document here in the nature of an apology."

McCarthy studied Dirksen's draft of the letter, the strongest of the three he had prepared. They had another drink, and McCarthy refused to sign the letter. Dirksen offered him another version of the letter, not quite as strong.

"Do you think you can sell this?" McCarthy asked Dirksen.

Dirksen argued for an hour with McCarthy, trying to persuade him. McCarthy was wary and reluctant. The two kept drinking, and McCarthy almost signed this letter. He threw down the pen.

"Have another drink," he said to Dirksen.

Dirksen still did not quit. He offered the third draft of the letter he had prepared, the least strong of all.

"This one you can sign," Dirksen said.

"No," McCarthy replied. "I don't crawl. I learned to fight in an alley. That's all I know."

On December 2, 1954, the Senate voted 67 to 22 to censure McCarthy for behavior unbecoming a senator. The names of those voting against censuring him read like a roster of the Taft wing of the Republican Party in the Senate. They included, besides Dirksen, the Republican leaders of the Senate: Knowland, Bridges, and Millikin. The Republican senators voting for censure were the Eisenhower bloc. Before the final vote Dirksen tried to plead leniency for McCarthy before the Senate. He asked how many senators had gone to McCarthy and tried to reason with him. "Had the milk of human kindness been a little sweeter," Dirksen told the Senate, "perhaps all this would not have happened." He made no converts. Then, in a final, futile gesture, Dirksen offered a substitute resolution to absolve McCarthy of all blame. The Senate summarily rejected it.

Long since, Dirksen had lost any remnant of the extraordinary prestige he had commanded as a member of the House of Representatives. He was bitterly hated by men who had once admired him. He was now almost as constant a target of the press as was Senator McCarthy. Indeed, journalists and senators too seemed to delight in an informal competition to find appropriate epithets to call him. Senator Robert Kerr of Oklahoma, a Democrat, called him

"Irksome Dirksen," and another wit in the Senate cloakroom described Dirksen as "The Voice of the Dented French Horn." One journalist called him "Old Bear Grease," mocking his fulsome manner. Another wrote that he "parts his metaphors in the middle," ridiculing his oratorical flourishes. Stewart Alsop, the newspaper columnist, called Dirksen "the Liberace of politics," and writers familiar with his relationship to Colonel McCormick acidly called him an "errand boy" for *The Chicago Tribune*. Another wrote that Dirksen in Congress resembled "a circus performer on roller skates" and said his voice was "like melted oleomargarine." A writer on *Time* magazine labeled him "the Wizard of Ooze," and that label stuck, repeated endlessly in the years that followed.

Even his record in the House of Representatives was now used to abuse him, despite the lavish praise he had received for it at the time. The flexibility he had then been honored for was now treated as a mark of his venality. Constantly journalists revived the tabulation from *The Chicago Sun-Times* stories of 1950 that purported that Dirksen had changed his position on military preparedness thirty-one times, on isolationism sixty-two times, and on farm policy seventy times. They never questioned the accuracy of these statistics. In mid-1954, at the height of the McCarthy furor, one reporter savagely criticized Dirksen's inconstancy, citing *The Sun-Times*'s articles, and damned him for his "bewildering pattern of expediency," his "strong stomach and politically convenient opinions," and "the corkscrew course that has placed him on every side of almost every issue in the past twenty years." Even the right-wing press, vitriolic supporters of Senator McCarthy, questioned Dirksen's faithfulness to their cause. For a brief period during the Army-McCarthy hearings Dirksen did not openly voice his support for McCarthy, and a Hearst writer immediately took him to task, obviously in some alarm that Dirksen might be thinking of changing sides again. "Dirksen," the Hearst man wrote, "may have forgotten that he drew the same smear campaign being accorded McCarthy by the Organized Red propaganda belt."

Dirksen's performance at these hearings drew the most severe criticism of all in the press. His flamboyant mannerisms, long cultivated, his sense of personal rectitude ostentiously worn at all times, fairly infuriated liberal journalists. "With his wavy pompadour, heavy-lidded eyes, loose full orator's lips, and imperturbable manner," wrote William V. Shannon in *The New York Post*, "he looks and sounds like an unfrocked minister who is never in doubt that he has found God's side on every issue." Michael Straight, in his study of the McCarthy-Army hearings, *Trial by Television*, titled one chapter "The Sanctimony of Senator Dirksen," and in that chapter he wrote this: "Dirksen wore the robe of judicial impartiality. As in the case of the Emperor's clothes, he alone supposed it covered him. And, as in the case of the misguided Emperor, there were chuckles whenever Dirksen rose to speak, throwing the robe around him."

For Dirksen, at the close of 1954, the future looked grim and unpromising. He was fifty-eight years old, almost fifty-nine. His reelection campaign now was hard upon him. His cup of bitterness was full. More than ever before, he was clearly isolated as a member of a minority and now discredited faction of his own Republican Party. The Senate vote did more than censure Senator McCarthy; it repudiated as well the men who had stood with him, none more than Dirksen. Dirksen had reached the nadir of his political career.

# Chapter 7

# Return of the Prodigal

*I've often said I should have been a woman,*
*I'm so easy to persuade.*

In the weeks immediately following the Senate's censure of Senator McCarthy, Everett Dirksen gave no public indications that he was unduly troubled by the fact of that censure, the Senate's most awesome rebuke of a member and only five times previously invoked in the Senate's history. Indeed, neither did McCarthy indicate that he was bothered by the Senate's censure. The Wisconsin Senator plunged right on in the course he had been pursuing for almost five years, slashing wildly at opponents, charging new Communist conspiracies, and even accusing the Eisenhower administration of treason. He apologized to the American voters for having supported Eisenhower in the 1952 election. It was his way of retaliating against the President. "They're shooting at me down there," McCarthy said of the Eisenhower White House, "and I've got to do something." There was in McCarthy's words unmistakably an increasingly hysterical tone, and a like hysteria was growing among his followers.

On February 12, 1955, Lincoln's Birthday, Dirksen and Senator McCarthy appeared together as speakers at a remarkable rally in Chicago. The rally was called to extol conservatism, and it was notable for the virulence of the invective against President Eisenhower. Among the sponsors of the event were such deeply conservative groups as the Committee of One Thousand Republicans, the Abraham Lincoln National Republican Club, and the Du Page County Patriots. At the rally J. Bracken Lee, the Republican governor of Utah, spoke the group's sense that Eisenhower had repudiated authentic Republican dogma. Lee called for the founding of a third party to restore, in his words, "constitutional government" to the nation. "I'd like to be loyal to the President," Lee said, "but loyalty is a two-way street. I have a feeling that the leadership in Washington hasn't been loyal to Republican principles." Senator McCarthy won the loudest applause of the day for his speech attacking the President. When Dirksen's turn came to speak, he made an attempt to praise Eisenhower; he asked the seventeen hundred conservatives there assembled to "salute and applaud" the President for his stand in defense of Formosa. The audience responded coldly to Dirksen's proposal, and Dirksen quickly changed his theme. Ringingly he proclaimed that he again would fight President Eisenhower in the Senate to adopt Senator Bricker's constitutional amendment to limit the President's powers over treaties. Dirksen thereby won thunderous applause.

Despite the outward seeming, Dirksen had never thrown himself totally into the camp of Senator McCarthy and the right-wing Republicans now so bitter against President Eisenhower. It was significant that if Dirksen had altered his speech at the Chicago rally to win the crowd's applause, he had also been the only speaker of the day who had even tried to speak flatteringly about the President. Four days after the rally Dirksen took care to disassociate himself publicly from Governor Lee's proposal of a third party; Dirksen called the idea "just nonsense." Earlier there had been other token actions privately executed, to suggest that Dirksen's commitments were mixed. For example, in the midst of the bruising quarrel between McCarthy and the Army in 1954, Dirksen intervened quietly to block McCarthy's plan to subpoena the members of the Army's loyalty and security screening board, thus sparing the Eisenhower administration an unwanted additional crisis with McCarthy. Later, when Army Secretary Robert Stevens had been humiliated by McCarthy, after the lunch meeting in Dirksen's office, Dirksen tried hard at the President's personal request to persuade McCarthy to accept a statement absolving Stevens from the worst of his public degradation. Dirksen failed to convince McCarthy, but he did try.

Even more significant than his obvious reluctance to be fully identified with the conservatives at the Chicago rally was Dirksen's reaction to another signal event a little more than a month later. On March 16, 1955, the Eisenhower administration made public the long-secret documents of the Yalta Conference, a summit meeting regarded with the darkest malignity by the Republican conservatives. Instantly Senator McCarthy rose in the Senate to denounce again this "great betrayal" by the Roosevelt administration, and McCarthy as well acidly accused the Eisenhower administration of "censoring" the Yalta documents before their release. Dirksen, pointedly, remained silent. In the past he had been among the foremost in denouncing the Yalta agreements.

Throughout his political career, Dirksen was always a big, hearty, gregarious man with the professional politician's amiability. From his earliest years in politics he eschewed the dogmatic and the doctrinaire. He tutored himself to the conciliation of jarring interests, not their alienation. If he had sided with Taft against Eisenhower, and then with Senator Bricker and Senator McCarthy, he had never totally spurned the President. Privately, at least, he had maintained friendly enough relations with the President to let the President and his aides believe that they might yet successfully coax Dirksen into their camp.

If flexibility was Dirksen's weakness, it was also his strength. He moved with the times, the way the country moved, or his state, and the times were changing in 1955. There were new realities for Dirksen to face. To win his seat in the Senate in 1950 and the support he felt he needed from the Illinois Republican oligarchy led by Colonel McCormick, Dirksen had abandoned his internationalism in favor of isolationism, his middle-of-the-road moderation in favor of stark conservatism. He had had his fling with Senator Taft, with his hopes high for national office, but Taft now was dead. After years of defiance, Dirksen had in 1950 knuckled under to *The Chicago Tribune* and Colonel McCormick. By 1955, however, McCormick, who was seventy-four, was grievously ill. On January 19 the publisher underwent abdominal surgery, from which he never fully recovered. He died April 1. It was significant that when McCormick's death was announced to the Senate, Dirksen did not join in the eulogies of him. Even earlier, during McCormick's long illness, *The Chicago Tribune* itself had begun to flag, with McCormick no longer physically able to give the newspaper the zest of his own peculiar brand of personal journalism. From a peak circulation of 1,076,866, *The Tribune* had shrunk to a daily issue of 892,058 copies at the time of the Colonel's death. Besides, the new managers of the newspaper had a somewhat less abrasive view of life and politics than McCormick. Less than five months after McCormick died, under pressure from Chicago's schoolteachers, the editors of *The Tribune* dropped the use in their pages of many of the bizarre, simplified spellings McCormick had ordered, such as "frate" for "freight" and "sofisticated" for "sophisticated." That change also betokened a softening of attitude in the most influential newspaper in Illinois, a change not lost on Dirksen.

As significant to Dirksen as the tempering of *The Chicago Tribune* was the altered status of Senator McCarthy. McCarthy's harshest critics had despaired at the Senate for punishing McCarthy with nothing more than merely censure, and even the language of the censure resolution had been diluted before it was adopted. At first there seemed no change. McCarthy continued as before, but in the end the Senate resolution of censure destroyed him. Senate correspondents reporting McCarthy's speeches at first treated them with the same gusto and urgency they had his earlier speeches, but they learned quickly enough to denigrate these speeches, even to ignore them, when their editors refused to give them the space and prominence they once had. In part, Senator McCarthy had been the creation of the American press, building a publicity crescendo with his vitriolic words spread brazenly across the front pages of the nation's newspapers. After the Senate's censure, he could no longer command such attention and interest. He kept hurling reckless accusations, but gradually he lost both his stature as a national hero to his admirers and as a national menace to his enemies. Wrenched by his fallen state, McCarthy became in time a somewhat pathetic figure in national politics, grateful to old associates for even recognizing him. He took to drinking heavily, and his health failed. He died May 2, 1957, ostensibly of hepatitis, but in the gossip around the Senate, he drank himself to death. Long before McCarthy died, Dirksen had quietly disassociated himself politically from the man he had once so ardently defended.

Above and beyond the deaths of Senator Taft and Colonel McCormick and the repudiation of Senator McCarthy, there were two other compelling facts that profoundly affected Dirksen in the spring of 1955. In the year ahead he would be running for reelection to the Senate, and President Eisenhower, patently the most popular man in the land, would be running for reelection too at the head of the Republican ticket. With his old allies gone, Dirksen needed to build a new political base or suffer defeat. He needed more than access to substantial campaign funds; he needed identification with his party's preeminent leader and with the party's new regulars. There were warnings aplenty for Dirksen. In the 1954 Congressional elections the nation had again elected a Democratic Senate and a Democratic House of Representatives. Even so, Eisenhower's personal popularity had not flagged. With his obvious benignity, his glowing smile, the President had created for himself an extraordinary "father" image in the minds of most Americans. Democratic politicians, acutely sensitive to Eisenhower's great popularity, normally shrank from criticizing him, an astonishing posture for the opposition party and one almost unknown in American political history. Ever since Eisenhower had taken office as President, Dirksen had been under assault in Washington and at home in Illinois for his political indifference to the President. In 1953 Senator Robert Kerr of Oklahoma had publicly mocked Dirksen as the man who "did less than any other to support President Eisenhower's program." Illinois newspapers like *The Chicago Sun-Times* had repeatedly carped at Dirksen's disinclination to follow the President's leadership. In 1954 the Democratic National Committee had even formally labeled Dirksen as one of a group of Republican "know-nothings" in the Senate and urged President Eisenhower to disavow him and the others in favor of creating a working coalition in Congress with the "loyal-opposition" Democrats. Eisenhower from the beginning had set a course with the Taft Republicans in the Senate that precluded any such action as the Democratic National Committee proposed, but as Dirksen contemplated his own coming reelection campaign, he could only regard such suggestions as dangerous and painful. They underscored and sharpened Dirksen's growing sense of his own political isolation.

In reality, President Eisenhower had tried hard to show Dirksen his desire for friendship, and the President's actions in this went far beyond yielding to Dirksen the federal patronage in Illinois. For example, on his return to Washington from a vacation in Colorado in September, 1953, Eisenhower went out of his way to stop at Chicago to attend a Republican rally where Dirksen was speaking. There, with Dirksen standing beside him, Eisenhower praised the Illinois Senator as a "very great associate of mine . . . absolute in his devotion." However much the President overlooked Dirksen's substantive opposition in this praise, he knew precisely what he wanted from Dirksen, and in private letters to Dirksen he made his plea even more plain. On August 3, 1953, at the conclusion of the annual session of Congress, President Eisenhower solicitously wrote a letter of "gratitude" to Dirksen for his help in support of the Republican program. "On every side," Eisenhower wrote, "I have received evidence of your effectiveness as a leader and your devotion to the 'middle way' political philosophy to which we both adhere. I most sincerely hope that the prospect of a continuing and closer personal and political relationship between the two of us holds for you the same appeal and satisfaction that it does for me." A year later, on August 23, 1954, Eisenhower sent Dirksen a similar flattering letter. "You have performed services of greatest importance to our country," the President wrote. Over the months, the President had often invited Dirksen to the White House, occasionally for a private breakfast and a quiet talk. Writing in his memoirs of one such instance in 1954, President Eisenhower said that Dirksen "had already shown the potential of a strong Republican leader, and I wanted to enlist his help." Eisenhower liked to believe that he could "count on" Dirksen. There were others in the White House watching the careful wooing of Dirksen by the President. One of these, writing years later, stated that Dirksen, "unflattered and uncourted," would never had shifted to support the President's program. The President himself quietly passed the word, certain it would reach the press and Dirksen, that he regarded Dirksen as "a good right arm." What Dirksen knew from all of this was that he would be totally welcomed by the White House; there would be no awkwardnesses raised from that quarter.

Dirksen had not been immune to Eisenhower's blandishments of friendship. Indeed, the President's cordiality toward him had already on many occasions blunted Dirksen's allegiance to the isolationist conservatives in the Senate. At some personal embarrassment, for example, Dirksen had broken with them in 1953 to support Eisenhower's proposal to admit an additional 240,000 immigrants to the United States. For that breach, Dirksen suffered a tongue-lashing from Senator Herman Welker of Idaho, one of Senator McCarthy's most ardent champions. Moreover, Dirksen did not hesitate to defend Eisenhower and his administration from the occasional attacks by Democrats. On the political stump Dirksen often had kind words for the President. In one speech he described him as "the gentle President." In the Senate Dirksen had also given indications that he was moving toward the President's stance in foreign affairs. In early 1954, for example, Dirksen reversed his long opposition to construction of the St. Lawrence Seaway, a project long regarded as inimical to the economic interests of Illinois. Dirksen stated that he had been persuaded by President Eisenhower's arguments that the seaway was a requirement of national defense. On the question of foreign aid, later in 1954, Dirksen also showed signs that he was softening his hostility. Not only did Dirksen defend Harold Stassen, the foreign-aid administrator, from a savage attack by Senator McCarthy, but Dirksen repeatedly voted against what he called "arbitrary" cuts in the foreign-aid program recommended by Eisenhower.

In June, 1955, Dirksen made another tour of Asia to study the need and use of foreign aid. His motivation this time was far different than it had been when he made a similar trip in 1953. Then he had gone on behalf of the Senate Appropriations Committee to find ways to cut the program; now he felt he went on behalf of President Eisenhower to find arguments to defend the program. He visited Formosa again, and Cambodia, Thailand, and Burma. He spent four days in Vietnam, and he returned to the United States via Israel and Berlin, where he also studied the effectiveness of foreign aid. He made this trip at a time of great international tension. In June President Eisenhower was making final preparations to meet the leaders of Russia, Great Britain, and France at Geneva in a summit conference the following month. Acutely alive to those tensions and to his own political problems at home and in the Senate, Dirksen returned to Washington utterly transformed in his attitude on foreign aid. The foreign-aid appropriations bill was brought before the Senate in July even as Eisenhower was meeting with the other heads of state at Geneva. Dirksen voted on amendment after amendment in support of Eisenhower's position. He defended the Eisenhower commitment in Vietnam, even then growing ticklish. "Shall we forsake them?" Dirksen asked about the South Vietnamese. "Shall we abandon them, or shall we stand by until the job is done?" He defended Eisenhower's commitment of funds to Communist Yugoslavia, arguing that this was no time to cut off those funds as an act of "retaliation" and thus stymie the American government's efforts to encourage Yugoslavia to move out of Russia's Eastern European bloc. Dirksen, however, did more than vote with the administration on this bill, more than defend specifics of the foreign-aid program. In a career marked with sudden reversals, Dirksen now publicly repudiated his own strident opposition to foreign aid.

"I believe the term 'foreign aid' is a very unhappy one," Dirksen told the Senate. "It implies and connotes a giveaway or welfare program. . . . This is the most selfish program I know of. We are not undertaking it out of the charity of our hearts. . . . We are doing it for our own skins. . . . I remember the day when I used to attack this program. I did it with a great deal of verve and vigor. I take it back. Publicly and privately, I take it back."

With those words Dirksen moved out of the isolationists' ranks back into the internationalists'. With those words and on this central issue of foreign policy Dirksen publicly abandoned the remnants of the Taft wing in the Senate and aligned himself with President Eisenhower. To Eisenhower, foreign affairs was his primary concern as President, the foreign-aid program his most significant legislative measure. Yet in executing his extraordinary shift, Dirksen managed not to offend unduly the senators whom he now appeared to forsake. In the inner life of the Senate there exists among the members a live-and-let-live attitude toward each other that transcends specific disagreements on any political matters. Personal friendships and alliances within the Senate are not dependent on such criteria. The senators mutually recognize the primary natural law of political survival. Dirksen's colleagues knew that he was up for reelection. Beyond that they accepted without cavil Dirksen's essential right in the final analysis to decide for himself what positions he had to take. Dirksen, in short, retained his intimacy with the Senate's Republican hierarchy. In the Senate cloakroom he was still one of them. Personally he remained closer to Styles Bridges of New Hampshire and William Knowland of California, the Taft men, than to such regular Eisenhower senators as Leverett Saltonstall of Massachusetts and James Duff of Pennsylvania. There was in this a personal equation of compelling importance to Dirksen. On maintaining his fellowship with the ruling Republican faction in the Senate depended Dirksen's future in the Senate.

Dirksen switched his public allegiance to Eisenhower at precisely the moment of Eisenhower's most astonishing public popularity. Eisenhower came home from the summit conference at Geneva in a rising national euphoria that he had worked there marvelously for world peace. At Geneva Eisenhower had dramatically proposed that the Russians and the United States fully disclose to each other their total military establishments and allow complete aerial reconnaissance of each other's country. Senator Lyndon Johnson of Texas, now the majority leader of the Senate, welcomed the proposal as "the daring, imaginative stroke for which a war-weary world has been waiting." Even Russia's spokesman, Nikolai Bulganin, left Geneva with the statement that the summit conference had markedly brought "the easing of tension" in the world. Americans and people everywhere talked hopefully of "The Spirit of Geneva" and agreed that the meeting of the four great powers had helped secure what Eisenhower there called the prospects of "lasting peace." The crescendo of approval for Eisenhower's performance at Geneva had fundamental implications for his own reelection campaign in 1956 and for all those running on the Republican ticket with him.

Dirksen knew this, and he was already hard at work getting ready for his own reelection campaign for the Senate. He and his Illinois operatives had scheduled a fund-raising dinner for him in Chicago on September 22, 1955, and he wanted to draw the mantle of President Eisenhower about his shoulders. Eisenhower was more than willing. From his vacation headquarters in Denver, Eisenhower sent Dirksen a letter of glowing praise to be read at the dinner. "Especially in the past three years," Eisenhower wrote, "I have come to know and appreciate the great value to our country of Senator Dirksen's labors in his influential position. Since 1952 Everett and I have not, of course, agreed on every public issue, but never have I had the occasion to doubt that sincerity and conviction have motivated every vote he has cast." The President's generous words amounted to an endorsement of Dirksen's reelection. The dinner helped Dirksen more than that. His political lieutenants sold sixteen hundred tickets to that dinner at one hundred dollars each, a handsome tribute to Dirksen's political prowess. He was off, obviously, to an auspicious beginning of his reelection campaign.

Two days after Dirksen's fund-raising dinner the news flashed from Denver that President Eisenhower had suffered a heart attack. For days there was uncertainty whether the President would survive the seizure. His illness had grave significance on the operation of the federal government, but politicians also knew the meaning to themselves and their political parties if Eisenhower could not run for reelection in 1956. The political world for all politicians, including Dirksen, was abruptly in great confusion. The Democrats began to believe that the Presidential nomination of their party the next year might be tantamount to election, but the Republicans tried to find solace in the doctor's diagnosis that the President's attack was moderate and without complications. For the politicians it proved a long wait before they knew whether Eisenhower could again carry on as President. It was more than a month before Eisenhower, at a Denver hospital, could try his first steps, almost two months before he could begin to pick up again the daily chores of the Presidency. Even after that the President's convalescence continued for many weeks.

Dirksen had no doubt at any time what he wanted the President to do. Almost with unseemly haste, he began to urge the President to run for reelection. Only three days after the President's heart attack, with the question of the President's survival still in some doubt, Dirksen confidently bespoke his expectation that Eisenhower would certainly run for reelection in 1956. "*Duty*," Dirksen intoned, "is the shining, iridescent word the President learned at West Point. The President knows and will know where his duty lies." There should be no mistake, Dirksen made plain, he was an

Eisenhower man. "I believe the President is my friend," he said, "and I try to be his." Earlier Dirksen had even proposed that the Republican Party draft Eisenhower for a second term if necessary. Dirksen knew the implications for himself if Eisenhower did not run for reelection in 1956, and if he had any tendency to gloss over the reality, the Chicago newspapers brought it starkly to his attention. On September 27 *The Chicago Sun-Times* surveyed the political meaning of Eisenhower's illness on Dirksen and stated flatly that Dirksen's chances of reelection would be endangered if Eisenhower were unable to seek a second term as President.

Not all Republican senators viewed the President's illness with the same fear for their own political prospects as did Dirksen. Senator Knowland, consumed with ambition and restlessly impatient, did not try to conceal his own deep interest in running for President at the first opportunity. "Observers here," reported a Washington correspondent of *The New York Times* the day after Eisenhower's heart attack, "expect to see Senator Knowland make his own bid for the Republican Presidential nomination if the President does not seek reelection." As the Republican floor leader, Knowland had not proved a success in the Senate. Bristling in manner, blunt in speech, he was a grim, unbending man with his colleagues. In the Senate's cloakrooms he was jokingly called "a young fogy." Ill at ease with his fellow senators, awkward in legislative tactics and maneuver, Knowland inadvertently made himself a ready foil to enhance the rising reputation of Lyndon Johnson, the Democratic floor leader, as a parliamentary master. Knowland often disagreed with President Eisenhower on foreign-policy questions and almost as often took the Senate floor to proclaim his disagreement. Less than three weeks after Eisenhower was felled, Knowland openly began to maneuver for the Presidential nomination. On October 13 he publicly urged that the President designate no one as "an heir apparent," an obvious ploy to try to block the nomination of Knowland's chief party rival, Vice-President Richard M. Nixon. Knowland asked publicly that Eisenhower announce his own plans early enough to give the Republican Party sufficient time to appraise "other possible candidates." Knowland also indicated that if President Eisenhower did not make up his mind by February 15, he would file in a number of Presidential primaries himself. More than anyone else, Knowland by his continuing clumsiness as floor leader had demonstrated to Dirksen, a student and practitioner of legislative legerdemain, how not to act in the United States Senate. More significantly now, however, Knowland's compulsion to become President opened the way for Dirksen's sudden elevation to Senate leadership. Dirksen could see in Knowland's maneuvers of late 1955 and early 1956 the opportunity for his own political promotion.

Not until February 29 did Eisenhower make his decision on running for a second term, and his decision then pleased Dirksen far more than Knowland. The President stated at a news conference that he would be available to run for a second term as President if the Republican National Convention wished to nominate him. "My answer will be positive, that is, affirmative," Eisenhower said. Knowland promptly withdrew from the Presidential primaries in which he had already filed, and Dirksen, heartened, continued his course of deepening his political commitment to Eisenhower on both domestic and international questions.

To a degree, Dirksen had already become the administration's spokesman and sponsor in the Senate. In January he had formally introduced in the Senate the Eisenhower administration's proposed civil-rights bill. In the months to follow, Dirksen took the leadership of the administration's struggle to enact that bill. At the Republican National Convention in San Francisco that summer, Dirksen chaired the platform committee's subcommittee on civil rights. As such he not only became the chief exponent of what he called the Republicans' "forthright" civil-rights plank, but he denounced the Democrats' version as an example of "serpentine weasling." In the thick of things, Dirksen obviously relished his role as subcommittee chairman and party defender. Questioned by reporters why the party's civil-rights plank did not include the word "force" in endorsing the Supreme Court's school-segregation decision, Dirksen fairly beamed.

"Oh, gentlemen," he wheezed, "I never use the word 'force.' 'Force' is an offensive word. I'm a lawyer, and I'm against force. Now, you take the words 'implementing the decision.' Those are fine, sixty-four-thousand-dollar words."

Dirksen knew what he was doing in thus aligning himself so closely to President Eisenhower. As early as February, 1956, according to a Gallup public-opinion poll, Eisenhower led Adlai E. Stevenson, his most probable opponent for the Presidency, by a 61-to-35 percentage of those polled. In political terms, it was advantageous for Dirksen, with his large Negro constituency in Chicago, to stand four-square with Eisenhower on civil rights. Not all the President's proposals were so helpful to Dirksen's own standing with the voters, and one in particular carried the gravest dangers to Dirksen's reelection chances. Nonetheless, Dirksen embraced the President's cause and made it his own.

This was the President's recommendation that the United States give Communist Yugoslavia American-made jet fighters. The administration's maneuver was part of a continuing attempt to encourage Yugoslavia and its dictator, Marshal Tito, to become more independent of Russia. When the President broached the idea to the Republican leaders of Congress, however, they indicated embarrassment. As working politicians, they had built for themselves postures of militant anticommunism. Giving military airplanes to a Communist nation ran sharply against their political grain. Eisenhower pressed his argument; the effort would help the United States by weakening the Soviet bloc. One by one the Republican leaders begged off. Indeed, Senator Knowland led the fight against the proposal when it reached the Senate floor. The President, seemingly helpless, could not persuade any of his party's leaders to sponsor the measure in Congress.

"Isn't someone going to help me?" he asked at last. "Isn't someone going to pick up this hot poker?"

Dirksen had more reason than Knowland to duck the politically odious chore. In a matter of months he was to face the Illinois voters. But also, now, he was an Eisenhower man.

"I'll do it," he said.

The funds for the jet fighters for Yugoslavia were carried in the 1956 foreign-aid program, and that meant the Senate had to approve the concept twice, first in the foreign-aid authorization bill, then in the foreign-aid appropriations bill. The process doubled the political hazards to Dirksen, but he did not flinch even though he was excoriated for this action in the pages of *The Chicago Tribune*. He was labeled "Tito's Senator," as though he were disloyal. He did not like it, but he went ahead. Briefed by the State Department, Dirksen made the administration's case to the Senate Appropriations Committee, reading to the members a secret memorandum on what was involved. The real test, however, came on the Senate floor, where the proposal came up for consideration on July 24. Senator Knowland opened the attack by offering an amendment to prohibit shipment of any military equipment to Yugoslavia. To underscore his opposition to the President, Knowland moved from his minority leader's seat in the Senate's front row, center, to the rear of the chamber "to make it clear," as he said, "that on this amendment I do not speak for the administration." Senator Bridges supported Knowland's amendment. So did Senators Bricker and Millikin. Senator McCarthy bitingly attacked the position Dirksen had taken. The Republican leadership was arrayed against Dirksen, and he could not count on the Democratic leaders either. Lyndon Johnson also supported Knowland's amendment.

Dirksen was in obvious difficulties. He argued that communism was not monolithic, as his colleagues suggested, but that it differed in Yugoslavia and Russia. His central argument, however, hung on the twin propositions that the Senate must not repudiate President Eisenhower and that he as a senator would be "derelict in my duty" not to decide the question on the basis of the public and secret testimony. He knew the risks he was taking politically, and he struck a heroic posture as he pleaded with the Senate against voting no confidence in the President.

"Are we going to do that to our President?" he asked. "Not I, no matter what my political fortunes may be. As Edmund Burke said to a constituent in England a long time ago, 'I must respect the opinions of my people, but when the time comes to decide, I owe it to myself to put one thing over and above everything else, and that is my independent judgment.' "

Despite Dirksen's forensic efforts on the Senate floor, the Senate adopted Knowland's amendment 50 to 42. Dirksen had been defeated, but his gallantry in taking on an obviously unpopular cause for the President did not go unnoticed at the White House. In fact, from this struggle dated the beginning of Dirksen's real intimacy with President Eisenhower, and Dirksen sensed the change. "It brought me closer to the White House," Dirksen said much later. "I got calls more frequently for help from 'The Chief.' " The Senate vote had come little more than three months before election day, and Dirksen felt then and for years later the political sting for standing by the President on this painfully controversial question. In private he had an explanation for his action that would beguile the most militant anticommunist. In the Senate debate, he explained, his lips had been sealed on the true inwardness of the administration's maneuver. Actually, he went on, although he could not say so publicly, the jet fighters were obsolete and useless, and the Defense Department only wanted to dump them on the Yugoslavs. It had the ring of a rationale he had thought up belatedly.

On August 9, scarcely a fortnight after his floor fight for military aid to Yugoslavia, Dirksen received a "Dear Everett" letter from President Eisenhower. The letter had been carefully drafted for use in Dirksen's reelection campaign. In it Eisenhower praised Dirksen for his "effective help" in passing administration legislation "for the public good." Discreetly the President neglected to mention the Yugoslav matter; that was better forgotten in the election campaign. "In your case," Eisenhower wrote, "I have been especially pleased by the way you have responded when I personally called on you for help in important legislation." This was a reward for Dirksen's services rendered, and he strove to make the most of it. He had the letter, on White House stationery, reproduced exactly in his campaign pamphlet for the voters of Illinois. For this pamphlet also Dirksen culled the newspapers for quotations complimentary of his work in Congress. The newspapers had not been kind to him in his years as a senator, and he had to reach back to his House service a decade earlier to find newspaper praise suitable for campaign use in 1956. He used a quotation from *The Chicago Daily News* of 1945 describing him as "Illinois' outstanding representative in Congress." From the same period Dirksen quoted what columnist Ray Tucker had said about him: that "the ablest man in Congress" was either Dirksen or James Wadsworth of New York. The press pickings were slim for Dirksen in the 1950's, and Eisenhower's letter therefore was all the more welcome.

In the campaign itself, Dirksen had a clear advantage over his less-known Democratic opponent, Richard Stengel. The Republicans in Illinois, however, had been badly shaken by a public scandal within their ranks, and this for a while threatened Dirksen's prospects. Organized labor also singled Dirksen out for special attack. His voting record was described as "consistently reactionary," and the AFL's Labor's League for Political Education reported he voted "100 percent wrong." He was described as a creature of the real-estate lobby and a spokesman for the liquor interests. President Eisenhower, however, had not finished giving help to Dirksen. In a limited campaign for his own reelection, Eisenhower chose to make one of his few appearances in Illinois. There, again, the President embraced Dirksen as a candidate and as "my very good friend." Over statewide television and radio, Eisenhower unqualifiedly recommended Dirksen to the voters. "These last years," the President said, "I have often asked his help, and always he has given it wholeheartedly. . . . Our country needs Everett Dirksen back in the United States Senate." When the votes were counted the day after election day, Dirksen had been reelected 2,307,353 votes to 1,949,883 for his opponent. Eisenhower had carried Illinois by a landslide, and he had clearly helped Dirksen into his second term in the Senate. In every one of the twenty-five Congressional districts in Illinois, Eisenhower ran comfortably ahead of Dirksen in the percentage of votes received. Dirksen had not been mistaken in choosing to hitch his political future to the President.

The 1956 elections did not alter the party balance in the Senate. The Democrats still held a two-seat margin, forty-nine to forty-seven, over the Republicans, but there had been significant changes in the Republican membership. Four Republican senators had not been returned, among them Eugene Millikin of Colorado, chairman of the Republican Senate Conference, or party caucus. Four new Republicans had been elected, including John Sherman Cooper and Thruston Morton, both of Kentucky. The retirement of Senator Millikin, Taft's ally over the years, was of special interest and concern within the Senate, because his departure opened up a principal position in the Republican hierarchy. Who would replace Millikin in the Republican leadership became automatically a question of the highest moment in the power structure of the Senate. In the weeks after the election there were most secretive consultations about the problem between Senator Knowland, the party's floor leader, and Senator Bridges, the chairman of the party's policy committee. Brought into these discussions also was Bridges' protégé, Everett Dirksen. The problem was further complicated by the uncertain plans of Knowland. He had, of course, already signaled his ambition for the Presidency by his abortive entry into the party primaries earlier in 1956. Now, with the reelection of Eisenhower, he appeared stymied politically for at least four years and possibly longer, for his chief rival, Vice-President Nixon, had moved swiftly into party prominence as the logical heir apparent to Eisenhower after the President's heart attack. Knowland saw that Nixon had a far more advantageous position, as Vice-President, to claim the Presidential nomination in 1960 than he. Only one senator, Warren Harding in 1920, had ever been elected President directly from the Senate. In short, Knowland was considering leaving the Senate to run for the governorship of California, a post of great power in the party's national convention. If he did make that move, he, of course, would vacate the Republican floor leadership in the Senate and create another opening in the party hierarchy. Thus the problem of replacing Millikin as chairman of the caucus had expanded into a question of the dynastic succession in the Senate. Bridges and Knowland, in their discussions, considered the question in that light. They wanted men of their own stamp in charge of the Republican Party in the Senate.

Under normal conditions the party's floor leader would be succeeded by the party's assistant floor leader, the party whip. This position was held by Leverett Saltonstall of Massachusetts, a political moderate and internationalist and a pre-Chicago-convention supporter of President Eisenhower. Saltonstall, the heir of an ancient New England family, had the becalmed, formal bearing of an aristocrat. Softspoken and kindly, he shrank from open quarreling. He had no taste for cut-and-thrust debate. When he rose to speak in the Senate, as the wiseacres in the press gallery often remarked, it was "to pour oil on the troubled waters." In both political and personal terms, Saltonstall could not be a satisfactory party spokesman, in the judgment of Senator Bridges, the party's most influential member in the Senate. With Knowland indicating he might leave the Senate, Bridges acted to secure the succession to the floor leadership for a political ally. Millikin's departure gave him the chance to execute the maneuver not only without precipitating a party quarrel but without even arousing suspicion of what he was doing. Overtures were made privately to Saltonstall. His moderating influence was needed to preside over the party caucus, to quiet there any incipient factionalism of the party members. No mention was made of the possible departure of Knowland from the Senate. The chairmanship of the caucus, the way the post was offered to Saltonstall, was to be a promotion in the hierarchy. Saltonstall accepted it as such. Then, with equal deftness, Bridges and Knowland brought Dirksen forward as their candidate for party whip, the assistant leader. A few of the party's liberals complained halfheartedly that a man of more liberal cast than Dirksen should be chosen, but they subsided quickly. "There was," said Dirksen, looking back at the stratagem, "no contest of any kind."

Dirksen at last had broken into the formal hierarchy of his party. Ever since he had entered the Senate, he had been part of the party's dominant wing in the Senate, but his position of influence had been in the secondary echelon of party power. Now he had risen into the formal leadership. He was sixty-one years old, in full physical vigor, and his prospects for advancement never looked brighter. He had the best of the two political worlds of the Republican Party. Not only was Dirksen the chosen of the Republicans' conservative leadership in the Senate, but he had also became the trusted ally in the Senate of the President, against whom the party's conservatives had long been feuding. It was not as though Dirksen were a bridge between the two warring factions; rather it was that he was separately a member in high favor with both. He functioned effectively and influentially in the inmost councils of each. In his extraordinary political career, marked by so many twists and turns, this was, perhaps, the most extraordinary paradox of all. When the time came that Senator Knowland did abandon the Senate in quest of the California governorship and the Presidency, Dirksen became the candidate of the Senate's conservative Republicans for the party leadership, and when he did, there were grounds to suspect that he also was Eisenhower's candidate for the post too, against the candidate of the Eisenhower wing of the party, John Sherman Cooper of Kentucky.

In the early months of the new session Dirksen applied himself to his Senate work as never before. Knowland gradually became more and more preoccupied with his own thrust for the California governorship and gave less and less attention to his duties as his party's floor leader in the Senate. The result was that Dirksen gradually became acting floor leader, rather than assistant floor leader, and the President's White House operatives liked that. No longer at the weekly legislative meetings at the White House did the President confront the glowering opposition of Senator Knowland. He could turn to Dirksen. Using the parlance of the military, Eisenhower repeatedly asked Dirksen "to carry the flag," and Dirksen did with pride and often with political courage. He supported the President's Middle East resolution of 1957 and won from Eisenhower's White House chief of staff, Sherman Adams, the compliment that he thus showed "considerable political gallantry." He again sponsored the President's civil-rights bill in 1957, and he was its leading advocate in the rough-and-tumble battling over the legislation on the Senate floor. He defended Eisenhower against criticisms by Lyndon Johnson that the President was frustrating the will of Congress by impounding funds designated for river-and-harbor projects. He moved away from the Congressional economy bloc to the extent that he supported Eisenhower's budget requests in case after case. He backed the foreign-aid program fully, as well as the rest of the Eisenhower domestic and foreign program.

His conservative allies in Illinois were angered by his performance. Repeatedly Dirksen and his aides heard their complaints. He had gone too far with Eisenhower. He should be leading the fight to cut the budget, not defending it. In these often abrasive sessions Dirksen defended his support of foreign aid on the grounds that the program had been pared down to military aid. He defended his support of the President on the grounds that he was the leader of the party. Occasionally Dirksen flared at the criticism. In one instance, he lectured a delegation from the Illinois Chamber of Commerce with unusual harshness. He told them that businessmen kept demanding budget cuts in Washington while they went on demanding federal money for their own pet projects at home. He cited as an example the case of the Chamber's own local in La Salle, Illinois. There the Chamber's unit urged approval of a $250,000 federal project to build a sewage-disposal plant in their city, and then the same men joined the state Chamber of Commerce in its plea that the federal budget be reduced. Some of Dirksen's most important backers in Illinois protested privately that Dirksen had deserted "the basic principles" of Senator Taft and the Republican

Party. A Dirksen lieutenant tried to explain away the change. Dirksen was now assistant floor leader in the Senate; he attended the White House sessions and helped make the decisions there. Senator Dirksen, the aide argued, was more valuable to "the Midwest point of view" if he participated in the decision-making at the White House than if he attacked those decisions from the Senate floor. Whatever the argument to try to quiet the party's conservatives in Illinois, he was hurting himself at home with those most influential in electing him to the Senate. In Washington, however, he was helping himself into a position of the greatest power he had ever held.

President Eisenhower obviously found Dirksen far more congenial than Senator Knowland, and the invitations to join the President at breakfast at the White House increased for Dirksen. In the inner world of Washington's upper echelons, this was, of course, well known, and it brought Dirksen the prestige of acting as the President's confidential adviser in the Senate. Within the Senate Dirksen was recognized as the man with "the best pipeline" to the White House, one of the very few senators who could breach the protective shielding thrown up around the President by his White House staff. Dirksen dealt directly with the President; his words and views were not filtered through staff aides. This brought Dirksen additional influence and the twin of influence, power. In personal terms, this intimacy offered by the President was a flattering unction for Dirksen's soul. It was heady stuff for Dirksen to return from the White House and say to his colleagues, as he did repeatedly: "When I had breakfast with the President this morning, he told me he wanted these things done." His confidential relationship with Eisenhower began to alter his views of the office of President. He began to see the Presidency as an office to be revered and to see the sublimating of himself and his ambitions to the President as a matter of considerable honor. "I carried the flag for him," Dirksen would boast in the years ahead. It was a matter of pride to him that he did so, and that he risked his own political fortunes at times in so doing.

Some of the Eastern Republicans were annoyed at the President for thus building up Dirksen's prestige. "It's the case of a man," one of these said, "who entered a revolving door after you, coming out in front of you." Yet the President had not erred in showing such favor to Dirksen. In the first Congress Eisenhower faced, the Eighty-third, Dirksen had stood far down on the list of senators giving support to the President's program. Even in the Eighty-fourth Congress, Dirksen was still closer to such Taft men as Bridges and Bricker in his Senate voting. Now, however, in the Eighty-fifth, Dirksen boasted: "I am the number-one Eisenhower man in the Senate." He was. By a statistical count, no member of the Senate supported the President more totally than Dirksen. He had a fluent, even pat explanation of his stance and what had happened to him.

"I'm just an old-fashioned garden variety of Republican," he said, "who believes in the Constitution, the Declaration of Independence, in Abraham Lincoln, who accepts the challenges as they arise and who is not unappreciative of the fact that this is a dynamic economy in which we live, and sometimes you have to change your position."

# Chapter 8

# The New Leader

*I am a man of principle,*
*and one of my basic principles is flexibility.*

In May, 1958, three Republican senators sent a formal letter to their party's conservative leaders. The three, all liberal internationalists, were George Aiken of Vermont, William Purtell of Connecticut, and Jacob Javits of New York, and their letter amounted to a challenge to the party's status quo in the Senate. Ever since Senator Knowland had announced he would not seek reelection to the Senate in 1958, Senator Dirksen had been regarded as the "heir apparent" to the party's floor leadership. That, of course, did not please the party's internationalists and liberals, nor did the party's ways of conducting its affairs. Long thwarted by the conservatives' dominance of the party in the Senate, these senators believed that they deserved, by right and common sense, a larger influence in the party's decision-making than they had wielded under existing arrangements. In their letter, Aiken and his two colleagues proposed basic alterations in the party's hitherto rigid seniority system.

Under traditional practice, the choice committee assignments were monopolized by the party's seniors, who normally were the party's staunchest conservatives. The system not only helped perpetuate the conservatives' control of the party in the Senate, but it also tended to allow them to formulate the party's public stance on the most consequential legislation coming before the Senate. In place of this system, the three liberal senators suggested that every Republican senator be assigned to at least one major Senate committee. This, they argued, would improve party morale, divide the Senate workload more equitably, and bring into use the talents and energies of all Republican senators.

On its face, the letter sounded like little more than a plea that the party's conservatives share their power in the Senate with their less fortunate colleagues. There was more behind the proposal, however, than the surface appearances. For one thing, the liberal bloc struck a sensitive nerve when they pointed to the party's dismal record of election defeats over the previous quarter-century. The Republicans had even failed to carry a majority of the Senate in the 1956 elections, when President Eisenhower had won again by a landslide. Inherent in those election failures lay the kernel idea that the party's leaders had failed to shape the party into a political instrument acceptable to the American voter. Obviously, behind the letter's polite rhetoric stood not only the assumption that the Republicans needed more modern and sophisticated leaders in the Senate, but the plain implication that Dirksen and his sponsors were not adequate to the party's future needs. In such a context, the conservatives had to treat the letter with delicacy and care. They dared not dismiss it.

"There is a general disposition," Dirksen promptly said, "to rearrange the current system to provide effective committees for everyone." Styles Bridges, Chairman of the Policy Committee, went further. He said that he liked "the general idea" and that he believed the "fresh ideas" of the younger and newer members might help. With the floor leadership at stake, Dirksen, of course, knew this was a time to placate, not offend, the senators who would cast votes at the party caucus. He had more in mind, however, than merely winning the party's leadership. He had watched and studied the legislative process for sixteen years in the House of Representatives and another eight years in the Senate. Year in, year out, he had frequently seen the blunderings of the party's leaders, and for the past five years he had watched in dismay Knowland's almost daily parliamentary gaucheries. Besides, the Republican Party in the Senate had long been bitterly divided, conservatives against liberals, isolationists against internationalists. Dirksen, as leader, wanted to unite the party, and across the Senate's center aisle Lyndon B. Johnson had done just that with the Democratic Party. On taking over the Democratic floor leadership in 1953, Senator Johnson had instituted a new system for allotting committee assignments, appointing each new senator to at least one important committee.* By so doing, Johnson had enormously enhanced his own position with his party members, and in the years that followed, on vote after vote, Johnson was able to bring to the Senate floor a party united or nearly united. Indeed, it had been the committee-assignment system Johnson had inaugurated that had given Senator Aiken and his colleagues the idea that the Republicans should do the same. Dirksen had to be impressed with Lyndon Johnson's success as a party leader and with Johnson's often astonishing legislative prowess. In the Senate Johnson stood in painful contrast to Knowland, his Republican counterpart, and Dirksen knew it. Dirksen wanted to pull the Republican Party together in the Senate, to end its internal dissensions and factionalisms, and Johnson had shown the way.

Dirksen had seen that Johnson had started to build what had become his extraordinary control over the Senate by his solicitude for the incoming freshmen senators. Johnson had persuaded John

---

* Senator Johnson used a story of his Texas boyhood to help persuade senior Democratic senators to go along with his plan. When he was a boy, he told them, he once invited a playmate named Cecil to spend the night at his house. Cecil's older brother, Bones, had already spent two nights away from home, but Cecil's mother decided that Cecil was too young. Cecil complained against the unfairness: "Bones been two wheres and I ain't been no wheres." Senior senators, Johnson said, scoring his point, had been two wheres on committee assignments, while some senators had been no wheres.

McClellan of Arkansas to resign from the Senate Public Works Committee to allow Albert Gore of Tennessee, the home of TVA, to take the position. He inveigled the party seniors to permit freshman Mike Mansfield a seat on the Foreign Relations Committee and freshman John Kennedy a seat on the Labor Committee. Dirksen knew what such committee assignments meant to the men receiving them. They brought immediate prestige and importance within the Senate, and an easier task when up for reelection. They also meant, inevitably, gratitude to the floor leader who provided them. Yet for Dirksen there was something beyond the personal benefits redounding to the floor leader by thus helping other senators, as he assessed not only what to do about Republican committee assignments but also his own coming role as party leader. He had played the partisan in the party's internecine warring over the years, and he had done so on different occasions as a member of *both* major factions of the party. He saw now the need to move in a different direction, to assume a stance to which both party factions could repair. He wanted to be the leader of the Republicans in the Senate, not merely of the dominant faction of the party there. Not surprisingly, Dirksen's desire to provide a different kind of leadership for his party reflected a remarkable change already under way in Dirksen himself.

Dirksen had run for the House of Representatives in the expectation that he could use the position as a springboard for national office, the Presidency or the Vice-Presidency. He had, plainly, similar motives when he first entered the Senate. Those ambitions had been killed by the party convention's decision in 1952, and Dirksen had lived in frustration and bitterness for years afterward. That malaise of spirit had augmented in Dirksen the tendency, common among green senators, toward personal arrogance and pomposity, an unhappy combination that made him an object of contempt to many in Washington. His reelection in 1956, the attentions paid to him by President Eisenhower, and now the imminence of his becoming his party's Senate leader had worked a change in

Dirksen, the beginnings of a fundamental change. He had already tasted the power and influence that were to come, and that power and influence were the fruits of his office as senator. The Senate had been to Dirksen a means to reach ends beyond the Senate. Suddenly, to Dirksen, the Senate began to appear an end in itself. This is a mystic phenomenon that in time shapes the understanding of some senators, but not of all senators, by any means. Those who are struck by the mystique of the Senate come to believe that service in the Senate is an ennobling experience, and that service *to* the Senate is a calling worthy of selfless devotion. Those who sense the Senate in this wise traditionally have been men who have found in the Senate the summit of their own political careers, and Dirksen was now becoming one of them. He was beginning to find a meaning in the office of senator that he had not found before, and to take his place with such Senate stalwarts as Richard Russell of Georgia and John Stennis of Mississippi. They believed in the Senate with a reverence that approached religious intensity. Dirksen's own rise to power within the Senate, of course, was accelerating this new view.

The change coming over Dirksen could not clearly be identified until some time later, when looking back the observer abruptly discovered that Dirksen was a different man, a different senator, than he had been before. The change was not one of degree; it was one of kind. Like the butterfly emerging from the drab chrysalis, Dirksen passed through a kind of metamorphosis. There had taken place in him a change in substance, and it was obvious, looking back, that it had begun with his altered attitude toward the President. He had become openly and willingly President Eisenhower's man in the Senate, sublimating himself to the President's cause. That this shift to Eisenhower's camp paralleled Dirksen's own political needs to win reelection did not alter the fact that the change was real. He worked now, in the late 1950's, on his legislative chores with the same prodigious energy that he had always given his work in Congress. To a reporter using Dirksen as an example of the hard-working member, he had joked: "It's gotten to the point where a senator needs a pair of roller skates to take care of even a minimum of his work." He was used to the long hours of committee hearings, conferences, reports, and bills taken home to be read before he slept. An energetic man physically, he had once enjoyed athletics, but he abandoned sports for his work. "You have to sacrifice so much time to go to play a game of golf," he said, "or even going down to the Y for a swim. I gave it all up."* He had always worked hard, exhaustively, but now there was a difference in intent. He had found a fuller meaning in his work, a meaning that went beyond himself.

Dirksen felt that his role went further than to support Eisenhower's legislative proposals. He not only defended the President from newspaper and Congressional criticism, but he took on as well the role of defender of everyone in the Eisenhower administration. When Senator Ralph Yarborough of Texas, a Democrat, proposed that the Senate ask Eisenhower's Secretary of Agriculture Ezra Taft Benson to resign and thus give the nation's farmers "relief" from his farm policies, Dirksen rose in the Senate to ridicule Yarborough and his idea. Yarborough's proposal, Dirksen said, was "a high piece of senatorial humor." When the Democrat Senate balked at confirming Lewis Strauss as Secretary of Commerce, it was Dirksen who carried the burden of defending him. Similarly, when the nomination of Clare Boothe Luce as ambassador to Italy ran into difficulties, Dirksen defended her from the Democratic objectors. In this instance, Dirksen's glib phrase-making got him in trouble, to his intense embarrassment. "Why thrash old straws," he asked shortly before the vote on her confirmation, "or beat an old bag of bones. . . ." Senators started to laugh at Dirksen's inadvertence. Senator Hubert Humphrey jumped to his feet. "I must rise to the defense of the lady," he told Dirksen in mock gallantry. Dirksen was badly flustered, an extraordinary turn of affairs for him. "I am referring to the old bag of political bones," he stammered, "those old canards."

* Dirksen's weight in this period rose to 227 pounds. He consulted a doctor who charged him twenty-five dollars for the advice he gave him to reduce by twenty-five pounds. By dieting Dirksen cut his weight to 172 pounds, and he joked that he got more for the doctor's fee that way.

In the summer of 1958, a House investigating subcommittee disclosed the financial relationship between President Eisenhower's White House chief of staff, Sherman Adams, and a Boston clothing manufacturer. Dirksen came to his defense. On his part, Senator Knowland demanded that Adams resign. So did other Republican senators, alarmed at the effect Adams might have on the fall elections. Dirksen, however, upheld Adams as a man of character.

Dirksen's commitment to Eisenhower and his men and measures only suggested the change now working in him. In his early years in the Senate Dirksen's admiration for himself had caused deep offense among those familiar with the Senate. His self-serving approach to politics, his often pontifical manner, and his obvious vanity made him the butt of the Senate's cloakrooms and galleries. "Senator Dirksen was long seen," wrote one Senate intimate, "by most Washington observers as a man of few fixed principles and many thousands of purplish words—an overripe Shakespearean actor tossing his graying locks and skipping nimbly among the issues." It was said that his promotion to the Senate from the House had been the House's gain and the Senate's loss. There was change now, however, in the man's view of himself. He still used the same grandiloquent language, at times to the point of the preposterous, but there was a tonal quality now different from what had been before. Where once he had seemed to believe that when he opened his mouth no dog should bark, now he turned his language against himself. A master of ridicule, he began to mock himself. He spoke of himself as "this old carcass," and self-deprecation slipped into his speeches. This scoffing at himself coincided with his sense of dedication to President Eisenhower and his growing affection for the Senate as a political institution. He came to describe the Senate as "an old, water-logged river scow. It isn't much to look at. It never moves fast, but it never sinks." There was a pride and love for the Senate in these words, despite the gentle derision, and there was in Dirksen even a sense of humility that he was allowed to serve in, to him, so majestic a legislative body.

This change in Dirksen did not alter or temper Dirksen's strident attitude toward politics or politicians. He remained what he had been, a formidable and skillful opponent, fully capable of assaulting the opposition with ridicule or facts, whichever served the purpose at hand. In cut-and-thrust debate, he remained a master, using all the varied skills he had amassed in his legislative career—sarcasm, mockery, humor, the pointed anecdote, the swelling Fourth of July fustian, and the intimate knowledge of men and affairs that he had long studied. He was abrasive one moment, conciliatory the next, and self-assured always. His ambition had not spent itself; it had taken a different course. He craved recognition as he had always craved it, but now he was finding it in the Senate. The sating of his ambition, indeed, lay at the core of his new selflessness.

The late summer and fall of 1958, even as Dirksen was considering how best to lead the Senate's Republicans, was an ill time for Republican politicians. Not only had the party been rattled by the public humiliation of Sherman Adams, but the nation's economy had slipped into another major recession. Combined with the traditional instinct of American voters to favor the party out of power in nonpresidential election years, these politically awkward circumstances guaranteed trouble for Republicans in the November elections. The election results, in fact, amounted to a party disaster. The Republicans lost forty-seven of their seats in the House of Representatives. In the Senate, the Republicans suffered comparable losses. Senator Knowland lost his attempt to become governor of California, and a Democrat won his seat in the Senate. Senator Bricker of Ohio was defeated, as were Payne of Maine and Thye of Minnesota. In all, the Republicans lost thirteen of their members in the Senate. When the new Senate met, there were only thirty-four Republican senators in the chamber. The Democrats had majorities in the House and Senate greater than at any other time in twenty years.

The election results had a shock effect on political Washington. Ever since 1938 Congress had been on balance a conservative legislature. Now, after the 1958 campaign, the Democratic liberals enjoyed clear majorities in both the House and the Senate. They could scarcely contain their elation as they contemplated the expected enactment of their legislative proposals that had been so long frustrated. Lyndon Johnson, as Democratic leader of the Senate, instantly saw in the election a new and expanded responsibility for himself. Just three days after the election, he made a speech in Texas that amounted to his own "State of the Union" address. The Senator recognized the dramatic shift to liberalism of his own party in the Senate, and he proposed his own legislative program for enactment by the new Congress. Whatever Johnson's pretensions in outlining his legislative agenda for the Eighty-sixth Congress, there seemed no doubt that the Democrats had the votes to pass the economic-welfare bills he sketched in his speech. President Eisenhower, until now a moderate on domestic legislation, looked with sudden apprehension at what was to come. Alarmed at the prospects of vast new federal spending for these Democratic programs, the President reacted by turning abruptly into a fiscal conservative. Even before the new Congress convened in January, 1959, Eisenhower resolved on his own strategy. He would block the Johnson legislative program with his veto. He conferred with the Republican Congressional leaders repeatedly on the need to prevent the Democrats from mustering the two-thirds majority to override his vetoes. "Remember," Eisenhower said to Dirksen at one such White House meeting, "one-third and one. That is the watchword for this year. That's what I mean." That was the margin needed in either the House of Representatives or the Senate to sustain the President's vetoes.

Within the ranks of the Republican Party in the Senate, there was dismay at the election results. The liberal Republicans wanted more now than better committee assignments; they wanted a share of the party leadership. They believed that the conservative party leaders, meeting weekly with President Eisenhower, had misled him on the party's political needs. Less than a week after the election, Senator Aiken publicly hinted that his colleagues might challenge Dirksen for the party's leadership.

"There's been this feeling for some time," he said, "that the conservatives would really put the party on the skids. And there will be more losses unless something is done. We have had the feeling that the President has been advised by ultraconservatives only. The liberal wing should have more access to the White House."

Aiken, the senior Republican liberal in the Senate, began the initial steps toward enforcing his faction's demands on the Senate party. He started conferring with his liberal colleagues on strategy for the January caucus of the party. These were the Eisenhower Republicans, still a minority among the Senate's Republicans, but stronger now than they ever had been. Most of the thirteen Republicans defeated in November had been conservatives. Styles Bridges, clearly the most influential senator in the party's councils, knew that the conservatives had to deal with the new situation realistically. He therefore suggested that a member of the liberal faction be made the party's assistant floor leader, and offered his support to that purpose. Bridges thus tried to prevent a direct challenge by the liberals to Dirksen's election as party floor leader. Privately Bridges made sure that Dirksen's candidacy would not be challenged from the conservative faction of the party. By an early count of the Republican ranks, the contest seemed close. There were only fourteen members of the Old Guard left, and they were nearly matched by the dozen Republican liberals and moderates. There were eight other Republican senators who, though conservatively inclined, were counted as "swingmen." They could presumably be won by either faction.

Dirksen also began maneuvering to avoid a party fight over his succession to the party leadership. He passed the word among his Senate colleagues that he wanted all Republican senators to help formulate party strategy, that he favored a more equitable distribution of committee assignments, and that he believed the liberal faction should be allowed to choose one of the party hierarchy. Thomas Kuchel of California, Dirksen said, would be acceptable to him as party whip and assistant floor leader. Dirksen and Bridges, however, were unable to prevent the challenge. The liberals regarded Dirksen, in Aiken's phrase, as the "hand-picked" candidate of the ultraconservatives. Senator Clifford Case of New Jersey, one of the most active insurgents, bluntly stated that Dirksen did not represent "what we believe the party should stand for."

By mid-December the Aiken Republicans had resolved to oust the entire conservative leadership of their party. They refused the compromise terms offered by Bridges and Dirksen. At the same time, however, the liberals' potential strength had been sapped by the offer to give the whip's post to a liberal. The swing Republicans found it reasonable, an appropriate compromise, and one designed to avoid a party quarrel. The Republican insurgents, however, were hurt even worse by President Eisenhower. They saw themselves as Eisenhower Republicans, fighting his fight in the Senate, as they understood it, but the White House proved hostile to their cause. The President in these crucial weeks welcomed both Dirksen and Bridges to the White House for private conferences, and the President urged on Bridges the appropriateness of electing Dirksen as the party's leader in the Senate. Bridges used the steps of the White House to reiterate his offer—"a damn fair proposition," he called it—to give the Republican liberals a larger share of the party control. Dirksen, after his visit, announced from the White House that he had already had the leadership won. Eisenhower publicly took the position that he was neutral in the struggle, but his own shift to the political right made the party's conservatives, long his opponents, seem a more attractive group to him now.

Indeed, the change in Eisenhower had already become so marked that Senator Aiken, the obvious choice of the insurgent group, declined to run against Dirksen for the leadership. "I just felt," said Aiken of Eisenhower's new conservatism, "that I could not carry the administration's banner." The liberal senators, meeting in Aiken's office on December 30, therefore picked John Sherman Cooper of Kentucky as their candidate for floor leader. Cooper immediately tried to draw Dirksen into a debate on the issues outstanding between the two Republican factions, but Dirksen simply ignored him. He conducted his campaign differently. "I buttonholed the right people," he later explained. Besides Bridges, there were several other conservative senators actively working for Dirksen, among them Barry Goldwater of Arizona, Roman Hruska of Nebraska, and Bourke Hickenlooper of Iowa. President Eisenhower and his White House assistants remained "rather circumspect," as Dirksen put it, about their interest in the struggle, and Dirksen himself did now know for sure whether they actually lobbied for him with doubtful senators. Dirksen did know, as did the other senators, that he had the President's tacit support, if not his open endorsement. Under the circumstances, Senator Cooper had no chance.

For many years Dirksen had been helping his Senate colleagues, and this now proved an enormous advantage to him. During two election campaigns, in 1952 and 1954, he had served as chairman of the Republican Senatorial Campaign Committee. He helped collect for those campaigns, by his own estimate, more than two million dollars, and this money he had distributed to Republicans running for the Senate. Beyond that, he had gone to these senators' states time after time to speak for them. "They looked on me," said Dirksen meaningfully, "with a very friendly eye." Such help in times of campaign difficulties amounted to political IOUs callable at a later date, and Dirksen called them now. The liberal faction had hopes of wooing to their cause a full majority of the party's senators, but Dirksen's earlier generosity to these colleagues scotched their efforts. One of these, for example, believed susceptible to the liberals' blandishments, was maverick Senator William Langer of North Dakota, a populist in political instinct. Langer, however, had been under severe assault from his own party in the 1958 primary, and Dirksen took a political risk in going into his state to campaign for him. Later, when Governor Mark Hatfield of Oregon sent Langer a telegram on behalf of Cooper, Langer promptly informed Dirksen. At the caucus Langer insisted on sitting next to Dirksen so that he could show Dirksen how he had marked his ballot, in capital letters, "DIRKSEN." Another senator the liberals hoped to win was Glen

Beall of Maryland, a moderate. They did not know that in 1952, as a member of the House of Representatives, Beall had been thinking of retiring from politics. Dirksen, who was not supposed to interfere in intrastate politics, not only persuaded Beall to run for the Senate but gave him every private help he secretly could to win the party's nomination. Senator Cooper had no chance of getting Beall's vote.

Well before the party caucus on January 7, Dirksen was certain of winning. The party's conservatives, in fact, had the votes to win all the leadership posts. This, however, did not suit Dirksen, nor Senator Bridges. They had been persuaded of the need to broaden the party's leadership to include the liberals and to give them as well a better share of the choice committee assignments. Therefore Dirksen and Bridges plotted to elect Senator Kuchel as the party whip. This was Dirksen's first maneuver in his strategy to become the leader of all the Senate's Republicans, not merely that of the conservative wing. Kuchel was the avowed candidate of the Aiken-Cooper liberal faction against the Dirksen-Bridges forces. Opposing him for whip was Senator Karl Mundt of South Dakota, a conservative. In the caucus Dirksen defeated Cooper, 20 to 14, and then the Republicans elected Kuchel over Mundt by the same margin, 20 to 14. The ballots, of course, were secret, but it was obvious what had happened. Bridges and Dirksen had switched their votes and those of four other senators to Kuchel. They were delighted by their success. "The leadership," Bridges announced, "now represents all the elements and the thoughts of the party, and now we can go forward united."

For Dirksen, his election as his party's Senate leader was his greatest personal triumph. At last he had become a political force in his own right. He had only the title, however, not yet the power. For one thing, Bridges remained, although somewhat indistinctly, immensely influential in the party. For another, the election of Kuchel would prove only a token gesture to the liberals unless more was done. Dirksen acted promptly and deftly to satisfy the liberal faction, and to make himself leader in fact as well as name.

He immediately began to rearrange the committee assignments. Most of the senior Republicans already had desirable committee assignments. Dirksen, with the help of Bridges, persuaded them not to ask for more of the party spoils. Using all his skills of private persuasion, Dirksen negotiated assignment of Case of New Jersey to the Labor Committee, Kuchel to the Appropriations Committee, and Carlson of Kansas to the Foreign Relations Committee. Javits of New York, two years a senator, had been serving on inconsequential committees. Dirksen moved him up to the Banking and Labor committees. Obviously Dirksen was not punishing those who had opposed him for leader. Traditionally the Senate's Republicans had given freshmen members the least important committees; Dirksen himself had had to suffer through such an initial hazing. As leader, however, Dirksen provided each one of the freshmen Republicans with prime committee assignments. Kenneth Keating of New York received the much-desired Judiciary Committee. Winston Prouty of Vermont went on the Labor Committee. "Every man got a top-flight committee," Dirksen explained. He sought out each senator and tried to accommodate his desires as best he could. There were not enough good committee assignments to go around, however, even with Dirksen's success in holding down the demands of the senior senators. Under the circumstances, Dirksen decided to sacrifice his own most important committee assignment, Appropriations. "I didn't want to waste it," he said, "so I put a price on it." He agreed to resign from the Appropriations Committee provided the vacancy went to Gordon Allott of Colorado. Allott would be up for reelection in 1960, and Dirksen knew membership on that committee would help him. The deal was made, one of the most remarkable in the Senate's modern history, for rarely has a senator willingly surrendered any prerogatives of power. Dirksen, however, had a different view now of party leadership than the traditional. He was willing to make sacrifices. He acted as a broker for the senators wanting special committees. "You shall have it," he told senator after senator, "provided everybody agrees." Then he proceeded to argue with the others to go along. Giving up the Appropriations Committee was not the only such instance of self-sacrifice by Dirksen. Two years later, in 1961, freshman Senator John Tower of Texas told Dirksen he wanted the Labor Committee. "You came to the right place," Dirksen told him. "I'm on the Labor Committee. I'll give you my spot." Dirksen's idea was to try to satisfy every Republican senator. "The leader," he said, "takes what's left." This was a new concept of party leadership. Not even Lyndon Johnson had gone so far to accommodate his Democratic colleagues. This was not uncompensated sacrifice by Dirksen, for he had a larger goal in mind. Like the maneuver to make Senator Kuchel the party whip, this also was part of Dirksen's strategy to unite the Republicans in the Senate under his leadership.

For Dirksen, distributing committee assignments on a more equitable basis was only the beginning of his plans to bring harmony and cohesion to the Republicans in the Senate, only the beginning of his plans to make himself an effective party leader. He had admired both Taft and Knowland, but he knew that each had proved awkward and maladroit as a party leader. Taft, shy and introspective, had no flair for the dramatic; he used no outside pressures on his party members; he had no gift of persuading them. A humorless, wooden man, Taft was stiffly formal. Knowland suffered from many of the same flaws, aggravated by a sense of his own rectitude and importance. "If he went to the latrine," one senator quipped, "he would announce it in stentorian tones." A grim man, stubborn and unyielding, Knowland expected from other senators the same dedication to their senatorial duties that he gave to his own. This bred animosity for him. On one occasion in 1958, for example, John Hoblitzell of West Virginia casually informed Knowland that he would be spending the next few days in his home state campaigning for reelection. Knowland did not reply; he just looked at Hoblitzell with shocked disbelief that he would even consider thus neglecting his duties in Washington. Hoblitzell stalked into the Republican cloakroom, angrily cursing Knowland. Hoblitzell was defeated in the election.

Dirksen had no such view of his colleagues. He understood the imperative of winning reelection, felt intensely by every senator, and he tried to do everything he could to help his Republican senators achieve that end. "You keep what you've got," he said once, describing his attitude toward Republicans seeking reelection. That meant soliciting money for their campaigns and then campaigning with them, as well as aiding them as best he could with appropriate committee assignments and other devices, like suggesting amendments to pending bills that they might offer to their personal advantage. Dirksen made it a point to be, in his phrase, "one of the boys" with his fellow senators. "I try to be cooperative," he said, explaining as leader how he dealt with his colleagues, "not to be selfish—to try to help." He was a pragmatic, flexible politician, not inclined to judge his colleagues in moralistic terms. "I am a man of principle," he once said, smiling, "and one of my basic principles is flexibility." He wanted power, influence, and the prestige that comes with them, and he wanted to shape and temper the course of American political affairs. "I am not a moralist," he had said. "I am a legislator."

Under Knowland's leadership the party's Policy Committee had ceased to operate as a functional organization. Dirksen reinstituted the committee as a vehicle of the leadership. He arranged to hold a lunch each Monday, after the meeting of the Republican leaders with President Eisenhower at the White House. There Dirksen discussed with the Policy Committee members the questions Eisenhower raised, as well as other matters coming before the Senate. This was a formality, deliberately contrived by Dirksen to give the members of the Policy Committee a greater sense of participation in the party's affairs. At first these lunches for the Policy Committee, held in the Capitol, were limited to the party leaders and the Policy Committee members, but gradually Dirksen expanded them until finally they were attended by all Republican senators. The Policy Committee did not, in fact, decide the party's policies, and Dirksen made no effort to use the meetings as a means to reach party agreements. With a membership split widely in political bias, from the arch-conservatism of a Barry Goldwater to the fiery liberalism of a Jacob Javits, any such attempt would have proved divisive and harmful to the party, not helpful. Instead Dirksen used the meetings to give each senator, of whatever political temperament, the chance to voice his views in the party's councils. More than this, Dirksen then reported these views faithfully to the President, letting Eisenhower know where the party's liberals stood, as well as the conservatives. Within months Dirksen had not only abated the hostility of the party's liberal wing toward himself, but he had actually won their admiration. "He was marvelous," said one liberal Republican senator, assessing Dirksen's efforts to represent all elements of the party at the White House. Dirksen made himself a bridge between President Eisenhower and all the Republicans in the Senate, transmitting not only what Eisenhower wanted from them but what they wanted from him. In this Dirksen did not pull away from his earlier commitment of full support for the Eisenhower program before Congress. No mean trick, he managed to act as Eisenhower's political lieutenant in the Senate and yet give those senators who disagreed with Eisenhower's specific requests the sense that their positions had weighed in the formulation of those requests.

On a less formal basis, Dirksen brought the party members together in a series of social affairs. He held cocktail parties at the Congressional Country Club outside Washington, inviting all Republican senators and sometimes their wives too. These were calculated by Dirksen to improve party harmony and to build a friendly feeling for himself with all the Republican senators. "You'd be surprised," he once said, "at the amount of goodwill they produced. You'd be surprised at how chummy they get at a party with a drink in their hands. It generates a fellowship that you can't generate in any other way."

Dirksen, however, was not content with the "social amenities" of cocktail parties. Occasionally he also held formal, black-tie dinners for the Republican senators and their wives, hiring a choice room in one of the downtown hotels for a "really swanky" party, as Dirksen put it. He did not want the senators, or their wives, to forget these dinners or the pleasantness there contrived, and he devised a tactic to make them remember. "You never gladden a heart so much," he said, "as to have a table favor that is durable and has a little value, and is most acceptable." For one dinner he went to a Chicago jewelry manufacturer to get such a table favor. "I would like a specially designed elephant," Dirksen told the businessman, "and I want a good one, and I want you to donate it to me. When you've done this, I want you to break the mold. This is special." The jeweler balked at first, but Dirksen insisted. For another dinner Dirksen decided he wanted to give each senator "a damn good watch" of special design. "I just went out and bummed it," Dirksen explained. He went to another jeweler. "This is for a dinner," he told him. "Don't expect anything in return. This is goodwill." The jeweler did not like the demand, but, as Dirksen said, "I got watches." If his methods of acquiring table favors for his colleagues were high-handed and brazen, he knew what he was doing. He was building goodwill for himself with his fellows.

In still another area, Dirksen brought remarkable change to the role of Republican floor leader. This was in his relations with the press. Taft had been almost indifferent to the reporters who covered the Senate, and Knowland had actually been hostile. Taft saw no reason to confide in the reporters, and Knowland reacted to their questions as though they were intruding improperly on matters that were none of their business. Dirksen saw not only that he could generate goodwill with the reporters by helping them in their work, but that he could better get publicity for himself and his party by cooperating with them. "I thought I could be a little more helpful," he said. He did more than take the time to answer the reporters' questions; he provided them with inside information, on a background basis, that they could not otherwise obtain. He made himself one of the most available and trustworthy news sources on Capitol Hill. This was a marked change in Dirksen himself, for he had not always been so. "Where once Dirksen was to be avoided by reporters for his fulsomeness and lack of candor," one reporter noted privately, "he became a man whom it was a pleasure to visit. He always found time to see you, where once he hadn't. He gave you what information he could, where before he tried to confuse you." Dirksen, however, did more than share private confidences with the reporters. He instituted his own weekly news conference, immediately after the luncheons of the party Policy Committee, and to make sure that he had a full complement of reporters present, he went to the Senate's press gallery himself for the meeting. There, perched atop a table, sipping black coffee from a paper cup, he reported on the Policy Committee's agenda. That done, he answered questions on any other subject the reporters wished to raise. It was not unusual for fifty or sixty reporters to attend these sessions, nor for Dirksen to run on for an hour or more, telling stories, cracking jokes, and amusing and beguiling the members of the press. His performances with the press, both in substance and appearance, were a far cry from the abrasiveness of both Taft and Knowland.

There was no question of the effect Dirksen had on the Senate's Republicans. Although badly outnumbered now by the Democrats, they were able to help blunt the drive of the liberal Democrats to enact their wide-ranging legislative proposals. Through most of 1959 a bitter quarrel raged between Eisenhower and the Congressional Democrats over federal housing legislation. Twice Dirksen led the Senate Republicans successfully to prevent the Democrats from overriding the President's veto on this legislation, and in the end the Democrats yielded to pass a bill palatable to Eisenhower. Similarly, there was a bruising quarrel in Congress that year over labor legislation, with the Eisenhower forces again successful. In the 1960 session Dirksen again seized the "hot poker," as Eisenhower called it, on bill after bill, battling the Democrats on civil rights, area redevelopment, aid to education, medical care for the aged, airport construction, and increasing the minimum wage. Dirksen and the Republicans in the Senate and the House of Representatives did not have the votes, even united, to impose their will on the legislation of this Congress, but they did block the Democratic efforts to pass *their* legislation. They made a mockery of the legislative program Lyndon Johnson had laid down in his "State of the Union" speech a few days after the 1958 election.

The improved morale of the Senate's Republicans was not unnoticed, nor was the extraordinary brand of leadership Dirksen had brought to his party in the Senate. The hostility of the press began to evaporate, and in its place appeared first reluctant approval and then open admiration for Dirksen. William S. White, the newspaper columnist, no friend of Dirksen in his dark days of alliance with Senator McCarthy, wrote in early 1960 of Dirksen's transformation with genuine surprise. "The plain truth today may seem surprising," White wrote. "Senator Dirksen has behaved with efficiency, with courage, with honor, with faithfulness to his partisan obligations, but with a higher faithfulness to the interests of the United States of America." White found special grounds to praise Dirksen for his tactical skills in leading his party, and he recorded the new respect Dirksen was finding among his own Senate colleagues. Similarly, *The New York Times*, often a biting critic of Dirksen, published a sketch of Dirksen candidly admiring his style of leadership, noting that when Dirksen had been elected leader nearly half the Senate's Republicans opposed him as a symbol of the party's Old Guard. "Since then," *The Times* reported, "most of them have been grudgingly won over by the hard cunning of a political master, by his refusal to take sides, and his insistence on giving all factions a full chance to be heard. . . . It began occurring to everyone . . . that he was probably the most effective leader the Republicans had had in the Senate for years."

Not all of his maneuvers proved successful, as he himself freely conceded. On one occasion, Dirksen suggested to President Eisenhower a way to ease the course of the foreign-aid appropriation through Congress. "I suggested to the President that we have Otto Passman in to negotiate," Dirksen said. Passman, a Democratic Congressman from Louisiana, was chairman of the House foreign-aid appropriations subcommittee and a bitter opponent of foreign aid. Eisenhower did invite Passman to the White House. "Otto started with a speech," Dirksen said. When the President tried to talk, to make a case for his foreign-aid proposals, "Otto made another speech," Dirksen said. Then Passman stalked out of the President's office. "Ev," Eisenhower said to Dirksen, "don't you ever suggest bringing that fellow around here again."

Dirksen adopted tactics similar to those used by Senator Johnson as leader of the Senate's Democrats. He polled his members privately before important votes, as Johnson did. He pleaded and cajoled with his own members, trying to persuade them to come along with the party on issue after issue, much as Johnson did. He carefully studied each parliamentary situation as it arose, as did Johnson, and he avoided the traps into which Knowland and Taft had fallen. "Bill Knowland saw the leadership primarily as a matter of stating a principle and standing on it," a Republican senator said privately at this time. "Dirksen doesn't stand on principle so much; he gets on the phone and lines up the votes for our side." Dirksen knew, from watching Johnson, the secret of delaying votes until a time when his own cause would have the advantage, either by the maximum attendance of Republicans or the maximum absenteeism of Democrats. Like Johnson, Dirksen crossed the Senate's center aisle whenever he could to inveigle Democratic senators to join him on given votes. The parallel between his operations and those of Lyndon Johnson became so striking that it was assumed by many that Dirksen was merely mimicking Johnson's successful techniques. An apocryphal story made the rounds that Dirksen insisted on the same tokens and marks of prestige that Johnson received. After much effort, so went the story, Dirksen managed to get a telephone placed in his official limousine just like the one in Johnson's limousine, and he called Johnson on it immediately. "Hello, Lyndon," Dirksen supposedly said. "This is Everett Dirksen. I'm calling you from my limousine with my new phone." "Wait a minute, Everett," replied Johnson in his limousine. "The other phone is ringing." In actuality, Dirksen had had the telephone that came with his limousine removed so that he might work undisturbed on his trips to and from home.

Dirksen and Johnson did have a similar view of the Senate and how to make it function, but there were substantive differences in their techniques of leadership and the function of leadership as they understood it. They were not far apart, however, in their legislative philosophy.

"The longer one is identified with public life, especially at the national level," Dirksen said privately, in words that Johnson would have approved, "the more one is persuaded, as the ancient philosopher said, that politics is the art of the possible. In any parliamentary body, you deal with many individuals who embrace different philosophies and represent different local interests. It would be strange indeed if members did not give attention to those items which meant the well-being and prosperity of their states and districts. So, in compounding legislation on the national field, there must be give and take. Nothing is ever black or white. If it were not for the adjustments made, it's doubtful that the legislative machinery could ever operate smoothly and effectively."

Dirksen admired Johnson's tactical skills as nothing short of parliamentary genius, but he had less than genuine respect for Johnson's approach to specific bills and their passage. Although they worked closely together and became intimate personal friends, Dirksen privately dismissed Johnson as "an operational senator." To Dirksen, Johnson was all tactics and cleverness; he did not deal with the substance of legislation. Johnson wanted to pass legislation, and he was not particularly concerned with its character. "What do you want?" Johnson would ask, "houses or a housing issue?" Given a problem, Johnson could work out a compromise, but he was normally indifferent to the terms of the compromise. Dirksen prided himself on his skills as a legislative draftsman, a field largely ignored by Johnson. Dirksen studied the bills, the committee hearings, and the committee reports, and he knew in detail the matters coming before the Senate. His emphasis was not so much on passing a bill as on influencing the substance of what it made law. In seeking the support of his colleagues for given proposals, Dirksen shrank from the heavy-handed pressures Johnson often applied to his rank and file. On occasion, as Johnson himself once conceded, he pulled on a colleague so hard that "the skin came with the hair." Johnson embittered many of his Senate colleagues, particularly Democrats like Paul Douglas of Illinois, with these tactics. Dirksen believed Johnson went too far. "Threats are not in my dictionary," he once said. "I never put anything in the form of retaliation. When a member walks in here, I never ask him to sit down and tell him the facts of life. What good would it do? It would make him hostile. It would make him bitter. It frustrates friendship. You probably would never get him again. That's not the Dale Carnegie school on how to win friends, but a lot of people still think the way to impress people is with a baseball bat."

All the same, Dirksen did learn from Johnson. Johnson, for example, took care never to be taken by surprise. "He knew who was present," Dirksen said of him, "and he knew whom he could rely on to provide a pair, or several pairs, to change a vote on final passage." Dirksen did not hesitate to do likewise. In the infighting prior to important votes, Dirksen made himself the master Johnson had become. "I know where the bodies are buried!" Dirksen liked to boast, half-humorously. He did not, however, try to overawe his colleagues. Unlike Lyndon Johnson, Dirksen could laugh at himself, and he did. He was engaged in serious, even fateful business, as was Johnson, and he treated it as such in dealing with it. He liked, however, to depict himself as a mock hero, even something of a rascal and charlatan, and to this end he adopted a slogan of his own: "The oil can is mightier than the sword!" That slogan, which he repeated constantly, captured his bubbling sense of humor. He intensely enjoyed his work, obviously. He had become a leader of men, and the great world of men's affairs beckoned to him as never before.

# Chapter 9

# The Loyal Opponent

*He has been my friend for fourteen years. He calls me to the White House. He sits in the rocker. I tell him what I think right from the bottom of my heart, and I think that's why he keeps asking me back.*

Senator Dirksen had scarcely consolidated his own position with the Senate's Republicans before he was confronted with the beginnings of the 1960 Presidential campaign. Dirksen himself had abandoned any ambitions for the Presidency, or the Vice-Presidency, but in the Senate he was fairly surrounded by Presidential candidates. Richard Nixon, the presiding officer of the Senate, had no real rival for the Republican nomination, although there was speculation about Senator Barry Goldwater of Arizona. Among Democratic senators, there were four competing for their party's Presidential nomination: John Kennedy of Massachusetts, Hubert Humphrey of Minnesota, Lyndon Johnson of Texas, and Stuart Symington of Missouri. With the Senate thus turned into a cockpit of Presidential intrigue, Dirksen could not have stayed aloof even had he so wished. An activist always, who wanted to play as large a role as he could in national affairs, Dirksen assumed for himself the role of defender of the Eisenhower administration against the oratorical attacks of the Democratic Presidential hopefuls. He saw himself as the special protector of President Eisenhower from the increasingly partisan Democrats.

Dirksen brought to the self-appointed chore the political and rhetorical talents he had been polishing all his life. Shrewd and calculating, a master of invective, Dirksen had a wide variety of oratorical flourishes with which to engulf his antagonist. He could be ferocious or beguiling, comic or sardonic, as the moment dictated. In the midst of the round-the-clock sessions forced on the Senate by Senator Johnson to break the filibuster against the 1960 civil-rights bill, Dirksen amused his colleagues with a recital of his difficulties responding to quorum calls. "One wearies in well-doing," he wheezed at the Senate. "The firebell rang at two o'clock in the morning, four o'clock, six o'clock, midnight, and ten o'clock. While I was trying to woo Morpheus, suddenly that awful clang occurred, and I thought, 'Goodness, who wants to go through all this again.' " In matching wits and barbs with the attackers of the Eisenhower administration, Dirksen could be less than amusing to his target. When Senator Symington tried to make some political publicity with an attack on the administration's military intelligence system, Dirksen mocked his speech. It reminded him, Dirksen said, of a man who was climbing trees to catch woodpeckers. "Some friends said," Dirksen went on, " 'You will never catch any woodpeckers that way.' 'Well,' he said, 'maybe not, but if I don't catch 'em I'll worry 'em like hell.' "

When Senator Hubert Humphrey teasingly suggested that the Eisenhower administration was suffering from what he called the dread disease of "budgetitis," an unwillingness to spend money for federal programs, Dirksen retorted in kind by diagnosing Humphrey's own illness as "spenderitis" and "squandermania." When a labor leader, James B. Carey of the International Union of Electrical Workers, accused the Eisenhower administration of betraying the nation's health needs, Dirksen turned savagely on him. "Just keep your mouth shut," he roared at Carey, and then Dirksen denounced him for his "stinking" remarks.

A more dangerous line of political assault came from Senator Kennedy and Adlai E. Stevenson, for they tried to take advantage of Eisenhower's obvious difficulties and political embarrassments in international affairs. In May, 1960, Soviet Premier Nikita Khrushchev abruptly canceled a long-planned summit conference with Eisenhower in Paris after the President had been forced to admit that the United States had been spying on Russia with U-2 reconnaissance planes. With far-fetched reasoning, Dirksen tried to blame the diplomatic disaster on Stevenson and a purported interview Stevenson had given a French journalist. Then, in June, Eisenhower had to cancel a planned goodwill trip to Japan after an outbreak of anti-American riots there. It made hectic work for Dirksen, trying to stave off the badgering critics of the President, but he did not shrink from it. Indeed, he went to the chore with the same zest as he did to the Senate's crowded legislative schedule. "We are going to have to be as busy," he said, "as a flock of bees that have had a shot of benzedrine." For his vigor in repelling the Democrats, Dirksen won the admiration and praise of his Republican colleagues in the Senate and at the White House.

President Eisenhower obviously appreciated Dirksen's endeavors and his willingness to grab "the hot pokers," in Eisenhower's phrase. After one such incident in March, Eisenhower sent Dirksen a "Dear Ev" note thanking him for his defense of the administration. "When there is need for a telling statement," the President wrote, "I know of no one who does a better job than you do. . . . You do credit to the Senate's finest traditions of oratorical power!" Again, in April, Eisenhower wrote a personal note to Dirksen offering "my thanks to you for continuing, as you have for so long, to keep the record straight and to challenge at once deliberately misleading statements of political partisans." Eisenhower had a still more significant way of thanking Dirksen. He chose Dirksen as the party leader to introduce him to the Republican National Convention in Chicago in July. It was a singular honor for Dirksen, in political terms, and Dirksen accepted it as such. Dirksen had traveled a long way to receive such a mark of esteem from Eisenhower. Eight years earlier, at the 1952 convention, Dirksen had led the attack against Eisenhower's candidacy. Now, when he faced the 1960 party convention, Dirksen forgot the old bitterness and spoke of his pride in serving Eisenhower. "It has been my privilege, ladies and gentlemen," Dirksen told the convention, "to be a part of his team. It has been my privilege to help carry the flag for his program. . . ."

Congress had not completed its work for the year by the time of the national political conventions, and so a rump session had to be called in August to wind up the legislative affairs. The circumstances were unprecedented. In the chair, as presiding officer of the Senate, sat Vice-President Nixon, the Republican nominee for President. On the Senate floor were John Kennedy, the Democratic nominee for President, and, across the center aisle from Dirksen, Lyndon Johnson, the Democratic nominee for Vice-President. All three would be President of the United States in the coming decade, though none could then foresee the course of the bitter events ahead. For Dirksen this unusual session of Congress posed painful difficulties. The Democrats seemed at the point of passing a series of major bills, including medical care for the aged, a major school-construction program, and an increase in the minimum wage. The legislation, if enacted, had to make the Democratic candidates appear to the voters as effective political activists, even as Nixon, silenced by Senate rule, would seem helplessly voiceless and inadequate in the Vice-President's chair. Rather than allow this to happen, Dirksen resolved to seize the initiative wherever he could.

He consulted with his fellow Republican senators and with Vice-President Nixon. Senator Hugh Scott of Pennsylvania, an acid-tongued politician in any fight, devised one tactic: he mustered a group of Republican senators to act as "shock troops." Their chore would be to see that at all times there were articulate Republicans in the Senate chamber to reply instantly to any Democratic speeches. "Our purpose," Scott said, "is . . . to keep the Democrats' feet to the fire." With considerable cunning, Senator Kenneth Keating of New York devised another tactic. He calculated a par-

Everett Dirksen, right, and his twin, Tom, left; older brother, Ben, center.

Young Everett and his dog on the front porch.

Pekin High School Football Team—Everett Dirksen at far right of second row.

Everett Dirksen, age 12.

**EVERETT McKINLEY DIRKSEN**
GERMAN COURSE

B. A. A. (1) (2) (3) (4).
Philo. (2) (3) (4), Treas. (4).
Deutsche Verein (1) (2) (3) (4),
 Pres. (4).
Colonel's Maid (3).
Football team (3) (4).
Ass't. Bus. Mgr. Pekinian (3).
Bus. Mgr. (4).
Class Treasurer (3). Vice-Pres. (4).
Track (4).
Debating team (4).
Manager Colonel's Maid (3).
B. C. C. C. (1) (2).

---

"Dirk, the man of many words," is that type of fellow with whom one must be intimately acquainted before he is fully appreciated. He merits the high regard in which he is held and is one of the ablest fellows of the class. He has all those sterling qualities that win the friendship of those with whom he is thrown in contact, and is truly a man's man.

Portion of page from the Pekin High School yearbook, *Pekinian,* 1913— graduating class of Everett Dirksen.

World War I photo of
Everett Dirksen, sent to his
mother.

Dirksen, aspiring politician.

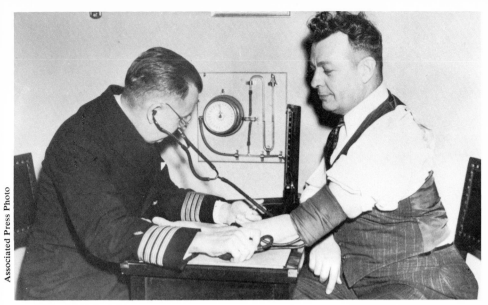

Congressman Everett Dirksen giving blood during World War II.

Dirksen at the Republican National Convention, Chicago, 1952.

Senator Dirksen with President Eisenhower.

Dirksen with Congressman
Charles Halleck, 1964.

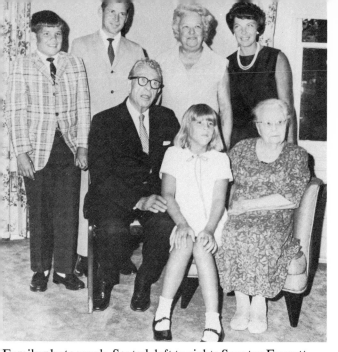

Family photograph. Seated, left to right: Senator Everett M. Dirksen, Cynthia Baker, Mrs. Lillie Carver (mother of Mrs. Dirksen). Standing, left to right: Derek Baker, Senator Howard Baker, Mrs. Dirksen, and Mrs. Baker (nee Joy Dirksen). Occasion was Mrs. Carver's ninetieth birthday, in 1965.

Dirksen with President Kennedy, September, 1963.

Associated Press Photo

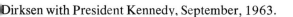

Senator Dirksen in the Senate hearing room, 1966.

In Ten Thousand Words Or
Less, Ev—Is It True You're
Verbose?

liamentary strategem by which the Republicans could force a civil-rights bill to the Senate floor, and thus disrupt the Senate Democrats. Any pending civil-rights bill had to split the Democrats into opposing camps. Behind the Republican maneuver lay an overall assumption that the Democrats had planned this rump session of Congress for purely political purposes. The Republicans therefore devised this strategy to knock the Democrats off balance and thus foil their efforts to enact the Democratic bills. "If the Democrats are going to play this kind of political game," Keating said, "you cannot expect us to take it lying down." Dirksen not only agreed to the Keating strategem, but he decided to give it the full endorsement of the party leadership by offering the necessary motion himself.

In substance, the proposed bill embodied two civil-rights proposals already rejected earlier that year by the Senate. Dirksen had not only voted then to reject them, he had in fact been the senator who proposed the motion to reject them. This did not unduly ruffle Dirksen. Always flexible on political questions, Dirksen did not believe that this disqualified him from asking the Senate in August to approve the very same proposals. To Dirksen there was more at stake in this postscript session of Congress than any mere matter of personal awkwardness for him. Thus, on August 9, Dirksen made the motion, and he caught Lyndon Johnson and the other Senate Democrats by surprise. Johnson was the more embarrassed in that he had no ready response. "It was a sneak play," he snapped privately. Senator Richard Russell of Georgia, the leader of the Democratic Southern bloc, and Joseph Clark of Pennsylvania, an outspoken civil-rights Democrat, both assaulted Dirksen for his about-face on the bill he now offered. Dirksen tried to deny that he had ulterior political motives in this calculatedly political maneuver. He did admit his about-face. "I offer no apology for it," he said in debate. "I confess my sins." Still the Democratic senators kept baiting him, taunting him about his extraordinary reversal on this measure.

"No one will ever embarrass the minority leader," Dirksen replied, "by charging him with having changed his mind or reversed his position on other occasions. One cannot have been in this man's town for twenty-eight years, in the House and the Senate, without developing a pretty tough skin and recognizing the verities of political life. I remember the old ditty:

> The King of France with 20,000 men
> Went up the hill, and then came down again.

I have marched up the hill many times. I have marched down. God willing, if I am alive long enough, I suppose I will march up the hill again and again."

Whatever Dirksen's own embarrassment, he had caught the Democrats in an awkward parliamentary trap. Instinctively the Southern Democrats reacted by starting to filibuster the Dirksen measure, thus threatening to block enactment of any of the bills on the Democratic agenda. On their part, the Northern Democrats could scarcely afford politically to oppose any civil-rights proposal, and on Senator Johnson rested the dilemma of what to do. After hurried consultations, he decided that the Democrats had best kill the Dirksen bill. It was an unsatisfactory solution politically on the eve of a Presidential campaign, but the alternatives were worse. Senator Clark, who had impeccable civil-libertarian credentials, volunteered to offer the necessary motion, thus sparing Johnson that mortification, and the Senate voted to table the Dirksen bill, 54 to 28. Kennedy and Johnson both voted for Clark's motion.

This was an ill augury for the Democrats in this post-convention session of Congress. Dirksen and his Republican militants had badly flustered the Democrats, and in the weeks that followed they put the Democrats to utter rout. "The sooner we get out of here," Senator Mike Mansfield, the Democratic whip, conceded privately, "the better it will be for the Democrats." Senator Johnson was humiliated, and he tried to find excuses why the rump session had been necessary. In the end the Democrats were forced to adjourn

Congress with none of the major bills enacted. It had been a clear triumph for Dirksen.

Dirksen's intrigues and maneuvers had been of a kind that in the hands of a less amiable man could have prompted bitter resentment from the Senate's Democrats. Whatever political somersaults he took, however, he played his role as party leader and played it well, without personal vindictiveness, and Senator Johnson did not fault him for so acting. Indeed, Dirksen and Johnson had already become intimate friends, and they did not let their political differences and scraps mar their personal relations. Dirksen had been on the Senate floor in 1954 when Senator Knowland, then majority leader, announced abruptly that he was holding the Senate in session that night. Knowland had not bothered to consult in advance with Johnson, then minority leader, and, to Knowland's humiliation, Johnson retaliated by moving successfully to adjourn the Senate immediately. "That," he lectured Knowland, "is no way to run the Senate—or a railroad, either." For Dirksen this was a lesson learned in the need for cooperation between the party leaders. Dirksen knew the necessity for a correct, and even cordial, relationship between the two party leaders, and he had cultivated such a relationship with Johnson. In the evenings, after the Senate's work was done, he liked to drop by Johnson's office, or Johnson would call on him. Both kept well-stocked liquor cabinets, and over bourbon and branch water they swapped yarns and confidences. A genuine affection blossomed between them. Johnson liked to josh Dirksen about his "big flannel mouth," but to others Johnson described Dirksen as "a great patriot." Dirksen was one of the rare persons who could taunt or tease Johnson without giving offense. Once, on the Senate floor, Dirksen baited Johnson by calling him "my distinguished and beloved friend from the greatest unfrozen state of the union," a reference to the fact that the new state of Alaska was larger than Texas. Johnson, replying in kind, corrected Dirksen by saying that Texas was rather "the largest state in the Union south of the North Pole." From such fluff and from their more meaningful cooperation on the Senate's business, their respect and understanding for each other grew.

By now Dirksen had reached a point of self-assurance that he took delight in burlesquing his own peculiar style of oratory and fustian, even to the point of the hilarious, but he did not burlesque his colleagues. He took pains to avoid giving personal offense to other senators. He had a distaste for slashing at his fellows in a personal way, in the manner of Senator Scott on the Republican side or Senator Robert Kerr on the Democratic. When he could, Dirksen liked to be helpful to his colleagues of either party, and he had friends in many odd corners of the Senate. Senator Joseph Clark of Pennsylvania, normally a legislative opponent of Dirksen, told of Dirksen's graciousness in teaching him how to muster enough senators on the Senate floor to order a roll-call vote. Dirksen's instincts were gregarious and friendly toward his colleagues, and, of course, he had no objections if his colleagues repaid his courtesies with courtesies of their own. Not all his colleagues took a kindly view of him, of course, and his fellow senator from Illinois, Paul Douglas, never forgave him for his utterly pliable approach to political questions. "He is a man of no principles," Douglas said privately of Dirksen many times. Dirksen did have a friendly, if somewhat distant, relationship with John Kennedy. They served together on the Senate's Labor Committee, and although Kennedy was a generation younger than Dirksen, and of a different breed, he was often amused by Dirksen's oratory and antics. Kennedy felt close enough to Dirksen to appeal to him privately in this post-convention session of Congress for some personal help. From constant speech-making, Kennedy's voice had suddenly grown husky, and he feared he might lose it entirely in the political campaign ahead. He had tried to spare his voice as much as possible in this rump session of Congress, even asking Senator Clark on one occasion to make a Senate speech for him. Dirksen, something of a student of oratory, was glad to help, even though Kennedy was the Democratic Presidential nominee. "There's a reason for it," he told Kennedy, analyzing his voice problem. "You keep talking off your vocal cords. I've been watching you. You need some exercises. You have to throw your voice down to your diaphragm." Dirksen a few weeks later noticed a news item that Kennedy had hired a voice teacher, Blair McClosky, and was mastering the trick of speaking off his diaphragm. That pleased Dirksen, for he had a kindly feeling for Kennedy.

In Senate debate at one point, Dirksen teased Kennedy, now his party's Presidential nominee, by saying he did not wish him to leave the Senate. "I want to keep him right here, sixteen blocks from the White House," he said. "The Senator from Illinois," Kennedy replied, amid the laughter, "is very generous." In the final moments of the rump session, Dirksen offered both Johnson and Kennedy "the warm hand of fellowship," as he put it. He said that he would be "lonesome" in the Senate without them. He did not hesitate, however, to speak his genuine affections for the two Democratic candidates.

"So, *au revoir*," he said to them. "We shall see you on the home diamond somewhere. And when it is all over . . . all the healing waters will somehow close over our dissidence, and we shall go forward as a solid phalanx once more."

The Senate, a sentimental place at sentimental times, gave Dirksen a standing ovation.

The home diamond where Dirksen met Kennedy was the White House, for Kennedy was elected President that November. That fact worked multiple changes within the political world of Everett Dirksen. The transfer of Presidential power from the Republicans to the Democrats, from Eisenhower to Kennedy, was a central fact with profound implications for Dirksen's political career and his course of action. Dirksen no longer could use the White House with its attendant publicity to speak for the President, as he had done for President Eisenhower. That, however, was but small loss in personal political terms for Dirksen against the automatic enhancement of his public stature brought about by the departure of the Republican President and his cabinet from Washington. Dirksen's role shifted from that of the President's lieutenant in the

Senate, as he had been for Eisenhower, to that of the leader of the opposition to the Democratic President. He and Charles Halleck, the Republican leader of the House of Representatives, had emerged from the defeat of their party in the 1960 election as the chief spokesmen of their party in national affairs.

Within the Senate itself, the elevation of Lyndon Johnson from majority leader to Vice-President had even more importance to Dirksen than his new role as one of the two principal party spokesmen in Washington. Johnson had surprised those closest to him when he agreed to run with Kennedy as his Vice-Presidential candidate, for few who knew him could conceive that he would willingly surrender his immense power in the Senate, built over the past decade, for the politically innocuous position of Vice-President. Johnson, however, had grandiose ideas. By the force of his own personality—his "imperious" manner, as Dirksen once described it—Johnson had transformed the traditionally secondary post of Senate floor leader into one of domineering command. As Johnson confided to a friend shortly before taking the oath as Vice-President, he intended to use that position to extend his "power" over the whole Congress, not just the Senate but the House of Representatives too. Quickly enough, however, Johnson learned that he could not, as Vice-President, dominate Congress, and even his old colleagues in the Senate let him know that he no longer could command them.* Johnson's sudden eclipse in the Senate left the chamber without a dominant leader. His successor as Democratic floor leader, Mike Mansfield, had neither the desire nor the will to adopt Johnson's autocratic methods. An aesthetic, self-effacing man, Mansfield preferred political anonymity to notoriety, and he invited the chairmen of the Senate's committees to take center stage when matters under their jurisdiction came before the Senate. For the moment, no Democratic senator assumed the real leadership of his party in the Senate, and that void opened the way for Dirksen to move into still greater national prominence and power.

* Johnson, for example, expected to preside over the Democratic caucuses in the Senate, but the Democratic senators would not allow it.

When Dirksen had been elected Republican floor leader in 1959, Senator Styles Bridges of New Hampshire, his principal sponsor, had been widely regarded as the real leader of the Republicans in the Senate. Bridges, however, shrank from such responsibility. Physically ailing, he did not have the strength or the interest to function as a dominant figure, much less *the* dominant leader, of his party in the Senate. Moreover, Bridges deliberately cast himself as a behind-the-scenes operator within the Senate. "He acted a mystic role, as it were," Dirksen said of him. He enjoyed the sense of intrigue and conspiracy that this role gave him. He did command influence within the Senate, but he used it, now, when he used it, primarily to assist Dirksen in his maneuvers and stratagems. Moreover, he encouraged Dirksen to assume the actual leadership of the party, not merely the title. Although Bridges was chairman of the Republican Policy Committee in the Senate, the post from which Taft had led the party, Bridges permitted Dirksen in effect to take over that position too. Dirksen had initiated the weekly lunches for the Policy Committee members, and then quickly expanded them by inviting all Republican senators to attend. With his regular news conference after these lunches, Dirksen thus made himself, in fact, the policy spokesman for his party in the Senate as well as its floor leader. Bridges did not mind. His illness grew worse, and on November 26, 1961, he died. Dirksen found himself without a Republican rival in the Senate.

Still another and somewhat unexpected phenomenon gave Dirksen a still larger scope as party leader than the floor leader traditionally exercised. Dirksen had always been a man of restless energy, an instinctive activist, and although he had deferred to his colleagues on committee assignments, he found that few of them actually bothered with the detailed work required to make them effective legislators on the Senate floor.

"I quickly discovered that," he said, "when a bill came to the floor. Normally you figured that the committee members would be on hand and would carry the ball. That wasn't always true."

On bill after bill, Dirksen found that his Republican colleagues had not done their "homework" and that many of them were not even willing to stay on the Senate floor during the actual consideration of the legislation. They were not prepared to offer amendments to these bills, nor to take on the exhausting work of rounding up enough votes to pass such amendments. This pervasive slackness within the Republican ranks allowed Dirksen to take a more active role on legislation than he had expected, and he soon saw what this meant to him in legislative terms. "You developed a work habit," he said of this unexpected role. "You learned where to look for things. Merely by habit you became a leader in almost all the legislation. This thing grew, of course." Traditionally the party floor leader's principal chore involved the *scheduling* of legislation. Dirksen's expanded role, stemming largely from his colleagues' uninterest, brought him added power and influence over the *substance* of that legislation. He had thought that he was sacrificing much of his direct influence on specific programs when he surrendered his seat on the Appropriations Committee, only to find that as floor leader he had an enlarged jurisdiction over the specifics of all legislation coming before the Senate.

In assessing his new role as the opposition leader in the Senate to a Democratic President, Dirksen sensed that something more was expected of him than sheer recalcitrance. There were two schools of thought on the role of the opposition leader. "The business of the opposition is to oppose," Taft had said during the Truman administration. "Minority leaders have no responsibility for presenting a program. Their role is one of opposition and criticism." When he became Democratic leader of the Senate at the start of the Eisenhower administration, Lyndon Johnson had announced a contradictory view. "It's not the duty of the opposition to oppose," Johnson said then, and for eight years Johnson consistently cooperated with the Eisenhower administration, notably in foreign affairs. Dirksen, so much like Johnson, agreed with Johnson's approach, not Taft's, that the opposition party had greater responsibilities than mere opposition. He would try to view national affairs, especially those involving international questions, from a national rather than a party stance. He had once sympathized with Taft's view that the Korean War was "Truman's War," but he had abandoned such blatant partisanship in the years since. "The Senate's primary function," Dirksen said privately, "is to serve the whole country. For that reason, it is the duty on the part of the Senate leaders never to forget the national interest. . . ."

That did not mean that Dirksen saw his role as merely cooperating with President Kennedy and his administration associates. On the contrary, Dirksen represented not only a different party but a different point of view from that of the Kennedy administration. These differences were substantive, especially in domestic affairs and in the government's approach to economic-welfare questions. Before he left the White House, President Eisenhower suggested that the Republican leaders in Congress in effect continue the weekly leadership meetings that they had been holding with him for the past eight years. They would need a different forum than the White House, of course, and Eisenhower proposed that they name the Republican national chairman, then Senator Thruston Morton, as their presiding officer. Dirksen and Halleck instantly adopted the idea. Such meetings would do more than allow the Republicans in Congress to act with more cohesion than would otherwise be possible. They would as well provide a means, through the press and television, for the Republicans in Congress to reach the American public each week with their view of the problems of the hour. They would have a formal platform from which to criticize the new administration and its measures. Thus it was that on January 24, 1961, just four days after Kennedy became President, the joint Senate-House Republican leadership held its first session. After the closed meeting, Dirksen and Halleck held a joint news conference to explain what had been discussed at the meeting and the Republican response to the Kennedy administration's unfolding program.

These leadership meetings and the news conferences following them were meant as a substitute for the Presidential conferences with Eisenhower, but from the start they lacked the essential ingredients of the earlier sessions. They were not held at the White House, but at the Capitol, alternately in the offices of Dirksen and Halleck, and they were not attended by the President. Without the prestige of either the President's presence or the White House, these meetings, or rather the news conferences held by Dirksen and Halleck after them, quickly fell prey to the wit and sarcasm of the reporters and the Democrats, and even of the Republicans in Congress. The news conferences, before television cameras, were immediately nicknamed "The Ev and Charlie Show." Despite the jest, Dirksen and Halleck actually were becoming television regulars, for every evening after their Thursday meetings the television networks carried film clips of them on their news programs. Repeatedly, Herbert Block, the cartoonist, depicted the two Republican leaders in cruel mockery as a vaudeville act, Dirksen as a melancholy, sad-faced clown, Halleck as a tubby buffoon and straight man. Senator Humphrey joined in the lampooning, describing their performance as "the twilight zone." President Kennedy joshed them by saying they reminded him of *The Untouchables*, a television series.

Halleck, an abrasive partisan, deeply resented this caricaturing of what he and Dirksen were doing. The ridicule angered him. "I'm no clown," he snarled at one point, in private. "I'm a gut fighter." The leadership meetings were serious business with Halleck, and he wanted them treated as such.

Dirksen had no such objections. He enjoyed the notoriety, and he was delighted with the attention he was getting. The publicity might be bad, but it was publicity. The "Ev and Charlie" label particularly offended Halleck, who found in it a deliberate attempt to make them both appear foolish, but Dirksen actually liked the nickname. He encouraged its use. He told Congressional reporters that he took no offense in the nickname at all, "any more than when you refer to some of the great duos in American life, like corned beef and cabbage, ham and eggs, the Cherry sisters, and Gallagher and Shean." Dirksen, a pragmatic politician and far more flexible than Halleck, knew that the public attention they were getting simply could not be bought, and that he could turn it to his own advantage. Within the Republican ranks there was some alarm at the ridiculing of the leadership meetings and the leaders. "They look like Mutt and Jeff," one Republican Congressman said privately. Others feared the image of the party they were giving to the country, a negative "prairie conservatism," and still others painfully compared Halleck and Dirksen to the handsome and graceful new President, John Kennedy. "Dirksen with his fuzzy hair," one Republican congressman said, "and Halleck with his big red nose!" None of this troubled Dirksen, for even as the criticisms were being made, he and Halleck were getting television and press coverage to make the opposition's case against the Kennedy administration. In time, he sensed, the criticism would wane, and he would be the better off for the national notoriety he was now receiving.

President Kennedy, although he occasionally would taunt Dirksen, from the start made certain that he and Dirksen had cordial official and private relations. He did not need to be told the influence Dirksen now carried with the Republicans in the Senate. Bryce Harlow, special assistant to President Eisenhower for Congressional affairs, had advised Lawrence O'Brien, Kennedy's liaison chief with Congress, to keep the President in close rapport with the opposition-party leaders in Congress, especially in all matters dealing with foreign affairs. Kennedy and O'Brien carefully courted Dirksen, and Dirksen responded much the way he had with President Eisenhower. Dirksen, indeed, felt so kindly about Kennedy that he continued to address him as "Jack" as he had in the Senate, even though all Kennedy's colleagues now carefully used the formal, deferential words, "Mr. President." Senator Dirksen's wife scolded him for taking such informalities with the President. The next time he saw Kennedy, Dirksen told him that Mrs. Dirksen believed he had committed a breach of etiquette in addressing the President by his first name. "Why, Ev," said Kennedy, "who more than you has the right?" Kennedy gave a formal lunch at the White House in early March for the Republican leaders of Congress, and Dirksen amused Kennedy by showing him a gold-plated key he had acquired inscribed "The White House—Back Door." Dirksen had bought it in a drugstore for twenty-five cents, and he conceded that he would not have felt free to have shown it to any other President. He felt no such constraint, however, with Kennedy. "He is quite a friend of mine, you know," Dirksen said. From time to time, on Kennedy's invitation, Dirksen slipped into the White House for private talks with the President, primarily on foreign-policy matters.

Dirksen, who had long sought power, relished these meetings. It was not alone his fascination with power, but his personal intimacy with the President, that gave these sessions a special savor to Dirksen. Dirksen was proud of his friendship with President Kennedy. "He has been my friend for fourteen years," he told one audience in Illinois. "He calls me to the White House. He sits in the rocker. I tell him what I think right from the bottom of my heart, and I think that's why he keeps asking me back." In these talks at the White House, Kennedy spoke candidly with Dirksen, and that candor warranted, in Dirksen's own mind, his giving the President his unstinted support in foreign affairs.

President Kennedy treated Dirksen gingerly. Unlike President Eisenhower, he did not send Dirksen private notes of appreciation for his help on administration measures. Kennedy did send such notes to helpful Democratic members of Congress, but he made it a rule never so to congratulate a Republican. Those notes could be useful politically to the recipient, and Kennedy knew it. When he wished to thank Dirksen, Kennedy thanked him by telephone. "I want to thank you for your help," he said in one such call in 1962. Kennedy normally telephoned Dirksen about once every two weeks, not always to thank him, of course, and he made it a point to invite Dirksen to the White House for a private talk about once a month.

"We have manifested over and over and over again," Dirksen

said on March 5, 1961, "that the opposition party must not follow an obstructionist or a hostile line. Our business is to think in terms of the well-being of the country."

Dirksen felt unusually sensitive about his relationship with President Kennedy, that there were proprieties he must maintain out of deference to this President. For example, Dirksen was invited by a Congressional correspondent to attend the 1961 dinner of the White House Correspondents Association for the President. Dirksen thanked the reporter but told him that on the particular night of the dinner he was scheduled to attend an important affair in Chicago and therefore would be unable to go to the dinner for the President. A little later Dirksen telephoned the reporter. He told him that he had been troubled by his refusal of the invitation, because he feared that Kennedy might take amiss his absence from the correspondents' dinner in Washington. He wanted to know if he could belatedly accept the invitation.

In April Kennedy triggered the ill-fated invasion of Cuba by Cuban partisans, and the resulting disaster created an international crisis and a personal humiliation for the President. Kennedy manfully shouldered full responsibility for the decision and the operation's failure, although there were others who rightfully deserved more than casual blame. Attorney General Robert Kennedy, the President's brother, in a secret report to the President stated: "You were told that this was guerrilla territory and failure of this invasion was very remote because these men if necessary could go underground. This was . . . the worst error in my estimation by the CIA planners and by the Pentagon military." President Kennedy, nevertheless, accepted the full guilt for himself, and Dirksen from the very beginning led the Congressional Republicans in full support of the President in this crisis. To Dirksen this was no time for fault-finding or criticism. "Republicans have supported President Kennedy in the Cuban crisis," Dirksen said, "in the belief that once a nation is committed by its President, we must present a united front to the world." Dirksen stated that Kennedy had been "generous indeed" in keeping the Republican leaders fully briefed on the crisis. "When the issue is resolved," he said, "it becomes the responsibility of the minority to uphold the hands of the President and commander in chief."

Cuba was not the only burgeoning international crisis for Kennedy and the country. For another, the nation's commitment to Laos seemed likely to force American intervention in that Southeast Asian country. Dirksen did not hesitate to stand with the President. "Once the President determines upon a course of action in a critical situation like this," Dirksen said of Laos, "every American is in his corner." In July, another crisis, this time in Berlin, suddenly confronted Kennedy, as the Russians threatened to seize that beleaguered city. Kennedy bluntly stated that the United States would tolerate no such thing, calling on the nation to be prepared for sacrifices, and Dirksen again came instantly to his support. "Let it be clearly understood," Dirksen said, "that President Kennedy has the complete support of the Republican leadership in Congress in the Berlin crisis." To Democrats with bitter memories of Republican exploitation of the Korean War a decade earlier, Dirksen's consistent and total support of the Democratic President in these crises suggested a remarkable maturity of purpose and responsibility. Dirksen was the leader of the President's opposition in the Senate, but in these international crises he made himself the leader of the President's loyal opposition. In the process, he made himself also the Republican spokesman on foreign policy.

"When you're in the field of foreign affairs," Dirksen said, explaining his approach as the opposition's leader, "and an issue or a policy or a course of action is once firmly resolved by the President as the conductor of our foreign relations, then, of course, we believe, and I think all like-minded Americans believe, that the President merits support. It simply wouldn't do under the fevers that beset the world today to have any differences of opinion or disunity. . . . We'll take no action and make no statements or indulge in any expressions that will add difficulty and obstacles to the course that the President may pursue. Sometimes we criticize, and freely so, before the final action has been taken . . . but when the action has been taken, then, of course, we cannot quibble, and we never do."

President Kennedy knew the value of Dirksen's support in this field, and he did not flag in the attentions he paid to Dirksen publicly and privately. On Kennedy's return June 6 from his summit conference in Geneva with Nikita Khrushchev, the Soviet premier, Senator Dirksen was among the large group of officials who greeted the President at the airport. Kennedy paid special attention to Dirksen there, greeting him amiably and chatting with him at length, and then inviting him to make the trip with him by helicopter to the White House. These tokens of personal approval and friendship by the President were more than his way of thanking Dirksen; they were as well his way of assuring continuance of Dirksen's support.

The extraordinary rapport between Dirksen and President Kennedy brought grumbling from within the Republican Party. Many Republicans in Congress thought Dirksen had been seduced by the President, and they did not like it. "That fellow down in the White House," Representative William Miller of New York said privately, "has certainly got Dirksen's number. Ev goes down there to a foreign-policy briefing and he comes out with stars in his eyes, and there's nothing you can do with him." Dirksen, however, was not unduly troubled by such complaining from his party members. He had clearly resolved his own stance on foreign affairs: he would support the President. On a more pragmatic ground, Dirksen could see the soaring popularity of the new President. A Gallup poll in May, 1961, indicated that eighty-three percent of the American people approved Kennedy as President, a higher degree of popularity than even President Eisenhower had ever attained. This popularity, however, appeared to apply only to Kennedy, not to the legislative program he had laid before Congress. Many Congressional Democrats and Republicans alike found that their constituents, while admiring Kennedy, were apathetic about much of the social-welfare legislation he proposed. Dirksen needed no such cue to prompt him to oppose these liberal bills, for he had been leading the opposition to them from the beginning.

Dirksen joined forces with Senator Goldwater of Arizona to try to reduce the President's minimum-wage bill. When Kennedy asked Congress for the largest increase in federal judgeships ever approved, Dirksen taunted him for playing "courthouse politics" with these "most desirable political plums." In his campaign for the Presidency, Kennedy had pledged immediate enactment of a far-reaching civil-rights bill, but when he failed to make any such request of Congress, Dirksen painfully embarrassed the President by introducing a Republican version of just such a bill. "Nothing has been done," Dirksen gibed at the Kennedy administration. "Nothing has been advanced." On the Senate floor, in news conferences, and through the "Ev and Charlie Show," Dirksen kept up a harassing critique of Kennedy's domestic program. On occasion he slapped at Kennedy's men. When Arthur M. Schlesinger, Jr., one of Kennedy's advisers, described the welfare state as the "best security against communism," Dirksen called the remark "a crisis in the mental history of Arthur Schlesinger." More often, however, he kept his criticism less personal. "Now the Kennedy program," he said in May, 1961, "is just what everyone expected—deficit spending, increased government controls, increases in the government payroll, more welfare statism, and that inevitable price which we must pay the piper, eventually more taxes. It may be called the New Frontier, but the Kennedy program is the old New Deal taken out of an old warming oven."

Thus Dirksen sharply differentiated his responses to Kennedy's proposals on foreign and domestic matters. If he gave Kennedy total support in international affairs, he used all his parliamentary wiles and wits to oppose Kennedy's plans to reshape the national economy and the federal government's role in domestic affairs. "President Kennedy is heading us toward the leviathan state," Dirksen complained of Kennedy's domestic program. He said that

Kennedy's 1962 State of the Union address read "like a Sears Roebuck catalog with all the old prices marked up." Dirksen, an old-fashioned rhetorician, could not accept the newfangled economics of the Kennedy administration; he believed in the "myths" Kennedy was trying to destroy. Dirksen played an activist's role in helping defeat Kennedy's plan for an Urban Affairs Department, his farm bill, and his school-construction bill.

Dirksen, however, did not oppose all legislation proposed by President Kennedy, especially if the measures involved the country's international relationships. He remained staunchly in favor of foreign aid, for example, and even the Kennedy Democrats gave Dirksen the full credit for passing the communications-satellite bill and a sensitive measure to lend the United Nations one hundred million dollars. In these two latter struggles Dirksen brought to play every tactic he knew to assure passage by the Senate.

The President's proposal to rescue the United Nations from a crippling financial crisis met unexpected difficulty in the Senate, where the Republicans in particular disliked granting the United Nations access to the United States Treasury even on a loan basis. Senator Dirksen did more than try to persuade his Senate Republicans to go along with the President on this question. He joined with Mansfield in working out compromise language that would assuage the objections of at least some of the dissident senators, but the proposed compromise was greeted with outrage by some of Dirksen's own colleagues. "A surrender," Senator Goldwater called it. Senator Homer Capehart of Indiana said it amounted to giving the President "a blank check." Dirksen was not to be discouraged from his course. In the Senate's debate he made an extraordinarily eloquent speech that actually changed votes in favor of the legislation. "This is not a financial question," Dirksen told the Senate. "This is a moral question. We must stand up and be counted in our generation. It does not make any difference what the mail from back home says to us." He left no doubt how he stood on President Kennedy as the nation's leader in foreign affairs. "I haven't forfeited my faith in John Fitzgerald Kennedy," Dirksen cried. "I'm willing, as always, to trust my President, because he is my President." Senator John Carroll of Colorado, a Democrat, openly acknowledged to the Senate that Dirksen's speech persuaded him to vote for the President's request. Such acknowledgments are rare indeed in the Senate, for they run counter to the normal pretension that every senator is sufficient unto himself. Senator John Pastore of Rhode Island, often a partisan Democrat, jumped to his feet to congratulate Dirksen for making "one of the finest speeches ever delivered in the Senate." Through Dirksen's efforts, the Senate passed the bill 72 to 22, the handsome margin of approval President Kennedy needed.

Dirksen's speech on the United Nations bonds hurt him in Illinois. This was no minor matter, for he was up for reelection this year. Some of his constituents mailed him news clippings of his speech with the word "shame" scribbled across the type. Dirksen knew there would be such a response. "There are people at home who do not like my attitude, believe me," Dirksen said in his speech. "There are those who would like to see the United Nations perish. . . . I will not charge my conscience with any act or deed which would contribute to the foundering of the United Nations, because I do not know how I would expiate that sin of commission to my grandchildren." Political safety lay in silence, but Dirksen eschewed such a course.

The communications-satellite bill posed a totally different question than the UN bond bill, for the measure was filibustered by a coalition of political liberals, led by Senator Morse of Oregon and Senator Douglas of Illinois. Not in thirty-five years, since 1927, had the Senate invoked cloture on a filibuster, and conservative Republican senators were almost as hostile to such a parliamentary maneuver as were the Southern Democrats. Dirksen believed that passage of the bill involved grave questions of national security, and he worked tirelessly to persuade his Republican colleagues to take the unusual step of approving cloture and ending the filibuster. "Votes don't flutter down like handbills from an airplane," Dirksen explained of his trouble. "They don't shake off a tree. Effort still counts around here." With persistence and patience he used what he called "gentle persuasion" on his colleagues, and in the end he had lined up all but two of the Republican senators in favor of cloture. In seeking to persuade his colleagues, Dirksen did not hesitate to remind them of his past favors to them. Even so, it was a hard struggle. "I got Milt Young to vote for cloture," Dirksen confided later about the Republican senator from North Dakota. "I got it on bended knees. I got it only by reminding him I'd gone twice to North Dakota. I thought he owed me a vote." Of the two senators who refused to yield to Dirksen's pleas to vote for cloture, Barry Goldwater privately made an agreement with Dirksen to hurt his efforts as little as possible. Goldwater opposed cloture ideologically. Coming from a small state, he could not and would not vote for cloture, but he agreed to duck the cloture vote if his vote would mean the defeat of the cloture motion. During the actual voting, Goldwater hid in the Republican cloakroom off the Senate floor until Dirksen sent him word that the Senate would invoke cloture however he voted. With the filibuster thus broken, the Senate passed the bill.

In one instance, surprisingly, Dirksen broke with his own Republicans on a purely domestic bill requested by Kennedy. This came on a proposal by the President to revise federal taxes, among other ways by tightening tax restrictions on savings accounts and allowing a tax credit for corporations under special conditions. In the House of Representatives the Republicans voted to the man against the bill, and their unanimity seemed to commit the Republican Party totally against the legislation. Dirksen, however, viewed the question differently. He felt pressures from a different quarter. The major industries in Illinois, including the railroads, wanted that tax credit, and they were supporting the bill. Dirksen moved cautiously, at first merely predicting that the tax credit would not be defeated by the Senate's Finance Committee. Then he began talking to one Republican senator after another. "I need your vote," he said. "Can you help me?" Gradually he mustered enough Republican senators, thirteen in all, to assure passage of the bill. One of the senators he talked to was Goldwater. "If you need my vote," Goldwater said, "I'll go with you." Dirksen's success here, as on the UN bond bill and the satellite bill, was proof of his growing influence within the Senate. In the case of the tax bill, of course, Dirksen was responding to home-state pressures, not to any private persuasion from President Kennedy.

Dirksen had long catered to such home-state interest groups, as did most senators, but his representation of their special interests was normally obscured by his more public participation in the compelling questions of national and international affairs as they arose. Now and then, however, he was put on public display for his cloaked activities in the half-world of the lobbyists and their sponsors. In 1954 a reporter for *The New York Post* excoriated Dirksen for his presumed role in such matters. "He is," the reporter wrote, "a down-the-line front man for various hungry special interests such as the real-estate lobby, the private power companies, and the big department stores." Dirksen was a political conservative, committed to the businessman's view of what free enterprise ought to be, and he could scarcely agree to such an interpretation of his sympathetic view of business interests. From time to time, however, there were public awkwardnesses for him. In 1959 there were published reports of a one-hundred-dollar-a-plate testimonial dinner for Dirksen sponsored in part by an official of the Standard Oil Company of Indiana. Dirksen blandly stated that he did not know anyone in the American Iron and Steel Institute, an alleged sponsor of the dinner too, and that he did not know who had arranged the testimonial. One of Dirksen's aides said the money collected, some ten thousand dollars, would be used to defray the costs of taped television programs Dirksen made weekly for Illinois stations.

Dirksen's office on Capitol Hill became a normal and regular stopping place for lobbyists, as it was for all those interested in the legislative process. Some of the lobbyists who called regularly on Dirksen, however, had less than savory reputations around Congress, like Sidney Zagri, the lobbyist for the Teamsters Union. There was a gaiety in Dirksen as he normally faced his day's chores and challenges, but with at least some of these lobbyists life was grim, and they faced it with a hard-bitten cynicism. Dirksen did more than tolerate their calls, and as a result they gave Dirksen a less-than-wholesome aura in this private world of pressure politics. "Every pressure group in the country has got it on Dirksen," a member of President Johnson's cabinet said privately. There was no direct evidence of Dirksen's receiving any personal gain from these power brokers, other than the usual campaign contributions they provided those who were cooperative, but Dirksen indicated by his almost open relationships with them that he was careless about whom he called friend. In the minds of skeptics, Dirksen was not above suspicion, and especially in his undisclosed relationship with a Peoria law firm with which he was associated. The skeptics assumed that the lobbyists and special interests repaid Dirksen's friendship to their cause through the law firm. To have done so would have been at least unethical and probably illegal, and Dirksen categorically denied any such improprieties. "I may lug some business in there," he said of the Peoria law firm, "maybe once a year, twice a year. As to fees, is that anyone's business but mine?"

When the interests of business came before the Senate, Dirksen did not shy away from defending them. He shaped an almost poetic argument to defend the billboard lobby from hostile legislation. "I am captivated by a billboard or a sign," he said. "I used to get a big kick out of reading Burma Shave signs. They will not be seen anymore under this bill. They had little slogans. These signs had two or three words. But good-bye Burma Shave. They will have to advertise some other place." Dirksen's attempt to charm a sense of nostalgia within the Senate for the long-gone cleverness of the Burma Shave signs blithely ignored the reality that commercial billboards had scarred the American landscape for a generation.

In another endeavor to protect business from federal incursions,

Dirksen was publicly embarrassed. For four years, 1959 through 1962, Dirksen served on the Senate's antimonopoly subcommittee. The chairman of this subcommittee, Senator Estes Kefauver of Tennessee, all through this period tried to bring forward legislation to control the excesses of the drug industry. Kefauver's thesis was that not only did the drug companies charge exorbitantly high prices for their wares, but they were negligent of the public's safety in their quest for profits. Kefauver was seeking safer drugs as well as lower prices for them. Dirksen battled Kefauver throughout, time after time forcing delays on any legislative action. Little of this struggle was known even around the Senate, for most of it was fought in the relative obscurity of a judiciary subcommittee's closed hearings. There, Dirksen was a master of the dilatory motion, the obfuscating amendment, and the gamesmanship of mustering the extra votes that meant a majority. Still Senator Kefauver persisted, and Dirksen, one of his chief antagonists, had to admire him for it. He said as much to Kefauver in the third-person formalized style of Senate debate: "I like his relentlessness. He is as single-purposed as an Apache Indian. He is as gracious as a Victorian lady. There is a rare diligence about him and a rare consistency too. The difficulty is that we do not agree on the fundamental thesis." Finally, in the summer of 1962, the Senate Judiciary Committee did approve a drug bill, but it had been savaged by weakening amendments offered by Dirksen and his cohorts in this struggle, Senators James Eastland of Mississippi and Roman Hruska of Nebraska. Throughout the long series of hearings Dirksen had been the apologist and defender of the drug manufacturers. It was his natural position, as an unblushing advocate of the capitalistic system. Less than a fortnight after the committee had acted, the nation was stunned by news from Germany that an inadequately tested drug, thalidomide, had caused widespread deformity in newborn babies. This had a shock effect as well on Congress and utterly changed the sentiment of Congress on the drug bill. Even the drug industry, shaken by the news from Germany, announced the formation of a special industry commission on drug safety. Dirksen joined with others in the immediate efforts to restrengthen Kefauver's bill and enact it into law.

This was a Dirksen that the public largely did not see, even though in these first years of the Kennedy administration the nation was becoming more and more aware of Dirksen. Not only had he become nationally known through his position as spokesman for the Republican Party, but his weekly performance on the "Ev and Charlie Show" was making him an ever more familiar personality to the nation's vast television audience. The Republican leadership meetings and the joint news conferences of Dirksen and Halleck had been mocked and ridiculed initially, but over many months the two Republican leaders persisted in their steady pummeling of the Kennedy program. By midsummer, 1962, the ridicule had been forgotten, for Dirksen and Halleck were winning substantial amounts of newspaper space and television time. Television was a medium peculiarly suitable—"felicitous," he would say—to Dirksen's unique style as a performing politician. His tousled hair, long his trademark, was an easily recognizable ensign. His deep-throated husky voice, his flamboyant manners, and his often astonishing use of a rococo vocabulary all tickled the viewing millions. "You'd be surprised," he once said in mild self-admiration, "what you can do with the flexibility of the English language." He was an amusing rascal, full of fun and thunder, and that's the way he deliberately tried to appear. He tantalized journalists who tried to capture his effects with words. "His homogenized prose is straight out of the Chautauqua circuit," one wrote in *The New York Times*. ". . . for students of TV performing there is something consistently fascinating in Senator Dirksen's savoring of a phrase and, more especially, the nuances of its timing. His style may be hopelessly out of date, but when those words come pouring out in measured cadence, there is no confusion over the identity of the actor." *The Fresno Bee* described Dirksen's voice as "suggestive of an unfrocked parson speaking through the bunghole of an empty rain barrel." A harsher critic wrote this: "To the public, Dirksen comes through as almost a burlesque figure, a honey-voiced old Throttlebottom." A writer for *Time* sketched him this way:

> He speaks, and the words emerge in a soft, sepulchral baritone. They undulate in measured phrases, expire in breathless wisps. He fills his lungs and blows word-rings like smoke. The sentences curl upward. They chase each other around the room in dreamy images of Steamboat Gothic. Now he conjures moods of mirth, now of sorrow. He rolls his bright blue eyes heavenward. In funereal tones, he paraphrases the Bible (" 'Lord, they would stone me . . .' ") and church bells peal. "Motherhood," he whispers, and grown men weep. "The Flag!" he bugles, and everybody salutes.

Yet his popularity was not confined to the country's television audience. He had a steadily growing following within Congress. Robert D. Novak, writing in *The Wall Street Journal*, reported that "the very characteristics of Mr. Dirksen that make the crew-cut young GOP politicians with their button-down collars shudder are those that endear him to the Senate—the mellifluous voice, the archaic hand gestures, the delight in the meandering anecdote." Ben H. Bagdikian, writing in *The Saturday Evening Post*, had a similar finding. "Fellow senators are inclined to forgive Dirksen his theatrics because they understand them," Bagdikian wrote. "The Senate has at least as much clever ruthlessness in it as any other working political body, but it is not supposed to show. Some hide behind an old-South courtliness, others behind Ivy League sophistication. Dirksen conceals his cleverness beneath oleaginous manners, the Old Testament lamentations, and the tremulo of his Shakespearean voice."

Dirksen, indeed, had worked his way into the affections of his colleagues. Their amusement at his postures and anecdotes was mixed with respect for the extraordinary dedication he gave his party and country, as senators understand such dedication. He was a difficult man to dislike when he engaged his colleagues on the Senate floor as he did Senator Morse of Oregon in a controversy over expanding the minimum-wage law. "Was it not Solomon," Dirksen said, "who pleaded with the Lord for understanding? The Lord said, 'Ask and I shall give thee,' and Solomon said, 'Give therefore thy servant an understanding heart.' " Dirksen turned to Morse and convulsed the Senate with his plea: "Have an understanding heart." Not always, however, did his fellow senators appreciate Dirksen's antics. Senator Albert Gore of Tennessee, who never took kindly to Dirksen's national notoriety, on one occasion in 1961 acidly described Dirksen's speaking style as "pompous verbosity." Dirksen, offended, called Gore to order under the Senate's rules and forced him to take his seat. The next day, by way of retaliatory reply, Senator Gore unctuously mocked Dirksen's style. He described Dirksen as "the inimitable and euphonious sockdolager from Illinois," who, he said, was "one of the most ariose, mellifluous, dulcifluent orators" in the Senate. Dirksen, in the face of such a verbal barrage, was speechless. Closer to the Senate's consensus was Prescott Bush of Connecticut, one of the Republican progressives who had opposed Dirksen's election as the party floor leader. Senator Bush took the Senate floor August 22, 1962, to speak his praise and admiration of Dirksen, whom he described as a public servant with the "elements of true greatness." Bush's laudatory speech touched off an afternoon-long eulogy of Dirksen, with senator after senator from both wings of the Republican Party voicing their admiration. They praised him for his fairness, his courage, his unselfishness, his eloquence, his erudition, and his patience, in a not unfamiliar pattern of fustian when senators praise one of their own. Yet there was something more than normal sentimental flattery here, for Dirksen had successfully managed to represent the interests of both wings of the party, the liberals as well as the conservatives, and he had brought to the party a cohesion that none of them before could remember. Moreover, the praise was not limited to Republican senators. Senator Mansfield, the Democratic floor leader, rose also to pay honor to Dirksen, telling the Senate he wished he had Dirksen's eloquence to praise him. "With words, I would lay bare the heart of a flower or pry open the fiery core of the atom that the Senate might appreciate the depth and breadth of the senator from Illinois," Mansfield said. Other Democratic senators joined in too, Pastore of Rhode Island, Humphrey of Minnesota, Kerr of Oklahoma. This was extraordinary, for Dirksen then was on the eve of another campaign for reelection to the Senate. It was a token of their respect for him that these Democrats gave Dirksen such glowing testimonials that he could use in the campaign ahead.

Privately these senators of both parties spoke of Dirksen even as they did publicly, which is not always the case in such matters. Their affection and admiration for him transcended party or ideological disagreements. Mansfield believed that Dirksen was the best man on the Republican side of the Senate's center aisle, and he did not care who knew it. "I've admired him as leader," Mansfield said privately. "At times he has literally stood by himself. . . . He is a man of responsibility, understanding, and integrity." A not dissimilar view of Dirksen was held at the White House. There the professional politicians, from the President down, had felt the sting of Dirksen's invective on their domestic programs, but they knew what he had done for them in foreign affairs. Besides, Dirksen did not let the disagreements with the President impair their personal friendship. "Who could dislike Dirksen?" asked Lawrence O'Brien, President Kennedy's chief political strategist. "He gets his arm around your shoulder and, well, he's a total pro, able, cute, and clever."

This obvious friendliness by the President and his men for Dirksen alarmed Sidney Yates, Dirksen's Democratic opponent in his race for reelection to the Senate. Yates, a talented liberal Congressman, became so upset that he went to the White House to plead with Kennedy to make firm commitments to come to Illinois and help him with his campaign against Dirksen. Kennedy made those commitments, but even so there was gossip all over Washington that Kennedy did not want Dirksen defeated. There were good reasons for the gossip, for it was no secret that inside the Democratic hierarchy the defeat of Dirksen, if it happened, would be regarded as a political catastrophe for the Kennedy administration. Robert ("Bobby") Baker, Secretary of the Senate Democrats and a long-time intimate of the Senate's inmost operations, believed Dirksen was the ablest leader the Senate Republicans had had in at least two decades. "He's been a fantastic help to the Kennedy administration," Baker said, "and Kennedy knows it. . . . I like Sid Yates, but my party would be in a hell of a mess—Kennedy would be in a hell of a mess—if Dirksen gets defeated."

On Friday, October 19, Kennedy met his commitment to Yates. He joined the Congressman in Illinois to campaign against Dirksen in both Springfield and Chicago. The next day Kennedy abruptly canceled any further campaigning, pleading he had a head cold, and he flew back to Washington. In reality, an international crisis was at hand; American reconnaissance planes had photographic proof that the Russians were mounting nuclear missiles in Cuba, threatening the nation's safety as never before. On Monday, October 22, Kennedy had resolved to act, and he summoned the leaders of Congress to appear "forthwith" at the White House for an urgent meeting with the President. Dirksen, like the other leaders, instantly returned to Washington, abandoning his political campaign. Dirksen came because he had no choice on such a summons, but he knew as well as any the enormous benefit such a call for him from the President had to have on his reelection campaign. "Chief," Dirksen joshed Kennedy about his alleged illness when he met him at the White House, "how's your fever?" Kennedy laughed, but then he turned to the grave business at hand. "I think," Kennedy began, "that the best thing is to bring you up to date on our intelligence." John McCone, director of the Central Intelligence Agency, briefed the assembled Congressional leaders on the installation of the missile sites. An aide to McCone showed the leaders the blown-up photographs showing those sites. Secretary of State Dean Rusk briefed them on the diplomatic situation, and Secretary of Defense Robert McNamara did the same on the military. President Kennedy, calm and sober, then took over the meeting. "We have decided," he said, "that we are going to take action." He was not asking for advice from the Congressional leaders. He was telling them what he had decided to do. He was placing Cuba in quarantine with a naval blockade, at least technically an act of war. He had called an immediate meeting of the Organization of American States, and he had asked for an emergency session of the United Nations Security Council.

The Congressional leaders listened somberly. When Kennedy asked them if they had any questions, most of them remained silent. Senator Richard Russell of Georgia, chairman of the Senate's Armed Services Committee, did not believe that Kennedy's response to the Russian threat was adequate. He told the President that he should hesitate no longer but immediately invade Cuba. He argued that the United States had blundered at the Bay of Pigs a year and a half earlier and that the United States should not make the mistake again of trying to resolve the Cuban crisis with an inadequate response. Senator Fulbright, chairman of the Senate Foreign Relations Committee, agreed with Russell. In 1961 he had advised Kennedy against the Bay of Pigs invasion; Cuba, he argued then, was a thorn in the flesh of the United States, not a dagger in its heart. Now, however, Cuba threatened the safety of the United States, he said, and direct action was required. He opposed Kennedy's proposed blockade of Cuba. It would be better, Fulbright said, to invade the island and destroy the missile sites.

Dirksen raised a question. He asked, in that tense room, whether the United States had the men and equipment necessary for such an invasion of Cuba. "Are we ready?" he asked. McNamara, chillingly, detailed the heavy cost in men and arms that such an invasion would require. Cuba had been heavily armed by the Russians; it was no longer weak militarily.

"It made my blood run cold," one of the leaders said later of McNamara's description of the estimated casualties.

Kennedy had no intention of altering his decision. Representative Charles Halleck, the Republican leader in the House of Representatives, asked him precisely whether the actions he had announced to them were finally decided. "Yes," the President replied. Dirksen, as the spokesman for the Senate's Republicans, offered Kennedy their full support. "We are in your corner," he said. Halleck made a similar pledge for the House Republicans. Those at the meeting quietly made note of the obvious: Dirksen, Halleck, and the Republicans were supporting the President more staunchly than the Democrats.

At Dirksen's suggestion, the President asked the Congressional leaders to stay in Washington for the next few days in case of immediate need for consultations. The grim meeting broke up just a half-hour before Kennedy went on nationwide television to announce the missile crisis and his decision to act. Dirksen asked the other Republican leaders to join him that night at his office in the Capitol. There they drafted and made public a formal statement endorsing fully the President's decision.

A few days later, after a second meeting at the White House, Dirksen suggested to President Kennedy that if the crisis had calmed enough, as it appeared to have, he permit the Congressional leaders to leave Washington. Dirksen said a number of the leaders, including himself, were running for reelection, and they wanted to get back to their campaigning. Amused, Kennedy teased Dirksen about his doubts at winning reelection.

"What are you talking about?" Kennedy joked, as Dirksen remembered. "You're not having any trouble. You're just as good as in."

"You and I are not novices in this," Dirksen replied. "We don't take anything for granted. There's work to be done."

Back in Illinois to resume his campaign, Dirksen casually mentioned these words of the President to him in the hearing of a reporter. The results were immediate news broadcasts and newspaper headlines all over Illinois to the effect that President Kennedy himself had written off any chance that Congressman Yates might defeat Dirksen. It was the final blow to Dirksen's Democratic opponent. Dirksen won reelection by a margin of more than two hundred thousand votes.

# Uncrowned King of the Senate

*I've only got thirty-three soldiers.*
*The Democrats have sixty-seven. That's why*
*the administration has legislative indigestion.*

"If you have some kind of trademark, like unruly hair," Senator Dirksen confided during his reelection campaign in 1962, "people get to recognize you."

Dirksen had more than his unruly hair to make him not only the best-known candidate up for election that year in Illinois but also the best-known member of the Senate in the nation at large. His frequent television appearances and the heavy press coverage he had been receiving had made him a national celebrity. Dirksen counted heavily on his notoriety to carry him successfully through the election campaign, and it proved an enormous advantage over his less-known Democratic opponent. Indeed, Congressman Yates had difficulty explaining to some voters who he was until he said: "I'm running against Dirksen." Then they understood.

In spite of his obvious advantages in the election, Dirksen did have some nagging doubts that he might have miscalculated his chances. He had repeatedly offended the conservatives and the isolationists in his state, and he had political enemies of formidable strength among the liberals. In any event, as a precaution, Dirksen composed in his mind the outlines of a speech he would make if he lost. In defeat, if it came, he wanted to thank the people of Illinois, his constituents, for their generosity in electing him so often. Publicly he wished to play the man, the gallant loser, and to exit gracefully from his political career. He had long since tutored himself to control his emotions, never to show anger unless anger served his purpose of the moment, and he did not want to end his political career with a show of bitterness. The fact was, however, that he was angry at the end of his campaign, and at no group more than the leaders of the Negro community. It was this anger that impelled him to compose the ungiven farewell speech.

In Dirksen's judgment, he had been shabbily and unfairly treated by the Negro leaders during the campaign. Principally he blamed the National Association for the Advancement of Colored People, and on his return to Washington in January, 1963, to begin his new term in the Senate, he bluntly so informed the NAACP's Washington director, Clarence Mitchell. Mitchell had called on Dirksen to ask that the Senator not hurt an effort then under way to liberalize the Senate's cloture rule on filibusters. Dirksen believed that the NAACP and the Negro leaders in Illinois had not shown "any real appreciation," as he put it, for all his efforts over the years to pass civil-rights legislation. "I carried the flag in the Eisenhower administration for all civil-rights legislation," Dirksen said, "and got a good deal of it through." He told Mitchell that the Negro leaders in Chicago had mocked him during the election campaign, and he cited hostile stories in the Negro newspapers, notably *The Chicago Defender*, ridiculing him as an enemy of civil rights.

"I was surprised," Mitchell said after their interview. "Senator Dirksen spoke rather frankly to me, and he seemed to be speaking from his heart. He said he really meant it. He said he did not feel he had any obligations to go out of his way for the Negro."

For Clarence Mitchell, as for any advocate of federal legislation, Dirksen's enmity had to be a cause for alarm, because Dirksen's power and influence on his return to the Senate were greater than they had ever been. It was not alone that he had won another six-year term with the prestige of that renewed mandate from his state, nor that he held enhanced command over the Republicans in the Senate. There were at work within the Senate and its leadership fundamental changes which had the effect of magnifying Dirksen's importance in the Senate's deliberations. A part of this stemmed from a basic alteration, under way for the previous decade, in the very anatomy of the Senate as a political institution. Another was the result of mere chance, the sudden death of the Senate's most powerful emerging leader, Robert Kerr of Oklahoma.

For more than half a century the Senate had been held in thrall by an organized bloc of Southern senators. They were Democrats to the man, and they were the chief beneficiaries of the Senate's seniority system, for they made their service in the Senate their life's career. Ably led by skillful parliamentarians, they could at will exercise an effectual veto over any legislation they opposed by the simple expedient of the filibuster. They talked such legislation to death. They were willing, if necessary, to impose their will, to obstruct the Senate's legislative routine this way for weeks and even months. Moreover, the Southern senators had silent partners in their filibusters, because the senators from the Middle West and mountain states feared they would risk their own prerogatives in the Senate if they voted for the parliamentary motion necessary to halt the Southerners' filibusters. The Southerners as well had entrenched themselves in the Senate's most powerful committees, and from those bastions of power they in large measure controlled the Senate's responses to the travails of the outside world. In the mid-1950's the South's power in the Senate had begun to erode and wash away. Senator Lyndon Johnson's practice of sharing more equitably the choice committee assignments among all Democratic senators played a significant role in diffusing the South's power in the Senate. The 1958 elections also played a part, for the sudden arrival of so many Northern and Western Democratic liberal senators deprived the Southern bloc of their almost unchallenged control of their party's caucus in the Senate and the party's Steering

Committee. With the 1958 elections too could be dated the beginning of a new working coalition of liberal Democrats and liberal-moderate Republicans that in the decade to follow took control of the Senate away from the old conservative coalition of Southern Democrats and Midwest Republicans. Public opinion also blunted and hampered the Southern bloc in the Senate, nowhere more obviously than in the way Southern senators conducted their filibusters in the 1960's. In the earlier years, a senator like Huey Long of Louisiana felt free to filibuster endlessly and aimlessly, offering recipes for "pot liquor" or reading the Constitution into the *Congressional Record*. In the 1960's the Southern senators in their filibusters felt compelled to speak directly to the legislation before the Senate. Perhaps, in this historic erosion of the South's power in the Senate, however, of most consequence of all were the sociological, economic, and political changes underway in the South itself. The industrialization of the South, the incursions of national press and television, and the Supreme Court's rulings had taken their toll on the South's regional isolation. The flagging energies of the aging Southern senators also played a part in this, as did the new breed of senators coming from such states as Texas and Tennessee. "The South is no longer solid," Senator Richard Russell of Georgia, long the leader of the Southern bloc, had said unhappily in 1960. The Southern senators were not helpless by any means, but they no longer held their once awesome veto power, as had been demonstrated by passage of the civil-rights acts of 1957 and 1960. In a sense, that veto power had shifted, although in considerably weakened form, to the Senate's Republicans, and it was held now principally by Senator Dirksen, as the deliberations of the new Congress would show. He could impose it, however, only as the Southern senators had imposed it, on questions requiring a two-thirds vote by the Senate: applying cloture to a filibuster, primarily, or approving treaties.

As important to Dirksen's new power was the changed leadership on the Democratic side of the Senate's center aisle. Senator Mansfield, the Democratic floor leader, had not tried to fill the power vacuum left by Lyndon Johnson when he had been elevated into the political ambiguity of the Vice-Presidency, and for a time there was confusion over who would emerge as the new Democratic power broker. By early 1962 it seemed evident that that senator was Robert Kerr of Oklahoma, an oil millionaire in private life and one of the most ruthless politicians ever to enter the Senate. Caustic and bruising in debate, utterly careless of his colleagues' sensibilities, Kerr had risen under the Senate's seniority system to a position of immense power, in effect controlling the decisions of both the Finance and Public Works committees while he chaired the space committee. He exacted a price for every favor he gave, even from the President. "Bob Kerr never does anything for nothing," said one of Kennedy's aides. Kerr bragged that he was against "any combine I ain't in on," and he once threatened to take Senator Paul Douglas out into a Senate hallway and thrash him. In 1962, according to Bobby Baker's testimony at his trial for tax evasion, Kerr wrung 99,600 dollars from officials of a California savings-and-loan association while the Senate was considering a tax bill they opposed. He had coerced at least one senator into changing his vote, thereby killing the medicare bill in 1962, by threatening to block Senate approval for a dam in the senator's home state. Kerr inspired fear among his fellow senators, most of whom hesitated to tangle with him in Senate debate. By mid-1962 Kerr had become so obviously dominant within the Senate, so influential in its decision-making processes, that Senator Douglas called him "the uncrowned king of the Senate." That title aptly caught the sense of Kerr's pervasive influence within the Senate, and President Kennedy's legislative aides planned their strategy for the 1963 Congressional session with Senator Kerr foremost in their minds. On December 16, 1962, however, Kerr suffered a heart attack, and two weeks later he died. Thus, by this chance, the Senate's most powerful member was abruptly removed, and that of itself augmented Senator Dirksen's growing importance. It was not at first obvious, but Kerr's death opened the way for Dirksen to become in his own turn the most influential man in the Senate, not merely the leader of the Republican faction there. Dirksen had the potential to assume, if from a totally different power base and by far less ruthless methods, the title Kerr had won, the uncrowned king of the Senate.

Senator Mansfield was not only willing but even anxious to defer to Dirksen. Mansfield, whose personal modesty all but defied the Senate's traditions, had but one objective as the majority leader of the Senate: to make the Senate function as a viable political institution. "When it comes to parliamentary tricks," he once said, "I have none. And if I had any, I wouldn't use them. An open-door policy is the only way I can operate. It's the only way I can hold the trust of my colleagues. I make no deals of any kind." Mansfield's deference to Dirksen annoyed some of his own Democratic colleagues, but Mansfield did not care. In this Mansfield had the support of President Kennedy and Kennedy's liaison man with Congress, Larry O'Brien.

"Yes," O'Brien once said, "they say Mansfield plays too close to Dirksen, but without Dirksen on these votes like civil rights, we're gone!"

Mansfield's perfect indifference to his own notoriety was a personal idiosyncrasy that offered Dirksen an unparalleled opportunity to build for himself both national renown and power within the Senate. The Senate's archaic rules and procedures offered Dirksen even greater opportunity, none more than the Senate's instinctive bias for unlimited debate. Dirksen had tutored himself, in his years in the House of Representatives, to speak tellingly and briefly to the point at issue, but in the Senate he came to love the lack of restrictions on debate. He could spread himself oratorically across an unlimited verbal landscape, and he took full advantage of the opportunity, evolving in time a meandering style of speech-making that was not only garrulous but delightful. Of far more consequence to him, however, were the political realities of the Senate's unlimited debate. The lack of inhibitions made possible the filibuster as a parliamentary tactic, and the potential of the filibuster gave Dirksen what became his great power in the Senate. In 1959, under pressure from the new liberal majority in the Senate, Dirksen had joined with Senator Lyndon Johnson in sponsoring a minor alteration of the Senate's cloture rule, making the halting of a filibuster slightly more easy, but he was a staunch defender normally of the cloture rule as it was, and of unlimited debate. "Over my dead body!" he once exclaimed when he was asked about changing the rules of debate. Indeed, he equated the Senate's unlimited debate with freedom itself. "Let us make no mistake about it," he once said in Senate debate. "If I read my history correctly, past and present, whenever the freedom of a parliamentary body is impaired, we go down the road to tyranny. Show me any place in the world where a parliamentary body and its freedoms are impaired, and I will show an instance of freedom in retreat." When Senator Pastore of Rhode Island acted to require the Senate's debate to stick to the subject pending in the Senate for the first three hours of each day's session, Dirksen vigorously opposed him. "Ha, ha, ha," Dirksen laughed at Pastore's resolution, "and you might add ho, ho, ho." At the beginning of each new Senate, the liberals normally tried to alter the rules to make cloture easier to obtain, and Dirksen stood in opposition to these efforts. "We are going through this quiet agony all over again," he once described the process. He resisted change in the rules of the Senate because he knew the power that those rules gave him.

As the 1963 session of Congress began, President Kennedy was acutely aware of Dirksen's importance to his administration, and he tried to maneuver Dirksen into a position where he would do the Kennedy administration the most good. Just before election day, 1962, the President privately invited Dirksen to join Senator Mansfield and a group of other senators on a tour of the world's trouble spots. The senators were to travel in the President's personal airplane. Dirksen begged off the invitation on the grounds that he needed rest after his election campaign. He was sixty-six years old, and the relatively short campaign he had made had exhausted him. President Kennedy did not desist in trying to inveigle Dirksen more fully into the foreign-policy field, where he could best help the Kennedy administration. There was a vacancy in the membership of the Senate's Foreign Relations Committee, and the President tried to persuade Dirksen to take it. Dirksen again declined. Kennedy had already indicated that tax revision would be his top-priority measure in the new Congress, and Dirksen wanted a major role in the drafting of that legislation. Thus Dirksen arranged for himself to be assigned to the committee that would have jurisdiction of that legislation, the Senate Finance Committee. He was more interested in the tax struggle ahead than in giving President Kennedy additional support in the international field.

When the Eighty-eighth Congress met, Dirksen had just become sixty-seven years old. He was beset with a variety of ailments, including periodic flareups of a peptic ulcer. A man of immense nervous energy, he smoked three packages of cigarettes a day, and when his doctor told him to cut down, Dirksen compromised by no longer carrying cigarettes on his person. Instead, he cadged cigarettes from everyone he met and thereby smoked about as many cigarettes as ever. He kept the same working hours he always had, normally up every morning by five-thirty and hard at work long before official Washington was stirring. He flew out to Illinois frequently, and with him always went his thirty-five-pound brief case, packed with official papers and reports he had yet to read. His colleagues worried about the strenuous pace he kept and whether his flagging health could stand it. Dirksen worried about his health too, and like a true hypochondriac he kept an array of bottled medicines in his Senate desk. On weekends that he did not return to Illinois, he liked to drive out to Leesburg, Virginia, where in 1959 he had bought a four-acre tract and built a home. There he conducted what he called "system repair," tending his garden of vegetables and flowers. "It freshens you up," he said, "for the combat of the next week."

His penchant for gardening, like his rollicking sense of humor, did not leave him, despite his ailments. For years before he purchased the property in Virginia, he had grown flowers and vegetables as a hobby at the residence he called home in Pekin, Illinois, the house of his mother-in-law. His wife canned the fruits he grew and made pickles from his cucumbers. "It's always been a great hobby with him," Mrs. Dirksen said, "to make things grow and watch them grow. He regrets very much when the summer season is over." He had a special fondness for flowers, and out of that fondness he was induced, half in earnest, half in fun, to propose the marigold as the national flower. In time, his annual speech on behalf of the marigold became something of a ritual in the Senate, a harbinger of springtime. He pulled a crowd into the Senate every time he began a verbal rhapsody on the marigold. "We shall be delighted with the earlier flowers—the tulips, the daffodils, the redbud, and the dogwood blossoms. A little later . . . the humble but beautiful petunia, the zinnia, and the calendula, and also the marigold. What a flower the marigold is!" Then on he soared into a paean of praise for the marigold.

"It is as sprightly as the daffodil," he said of the marigold at another time, "as colorful as the rose, as resolute as the zinnia, as delicate as the chrysanthemum, as aggressive as the petunia, as ubiquitous as the violet, and as stately as the snapdragon. It beguiles the senses and ennobles the spirit of man. . . . Since it is native to America, and nowhere else in the world, and common to every state in the Union, I present the American marigold for designation as the national floral emblem of our country."

Dirksen still laced his speeches with humor, as he always had, and he persisted in telling the same jokes and anecdotes that had been in his repertoire for many years. When the occasion arose, for example, he would use his story about the ship's captain and his first mate who did not get along. "One day," Dirksen said, in one telling of this story, "the mate made a note in the log: 'The captain was drunk today.' The next day the captain made a note in the log: 'The mate was sober today.' " As time-tested as any of Dirksen's stories was his anecdote about a schoolboy named Johnny, and Dirksen usually used it when he spoke of freedom. "I take my freedom straight," he said in one such instance. "I am like little Johnny. His teacher asked him, 'How do you spell "straight"?' He said: 's-t-r-a-i-g-h-t.' The teacher then asked, 'What does it mean?' He replied, 'Without ginger ale.' That is the way I take my freedom. I take it without ginger ale. I take it straight."

Occasionally Dirksen was inadvertently funny, as when he tangled his metaphors in an unravelable chaos. "It's not a secret," he said in one such case, "that all Republicans don't look through the same pair of spectacles. This is eloquent testimony of the size of the umbrella over the Republican Party." Sometimes he jumbled his facts in confusion, as he did one afternoon in Senate debate when he and Senator Douglas successfully defeated an effort to restrict the importation of dates. The thesis of the two Illinois senators was that cookie manufacturers—Dirksen called them "the cookie processors of Chicago"—needed dates to make Fig Newtons. "Unless in his lifetime," Dirksen said, "one has indulged in the delight of sinking a molar into a succulent Fig Newton, much of life has gotten by him." It bothered neither Douglas nor Dirksen in the least that Fig Newtons are made with figs, not dates.

As the new session of Congress got under way, Dirksen made plain that he would combat the President's domestic legislative program at just about every point. He was the leader of the opposition party, and in the domestic field at least he intended to oppose the President's bills as stiffly as ever. He opposed the establishment of a youth-unemployment program and the extension of the area-development program. He led the Republicans in opposing the President's plan to establish a 375-million-dollar program to help improve transportation in the country. He made a motion to kill the President's plan for a domestic Peace Corps and then, when that motion failed, he voted against the bill. He opposed the President's farm bill, and he joined Charles Halleck, the Republican leader in the House of Representatives, in belittling the administration's fiscal policies. On vote after vote Dirksen opposed the President, and he and other Republicans maneuvered to try to slash the President's proffered budget for fiscal 1964. By the Easter recess the Democratic leaders of Congress were indicating growing concern about their ability to carry the Kennedy program through Congress. "We have to work on those bills," Speaker of the House John McCormack said. "The Republicans have become completely obstructive." By early summer there was genuine alarm in the Democratic leadership. The entire Kennedy program appeared stalemated. The principal difficulty for Kennedy lay in the House of Representatives, where Speaker McCormack and Democratic floor leader Carl Albert could not find enough votes to pass the Kennedy bills. From the Senate's Republicans, however, there also came continual harassment, and the Southern senators had turned sullen toward the President and his program.

Kennedy's prospects for passing his legislation had been hurt by the unifying of the Republicans against him. In the previous Congress he had received substantial support from Southern Democrats for his bills, but now that support was vanishing. In the South, Negro protest marches had begun and would shortly lead to a nationwide racial upheaval. President Kennedy had failed to meet his election-campaign pledge to pass an omnibus civil-rights bill in his first year as President; he had held off the request to avoid offending Southern Congressmen whose votes he needed for other legislation. National sympathy went to the Negro demonstrators, who were attacked with cattle prods and police dogs by the Southern constabulary, and, as the Southern Congressmen had anticipated, Kennedy finally could hold off civil-rights legislation no longer. On June 11, 1963, the President announced that he would ask Congress to enact an omnibus civil-rights bill. "The fires of frustration and discord," Kennedy said, "are burning in every city, North and South, where legal remedies are not at hand."

Dirksen, like every other Congressman, had been closely watching the rising racial discord. Like them, he tried to fathom the political implications involved and how best to act in the growing crisis. He sensed the national sympathy for the Negro demonstrators and the feeling that something must be done. All but forgotten now was his bitterness against the Negro leaders who had ridiculed him in his election campaign. Dirksen now was willing to go out of his way to help the Negro, but he was not willing to go as far as President Kennedy proposed. Dirksen agreed to co-sponsor an omnibus civil-rights bill with the Democratic Senate leader, Mike Mansfield, as a demonstration of unity, but he was not willing to write into law federal guarantees of the right of Negroes to use all public accommodations, like restaurants and hotels. There were private-property rights here, in Dirksen's mind, and he believed they should be protected too. The public-accommodations section, however, was the emotional heart of the Kennedy proposals, of immense symbolic significance, for the Negro demonstrators had begun at all-white lunch counters. Dirksen did agree to co-sponsor the rest of the Kennedy proposals, including a federal option to cut off federal funds wherever discrimination was practiced, and such a bill he and Mansfield introduced in the Senate on June 19. Thus Dirksen came part way, and a long way, with President Kennedy on this legislation intended to quiet the racial turbulence enveloping the land, but he placed himself squarely athwart the single proposal that was to become the central issue of the ensuing Congressional struggle.

Meanwhile, in another area, Dirksen also placed himself, as the Republican leader of the Senate, against the President. On June 10, the day before he announced his civil-rights proposals, President Kennedy declared that the United States was resuming negotiations with Russia to draft a treaty banning atmospheric testing of nuclear weapons. Dirksen's opposition was immediate. He rose in the Senate to question whether this was not "another case of concession and more concession" to the Russians. Dirksen, who often described himself as a "hard-liner" against communism, did not trust the Russians. He and Charles Halleck, the House Republican leader, issued a joint statement that the proposed treaty might mean the "virtual surrender" of the United States.

On July 15 the American, Russian, and British negotiators met in Moscow, and ten days later they initialed a test-ban treaty agreeable to them. Dirksen already had some doubts that he had taken too strong a position against the treaty. Editorial support for the treaty was overwhelming. Some Republican senators had already indicated they intended to vote for the treaty. Significantly, former President Eisenhower remained neutral, stating that he wished to hear what the military and scientific experts had to say about the treaty. The Republican leaders of Congress, including Dirksen, met privately to discuss the question, and they decided formally to wait before passing judgment, as Eisenhower had suggested. President Kennedy maneuvered cautiously to win the support of Republican senators for the treaty. Senator Dirksen, anticipating a Presidential invitation to fly to Moscow as part of the U.S. delegation signing the treaty, passed the word that he would not accept. However, Senator Aiken of Vermont, a ranking Republican on the Foreign Relations Committee, and Senator Saltonstall of Massachusetts, the senior Republican member of the Senate Armed Services Committee, did accept the President's invitation, thus suggesting how they differed with Dirksen on the treaty. When the White House reported that the President's mail was running twelve to one in favor of the treaty, Dirksen sounded out almost half of the other senators to find out what their mail indicated. On balance, they told him that their constituents seemed about equally divided, just the way Dirksen found his own. Dirksen knew by then, however, that among senior Republican Congressmen there was a view that the party should not take a merely negative stance against this "first step," as President Kennedy called it, away from nuclear war.

There were, indeed, deep political implications in this vote on the treaty. Dirksen, somewhat belatedly, discovered that the Republican Party platform of 1960 had advocated the termination of atmospheric testing of nuclear weapons. Kenneth Crawford, *Newsweek* magazine's Washington columnist, in early August noticed Dirksen's hesitations on his opposition to the treaty. "Dirksen is not one to guess wrong about a thing of this kind," Crawford wrote. "His associates, unlike some television viewers, never mistake his cultivated eccentricities—the gamin hair-do and the syrupy rhetoric—for clownishness. Nobody gauges the velocity of a political wind with a wetter finger." Dirksen could sense the growing confidence of the White House that the President had clearly enough votes in the Senate to win approval of the treaty. In testimony before the Senate Foreign Relations Committee, an array of military and scientific authorities endorsed the treaty, and on August 26 Eisenhower let it be known that he also supported it now. A few days later, on August 21, a Gallup poll indicated that only seventeen percent of the American people opposed the treaty.

On Wednesday of the following week, September 4, Dirksen decided to act, to change his position completely on the test-ban treaty, and in doing so to obtain guarantees from the President that the interests of the United States would not be harmed by ratifying the treaty. To a cynic, what Dirksen had in mind would also give him a rationale for shifting to support the treaty. Dirksen went to Senator Mansfield and told him the feeling he sensed of anxiety that the United States might slacken its efforts in the nuclear field. "There's a pattern to it, the pattern of fear," Dirksen said, by his own account, "that if we sign this treaty, we won't keep on our toes. If anything happened, if the treaty were abrogated suddenly, we could be in trouble. You and I ought to get on our horses and go down to the White House." Mansfield acquiesced in Dirksen's request. He telephoned Larry O'Brien at the White House, and O'Brien arranged for Dirksen and Mansfield to meet with the President the following Monday morning. When President Kennedy learned the next day of the appointment O'Brien had scheduled, he was furious. He was annoyed at Dirksen for his long harassment of the administration's legislative program. Furthermore, Kennedy did not want Dirksen to use the White House for his own purposes, especially since he had opposed the treaty when Kennedy thought he needed Dirksen's support for it. The next day, Friday, however, Kennedy abruptly changed his mind, for on that day the approval of the treaty by the Senate suddenly seemed in doubt. Senator Russell, chairman of the Armed Services Committee, and Senator Stennis, chairman of the Senate's preparedness investigating subcommittee, both announced formally that they opposed the treaty and would vote against it. Russell and Stennis were men of great influence in the Senate on military matters, and so Kennedy was pleased enough to greet Dirksen in his office the following Monday. The situation had changed, and the President needed Dirksen's support.

Kennedy did not know what Dirksen had in mind as the Senator in his husky voice started to explain to the President the fears and doubts that many had, by Dirksen's reckoning, about this treaty. Dirksen talked on, and Kennedy, who normally was amused by Dirksen's antics, tried to guess what Dirksen was about. Finally he caught Dirksen's meaning. He wanted the President to do something specific.

"You got your notes?" Kennedy asked Dirksen.

"Yes," Dirksen said.

"Can I have them?"

"Yes, Mr. President."

Dirksen reached inside his coat and pulled out the draft of a letter he had written. He intended that the President send this letter to him and Mansfield, giving them assurances that the government would not relax its nuclear-weapons program if the treaty were approved. The President laughed.

"It will be done," he said.

Two days later, a revised version of the Dirksen draft, signed by the President, reached Dirksen at the Senate. For Dirksen it was a moment to savor. The President had pledged even more than Dirksen had asked. In the letter he gave his "unqualified and unequivocal assurances," that he, as President, would maintain a vigorous program of weapons development after the treaty was approved. Dirksen read the letter to the Senate with a flourish in the midst of his own thunderous speech endorsing the treaty in its entirety, now that the President had given the appropriate assurances that the nation's safety would be protected. In his peroration, Dirksen spoke movingly. "I am not a young man," he said. "One of my age thinks about his destiny a little. I should not like to have written on my tombstone: 'He knew what happened at Hiroshima, but he did not take a first step.' " Dirksen's speech and his change of position came at a propitious moment in the Senate's debate. He was credited not only with effectively countering the opposition of Russell and Stennis by steadying those senators beginning to waver, but also with actually gaining additional votes for the treaty. The Senate approved it 81 to 19, well over the two-thirds margin required.

While the treaty was under consideration, the preliminary steps were under way on the President's proposed civil-rights legislation. The House Judiciary Committee opened hearings on the legislation on June 26, with Attorney General Robert Kennedy as the lead-off witness. On July 16 the Senate Judiciary Committee, of which Dirksen was now the ranking Republican member, began similar hearings. All summer long, as these hearings were held, the pressure mounted for legislative action. In early August the NAACP held a legislative strategy conference in Washington to lobby for the bill. When Dirksen met with these Negro leaders, he told them Congress would pass a "reasonable" bill but that it would not contain a section on public accommodations. On August 28 a coalition of Negro organizations held a "March on Washington" on behalf of the President's bill. It was a dramatic and moving ceremonial, with some two hundred thousand demonstrators massed before the Lincoln Memorial to signal their support for the legislation.

From the start Dirksen held the central position in this legislative struggle. In effect, he had the power of veto, and President Kennedy and those trying to enact this bill planned their strategy with that in mind. A clear majority of the Senate obviously favored the omnibus bill in its entirety, but that was not the problem. The bill could not be brought to a vote to let that majority act unless the inevitable filibuster by the Southern senators could be broken. A motion to invoke cloture against the filibuster would carry only with a two-thirds vote of the Senate, and the problem was the more ticklish in that the Senate had never imposed cloture on itself on a civil-rights bill. The advocates of the President's bill had no hope of invoking cloture without Dirksen's active help, because Dirksen alone had the necessary leverage to persuade enough Republican senators to go along. By the advance hard counts, not more than sixteen Republican senators were likely to vote for cloture and at least eight more had to be recruited. Thus the parliamentary procedures of the Senate gave Dirksen in substance a veto over the bill. He could dictate not only whether any bill would be passed, but the legislative substance of that bill. If any given civil-rights bill displeased him in any of its parts, Dirksen could refuse to make the effort to have it passed, and that refusal had to prove fatal to the bill. Dirksen himself did not see his role in simplistic terms, for he knew that these senators who had to be persuaded might refuse to be persuaded. They came, mostly, from small states, with negligible numbers of Negro voters, and they were jealous of losing the special prerogatives the Senate's procedures gave them. At best they would be reluctant converts.

For strategic reasons, the Kennedy administration decided to have the House of Representatives act first on the President's civil-rights bill. There were obvious reasons, both parliamentary and psychological, for choosing this course, but the principal reason was to try to influence Dirksen. By having the House of Representatives act first, the administration had the opportunity to carry Dirksen further in civil-rights legislation than the Senator intended to go. The President's men hoped to find a way to persuade Dirksen to agree to some kind of federal protection for Negroes to use public accommodations. They hoped it could be done by bringing the Republicans in the House massively behind the whole bill. It would be no easy task. Indeed, there were widespread rumors around the Capitol in the early stages of the struggle that the Kennedy administration had already abandoned its public-accommodations proposals because of Dirksen's opposition. In the hearings before the House committee, Representative John Lindsay of New York went so far as to question Attorney General Kennedy about these rumors.

In keeping with their strategy, the administration's officials concentrated on William McCulloch of Ohio, the ranking Republican on the House Judiciary Committee. McCulloch, a talented lawyer in his own right, carried great influence among the House Republicans, especially on legal and constitutional questions. The plan of the President's men was to persuade McCulloch to support the whole Kennedy bill in substance, and then through McCulloch to win the mass of the Republicans in the House, including the Republican floor leader, Charles Halleck. By so doing, the administration's strategists calculated to put Dirksen in such a position with his party that he would have to go along with at least some kind of public-accommodations guarantees. The wooing of McCulloch was thus begun, and it included conferences at the White House with President Kennedy. All summer and fall the struggle went on, complicated by the intransigence of the Southern Congressmen, desperate to block this legislation. "Our backs are to the wall," cried Senator Strom Thurmond of South Carolina, "but we are not without weapons. . . ." In the process, the President made concessions to the Republicans, and in the end McCulloch and Halleck and the mass of the House Republicans moved behind an omnibus civil-rights bill including public accommodations. The strategy had worked, and now the burden fell on Dirksen to make his decision.

President Kennedy, of course, had not neglected Dirksen in the long negotiations with the House Republicans. Even before Kennedy announced his omnibus bill, he had invited Dirksen and other Republican leaders to the White House to discuss the growing civil-rights crisis. He sent Dirksen an advance copy of the bill before he formally proposed it to Congress. The President as well conferred frequently and privately with Dirksen about the bill, and so did the President's brother Attorney General Robert Kennedy. Neither the President nor Dirksen had any illusions about the Senator's power over this legislation, and Dirksen left the President in no doubt that he intended to use that power. "Mr. President," he told Kennedy early in the negotiations, "you may be sure I will try for some modifications in this bill." Kennedy assigned Larry

O'Brien, his chief liaison man with Congress, and Michael Manatos, his special liaison man with the Senate, to pay close attention to Dirksen, and they conferred periodically with him too throughout the long struggle.

Dirksen had long prided himself on his craftsmanship in handling legislation, not only its substance but also its technical language as well, and on this bill he devoted every spare moment. He worked on it at his office in the Capitol and at his home in Leesburg. He carried it with him when he traveled. "I kept annotating the bill," Dirksen explained, "and making a list of prospective amendments." He borrowed three lawyers from the staffs of subcommittees of the Senate's Judiciary Committee and assigned them to the civil-rights bill. They were Republican counsel on their respective subcommittees, responsible to Dirksen therefore, and they were later to be nicknamed "Dirksen's Bombers" in this struggle to enact a law. Dirksen depended on them for advice and ideas, and they played a crucial role in drafting the final bill. "I have to rely on staff," Dirksen once said. "You can't work any other way, or you flounder." There was more to this, however, than merely drafting a "good, workable, equitable, practical bill," as Dirksen described his goal. His most ticklish problem was maintaining his control over his own rank and file in the Senate. The Republican senators were badly divided over this legislation, and by bluntly stating his original objections to the bill Dirksen increased his influence with the very senators inclined to oppose it. Later he used that influence as his leverage not only to change the bill but to persuade the doubting Republican senators to support it. Dirksen had other problems too. He warily watched the maneuvers in the House of Representatives, and he, like every other politician, sensed the ever-mounting demand in the country for legislation. The death of four Negro girls in the bombing of a church in Alabama had a shock effect on Congress. So did the cold-blooded murder of a civil-rights marcher. These outrages brought to the legislation an extra dimension of moral fervor and made enactment of a bill a political imperative. Dirksen had learned long before, as part of his political

self-education, to look ahead of any crisis of the moment to antici-
pate its implications in the future. By the fall of 1963 he knew that
the racial upheaval had to be the crucial domestic issue of the
nation's elections in 1964. In his planning, therefore, he carefully
calculated how best to position his own party and its Presidential
candidate, whoever he might be, on this question.

On November 22 an assassin killed President Kennedy in Dallas,
Texas, and Dirksen, his melancholy face contorted in grief and
shock, was on the Senate floor when the dreadful news was announced. Dirksen had a genuine affection for Kennedy and he felt
a special anguish at the murder of his friend. The Senator had even
closer personal rapport with Kennedy's successor, Lyndon Johnson,
and in the weeks of the political moratorium that immediately
followed Kennedy's assassination Dirksen was among those most
frequently called to the new President's side. Johnson publicly endorsed the entire Kennedy legislative program, including the civil-
rights bill and the pending bill to revise the tax code, and Dirksen
altered not a bit his approach to these administration measures.
"Congress hasn't changed," Dirksen said in the immediate aftermath of Kennedy's murder. He did not intend to give Johnson what
he would not have given to Kennedy. "Believe me," Dirksen said,
"there's not going to be a political truce." When Johnson made his
first State of the Union address in January, 1964, Dirksen mocked
his view of the nation and its needs. He went so far as to suggest
that President Johnson was practicing "financial legerdemain" in
his pledges to do more for the country at a lower cost.

For Dirksen, his first legislative collision with the new President
came not on civil rights but on the tax bill Kennedy had proposed.
Dirksen had not ignored this legislation, despite his increasing
preoccupation with the civil-rights bill. The House passed the tax
bill in September, 1963, and the Senate Finance Committee completed its formal hearings on the measure in December. Thus, it
was not until January, 1964, and under President Johnson's goading, that the committee finally began to mark up the bill. In the
ensuing struggle one of Dirksen's primary goals was to repeal many

of the existing excise taxes. On January 23, in committee, he made his move. He and other senators with whom he had consulted offered a series of amendments, and in rapid order the committee voted to repeal excises on luggage, jewelry, cosmetics, furs, and a variety of other commodities. By the noon recess, the senators had voted to repeal excises that brought the government revenues of almost five hundred million dollars a year. President Johnson reacted instantly. He telephoned Harry Byrd of Virginia, chairman of the committee, and appealed to his patriotism. He telephoned Abe Ribicoff of Connecticut and let the Connecticut senator know bluntly how seriously he took this committee action. He dispatched Larry O'Brien and the Treasury's ranking officials to the Senate to undo the committee's votes, and by the time the committee reconvened at two-thirty for its afternoon session, Johnson and his men had switched enough senators to reverse the morning's decisions. It was the first illustration of Lyndon Johnson's extraordinary talent, as President, for pressure politics, and he did not quibble about the rough tactics he used.

Dirksen, who knew Johnson's prowess in such a fight, was naturally chagrined to see his own maneuver thus foiled, and leaving the committee room that afternoon, he taunted Ribicoff for switching sides.

"Ah, you are a fine goddamn guy," Dirksen said to him. "You were in my corner. What about all those little manufacturers in Connecticut?"

"Well," Ribicoff replied, "what do you do when the President gets you on the phone and eats your consummate ass out? He told me what a low-life bastard I was: 'You better get right with God before it is too late!' "

Dirksen did not give up his efforts to repeal these excise taxes. He and Senator Morton of Kentucky joined forces to offer an amendment to repeal them when the tax bill reached the Senate floor in early February. Other Republicans offered similar proposals. The crucial vote came on February 5, and the Senate rejected the Dirksen-Morton amendment 45 to 48. The new President's hand was visible on this vote too. Several Democratic senators refrained from voting until they saw that with their votes the amendment would carry. Only then did they vote against it. On the date of the vote, Dirksen was absent from the Senate, confined in a Washington hospital with a bleeding ulcer, but he knew from there well enough the role President Johnson had played in defeating the Republican amendments. He sent a message to his Senate colleagues, mocking Johnson's success in blocking the Republican efforts to bring tax relief. "So perhaps you can understand my bedridden amazement, my pajama-ruffled consternation, yes, my pill-laden astonishment this week," he wrote, "to learn that three Republican-sponsored proposals to assist in achieving these laudable goals had been defeated by very narrow margins, victims of that new White House telephonic half nelson known as the 'Texas twist.' "

In his hospital bed Dirksen also was working on the civil-rights bill, figuring what amendments he wanted to propose. The civil-rights bill had not yet been passed by the House of Representatives, and it was not passed and sent to the Senate until February 10. Senator Mansfield's strategy was to keep the House bill before the Senate, not allowing it to be referred to the Senate's Judiciary Committee, where it might have languished. Mansfield openly announced to the Senate that he relied on Dirksen to pass the bill. "I appeal to the distinguished minority leader," Mansfield said in Senate debate, "whose patriotism has always taken precedence over his partisanship, to join with me, and I know he will, in finding the Senate's best contribution at this time to the resolution of this grave national issue." Dirksen disagreed with Mansfield's strategy. He wanted the House bill sent to the Judiciary Committee, but the Senate supported Mansfield's motion on a vote of 54 to 37. Mansfield also wanted the Senate to pass the House bill without amendment, but here Dirksen had absolute control, for it was utterly obvious that no civil-rights bill at all could be approved without Dirksen's commitment to it. These procedural and substantive disagreements between Dirksen and Mansfield did not ruffle either of them, for by now they were close personal friends. "Dirksen is an old pro," Mansfield said in admiration. "He's got what it takes. It's a pleasure to be associated with a man like that." Dirksen had equal respect for Mansfield. "Another leader might have got his hackles up," Dirksen said, "but there's no false pride about Mike Mansfield." Mansfield did not confuse his personal fame with his goals. "I am not interested in a headline or an issue," he said at one point when his strategy was challenged. "I am interested in results." Mansfield deferred so totally to Dirksen that even Senate correspondents began to confuse Dirksen's functional role in the Senate as that of the majority leader, not the minority leader. Dirksen was not unappreciative of Mansfield's generosity to him, and he was prepared to requite Mansfield's friendship to the full. He had already done so in two ugly incidents on the Senate floor where a truly partisan leader might well have stood aloof. Both involved Democratic senators nastily attacking Mansfield, and in both Dirksen leaped to Mansfield's defense. In Senate debate in 1962 Senator Wayne Morse of Oregon publicly renounced Mansfield as his party leader and in effect called Mansfield a liar. Instantly Dirksen was on his feet, and he silenced Morse by calling him to order under the Senate's rules for his "indecorous language." Dirksen forced Morse to take his seat, a severe reproof rarely imposed on any senator. The next year Senator Thomas Dodd of Connecticut in a Senate speech acidly criticized Mansfield's leadership. Dirksen unleashed on Dodd a furious verbal assault, even suggesting that Dodd was drunk. He charged Dodd with "cerebral incoherence" and "emotional inconsistency," and he accused Dodd of trying to use the Senate as "a glorified wailing wall." Dodd apologized to Mansfield. Dirksen said he was prepared to defend Mansfield at any time. Mansfield regarded Dirksen as nothing less than his "partner" in running the Senate, and he described their unique relationship this way: "You get a partner like Dirksen and form a dream relationship once in a century."

For the civil-rights bill Mansfield depended completely on

Dirksen. "Dirksen is the real leader of the Senate," one senator said privately at the time. "He understands Mike, and Mike turns to him." Mansfield was quite open about his reliance on Dirksen to pass the civil-rights bill. "The key," Mansfield said, "is Dirksen." President Johnson and his White House lieutenants were saying precisely the same thing, in the very same words, and it bothered Dirksen. "I know the White House is saying that about me," Dirksen said. "I wish they wouldn't." In his own terms, Dirksen foresaw the great difficulty in persuading the needed Republican senators to vote for cloture. He was not sure he could do it, and he felt that that kind of talk from the President and his men complicated his chore. "Getting cloture," he said, "is going to be as difficult as hell. I don't know that we can do it." Some of his Republican colleagues were already annoyed at Dirksen's open intervention on this legislation. They felt he was rescuing the Democrats from a painful political dilemma. A few Republican senators, including Bourke Hickenlooper of Iowa, resented the national attention Dirksen was receiving.

Mansfield based his strategy for passing the civil-rights bill solely on invoking cloture, because he saw no other way feasible to halt the Southern filibuster. He rejected out of hand any thought of holding the Senate in session around the clock to try to exhaust the filibustering senators. For one thing, Mansfield feared that some of the aging senators might not survive such an ordeal. For another, he shrank from exhibiting the Senate in such an undignified posture as all-night sessions invariably produced. "This is not a circus or a sideshow," Mansfield said. "We are not operating in a pit with spectators coming into the galleries late at night to see senators of the republic come out in bedroom slippers without neckties, with their hair uncombed, and pajama tops sticking out of their necks." The Southern senators, led by Richard Russell of Georgia, prepared for any eventuality. They would fight the bill "to the last ditch," Russell said. "We don't mind around-the-clock sessions," he said. "We will be there twenty-four hours a day."

To keep himself free to negotiate with Dirksen and the others engaged in this controversy, Mansfield assigned Senator Hubert Humphrey of Minnesota, the assistant Democratic leader, as floor manager for the bill. Dirksen did likewise. He placed Thomas Kuchel of California, the assistant Republican leader, in command on the Senate floor, and he appointed seven other senators to assist Kuchel. He selected these seven senators carefully so that they represented the Northern, Western, Midwestern, and Southern ranks of the party. "This way," he explained privately, "no one can come up on your blind side." An additional special chore assigned Humphrey by Mansfield was to prevent the advocates of civil rights from unduly provoking Dirksen. Some protesters had already angered Dirksen by throwing up picket lines at his home. Dirksen did not like it. "If the day ever comes," he told the Senate, "when, under pressure, or as a result of picketing or other devices, I shall be pushed from the rock where I must stand to render an independent judgment, my justification in public life will have come to an end." Senator Russell had seized the incident to try to pull Dirksen into opposition to the bill. He flatteringly praised Dirksen for his courage. "It gives one hope for the republic," Russell said, "to see a man who has convictions and the courage to sustain them even though it may endanger his seat in the Senate." Dirksen was not to be so easily wooed from his course, but the incident alarmed Mansfield. He and Humphrey both warned the civil-rights bloc against any action that might alienate Dirksen. "I don't want such tactics used," Mansfield said. "They are not beneficial."

For weeks Dirksen kept his own counsel. It was known that he had been drafting amendments to the bill, but their details he largely kept secret. Meanwhile, he continued in negotiation with Mansfield and the others involved. Early in these negotiations Humphrey revealed a major breakthrough. There would be a public-accommodations section to the bill; Dirksen had softened his opposition to that proposal. He had been "mouse-trapped," as one Republican senator phrased it, by the approval of the omnibus bill by McCulloch and Halleck in the House of Representatives.

The support of those Republican leaders for the whole bill, including public accommodations, had had the planned effect on Dirksen. Still the proposal went too far for Dirksen, and the public-accommodations section was only one of several parts of the bill that Dirksen wanted altered. The debate on the bill droned on week after week as the negotiations went on behind the scenes. Not until the very end of March did Dirksen begin to move, and then only cautiously. Up to then he had hung back, talking with the other senators and assessing their positions. On March 31, at a closed meeting of the Senate Republican Policy Committee, he first discussed formally the amendments he had prepared. The next day he had a similar conference with all Republican members of the Senate. "I was trying to condition them a little as to what I had in mind for this bill," he said. He had more in mind than that, however, for he was also sounding out the Republican senators. Some of them were not pleased with Dirksen's initial ideas. He was seeking a consensus of these senators, for he could not persuade them to vote for cloture if they opposed the bill itself. For a fortnight he continued these sessions with the Republican senators, normally at the lunches of the Policy Committee, which were now held on Tuesday each week. He was circumspect in what he told the reporters. "Not being Houdini," he said after one of these sessions, "I didn't find the right answer." He kept at work, however, trying to find the legislative language that would turn his party members in mass for the bill. "If you don't get a whole loaf of bread," he said, "you get what bread you can." Some of the Republican senators, troubled by Dirksen's vagueness on some points, believed he was using the amendments only as a "smoke screen" behind which he was carefully maneuvering to find his own way on the bill. "He's playing a role," one Republican said. "He's a master of timing and the dramatic." Piecemeal, Dirksen began formally introducing a variety of amendments in the Senate, presumably to be called up later for the Senate's approval. Actually, Dirksen's goal was an omnibus, substitute bill which both Democratic and Republican senators could support, as well as the Johnson administration.

"I have a fixed Pole Star to which I'm pointed," he explained in mid-April. "This is, first, to get a bill; second, to get an acceptable bill; third, to get a workable bill; and, finally, to get an equitable bill."

By early May Dirksen began to feel confident of his Republican senators. He discussed with Humphrey the advisability of holding private sessions with all the principals engaged in the continuing struggle. The basic purpose would be to produce a package proposal that all could agree to support. Thus, on May 4, in Dirksen's leadership office just thirty-three paces down the hall from the Senate chamber, the final negotiations on the substance of the bill began. Attending the sessions besides Dirksen, Mansfield, and Humphrey were Attorney General Robert Kennedy with the senior officials of the Justice Department, a number of interested senators from both parties, and several staff lawyers. Dirksen had some seventy amendments drafted, most of them technical changes in the bill, but many of substance. These became the primary concern of the conferees. All that week, cluttered around the large mahogany dining table in Dirksen's office, under the tinkling crystal chandelier, the conferees argued back and forth. After one session Dirksen was asked what he was doing. "I am trying," he said with a grin, "to unscrew the inscrutable." Attorney General Kennedy in particular tried to resist Dirksen's proposals on public accommodations and fair employment practices, but Dirksen was insistent. He had the compelling argument that he could not deliver the Republican votes for cloture unless he had a "salable" package. Even when the administration officials reluctantly gave way to Dirksen, some of the Republican senators balked at the final bill. The concessions, said Senator Hickenlooper, did not go far enough. Milward Simpson of Wyoming echoed that view; to him the conferees had just warmed over the bill "like hash to make it more palatable." All the same, Dirksen had his bill, drafted to his specifications, and he proceeded now to try to round up enough votes to apply cloture on it.

For Dirksen this was to be the hardest legislative chore he had yet tried to accomplish, and he put into it all the wiles and beguiling talents he had learned in his long career. "Sometimes," he said, "you just have to glower at them as they go by your desk." Few of the averse senators succumbed so easily. They were conservatives out of the Middle and Far West, instinctively hostile to invoking cloture. Dirksen made the bill the subject for discussion at the next weekly meeting of the Republican Policy Committee, and he argued there the gains wrung from the administration in the concessions he had forced. There was still hesitation among many of the Republican senators, but Dirksen, a talented nose-counter, sensed that he was making gains. "Today," he said, after that session, "there are members talking about cloture who yesterday wouldn't be caught dead with it. There comes a moment when the time calls for action. That time is now."

The following week, on May 19, Dirksen summoned a conference of all Republican senators, and there he again presented the bill. He again felt he had made gains, but there were senators criticizing that he had gone too far, others that he had not gone far enough. It reminded him, he said, of a young airman on his first bombing mission. As their plane reached enemy territory, enemy batteries opened up. "Sarge," said the youngster to a grizzled veteran, "they're shooting at us." "Yes," the sergeant replied, "they're allowed to." Dirksen was in an ebullient mood, with growing confidence in his powers of persuasion. He told his weekly news conference that he tried to study history carefully, and he had found great truth in a line he remembered from Victor Hugo's diary: "Stronger than any army is an idea whose time has come." To Dirksen the idea of this sweeping legislation to guarantee the rights of Negroes was one whose time had come. At one of his regular Tuesday press conferences he recited a list of similar events in American history—civil-service reform, the popular election of senators, the women's suffrage movement, the pure-foods act, the child-labor law.

"They would not be stopped," he fairly shouted. "Let editors rave as they will. Let statesmen fulminate as they will. No one on that floor," he said, gesturing toward the Senate chamber, "is going to stop this. It is going to happen. . . . There's no way you are going to stop it."

Appropriately, Dirksen was given the honor of formally introducing the agreed-upon bill as a substitute for the House bill pending before the Senate.

"As a result of the various conferences and by the processes of give and take, we have at last fashioned what we think is a workable measure," he said in his speech. "I hope it will commend itself to the Senate."

The long, harrowing days of pressure had told on Dirksen. His face looked like a collapsed ruin, drawn and gaunt. He smoked too many cigarettes. He was suffering from a half-dozen ailments, besides the persistent ulcer. He took solace in stiff drinks of bourbon at each day's end, swallowing Aludrox tablets to soothe the ulcer. "Listen," he growled in private, "they forget I'm no spring chicken anymore. I get out of this damn place every day at eight, nine, or ten o'clock, drive home, have dinner at eleven, and get up in the morning at dawn. My main problem is getting enough restorative sleep." Still, he drove himself, for the work was not done with the formal introduction of the substitute bill.

In the process of his performance over the preceding weeks, Dirksen had done an extraordinary thing. On this most painful of domestic issues, with great skill and energy, Dirksen had simply imposed himself as the arbiter of the Senate. On him alone now depended whether the civil-rights bill would become law, and everyone in Congress knew it. All over the Capitol, members were no longer discussing the civil-rights bill. They were talking about "the Dirksen package" or "the Dirksen formula." They were talking as well about the remarkable talents of this senator and giving him credit for the Senate's approval of the test-ban treaty. Even Senator Russell, leader of the Southern bloc, began to suggest privately that the Southern senators no longer had a chance to win this struggle. Dirksen was proving too strong. Correspondents who in the past had questioned whether Dirksen had any principles now began to see him as the one emerging statesman in the Senate. He had achieved at this moment command of the Senate. With but thirty-three Republican senators, he had accomplished what his predecessor as Republican floor leader, William Knowland of California, had not been able to accomplish with a majority.

Yet all was not done. Still Republican senators held back, unwilling to follow Dirksen on this perilous course, unwilling to vote for cloture even now. Dirksen went to them, one by one, and pleaded with them. He reminded them of past favors he had bestowed upon them, and he appealed to their sense of responsibility to try to quiet the gathering storm of racial upheaval in the nation. These senators protested that voting for cloture was difficult for them; their constituents believed they betrayed their states' interests by so doing. Senator Young of North Dakota had reluctantly agreed to vote for cloture on the communications-satellite bill in 1962 at Dirksen's urgent pleading, but he had heard from home about it. "Damn you," he told Dirksen, "don't you ever ask me again for cloture." Young thus turned Dirksen down, but Dirksen persisted with his other Republican colleagues. Finally he was ready. He knew he had persuaded enough senators. Thereupon, he and Mansfield jointly offered a motion to invoke cloture.

Dirksen, in Senate debate, argued for the bill. He recited again his view that this was an idea whose time had come, and he urged his colleagues that they had no other course. "Any man's death diminishes me," Dirksen said, "because I am involved in mankind. I am involved in mankind, and whatever the skin, we are all involved in mankind."

On June 10, 1964, almost four months after the struggle had begun in the Senate, the Senate approved the cloture motion, 71 to 29. The rest was anticlimactic. In due course the Senate approved the Dirksen bill on June 19, and the House of Representatives accepted the bill without change. The House leaders dared not try to change the bill for fear of endangering final passage of the bill. In the Senate vote on cloture, the crucial vote, twenty-seven Republican senators voted "aye." Those persuaded by Dirksen were the difference between the success and failure of the bill. The bill could not have become law without his grinding labors for its enactment.

Dirksen stood at the peak of his power in the Senate, at a peak where few men have ever stood in the Senate's history. Yet, in one extraordinary way, he had failed. In large measure Dirksen had predicated his efforts for this bill in terms of positioning his party and its Presidential candidate on this question for the coming election. Six Republican senators refused to accede to Dirksen's pleas for this legislation, and one of these was Barry Goldwater of Arizona, by then almost certain to become the Republican nominee for President that year. The nominating convention was hardly a month away, and Dirksen had argued desperately with Goldwater to support the bill, and cloture on the bill. "You just can't do it," Dirksen told him of his refusal, "not only for yourself, but you can't do it for the party. The idea has come!" Still Goldwater refused. He had constitutional objections to the bill that he could not reconcile. Goldwater voted "no" on cloture and "no" on passage of the bill. For Dirksen, Goldwater's votes took away part of the savor of his greatest legislative triumph. Dirksen had imposed his will on the Senate, but not on the leader-to-be of his own Republican Party.

# Chapter 11

# The Dirksen Veto

*When you make a trade, you've got to get a little something.*
*Don't you know that you can bargain and swap a hat*
*for a monkey wrench?*

For Senator Dirksen, Barry Goldwater's votes against cloture and the civil-rights bill amounted to something more than an embarrassment to the Republican Party. Dirksen knew, as did every other politician, that however sympathetic Senator Goldwater might actually be to the aspirations of the Negroes, his votes made him appear a racist. Dirksen's long effort to position his party on this question had gone for naught. Goldwater had undone his strategy, and Dirksen found himself trapped in an awkward personal predicament. "I've got some people to live with around here," he said, "and I've got a kettle of fish to get out of." Dirksen had been angered by Goldwater's balking on the civil-rights bill, but as a Republican leader Dirksen had to reconcile himself to the fact that by mid-June Goldwater had become for all practical purposes his party's nominee for President. Not only this, but Dirksen himself was a delegate to the Republican National Convention that would nominate Goldwater. Dirksen, indeed, had been chosen chairman of the Illinois delegation to that convention in San Francisco. He could not escape making a choice, even if he had wanted to do so. A political activist by instinct, a man who wanted to be where the decisions were made, Dirksen had no other intention than to play a continuing role in the proceedings of that convention and its aftermath.

Goldwater's vote on cloture caused reverberations throughout the Republican Party. Because of it Governor William Scranton of Pennsylvania decided to make what proved a desperate and abortive attempt to wrest the nomination away from him. Scranton announced himself as a candidate for the Republican Presidential nomination, and the party's liberal-moderate wing rallied to his candidacy as the only way to stop Goldwater. In his quest for support, Scranton came to Washington, and he called on Dirksen in his office in the Capitol. "You know," he said to Dirksen, "you'd make a great favorite son." Scranton touched a delicate nerve with Dirksen, for there were among Dirksen's intimates and immediate family those who wanted him to make a real effort to win the nomination. Dirksen himself had squelched their talk, and he had no temptation to take Scranton's suggestion. He knew what Scranton wanted, for him to offer himself as Illinois's "favorite-son" candidate for President and thus deprive Goldwater of Illinois's fifty-eight votes at least on the first ballot. He turned Scranton down. He was sure that there was no way for anyone to stop Goldwater's nomination. "This thing has gone too far," he said. Moreover, Dirksen already knew that the overwhelming majority of the Illinois delegation to the convention favored Goldwater. He had asked an aide, Harold Rainville, who operated Dirksen's Senatorial office in Chicago, discreetly to poll the Illinois delegates. The Illinois delegation, Dirksen said later, was "as tight as the paper on the wall for Barry Goldwater." Dirksen was one of Goldwater's closest friends in the Senate; he confided in Dirksen. Dirksen had his own doubts as to how effective Goldwater would prove as a Presidential candidate. "The secret to understanding Barry," he had said privately a year before, "is that there's a little voice deep down inside of him that tells him: 'You can't win, you can't win, you can't win.' "

In this dilemma Dirksen acted to recoup what he could. He announced that he not only supported Goldwater for President but that at the convention, at Goldwater's request, he would place his name in nomination. Dirksen's announcement took the Congressional correspondents by surprise, and he had to scramble to find an explanation for them why he was so acting. "This guy," Dirksen said of Goldwater, "has won his spurs in the Republican Party. For thirteen years he's flown all over the country in support of Republican candidates." Dirksen said he understood Goldwater's vote against cloture: no senator from Arizona had ever voted to limit Senate debate. His contrived rationale sidestepped the political realities, but those realities were not missed by other Republican leaders. "Ev's not a man to swim upstream," explained Senator Thruston Morton of Kentucky privately. "So he just went the way he had to go. And, in his way, once he decided to go, he grabbed the banner and led the way. Ev's a man who flows with the stream."

There was some speculation that Dirksen, by joining Goldwater, might be seeking the Vice-Presidential nomination. Dirksen quickly scotched that idea. He did not want to be Vice-President. "I'd have to dedicate roads and courthouses and bow to visiting princes and kings," he said. That was not his idea of attractive work. "I am not a candidate." More than this, however, Dirksen explained that he preferred his place on the Senate floor to the political ambiguity of the Vice-Presidency. A decade earlier he would have rejoiced at such a nomination, but his status had changed radically since then. "There are only one hundred votes out here in the Senate," he said. "I have one of them, and there are four years of my term left to serve. I want to leave a little mark on the pages of history."

In deciding to sponsor Goldwater as the Republican Presidential nominee, Dirksen had more in mind than merely bowing to the inevitable. The odds against Senator Goldwater defeating President Johnson in the November election were prohibitive, but as the nominee of the Republican Party he would have to be conceded at least a chance. In these weeks Dirksen was considering that possibility as well as the immediate fact of Goldwater's imminent nomination. At his home in Leesburg, Virginia, Dirksen tapped out the nomination speech on his portable typewriter, and that speech in sepulchral tones he delivered to the massed convention on July 15. In his speech Dirksen described Goldwater as a peddler's grandson who had risen to his present stature through his moral courage and his conscience. "The time is here," Dirksen said, "for America to retrieve her self-respect." The editors of *The New York Times*, in a moment of whimsy, had sent theater critic Brooks Atkinson to review the convention, and he found little there to admire in theatrical terms except Dirksen's performance. "But none of them," Atkinson wrote of the other Republican orators, "can equal good ol' Ev Dirksen of Illinois, who brings to the rostrum the poised eloquence of the 19th Century thespian. He practices the pregnant pause perfectly. His voice is like the froth on a warm pail of milk just extracted from a fat Jersey cow." Dirksen's nominating speech, however, met less than rave reviews elsewhere, and he himself had doubts about the tastefulness of presenting Goldwater to the convention as a peddler's grandson. A week before the convention, in fact, in Goldwater's Washington apartment, he had read the speech to the senator. They were alone, and at the conclusion Dirksen waited for Goldwater's response. Goldwater was sobbing. "My God," Dirksen thought, "what have I done?" He feared he had offended Goldwater by his references to his peddler grandfather. Goldwater got control of himself, and then he told Dirksen that he had never heard anyone say anything about him that had touched him more deeply. On the night Dirksen delivered the speech to the convention, Goldwater in his suite at the Mark Hopkins Hotel scribbled a note of thanks to Dirksen: "Dear Ev, My prayer is that I will always merit the wonderful words you bestowed on my name today. To a large measure—in fact the largest measure—I was able to hear those words because of you, my political godfather, my friend, and my adviser. With humble thanks, Barry." Dirksen and Goldwater were intimate personal friends, with twelve years' service together in the Senate, and should Goldwater be elected President, Dirksen intended to remain his political godfather, his friend, and his adviser.

Even though he nominated Goldwater for President, and despite the glowing tributes he paid him in that speech, Dirksen had serious reservations about Goldwater's capacity to serve as President. Goldwater had caused widespread alarm by his tendency to "shoot from the hip" in response to questions put to him, and if his remarks were candid, they were also often careless. As a senator Goldwater did not create national or international difficulties with such statements, but as President he would, and that troubled Dirksen. To a friend, as he relaxed after making his speech nominating Goldwater, Dirksen confided his doubts and what he thought ought to be done. "We have got to stop this hip-shooting," Dirksen said. "It is simply too dangerous in the world as it is." Dirksen cited the growing crisis in Vietnam and Southeast Asia, the painful difficulties in Latin America. What Dirksen proposed to do was to persuade Goldwater to abandon any further news conferences with the press, either as Presidential candidate or as President. Dirksen intended, instead, for Goldwater to answer only written questions submitted in advance. This would allow study and care in preparing his answers and avoid rash and unconsidered replies. Years before, Dirksen had seen this technique used in the British government, during the question period of the House of Commons, and he figured it would be best for Goldwater to adopt it. Dirksen knew that Goldwater would be hurt politically by refusing to answer questions directly. "We will have to pay that price," Dirksen said. There was more at stake to Dirksen than that political embarrassment, or even than the ruffling of international affairs by Goldwater's too prompt replies. Dirksen, in combination with other party leaders, wanted to temper the very substance of Goldwater's responses to national and international problems, not just their outward impression. "We must control him," Dirksen told his friend. If there were to be a Goldwater administration, Dirksen obviously intended to be President Goldwater's first minister, his counselor, his adviser, his guide. He wanted, in effect, a form of veto over President Goldwater's decisions.

Dirksen was not alone among Republican leaders disturbed by

Goldwater's responses. Governor Scranton had heard with dismay Goldwater's acceptance speech, in which, for practical purposes, he read the political moderates out of the Republican Party. Scranton was, as well, disquieted by Goldwater's stance on civil rights and the swelling opposition to him by the Negro militants. Governor Scranton believed that the summer and fall of this campaign year would be scarred by continuing racial violence, made worse by Goldwater's candidacy, and he asked an associate to relay to President Johnson his expectations for the summer and fall and his advice to the President on what to do about it. Through this intermediary Scranton asked President Johnson to use his "good offices" to persuade the Negro leadership to declare a "moratorium" on racial demonstrations until after the election. Three weeks later the Negro leadership did so.

Dirksen, by the force of his personality and talents, had wrung from the Senate what amounted to a veto over the legislative process, as he had demonstrated by dictating the language of the civil-rights act of 1964. At the Republican convention he had maneuvered to give himself a somewhat similar influence over the Goldwater administration, if the nation elected Goldwater President. Now, in the late summer of this year, with Congress reconvened, Dirksen began a personal campaign against the third branch of the federal government, the Supreme Court. Dirksen's essential philosophy of government, however sophisticated and pragmatic he had become during his three decades in Congress, did not differ in its emotionalism from that which he had brought with him to Washington from his rural constituency in 1933. He had long since appropriated as peculiarly his own the words and pathos of Abraham Lincoln, and he normally approached national problems with a simplistic fundamentalism common to "the folks" he felt he represented. Using a rhetorical ready-mix of melancholy and country humor, Dirksen mouthed the platitudes of an earlier America as though they were beatitudes, and he sensed himself as the appointed guardian of those values. As such, he resented the current course of the Supreme Court, and he felt called upon to correct the court's mistaken judgments. Specifically, Dirksen objected to the Supreme Court's ruling on school prayers, denying their use in public schools, and its decisions in the apportionment cases that required equal representation of all the citizenry in both branches of the state legislatures. The effect of the apportionment decisions would be to lessen the rural influence on the state legislatures. Dirksen set out to overturn those decisions, to veto them, as it were, by constitutional amendment.

The Supreme Court's initial decision on prayer in public schools came in June, 1962, and a year later the court broadened that decision to declare unconstitutional the reading of the Bible or the Lord's Prayer in classrooms. Fourteen senators introduced bills to cancel the decisions, and the Senate Judiciary Committee held abbreviated hearings on the subject in late July, 1963. More important than Senate consideration, however, was the stiff opposition to any such action by Representative Emanuel Celler of New York, chairman of the House Judiciary Committee, and the principal contest evolved therefore in the House of Representatives. By deliberate stalling, Celler delayed committee hearings, then extended those hearings well into 1964, and thus prevented action by Congress that year. By summer there was no chance of action until a new Congress convened the following January, and Dirksen necessarily gave up any effort to overturn the school-prayer decision for the time being. Of more immediate moment, however, was the Supreme Court's "one man, one vote" decision on state legislatures. Acting under the court's mandamus, the state legislatures were already reconstituting themselves to meet the court's requirements. Senator Dirksen, if he were to halt this alteration of the state governments, had to act immediately, but there was not enough time left in this Congress to approve the constitutional amendment needed.

On July 23, with twenty other senators as co-sponsors, Dirksen did introduce a constitutional amendment to allow each state's voters to determine the structure of its legislature, but he did not stop there. He also introduced a bill the legal effect of which would be to stay the Supreme Court's rulings in these apportionment cases for at least two years. As Dirksen explained, he wanted to buy time enough to pass a constitutional amendment; the bill he offered was only a vehicle to achieve his ultimate end. The day after he introduced the bill, quickly labeled "the Dirksen breather," the Senate Judiciary Committee approved it, without hearings. Dirksen then had to figure not only how to bring it swiftly before the Senate but also how to do so in such a way as to force President Johnson to sign it. Dirksen took unusual precautions. He visited Johnson at the White House July 30 to explain what he planned. "I didn't want to take him by surprise," he said. Then he got ex-officio rulings from the Justice Department's ranking lawyers that his legislative injunction on the Supreme Court was constitutional. Thus armed, he maneuvered to bring his proposal directly before the Senate. "Mr. President," he had said to Johnson, by his own account, "I'm sure you probably won't like this, but I feel duty bound to do it. I have to find a vehicle where my amendment can take its ride and land right in the middle of that big desk of yours." Dirksen, in short, offered his bill as an amendment to the foreign-aid appropriations bill, a measure that had to be approved that year.

Dirksen, with a clear majority of the Senate behind him, anticipated with great relish his expected victory. There was righteousness in his words as he addressed the Senate. "It is the court that has brought it upon itself," he said. "We're fighting over the chaotic condition that the court has created." Dirksen, however, had not calculated the response from the Senate's liberals of both parties, who regarded Dirksen's maneuvers as an attempt to perpetuate the "rotten boroughs" of the state legislatures. "The Constitution guarantees a republican form of government," Dirksen said. "It contains no authority to take away the authority from the states to determine the composition of their own legislatures." Somewhat reluctantly, faced with Dirksen's majority on this question, the Senate's liberals began to filibuster his rider. In this tactic they were led by Senator Douglas, Dirksen's Democratic colleague from Illinois. "This is not something to be rushed through quickly or hastily," Douglas said. "We do not want to repent at leisure." Dirksen would not give up.

"I am prepared," he said, "to fight this one out until hell freezes over." He was caught, however, in a painful quandary, for he could not muster all those senators supporting his bill to vote for cloture; many of them were from the South and West and therefore opposed to cloture under any conditions. Dirksen had to let the filibuster run its course. "I have been charged with working miracles," Dirksen protested. "I have been classed with Houdini as a magician. I have been charged with masquerading. I believe the only thing I have not been charged with is sorcery." (Actually, Douglas had accused him of sorcery, and necromancy too.) Dirksen could not persuade the necessary senators to vote with him, but he refused to yield. The Senate recessed over the final week of August, for the Democratic National Convention, and then over the long Labor Day weekend. Finally, on September 11, Dirksen asked for cloture, and when the vote came two days later the Senate rejected his motion resoundingly, 30 to 63. Embarrassed by that poor showing, Dirksen's supporters forced a test vote on his rider-amendment itself. The Senate on this voted 38 to 49 against rejecting Dirksen's proposal, demonstrating the majority favoring the measure, but still the Senate's liberals continued their filibuster.

For a fortnight more the struggle went on, and Dirksen could not find a way to break the liberals' filibuster. Anxiously he searched for some kind of compromise language by which he might pull to his side at least a few of the filibustering liberals. At one point he sought converts by eliminating from his proposal any direct mention of the Supreme Court. That did not work either. "We can defeat the Dirksen rider," Senator Douglas said, "by a combination of talk and persistence, and we have plenty of both." Unused as the liberals were to the arts of filibustering, they nevertheless prevented any advance by Dirksen for his amendment, and Dirksen was stymied. At one point the liberal bloc tried to undo Dirksen's campaign by offering a substitute for his bill that would have had no legal force. Dirksen argued against it, that he wanted substantive action against the Supreme Court's rulings, not superficial gestures. "I remember," he said, "a story about an English rector who was describing the glories of heaven and all the felicity there. He said there would be ambrosia and nectar for everybody, no cares, no worries, no anxieties. When he finished his sermon, an old man came up and said: 'Rector, what am I going to do when I get to heaven? I don't have any teeth.' The rector looked at him and said: 'Mister, teeth will be provided.' " Amid the laughter, Dirksen made his point that he wanted "teeth" in the measures against the Supreme Court. The Senate rejected the substitute, but Dirksen could not break the filibuster. The effect of that filibuster was to veto his efforts to veto the rulings of the court. "When the immovable object and the irresistible force come together," Dirksen said, "something has to give." In the end his force proved resistible. Senator Mansfield, as the Senate's majority leader, could not permit the Senate to remain deadlocked indefinitely. He had the responsibility to bring forward the other measures on the Senate's agenda. "The Senate," Mansfield said, "is reduced to a gross impotence and demeaning futility." Mansfield had supported Dirksen's amendment, for reasons other than Dirksen's, and he felt he had a commitment to Dirksen on his proposal that conflicted with his responsibility as majority leader. He approached Dirksen on the Senate floor. "I've got to talk to you," Mansfield said. "Let me buy you lunch." The two leaders slipped off the floor to Mansfield's offices across the hall from the Senate chamber, and there, in Mansfield's back room, over Delmonico steaks, Mansfield explained his dilemma to Dirksen.

"I'm under obligation to you on this," Mansfield said, referring to his sponsorship of Dirksen's amendment.

"No, you're not," Dirksen replied, releasing Mansfield from his commitment. "You don't owe me anything. You have a higher responsibility here—to make this place work."

Thus freed, Mansfield returned to the Senate floor and offered his own substitute for Dirksen's measure. Mansfield's substitute merely expressed the sense of Congress that the Supreme Court ought to allow the states adequate time to meet its directives on their legislatures. Senator Douglas, on behalf of the filibustering liberals, accepted Mansfield's surrender. "It is the mark of a great man," said Douglas, an inflexible man himself, "to adjust himself to circumstances." The Senate approved Mansfield's amendment, 44 to 38, and moved on to other matters, but Dirksen had not surrendered. He would resume his fight against the Supreme Court's rulings in the new Congress.

The shape of that new Congress, meanwhile, was being forged in the election campaigns already under way. By early October the Republican Party stalwarts knew that they faced an election disaster the following month. "Oh," Dirksen said earlier in the year, "you know the Republican Party never goes to hell. It just gets close to it sometimes." Despite an embargo on on-the-record news conferences, Goldwater throughout his formal campaign confronted an electorate well aware of his penchant for the abrupt and unexpected in political reaction. He was savaged for his stand on nuclear weapons and on a host of domestic issues, including the race question. He lost to Lyndon Johnson in the worst defeat for the Republicans since 1936, and with him lost scores of Republican candidates for Congress. The new House of Representatives would have only 140 Republicans, against 295 Democrats, and the Senate would have but 32 Republicans, against 68 Democrats. With ranks so depleted, Dirksen would have a more difficult job impressing his stamp on the Senate's decisions.

In the wake of the election calamity, Republicans privately and publicly vented their bitterness toward each other in an extraordinary display of self-recrimination. Party conservatives blamed party liberals, and the liberals blamed the conservatives, for the party's defeat. In the House of Representatives, a group of younger Republican activists coalesced behind Gerald Ford of Michigan and deposed Charles Halleck as party leader. Halleck and Dirksen had been friends and competitors for thirty years, and Dirksen resented the party uprising against Halleck. He regarded it as an act of ingratitude. In the Senate Dirksen himself was immune from such an assault, despite the election disaster. He had undisputed com-

mand of the Republicans in the Senate, even though the members
of his rank and file were smarting angry at the campaign's outcome.
Two Midwestern conservatives, Karl Mundt of South Dakota and
Carl Curtis of Nebraska, decided to punish the liberal wing of the
party for its hostility toward Goldwater in the campaign, and they
chose Thomas Kuchel of California as their special target. They
began a campaign to remove Kuchel, an outspoken liberal, from
his post as Republican whip of the Senate. It had been Dirksen,
with the help of Senator Styles Bridges, who in 1959 had maneuvered to elect Kuchel to that post. Kuchel, as a member of the
"coalition" leadership of the Senate's Republicans, was the representative of the liberal wing in the party hierarchy. He had often
offended the party's conservatives, not only with his liberal views
but occasionally with his offbeat earthy characterizations of his
colleagues' eloquence. "It seems to me," he once said in Senate
debate to the orator of the moment, "that the soil of the Senate has
been enriched and fertilized sufficiently for one evening. . . ." That,
to the traditionalists, was not a proper way to describe a colleague's
words. More importantly, and with considerable courage, Kuchel
had conducted a continuing campaign against the right-wing
extremists of his own state, people he called "the fright peddlers."
The Republican conservatives in the Senate were especially angered
by Kuchel's performance in the 1964 Presidential campaign. In the
bitter California primary he had acted as campaign manager for
Governor Nelson Rockefeller of New York, then Goldwater's principal opponent. Kuchel and Goldwater had long been political and
personal enemies, and Kuchel refused to support Goldwater after
he was nominated. Indeed, privately Kuchel mocked Goldwater's
pretensions to be President. The Goldwater managers had chosen a
slogan for their candidate: "In your heart you know he's right."
Kuchel altered that slogan for his own use: "In your guts you know
he's nuts." Indiscreetly he repeated his version of the slogan in his
private talks. For these reasons Senator Mundt and Senator Curtis
felt justified in retaliating, and they began soliciting votes among
their colleagues to replace Kuchel in the leadership. Dirksen, how-

ever, quashed that maneuver in the making. He and Kuchel had developed a genuine personal liking for each other, but beyond that Dirksen was not prepared to let the liberals' spokesman in the party leadership be summarily deposed. Dirksen let it be known among the party conservatives in the Senate that he supported Kuchel in the leadership, and the plotting against Kuchel was abandoned. It was a demonstration of Dirksen's latent power within his party in the Senate.

In the second session of the Eighty-eighth Congress in 1964, the Democrats had abruptly reversed the legislative stalemate that had blocked so many of President Kennedy's proposals. In rapid order Congress approved the urban mass-transportation bill, a newly conceived antipoverty program, the Peace Corps, a food-stamp plan for the poor, and a broad array of bills dealing with conservation, airports, highways, and food marketing, besides the landmark legislation of civil rights and taxation. With Kennedy's assassination and the succession to the Presidency of a Texan, the Southern senators and representatives swung behind the new President and voted for bills they had hitherto opposed. The effect, legislatively, was to build momentum for the entire Democratic program that carried into the opening session of the Eighty-ninth Congress. In that 1965 session the Democratic liberal activists had clear and compelling majorities in both the House and the Senate. At hand, obviously, as the new Congress convened in January, was a period of intense legislative action, and the Democrats moved swiftly to enact into law the extensive agenda of legislation they had been urging for the previous decade and more. Within weeks the approved bills began arriving at President Johnson's desk at the White House, starting with a plan to rebuild the Appalachian region economically and moving on to such proposals as medicare, federal aid to primary and secondary schools, air- and water-pollution control, vocational rehabilitation, highway beautification, and creation of a Department of Housing. The Democratic legislative thrust seemed irresistible, and the role of the Republicans merely superfluous, but Dirksen instinctively could not permit such a status to envelop himself or his party in the Senate. Insistent as always that he play a major role in the Senate's affairs, Dirksen sought ways to divert and staunch the headlong Democratic legislative rush and to make himself the arbiter of the Senate's decisions where he could. He had not long to search, for abruptly and unexpectedly he found himself again the central actor in still another legislative crisis.

Dirksen and the others engaged in the omnibus civil-rights act of 1964 had assumed that they had enacted the final such measure for years to come, but the opening months of 1965 brought new racial turmoil and, with it, a swelling demand for still more legislation. Dr. Martin Luther King, Jr., president of the Southern Christian Leadership Conference, on January 18 opened a campaign in Selma, Alabama, to demonstrate the discrimination against the right of Negroes to vote. Within days the brutality of the state police in suppressing King's peaceful protest shocked the country and Congress. In the first week of February, 1965, President Johnson summoned Dirksen to the White House, and there they discussed the possible need for a new civil-rights bill. They made no decision, but in the days that followed, the repressive measures ordered by Alabama's governor, George Wallace, embarrassed even the racists among the Southern politicians. They made no effort to defend Wallace in Congressional debate, and some few Southern Congressmen spoke out publicly against Wallace. Senator Ralph Yarborough of Texas took the Senate floor to denounce, as a Southerner, Wallace's "brutality . . . for the wet ropes that bruised the muscles, for the bullwhips that cut the flesh, for the clubs that broke the bones." By the second week in February, Dirksen, Mansfield, and the Johnson administration knew that a new law would have to be enacted. This was an unexpected turn of events, for the sponsors of the omnibus civil-rights bill of 1964 felt that it was a comprehensive bill. "We felt," Dirksen said in the midst of the new racial crisis, "we had made some real honest-to-God progress last year. We felt everything would fall into its slot. We thought we were out of the civil-rights woods, but we weren't." On February 11, in Dirksen's office in the Capitol, at Dirksen's invitation, he met with Senator

Mansfield and Nicholas Katzenbach, the new Attorney General, to consider the new emergency and what to do about it. In principle, they agreed on enacting a stringent new law to guarantee the right to vote, one that would inflict severe penalties on anyone obstructing any citizen's right to vote. Dirksen was enraged at the police atrocities, as he described them, in Alabama, and he told his associates privately that he was prepared for "revolutionary" legislation if necessary to prevent any repetition of them.

To agree to act is not to agree on what to enact, and Dirksen and Katzenbach were far from agreement on what course the federal government should take. They were closer, however, to each other's views than to those of some members of Congress who were talking of denying Alabama representation in Congress as punishment for the outrages committed by its state government. Katzenbach favored creating federal registrars to protect the right to vote in the South, but Dirksen shrank from that idea. He wanted some alternative less inflammatory to the South than a federal inspector of their election processes. Unlike his Republican colleagues in the House of Representatives, Dirksen carefully avoided any criticism of the Johnson administration in this domestic crisis. "I'd rather not throw any stones," he said. "We are trying to find a common approach." Mansfield, rarely an angry man, gave his staff instructions to draft the simplest and harshest of bills, no more than one page long. "I want a bill," he told his staff, "that a man with a first-grade education, colored or white, can understand." Dirksen continued to confer with President Johnson, and Johnson relied on Dirksen's goodwill to fashion and enact the new law. "I feel a kinship for him," Johnson said of Dirksen privately. "We've had lots of battles, mostly on opposite sides of the aisle, but he always comes to the top."

As the tension mounted in Alabama, week after week, Dirksen, Mansfield, and Katzenbach continued to seek common agreement on a legislative remedy. Dirksen and his lawyers produced a bill that gave the federal courts responsibility for enforcing the right to register and vote. "My real concern," Dirksen said, "is not to put anyone in jail, but to get people to vote." In the candid private sessions he held with Mansfield and Katzenbach, Dirksen finally gave way on his position of relying for enforcement on the federal courts. Katzenbach argued that the federal judges in the South, cleared for their judicial posts by Southern senators, could not be expected to uphold the rights of Negroes. "Some of the federal judges in the South," one of Mansfield's lawyers argued, "are just not to be trusted." Dirksen agreed to Katzenbach's federal registrars, and Katzenbach, out of deference to Dirksen's objections to the registrars, agreed that they be called by the less grating title of "examiners." The group also agreed, after their long series of meetings in Dirksen's office, that the federal voting restrictions apply only to seven Southern states. "These states are on parole," Katzenbach said. "Because of their past history, we have the right to put this restriction on them."

With Dirksen agreed on a bill, President Johnson took the formal initiative. He went before a joint session of Congress on March 15 and asked that this legislation be passed. In solemn tones the President declared that every citizen must have an equal right to vote, and he made the cause of the Negroes his own in asking for the end of "the crippling legacy of bigotry and injustice." Dramatically and with great deliberation Johnson adopted the slogan of the protesters for the legislative fight ahead: "And we shall overcome!"

On March 18 Dirksen and Mansfield jointly introduced the President's bill, which had been drafted in Dirksen's office. Dirksen wanted the bill referred to the Senate's Judiciary Committee in normal fashion, but when its chairman, James Eastland of Mississippi, told him that he would resist the bill in every way he could, Dirksen changed his mind. He joined Mansfield in asking the Senate to send the bill to the Judiciary Committee but to instruct Eastland to report the bill back to the Senate by April 9. This the Senate did by a vote of 67 to 13. Eastland's response did not characterize that of all the Southern senators. A few, like William Fulbright of Arkansas, indicated that they might even vote for the bill. For the Southerners in the mid-1960's it was difficult to argue against the right to vote, and most of them did not try. At the committee hearings, one Southern racist, Leander Perez, the tyrannical boss of Plaquemines Parish in Louisiana, tried to argue that the proposed legislation was really a Communist plot. Dirksen excoriated him on the instant. "That," Dirksen said, "is about as stupid a statement as has ever been uttered in this committee room, and it's a reflection on senators here to say that." As a political bloc, the Southern senators had been demoralized, partially by Governor Wallace's excesses and partially by their own weakened ranks. Senator Russell of Georgia, nominally the leader of the Southern bloc, was ill, suffering from emphysema, and he was unable to help in the effort to prevent passage of this bill. Russell sensed the hopelessness of the South's cause. "If there is anything I could do, I would do it," he said, "but I assume the die is cast."

Still, the Southerners would be able to conduct a filibuster against the measure, and to halt that filibuster Dirksen again would have to rally his Republican colleagues for cloture. It would be, presumably, easier to execute than in 1964, but still a difficult chore in the tradition-bound Senate. The necessity to invoke cloture, and Dirksen's command of the Republican ranks, made him on this new bill what he had been to the 1964 act, the senator who had control of the fate of the legislation.

In the Judiciary Committee began the first skirmishing between the advocates of legislative action. A group of Northern Democrats believed the bill did not go far enough in abolishing literacy tests, and they maneuvered to add a complete ban on all poll taxes, state and local. Dirksen, resisting their efforts, managed to add to the bill an amendment that would allow any state to "escape" the strictures of this legislation if sixty percent of its eligible voters were registered. The Democratic liberals on the committee accused Dirksen of "gutting" the bill, and he retorted by citing Katzenbach's judgment that their anti-poll-tax amendment was unconstitutional. The quarreling went on, and Mansfield anxiously tried to persuade both sides to yield their proposals, to pacify the two camps. Dirksen made no pretensions but that he was playing a game with the Democratic liberals. "When you make a trade, you've got to get a little something," he said. "Don't you know that you can bargain and swap a hat for a monkey wrench?" Dirksen, in effect, offered to swap his "escape clause" for their anti-poll-tax amendment. The Democratic liberals, however, would not negotiate. Vice-President Hubert Humphrey tried to talk them out of their amendment, but they would not listen to him either. Dirksen, frustrated by the unwillingness of the liberals to abandon their cause, dropped his amendment and tried another tactic. "If the poll-tax abolition is written into this bill," he said, "I would have difficulty going to any other senator and asking him to vote for cloture. Then it would be a fielder's choice. It would be every man for himself." Thus Dirksen threatened the liberals, now led by Senator Edward Kennedy of Massachusetts, that if they attached their amendment to the bill, he would let the bill, as he said, "go down the drain."

Dirksen did more than threaten; he campaigned hard in private to persuade his colleagues to vote against the Kennedy amendment. In this effort he had the active help of President Johnson's White House lieutenants, led by Larry O'Brien. The President's aides lobbied the Democratic senators while Dirksen concentrated on the Republicans. One of these Republicans, Clifford Case of New Jersey, described Dirksen's technique as considerably different from "The Treatment" that Lyndon Johnson, as a senator, used to apply on reluctant colleagues. Johnson, Case said, used to put his arm around his intended victim's neck and look up his nose until he said yes. "Senator Dirksen doesn't work this way," Case said. "He takes a little longer. He does it with oleaginous applications of one kind and another, oral and other kinds too." Dirksen was pleased with the results he was getting. "I brought three lost sheep back into the fold," he said the day before the vote, "and I'll get another one tomorrow." He was understandably somewhat vague on just what he had done to persuade the strays to return. "You have to know where to go," he said, "and what to remind them of." The Senate rejected the Kennedy amendment 45 to 49.

For weeks, while these negotiations were underway, the Senate had been conducting a desultory debate on the bill itself. Now, with the poll-tax question resolved, Mansfield and Dirksen acted to bring the bill to a final vote. In mid-May they announced that they were preparing to invoke cloture once more. The Southern senators, demoralized and weakened, still had the bloc strength to mount a filibuster, and they informed the party leaders that they would not submit to this legislation unless forced to by cloture. All along Dirksen had been canvassing his Republican ranks, and he knew that many of his Republican colleagues were unusually reluctant to vote to cut off this debate. When he appealed to them, they protested that the voting-rights bill had not yet been adequately debated and considered. "We are in difficulties at the moment," Dirksen confided after a week of such private consultations.

Dirksen was too knowledgeable of the inner workings of the Senate not to uncover soon enough the real cause for his trouble in persuading Republican senators to go along with him. The resistance to Dirksen's arguments had a source—Senator Bourke Hickenlooper of Iowa, chairman of the Senate Republican Policy Committee and a man of considerable influence with the very Midwestern senators Dirksen now was trying to persuade. Hickenlooper had voted for cloture on the civil-rights bill in 1964, but now he was urging his Republican colleagues to vote against cloture on this bill. "I have never believed," Hickenlooper said, "in trying to kill a cold by cutting off the patient's head." There was more to Hickenlooper's opposition, however, than a disagreement on the correct legislative diagnosis of the problem at hand. In the Senate cloakrooms the gossip was that Hickenlooper was retaliating against Dirksen out of spite for the extraordinary notoriety Dirksen had achieved as *the* Republican leader of the Senate. "Hickenlooper is a little jealous about all this," one Senate intimate said privately. "Dirksen holds all the cards, not Hickenlooper." There was substance to Hickenlooper's complaint, and that complaint ran far deeper than the immediate question of the voting-rights bill. In fact,

Dirksen had usurped the traditional prerogatives that by the Senate's traditions belonged to Hickenlooper as his party's Policy Committee chairman. Senator Taft had once led the Senate's Republicans from that post, and Hickenlooper blamed Dirksen for denying him a similar influence within the Senate. "I'm only the Republican leader," Dirksen said at one point, "not the Policy Committee." The reality, however, was that Dirksen had taken over the function of party policy spokesman back in 1959 and 1960. At that time Senator Styles Bridges, then the Policy Committee chairman, had acquiesced to Dirksen, and when Hickenlooper became Policy Committee chairman in 1961 Dirksen felt no compunction to surrender the prerogatives he had already assumed. That bred resentment in Hickenlooper. At the start of the struggle over the voting-rights bill there had been a presumption even at the White House that Hickenlooper would play a crucial role in enacting the law. Dirksen, by the very force of his own driving personality, prevented that from happening. He simply monopolized the Republican position on this issue, and, by so doing, shunted Hickenlooper aside. Thus goaded, Hickenlooper quietly maneuvered to bring about Dirksen's defeat and humiliation on this bill. He met privately with his Republican colleagues, and with them he argued the "real evils" of this Dirksen bill.

At the White House this intraparty Republican bickering was watched nervously. "You can't get cloture in the Senate," Larry O'Brien said, "without Dirksen working like hell for it." The question became whether cloture could be achieved even with Dirksen working furiously for it. There was in this a bitter irony for Dirksen, for the Southern senators had already in effect conceded their defeat. The struggle had changed to a personal challenge to Dirksen's leadership by the ranking member of the Republican hierarchy in the Senate. The principal battleground between Dirksen and Hickenlooper was for the votes of the conservative senators of the Middle West, men instinctively reluctant to vote for cloture and hardly susceptible to pressure from the Negro and labor lobbyists working for the bill. Dirksen knew what Hickenlooper was doing, and why; he had informants aplenty among his Senate colleagues. He argued tirelessly with the Midwesterners to stick with him on this question, and he couched his pleas in a mix of party and personal terms. "This involves more than you," Dirksen told one hesitant Republican senator. "It's the party. Don't drop *me* in the mud." He concentrated especially on the senators from Nebraska, Kansas, and the Dakotas. It was a grueling process. He found Carl Curtis of Nebraska weakening. Curtis had voted against cloture on the civil-rights bill the year before, but he would be up for reelection the next year and he was nervous about his prospects. Finally Curtis decided to take his chances with Dirksen, not Hickenlooper. Dirksen turned immediately to Curtis' Nebraska colleague, Roman Hruska. Hruska, Dirksen argued, could not embarrass Curtis by voting against cloture, and that argument worked. By the end of the second week Dirksen knew he was making headway. With the fate of the bill depending on his persuasiveness and with his own reputation at stake, Dirksen did not flag in his efforts. Finally he had wrung enough commitments from his Republican colleagues to assure cloture, and he so informed Mansfield. Acting together, they brought a cloture motion on the bill to a vote on May 15. The Senate approved it, 70 to 30, with a margin to spare over the two-thirds vote needed. The next day the Senate passed the bill itself.

On the 1964 cloture vote on the civil-rights bill, twenty-seven Republicans voted for it, six against. In this new cloture vote, on a bill far less controversial, only twenty-three Republican senators voted for it, and nine voted against. The difference marked the inroads in Dirksen's influence made by Hickenlooper's assault on his leadership. Dirksen knew he had to be wary of Hickenlooper.

Even so, despite the smaller margin, the passage of this second civil-rights bill, tailored largely to his specifications by an overwhelmingly Democratic Congress, was an extraordinary achievement for Dirksen. He was hailed anew for his statesmanship and parliamentary skills. When President Johnson signed the bill into law at a special ceremony at the Capitol, he drew Dirksen aside. "Well, Ev," he said, "you'll never know how much I appreciate your help." Among his own Republicans, there was growing distress at the help Dirksen was giving the Johnson administration, and some verbal sniping at him too, as Senator Hickenlooper had illustrated. Some of the conservative senators did not like Dirksen's penchant for rescuing the administration from ticklish dilemmas like the filibusters by Southern Democrats against civil-rights measures. On balance, however, he was admired by his colleagues to a greater degree than by the world outside the Senate. "There are a lot of senators who are worse than they look," one senator said. "Dirksen is the only one who is better than he looks."

Even as Dirksen was arguing with his colleagues to assure passage of the voting-rights bill he was working on another project of national consequence that made him the ally of the very senators he opposed on civil rights. In late 1964 he had been prevented by the liberals' filibuster from enacting a legislative injunction against the Supreme Court's directives on state legislatures, but he had not abandoned that campaign. Indeed, in the following winter he helped organize a nationwide campaign to amend the Constitution and cancel these judicial rulings. One phase of this campaign was to urge the state legislatures to petition Congress for a federal constitutional convention to adopt Dirksen's proposed constitutional amendment. If two-thirds of the states, thirty-four of the fifty, so petitioned, Congress would have to call such a convention. Another Dirksen maneuver was to build grass-roots support for the amendment and thus bring another form of pressure on Congress. Dirksen himself introduced his proposed amendment on January 6, 1965, and a subcommittee of the Senate Judiciary Committee began formal hearings on the measure March 3. "We are confronted with a basic issue of free government," Dirksen said in opening those hearings. Not all his colleagues saw the issue that way; the liberals believed his proposal a raw effort to protect the rural domination of those state legislatures. The subcommittee approved the amendment without difficulty, but Dirksen found he could not obtain a majority of the full Judiciary Committee. The crucial vote in the committee was that of Jacob Javits of New York, who was torn by the conflict of his own state's constituency over the issue. Dirksen tried to persuade him. "You are my friend," he told Javits. "I am your friend. I say only one thing: pray over it."

When Javits failed him, Dirksen seemed trapped, but he did not quit. "In the pinches," he said, "I always have a strategy." Unable to bring his amendment to the Senate floor with the endorsement of the Judiciary Committee, Dirksen used another tactic: he proposed it as a substitute amendment for a minor resolution pending before the Senate. As with a treaty and a motion for cloture, a constitutional amendment requires a two-thirds vote of the Senate, and Dirksen tried desperately to muster that many senators to his cause. With equal determination the Senate's liberals, led by Paul Douglas, solicited support against the Dirksen amendment. Dirksen had a pledge from President Johnson to remain neutral in this struggle, but when he discovered Vice-President Hubert Humphrey helping the Senate's liberals, he hurried to the White House to see the President. Johnson assured him that he was playing no part in this contest between Congress and the Supreme Court. "Then," Dirksen demanded, "what's Hubert doing lobbying for it on the Senate floor?" Johnson protested that he knew nothing about that except what he had read in the newspapers. "Well," Dirksen said, "then call him up and give him hell."

Try as he did, Dirksen could not find enough votes for his amendment. "I am not so blind," he said, "as not to know when I am up against a stacked deck." Douglas and the other opponents of Dirksen's proposed amendment had intended, if necessary, to filibuster again against Dirksen, but by late July they knew they had enough votes to block the Senate's approval of his amendment. They had hard commitments from thirty-five senators, enough to prevent the two-thirds margin of the Senate Dirksen needed. With such an assurance, they wanted a vote on the measure. Dirksen could not deny it. "What do you do when you believe in something and are heartsick and you think the Republic is at stake?" he asked. "You have to use every weapon in the arsenal." On August 4 the Senate voted on his amendment, and a clear majority of the Senate supported it, 57 to 39, but the margin was short of the two-thirds necessary. "This is not yet over," Dirksen said after the vote.

"From the day I was able to put a milk bottle in my mouth," he said, "life has been a conspiracy to bury me. But I am not going to be buried, and my brainchild is not going to be buried either."

Just a week after the vote, Dirksen introduced a new resolution proposing a constitutional amendment similar to the one on which he had failed. The resolution was referred to the Judiciary Committee, and again Dirksen found it was blocked there. "I've got some rights around here," he said, "and I know how to use them." Pending before the same committee was the Johnson administration's bill to rewrite the immigration law, abolishing national quotas. Dirksen threatened to block any action on that bill unless the committee voted to send his new constitutional amendment to the Senate floor. His earlier effort had been handicapped both by his failure to get the endorsement of the committee and by the necessity of calling it up merely as an amendment to another measure. Dirksen's terms were harsh, for immigration was a priority measure for President Johnson and the Senate's liberals. Senator Joseph Tydings of Maryland angrily accused Dirksen of legislative "blackmail." That did not bother Dirksen; he meant the threat that way. He had, in fact, presented his terms that way to President Johnson himself.

"I want an immigration bill," Johnson told Dirksen in a private conversation at the White House.

"You're going to get an immigration bill," Dirksen said, "when I get the necessary vote on the resolution on reapportionment."

Dirksen could make good his threat on the immigration bill because he not only was a member of the Judiciary Committee himself, but he had allies on the committee who would support him. Finally, to clear the immigration bill, Senator Dodd of Connecticut reluctantly agreed to change his vote on the Dirksen amendment and thereby gave a one-vote majority of the Judiciary Committee for it. Dodd was an intimate friend of President Johnson, responsive to his requests. Dirksen was delighted.

"Somehow," he said, "there seemed to be a telephone call from some source, and a vote was changed, and I got a one-vote majority."

Dirksen had not ignored the immigration bill in its own right, for one of his allies on the Judiciary Committee, Sam Ervin of North Carolina, had wanted a change in it. Ervin, a senator who made speeches not unlike Dirksen's, filled with fustian and country anecdotes,* supported Dirksen in his battle against the Supreme Court's rulings. Dirksen was more than willing to help him. He telephoned Attorney General Katzenbach and asked him to come to his office to negotiate further terms on the immigration bill. "Whenever there's a Gordian knot to cut," Katzenbach joked to Dirksen, on his arrival, "we have to do it in your office." Senator Ervin wanted a limit placed on Latin Americans immigrating into the United States, an idea stiffly opposed by the State Department on the grounds that it would offend the sensitive Latin-American governments. With Ervin present, Dirksen suggested to Katzenbach that Latin-American immigration be limited to 120,000 persons a year. Katzenbach argued against the proposal, but he did not want to risk defeat for the immigration bill. Finally, for the Johnson administration, he agreed.

"I think we can live with it," he said.

"I think I can live with it too," Ervin said. He had wanted a lower number admitted.

"Say nothing about it," Katzenbach asked as he left. "I have to sell this to the State Department."

Dirksen did not press immediately for further action on his

* This is one of Ervin's stories deriding the Supreme Court's prayer decision: "This North Carolina schoolteacher entered her classroom one morning fifteen minutes earlier than the time to convene, and she saw a group of boys on their hands and knees huddled in a corner of the room. She demanded of them, 'What are you doing?' One of the boys yelled back, 'We are shooting craps.' The teacher said, 'That is all right. I was afraid you were praying.'"

constitutional amendment because time was running out in the 1965 session of Congress, but he brought it forward again the following year in the new session. When it came to a vote, on April 20, the Senate approved it 55 to 38, but that vote was still short of the two-thirds needed. By now the question itself was becoming moot, for most of the state legislatures had already reconstituted themselves under the Supreme Court's directives. The campaign, supported by Dirksen, to force the calling of a constitutional convention had not been successful, falling short of the prerequisite number of state-legislature petitions. Dirksen had the support of a majority of the Senate, but that was not enough. He was forced to put off any further effort until a new Congress was elected.

If Dirksen failed in this campaign, one rooted in his pastoral sense of American traditionalism, he did not fail in still another campaign he conducted at the same time. The priority demand of organized labor from the Eighty-ninth Congress was to repeal Section 14(b) of the Taft-Hartley labor-management law, the provision allowing state legislatures to prohibit the negotiation of union shops. President Johnson, anxious not to impede his other measures, hesitated to ask Congress to repeal Section 14(b), and he delayed doing so until May, 1965. The issue itself carried intense emotionalism for both sides: the liberal supporters of labor unions argued that labor unions had the right to prevent "free riders" from enjoying the benefits they negotiated for their members, and the conservative defenders of management insisted that nothing less than "the right to work" was at hazard. Senator Dirksen, who never forgot his special relationship to Robert Taft, automatically opposed repeal of any provision of the law that Senator Taft regarded as his legislative monument, but Dirksen knew that he faced fearful odds in the overwhelmingly Democratic Congress. For months he put off making a decision on what he would do. In July the House of Representatives voted to repeal Section 14(b), and the issue came squarely before the Senate. In mid-August Dirksen consulted with two of his most conservative Republican senators, Carl Curtis of Nebraska and Paul Fannin of Arizona. They had been taking soundings, and they gave Dirksen a list of eighteen senators who had expressed a willingness to try to kill the repeal bill by filibustering. Dirksen called on President Johnson to sound him out, for the President's hesitation on the proposal indicated that he might be less than adamant about its approval. "I'm committed," Johnson told Dirksen. "Mr. President," Dirksen replied, "I am also committed." Dirksen had resolved to defeat this measure by whatever means were necessary. He began the detail work necessary to organize a successful filibuster. That he would do so was feared by organized labor, and George Meany, president of the AFL-CIO, called on Dirksen to try to dissuade him.

"George, I'm glad to see you," Dirksen said to him. "How's Mrs. Meany?"

"Everett, you know why I'm here," Meany replied.

"Oh, sure, I can guess."

"All we want is a straight up-and-down vote."

"George," Dirksen said, "you're not going to get a straight up-and-down vote."

Meany knew, as did Dirksen, that a clear majority of the Senate favored the repeal bill. Larry O'Brien, the President's chief liaison officer with Congress, had commitments already from fifty-two senators, and others still could be persuaded, but it was doubtful that enough senators could be found to cut off the filibuster Dirksen was planning. "I am no spring chicken," Dirksen said, "but so long as there is any breath and energy in this carcass, we will go ahead. We mean business."

Meany appealed to Senator Mansfield, asking him to hold the Senate in continuous session and thus break the filibuster by exhausting Dirksen and the others supporting him. That was not Mansfield's way, and he refused Meany's plea. "There will be no mock trial of this question by physical endurance," Mansfield said, explaining his position to the Senate. "There will be no pajama sessions of the Senate." Dirksen, of course, counted on Mansfield taking that course. Mansfield's distaste at making a public spectacle of the Senate, in this instance as in others, gave Dirksen a pronounced advantage and in a real sense had helped Dirksen achieve the power he held in the Senate. "He can really sweat you some," Dirksen said privately, glad that Mansfield would not try to break the filibuster by exhaustion, "but that's never Mike's way." When Mansfield brought the bill to the floor in early October, Dirksen was prepared.

"The lines are intact," he said privately. "The boys are ready. The captains are on duty at the appointed hour in the appointed place. The speakers are ready. The floor monitors are on duty, and they remain on duty."

He had prepared as though for a siege; he had arranged his supporting cast of senators to hold out until Christmas. Mansfield could not permit the already long session of the Senate to continue indefinitely and futilely, and on October 11 he brought a vote of cloture on this filibuster. The Senate voted 45 to 47 against the motion; Mansfield had not received the support of even a majority of the Senate, much less the two-thirds required for cloture. "I no longer find myself looking through a glass darkly," Mansfield said. "The image is clear."

He gave up for the moment, but in January, at the start of the 1966 session of Congress, Mansfield again tried to pass this bill. Dirksen, however, was as well prepared as before. "Knowing the rules," he said, "we knew what to do." He and his conservative allies refused even to let the repeal bill be taken up for consideration, and they frustrated Mansfield's various maneuvers to bring the legislation directly before the Senate. In one instance Mansfield tried to bypass Dirksen's filibuster and bring the bill formally before the Senate with the use of a technicality available to him through the procedures of the Senate's morning hour. Senator Ervin, Dirksen's ally, frustrated this Mansfield tactic by offering a motion to require the opening prayer of each day's session to be included in the Senate's journal. He then filibustered his own motion. "Hereafter," Ervin cried, "prayers are to be recorded in the journal of the Senate from now until the last lingering echo of Gabriel's horn trembles into ultimate silence." Mansfield still resisted the demands from organized labor and some of his own senators to force round-the-clock sessions and thus try to break the filibuster. Dirksen knew what this meant to his side in this quarrel. "Thank God," he said, "for the majority leader." Again Mansfield had to give up, this time finally on this legislation. For Dirksen, as in the struggle to enact the civil-rights bills, this was another remarkable personal triumph: he had again imposed his will on the Senate and the Congress. He had vetoed a major bill he opposed by the sheer will to stand and deny it passage.

In still another area Dirksen imposed his veto, this time on a nomination made by President Johnson to fill a vacancy on the federal bench. At the request of Senator Edward Kennedy of Massachusetts, the brother of President Kennedy, Johnson nominated Francis X. Morrissey, a municipal judge in Boston, to be federal district judge in Massachusetts. Morrissey's principal qualifications for the post, as quickly disclosed by the Senate Judiciary Committee, were his long service and friendship with the Kennedy family. In 1961 President Kennedy had decided against appointing him to the federal bench after the American Bar Association had reported he was not qualified. President Johnson, sensitive to the Kennedy family and anxious to please the surviving brothers, submitted Morrissey's name despite the findings of the bar association. The nomination met immediate difficulty in the Senate, and Morrissey harmed himself further by his self-contradictory testimony before the Judiciary Committee. Even so, the Judiciary Committee recommended his confirmation by a vote of six to three.

Senator Dirksen, senior Republican on the committee, was one of the three senators voting against the recommendation. He did not let the matter rest there. He proceeded to compile what he called a "dossier" against Morrissey. The materials he gathered went beyond what had been revealed by the committee hearings and were sufficient, in Dirksen's judgment, to persuade the Senate to reject Morrissey. In this Dirksen had not set himself against President Johnson, who had merely acquiesced in the nomination, but against Edward Kennedy, a fellow senator. This raised not only delicate questions of senatorial courtesy but also, in Kennedy's terms, a challenge to the Kennedy clan. Well aware of these sensitivities, Dirksen decided to try to negotiate a settlement rather than let the nomination go to a vote in the Senate.

Dirksen was reluctant to talk to Edward Kennedy. Instead he invited Edward's older brother, Robert Kennedy, now a senator from New York, to his office. "Bobby was the knowledgeable one," Dirksen explained. "He'd been in the Justice Department as Attorney General. I could talk to him a little better. Teddy might become a little uneasy with the frank way I talk."

When Robert Kennedy arrived, Dirksen handed him his file on Morrissey, and Kennedy thumbed through it. Dirksen urged Kennedy to persuade his brother to withdraw the nomination.

"There's my case," Dirksen said, by his own account.

"I've seen it," Kennedy said testily.

"You can do as you like," Dirksen said.

"You hate the Kennedys," Kennedy said.

Robert Kennedy left Dirksen's office angrily. He had made, of course, no commitments. Clearly, however, the Kennedy brothers were in trouble with this nomination, and in the end they had no choice but to back down. Senator Edward Kennedy so informed Dirksen. For Dirksen this was not the kind of victory in which he had any desire to exult. His opposition to Morrissey ran against the grain of the Senate's usual live-and-let-live philosophy. He had no desire to embarrass either Kennedy, and, indeed, he acted to blunt the blow he had struck at them.

"When Teddy came over to tell me he was going to withdraw the nomination," Dirksen said, "he had tears in his eyes. I could have made enemies forever of the Kennedys. Then Bobby walked across the chamber and said, 'Could you say a good word about Teddy? He feels terrible.' Well, of course I could. So I talked about Teddy's courage as a freshman member in withdrawing that name. Instead of an enemy, I made a friend."

In these struggles Dirksen's already commanding stature with his own Republican colleagues in the Senate had taken on a new dimension. Tirelessly he worked at his job, awake before dawn as always and not returning to his home before mid-evening. In his early years as party leader he had shown deference normally to his colleagues even in their private dealings off the Senate floor, but now he had assumed some of the imperiousness that had marked Lyndon Johnson's manner in the Senate. He kept careful tally of the whereabouts of every one of his Republican senators, and when they were needed in the Senate for an important vote he literally ordered them to be there. He took no chances himself on missing important votes, and when necessary he stayed at a downtown hotel. "I wouldn't take a chance on another snow in Leesburg," he explained of one such stay in town. The day before a crucial vote on the repeal of Section 14(b) of the Taft-Hartley law, in February, 1966, a half-dozen Republican senators were scattered around the country, one of whom, Hiram Fong of Hawaii, was as far away as Honolulu. Dirksen telephoned them all and ordered them to return to Washington. He called Senator Hickenlooper in New York. "By God," he said, "you're going to be here." On the vote there were no Republican absentees. Similarly in the case of the Morrissey nomination, several Republican senators were out of town. Dirksen telephoned John Tower in Texas: "You get yourself back here." He called Senator Thruston Morton and ordered him back: "I don't care what kind of a speech you have." Senators Gordon Allott and Hugh Scott had flown to Denver to make speeches. "Both of you cancel," Dirksen told them by telephone, "and consider that an order."

In times of travail, when he was seeking to persuade reluctant or hesitant senators to join him in a cause, Dirksen could wheedle and cajole his colleagues with a finesse and charm second to none in the Senate. He helped himself in this process with his mastery of the legislation under consideration and with the bluntness he did not hesitate to use to remind the senators of the personal debts they owed him from his favors of the past. He tutored himself to the foibles and idiosyncrasies of each of his colleagues, and he played upon them with a remarkable talent. In his oratorical flourishes Dirksen had become master of what Senator Douglas called "spontaneous irrelevance," but in the earnest business of mustering the votes he needed to execute his purposes he had now no peer in the Senate. He did not always succeed in his purposes, for he was handicapped by the very smallness of the Republican contingent in the Senate.

Dirksen had especially close relationships with several of the Republican senators like Roman Hruska of Nebraska and Wallace Bennett of Utah, and to these senators he could appeal for support on a purely personal basis. With other senators he often felt harassed, either because they neglected their legislative duties or because they would annoy him with their constant petty demands. One of these latter was Jack Miller of Iowa, who frequently tried Dirksen's patience with the constant stream of last-minute amendments he would tap out on the typewriter in the Republican cloakroom just off the Senate floor. "I know how to fix him," Dirksen finally said. "I'm going to take the typewriter out of the cloakroom." And he did. "All I know," Dirksen said of his techniques in rounding up votes, "is that arithmetic is the greatest of the sciences. There you add and subtract. . . . I try to count and count hard." The combination of his seemingly contradictory skills—his beguiling Steamboat Gothic oratory and his resolve to decide public questions—brought him a personal power in the Senate that few men before him had ever matched. He could not, necessarily, dictate what the Senate would do, but he had the power when he chose to use it to decide what the Senate would not do.

# Chapter 12

# The President's Special Friend

*We are like two horse traders who knew
they were sometimes indispensable to one another.*

"We have a duty to support the President," Senator Dirksen said in early 1965.

He spoke the words during the Senate's anguished debate over President Johnson's urgent request for a special appropriation to pay for the men and military equipment he was dispatching to Vietnam. Without specific approval from Congress, Johnson had begun to send more and more troops to fight in Vietnam, and especially among Democratic senators there was alarm and deepening skepticism at Johnson's decision. A clever parliamentary tactician, Johnson had so couched his request for the seven-hundred-million-dollar appropriation that approval of it amounted to ratification of the commitment he was making in Vietnam. Because of the doubts expressed by these Democratic senators, Dirksen's endorsement of the President's action was the more welcome by Lyndon Johnson. To Dirksen, who made no fetish of consistency, there was nothing incongruous in giving Johnson his unquestioning support in Vietnam. From the start Dirksen chose to take a simplistic view of the Vietnam War. "When you are at war," he said, "and the enemy refuses to talk except on terms that would mean your surrender, you turn the screws on him. You do everything that is necessary to bring him down." Dirksen repeatedly mocked his own capacity to contradict the military chiefs advising President Johnson. "If they don't know," he said, "I ask you how should a humble shavetail who served in World War I know?" Dirksen had long approved U.S. policy in Vietnam. He had approved in the mid-1950's President Eisenhower's initial commitments of foreign aid to South Vietnam. Dirksen as well had approved President Kennedy's actions increasing that aid and sending as well military "advisors" to Vietnam in 1962 and 1963. On one occasion Dirksen even publicly rebuffed the Republican National Committee for criticizing Kennedy's policy toward Vietnam. From Eisenhower, Kennedy, and Johnson, Dirksen had expected and received candid briefings on all emerging foreign-policy questions, and, once briefed, Dirksen supported these Presidents in whatever decisions they made.

"I may not always approve what you do," he told President Johnson at a 1965 White House conference with the leaders of Congress, "but when I have had my day in court, I support you."

With President Johnson, Dirksen enjoyed a unique personal rapport, one that transcended the relationship of any opposition-party leader with a President in the history of the American republic. "I don't attempt to drive the President . . . ," Dirksen said, "but I do talk to him like a Texan. I talk to him like he ought to be talked to. We use firm, understandable language. And we're good friends." They were more than friends. They were intimates and they shared a confidential political kinship that negated traditional partisanship. Because of that special relationship, Dirksen gave to Johnson his unflagging support through the long ordeal of the Vietnam War. In this Dirksen stood against some of the most influential senators of the President's political party and, with even more telling effect, against the stalwarts of his own Republican Party. Repeatedly Dirksen acted to blunt, and even to silence, criticisms by Republican leaders of Johnson's policies in Vietnam. He used what talents he possessed to defend the President against all faultfinders. He mocked the Democratic senators protesting

Johnson's actions; they were engaged, he said, in "a chorus of despair sung to the tune of a dirge of defeat." When Melvin Laird of Wisconsin, chairman of the House Republican caucus, threatened the withdrawal of Republican support of the President in Vietnam, Dirksen did not try to hide his annoyance. "Lyndon Johnson," he said pointedly, "is the commander in chief." This was Dirksen's position from the start, and at the beginning Dirksen even opposed seeking negotiations on the war. "To negotiate in South Vietnam, while the Communist aggression is spreading throughout the entire Southeast Asian peninsula," he said, "is like a man trying to paint his front porch while his house is on fire." Within the Republican Party there were those who wanted a more rigorous military prosecution of the war and those who wanted a more diligent effort to negotiate peace than President Johnson proposed, and Dirksen opposed both groups. Dirksen by now had achieved a commanding presence over his Republican colleagues in Congress, not in the Senate alone, and he used his prestige and power to smother the instinctive impulses of his colleagues to attack the President and his war policies.

Dirksen's attitude was uncomplicated. "Congress," he said, "has the job of raising and supporting the Army, but the direction of the military is the business of the President." Dirksen placed absolute confidence in General William Westmoreland, the American commander in Vietnam, and in the other military chiefs. "Who am I to swap my judgment for his?" Dirksen asked of Westmoreland. When Westmoreland repeatedly asked for more troops, Dirksen treated those requests with equanimity. "That's a military decision," he said. "You don't quarrel with him. You're in no position to quarrel with him." At private conferences at the White House, where he was invited to consult about the war, Dirksen had but one standard message for President Johnson: "I support you." That unquestioning support gave Johnson a freedom of decision in prosecuting the Vietnam War that he would not otherwise have had. Dirksen's behavior in this stood in marked contrast to his performance during the Korean War. Then he had been among the bitterest critics of

President Truman. As the leader of his party in the Senate, Dirksen had a different sense of responsibility than he had as a freshman member in the party's ranks. During the Korean War Dirksen savagely criticized the Truman administration on the management of the war, often in simplistic, emotional terms. "In heaven's name," he exclaimed in 1951, "let us not slaughter any more youngsters over there when it looks as if they are going to run us out of the place anyway." During the Vietnam War Dirksen became President Johnson's most important supporter on his management of that war. He stood staunchly with Johnson on Vietnam from the very beginning and never really flagged in that support, even when Democrats and Republicans alike fled from Johnson's Vietnam policies. The rising opposition to the war only seemed to drive Johnson and Dirksen closer together on their views of the war. They spent long hours alone consulting at the White House. There were reports, only halfheartedly denied by Dirksen, that not only did he help the President select bombing targets for American airplanes in North Vietnam but that on occasion he alone picked some of the targets. Dirksen's sense of responsibility to the President on international questions no doubt was enhanced by the fact that this President, Lyndon Johnson, was his cordial friend. Dirksen could be faulted, as he was, and by his own party members, for yielding so totally to President Johnson on so momentous a question as the Vietnam War. Acting as he did, he made himself a partner in responsibility for the military commitments that Johnson made.

Not even the President's staunchest Democratic supporters gave Johnson the unstinted approval that Dirksen offered. Senator Richard Russell, chairman of the Senate's Armed Services Committee, supported the commitment in Vietnam, once made, but he disagreed with the commitment. "We never should have got involved in Vietnam in the first place," he said. Senator John Stennis, chairman of the military-preparedness subcommittee, took a similar position: "I regret that we got in there." Among senior Republican senators a similar view prevailed. Senator George Aiken spoke of the need to blame Johnson for the "mess" he had made in Vietnam.

"We're in the quicksand," Senator Hickenlooper said, "and we've got to get out." Some of the most senior Democrats openly opposed the President. Senator William Fulbright of Arkansas, chairman of the Senate Foreign Relations Committee, hesitated for more than a year to speak publicly his growing dismay at the President's Vietnam policy. At a leadership meeting at the White House in January, 1966, Fulbright earnestly tried to argue that a then existing halt in bombing of North Vietnam be continued. As Fulbright began to speak, President Johnson coolly turned to Secretary of State Dean Rusk, at his immediate right, and engaged him in animated conversation until Fulbright had finished. Thus grossly snubbed by the President, Fulbright immediately became an open and avowed opponent of the war. Senator Mansfield, the Democratic leader in the Senate, acted with more discretion than Fulbright, but he made his opposition to the war perfectly plain to the President. Johnson often was vindictive, a man who brooked opposition badly, and he chose to punish Fulbright and Mansfield for their intransigence, as he felt it. He declined to invite Fulbright to state dinners at the White House, affairs which the chairman of the Foreign Relations Committee normally was expected to attend. Mansfield was invited, but he was shunted to a table in the far corner of the state dining room. Johnson insisted that at these dinners Dirksen sit at his table, the seat of honor. Dirksen was troubled by this pettiness of the President. Partly Dirksen feared that even selfless Mike Mansfield, his friend, might be hurt by these personal rebuffs; partly he feared that Johnson, out of personal spite, was damaging the country's best interests by these antics.

In December, 1965, Dirksen joined with other Republican leaders, acting jointly as the just-created Republican Coordinating Committee, to criticize Johnson's handling of the war. The Republicans proposed a more strident prosecution of the war, concentrating on "maximum use" of air and sea power, including a quarantine against North Vietnam. A month later, however, Dirksen returned to his true position of total support for the President in Vietnam. He did so under unique circumstances, as the Republican Party's spokesman in the first "State of the Union" address ever formally made by the leaders of the opposition party in Congress. On the demand of Republican leaders, the television networks had agreed to give the Republican Party the free air time to reply to President Johnson's State of the Union address. Dirksen and Gerald Ford, the new Republican leader of the House of Representatives, divided the television time, and Dirksen preempted for himself the field of foreign policy, confining Ford to domestic matters. In his speech Dirksen endorsed anew Johnson's handling of the Vietnam War. "Let the peace efforts continue," he said. "Let the military efforts continue. Let it be intensified if necessary as sound military judgment dictates." The Republicans had been granted the television time to reply to the President, presumably to differ with him, but instead Dirksen sanctioned precisely what Johnson was doing in Vietnam. Dirksen knew that he did not speak the views of all his Republican colleagues on the Vietnam War. "If they want to try me for party deviation," he said, "they can."

Dirksen had known Johnson for more than thirty years, and the friendship of their Senate years together grew to extraordinary intimacy in the years of Johnson's Presidency. Johnson consulted with Dirksen about many difficult questions besides Vietnam, and on foreign-policy questions Dirksen steadfastly supported Johnson at every point. When U.S. relations with President Nasser and the United Arab Republic suddenly worsened in early 1965, from Congress came a rising demand to retaliate and punish Nasser for his intransigence. The State Department took alarm, but Dirksen acted to dampen the anger of his colleagues. "Should we clench our fist," Dirksen asked the Senate, "and talk through our teeth in language that even Nasser can understand? No! We had better leave this matter where it is—with the President of the United States." When in July of that year Johnson intervened in a revolution in the Dominican Republic by dispatching U.S. marines there, Dirksen again supported him. Dirksen did have later reservations about Johnson's strategy of replacing the marines with troops from Latin-

American countries, but he did not want them published. "When you sick a Latin on a Latin," Dirksen remarked informally to a group of reporters, "they're likely to start a pool game. Don't put that down, because Lyndon would call me up and give me hell. And don't put that down either!" In the summer of 1966 a group of Democratic senators, including Mike Mansfield, demanded a reduction of American troops stationed in Europe. President Johnson turned to Dirksen. At the White House Johnson outlined to Dirksen his objections to formalizing that demand by the Democratic senators in a Senate resolution. Dirksen returned to the Senate to argue the President's case. He told his colleagues that before any such resolution could be brought before the Senate, the Senate needed "a lot more factual information" than its members had. In the field of foreign policy, to a remarkable degree, Senator Dirksen became in effect President Johnson's spokesman in the Senate, an unprecedented role for the leader of the opposition party.

"I've seen a lot of the President the last few months," Dirksen said privately in the fall of 1966. "I've spent hours and hours with him alone. He talks to me more than he does his own people."

Their conversations were extraordinarily candid. "Several times," Dirksen said, "he has leaned over and put his face right close to mine and said: 'Remember this—I'm not a candidate for anything.' He has repeated it over and over again. I don't really know what he means. Maybe he's just trying to get me to think he won't run again." Johnson, in fact, was doing just that, and a year and a half before he startled the world with his dramatic announcement that he would not seek reelection. Their private talks, either at the White House or more frequently by telephone, were often lighthearted and bemused, but sometimes they carried the edge of two men who led opposing political parties. On one occasion, for example, Dirksen flew to Texas to make a series of political speeches, and Johnson telephoned him to ask what he was doing.

"Well," said Dirksen, "I have to brush you off and brush off the Great Society."

"I thought you were my friend," Johnson said.

"You have no better friend in the United States," Dirksen said, "because my mission in life is to save you from yourself."

Dirksen normally opposed President Johnson's domestic legislation, but not to the degree that he had opposed Kennedy's. He attacked Johnson's bill to establish model cities as potentially "one of the greatest boondoggles this country has ever witnessed." He offered no less than six amendments to cripple the truth-in-packaging bill supported by the Johnson administration. More effectively, Dirksen persuaded the Senate to slash two hundred and fifty million dollars from the funds Johnson wanted for the Development Loan Fund. In the spring of 1966 Johnson made a concentrated effort to hold down the federal budget, and he read with annoyance news reports quoting Dirksen that he and the Congressional Republicans would really cut Johnson's budget. The President dashed off a note to Dirksen, taunting him for his claims. "What do you think I did in preparing my budget this past winter?" Johnson wrote testily. Johnson cited recent examples of Congress increasing his budget. "I am afraid *my* economy hunt—which most people in the executive branch thought the strongest they had ever seen—is suffering up there. Can't you help?"* Johnson and Dirksen scrapped repeatedly about federal spending, and over who was to blame for its increase.

"Ev," Johnson said at one point in 1966, "you people are going to increase my budget by two and a half to three billion dollars."

"Mr. President," Dirksen shot back at him, "you've lectured the business community. You've lectured the grocers, and you've lectured the housewives. You've lectured everyone but the right crowd, the members of your own party. Why don't you lecture your own guys?"

---

* President Johnson plainly regretted sending Dirksen this carping letter. The very next day, March 31, 1966, he wrote Dirksen another note, congratulating him effusively on a minor statement Dirksen had made in the Senate on the Indo-American Foundation. "I am very much appreciative," Johnson wrote, "of your leadership in putting your country's cause above all things."

Despite this abrasiveness on domestic matters, Dirksen did cooperate with Johnson periodically on these questions when he could, but not always out of any special desire to help the President. Dirksen, for example, declined to oppose any of Johnson's repeated requests to increase the legal limit on the national debt. In this he worked at cross purposes with Gerald Ford and the House Republicans, who united against these bills; Dirksen believed the question was not a valid political issue. In 1966 Dirksen vigorously opposed enactment of a federal program to provide rent supplements to the poor; the following year, abruptly, Dirksen reversed field and supported the program. He had discovered that the leaders of the real-estate industry favored the program, and he altered his position because of them rather than any kindliness for President Johnson. "All of them," Dirksen said of the businessmen, "seem to believe that rent supplements may be the best answer to low-cost housing." The home builders were making money under this federal program, and that had changed their view of its social value to the country. Dirksen was more than candid in acknowledging why he changed his mind; he conceded plainly he shifted because of the businessmen. "I didn't get myself too well informed on this rent-supplement program and how it operates," he said somewhat sheepishly. "No one seemed to be for it except the administration." Only belatedly did he learn that the real-estate industry favored it. "I now think I understand the program a little better," Dirksen said. "Now we may be able to get the government out of public housing." He had a pat answer to justify his change of mind. "Haven't I told you?" he said. "The only people who don't change their minds are in the insane asylum or in the cemetery." Occasionally Dirksen did take the President's side openly on domestic legislation, as in the instance in 1966 when the Senate Democrats tried to approve a 2.5-billion-dollar antipoverty program, some 750 million dollars more than Johnson wanted. It was Dirksen who offered the amendment to reduce the authorization to the President's requested amount. "Brethren," he addressed his colleagues then, "weep with me. . . ." This was an isolated case of Dirksen and Johnson working together in this field. Normally they were at total odds on this program, with Dirksen scathing in his criticism. "Most of the controversy within the Great Society itself," Dirksen said at one point, "has not been about the poor, but about who was going to control the loot. . . . The poverty program has theories sounding as wholesome as blueberry pie, but right away it ran afoul of hanky-panky."

During the airline strike of 1966 Dirksen also cooperated fully with President Johnson, but in this case he inadvertently misspoke the President. Dirksen announced, in effect, that the President "very much" wanted Congress to pass legislation to bring the strike to an end. Dirksen, of course, had conferred with the President that day, and he believed he knew the President's position. He was therefore somewhat embarrassed to receive a telephone call from Johnson almost immediately after the wire services carried his remarks. "I told you I didn't want a bill," Johnson told him. Dirksen had to go before the Senate and correct himself. He had been, he said, "abysmally wrong" about the President's position.

Dirksen liked to jest at his double relationship with the President, that of formal opposition-party leader and that of intimate personal friend. On one such occasion, Dirksen attended a Republican women's gathering dressed in formal dinner jacket. When it came his turn to speak, he roundly berated Johnson's legislative program, not sparing the President himself in his partisan words. Abruptly he stopped his denunciation. With studied timing and exaggerated deliberation he looked at his wristwatch. "Oh, my," he said, "I'll have to leave you girls or I'll be late for dinner at the White House." He was as amused as the Republican women.

Dirksen's unique friendship with President Johnson, his full cooperation on the Vietnam War and other foreign questions, and his occasional help on domestic matters gave credence to the view that Johnson and Dirksen were reveling in a political "honeymoon" that encompassed all questions coming before the Senate. The President himself helped create this impression. On invitation from Dirksen and Mansfield, Johnson lunched in the Capitol with the Senate at the end of the 1966 session. In his address to the senators he thanked them for their cooperation. Then he turned to Dirksen. "You have been fair with me, and you have been just with me," Johnson said to him. "You have been good to me, but that is not very important to anybody how you have been to me. You have tried to put the interest of the country first and to serve it." The President was obviously moved as he spoke. Their open friendship sometimes led to public confusions, as when the President's request for a ten-percent income-tax surcharge became stymied in the House Ways and Means Committee in 1967. Dirksen offered a compromise, designed to break the stalemate, and "the Dirksen Plan," as the proposal was quickly labeled, was interpreted by some reporters as a "trial balloon" he offered on behalf of Johnson. In actuality, Dirksen got the idea from his own Republican colleagues, and Johnson did not support it. The very frequency with which Johnson and Dirksen conferred let Dirksen speak with confidence on how the President stood on almost any public question and encouraged the view that they worked out their differences in private. Where President Kennedy invited Dirksen to the White House perhaps once a month and telephoned him only a little more frequently, President Johnson was constantly talking to Dirksen, to the extent that he seemed to depend on Dirksen for advice. Johnson asked Dirksen to the White House two or three times a week in normal times and even more frequently at times of travail. His telephone calls to Dirksen were numberless, sometimes as many as ten in a single day.

Their friendship was not marred by their public disagreements, and Dirksen on occasion took pains to make sure of that. Every week that Congress remained in session, Dirksen held a joint news conference with Gerald Ford, a series like the "Ev and Charlie Show" when Charles Halleck had been the leader of the House Republicans. At these news conferences Dirksen was avowedly partisan, and he and Ford belabored the President and his legislative program with regularity. "The President has referred to the Republican Party as the party of fear," Dirksen said at one of these meetings in 1966, "and moreover, as having no constructive programs to fight inflation, no programs to ease racial tensions. . . . Is the President bewildered? Was he referring to his administration? His statements spell out the most damning self-indictment in modern political history." There was reason to doubt that Dirksen really meant these tirades against the President. After one of these meetings he met Larry O'Brien in a corridor of the Capitol and he told O'Brien not to take these tongue-lashings of the Democratic administration to heart. Dirksen explained, certain that O'Brien would relay the message to the President, that on these occasions he had to placate his own Republican ranks. "I have to throw them a piece of raw meat now and then," Dirksen said. He spoke to O'Brien as though he were using these denunciations of the Johnson administration merely to pacify his Republican colleagues for the cooperation he normally gave the President.

From their obvious friendship grew the assumption, common among journalists not familiar with their operations, that Johnson and Dirksen spent their time together at the White House swapping favors. The assumption was that Dirksen traded his votes on legislation in return for appointments for his friends to federal office, that he bargained his support of the President's foreign policies for federal buildings in Illinois. Their relationship ran deeper than that. It was true that all through his political career Dirksen paid special attention to political patronage, a major concern for every professional politician. Patronage was a means of building his own personal network and power within the federal establishment, and it was a point of pride with Dirksen that he managed to place friends and allies all through the federal establishment despite the long Democratic dominance of national politics. President Johnson tried to be cooperative with Dirksen's desires for patronage, more so than President Kennedy, and Dirksen had no qualms at all about simply asking for appointments for his friends and associates. "I wanted to get something out of him," Dirksen once bluntly stated after a visit to Johnson at the White House. He calculated that he had made his case well and that his nominee would receive the post from Johnson. A skeptical reporter questioned Dirksen: what did he have to give in return? "Nothing," Dirksen snapped. He thought a moment. "I done 'guv'!" he said, grinning. His dealings and negotiations with President Johnson were not fragmented, a tit for a tat. Rather their relationship was a continuous, seamless fabric. Out of mutual sympathy, they tried to help each other whenever they could; it was an understanding they had with each other, sealed with many a friendly handshake, and needed no signatures on any contracts. That they were leaders of opposing political parties ironically seemed to make their relationship easier, not more difficult. They met and dealt with each other in roughly the relation of peers and equals, not rivals.

Dirksen took care that no act of his would jar their curious alliance. He was direct with Johnson; he used no guile. "I never threw him a curve," Dirksen said once. "A curve is a device to give a spirit of revolution to a ball, the purpose being to deceive the batter. I never threw a curve at the President in my life."

None mentioned it during the painful course of the Vietnam War, but Dirksen's staunch support of President Johnson there had the effect of mollifying the political debate over that war. Notably, there was no repetition in this war of the "McCarthyism," in which Dirksen had then joined, that played havoc with American politics during the Korean War. Dirksen's support sheltered Johnson from such attacks as Senator Joseph McCarthy had launched on President Truman and the Truman administration. No responsible Republican felt free to raise such demagogic cries against the Democrats during the Vietnam War. Dirksen kept in check whatever instincts they had for such partisanship. Indeed, in the 1968 elections, when Spiro Agnew, the Republican candidate for Vice-President, called Vice-President Hubert Humphrey "soft on Communism," it was Dirksen who acted to correct him. He talked to Agnew by telephone, and he repudiated the charge publicly. "I'm not aware of any evidence," Dirksen said. "I'm rather restrained in the statements I make." Agnew publicly apologized for the remark. "I'm not proud of it," he admitted. In election year 1950 Senator Taft, as the leader of the Republicans in the

Senate, had encouraged McCarthy to continue his attacks on the Democrats.

The obvious cordiality between Dirksen and Johnson disturbed the Republicans in Congress. Their distress grew as the Dirksen-Johnson friendship became more obvious and open, and in the gossip of the Senate cloakrooms there were doubts raised as to where Dirksen truly plighted his political loyalty. President Johnson himself continued to feed these suspicions by his acts and words. In 1967, for example, he dropped in unexpectedly at a dinner honoring Dirksen. "The man you honor tonight," Johnson told the diners, "is often accused of being my fifth column on 'The Hill.' I want all of you to know that Everett Dirksen is the only column I haven't complained about all year long." That kind of praise pleased Dirksen, but it did not please his Republican colleagues. His confidential relationship with President Johnson had begun to weaken his command over the Republicans in the Senate.

Dirksen, of course, did oppose most of the Johnson domestic legislation, and in 1966 he alone defeated the most consequential Johnson bill of that year. He vetoed, in effect, the President's proposal for still another civil-rights bill. Searching for new legislation to help quiet the continuing Negro protests throughout the country, Johnson had asked Congress to enact a bill that would, among other things, establish federal guarantees for the right of Negroes to buy and rent homes where they wished. Dirksen promptly rejected this "open-housing" proposal; it was, he said, "absolutely unconstitutional." Dirksen denied federal jurisdiction over the sale and rental of houses; he rejected the administration's argument that these transactions came under the Constitution's interstate-commerce clause. "If you can tell me what interstate commerce is involved in selling or renting a house fixed in the soil," Dirksen said, "or where there is federal jurisdiction, I'll go out and eat the chimney off the house." President Johnson assigned Attorney General Katzenbach the chore of shepherding this bill through Congress, and Katzenbach, who had been the chief negotiator with Dirksen on the 1965 voting-rights bill, felt confident that he could work out another such accommodation with Dirksen. He knew also that he had to have Dirksen's support and active help to get the bill approved by the Senate. "We want Dirksen's support," Katzenbach said in the early stage of the struggle. "I think we will get Dirksen's support. He is a very reasonable man." Katzenbach knew Dirksen's flexibility on public questions, and he relied on that to win Dirksen's support eventually. The Attorney General was not alone in assuming that Dirksen could be persuaded to join the proponents of this new civil-rights bill. Senator Jacob Javits of New York, who had long watched Dirksen at close hand, figured he would finally come to terms. "Senator Dirksen," Javits said, 'is a consummate master of the parliamentary art, and I have no doubt that he is going to hold the line tightly until he feels the time has come to work something out." Katzenbach knew, as did the others engaged with this legislation, that only Dirksen could muster the necessary votes to halt the inevitable filibuster against the bill by the Southern senators. Katzenbach assumed that he would have to meet Dirksen's terms on the substance of the ultimate bill, and he also assumed that Dirksen's initial rebuke to the proposed legislation was merely his way of announcing that political reality.

Lawrence O'Brien, now Postmaster General but still President Johnson's chief liaison officer with Congress, made no such assumptions. O'Brien tended to see the world and its affairs in practical political terms, and he had long since learned that Dirksen did the same. From O'Brien's political perspective, he believed that Dirksen this time meant to remain in opposition to this civil-rights bill. Conferring privately with Katzenbach, O'Brien warned him of this danger. What O'Brien sensed was Dirksen's instinctive reaction to the growing hostility in the country to the Negro protests. The riots in the cities and the cries of "black power" by militant Negroes were alienating many of those who had sympathized with the earlier Negro protests. The issue had been fought in California on a statewide basis, and the advocates of open housing had been defeated. O'Brien knew that Dirksen had not missed the implications of that skirmish for the national scene. For political managers, this was not a question of prejudice or cowardice: it was merely the current trend of the country. "This is as tough an issue as you can find," O'Brien said privately. "Some of our Democrats are going to vote for it and be defeated in November as a result." O'Brien therefore believed that Dirksen would follow the political pollsters, who already were recording this change in national attitude.

Katzenbach, nevertheless, did his best to persuade Dirksen to agree to some form of the legislation. He received little encouragement; Dirksen refused to change. "Nick," he said to Katzenbach after one of their many conferences, "it's just no dice. I see no way out that doesn't violate principle." Dirksen did not always couch his objections on such high grounds; occasionally he cited the political realities. "Nothing has been suggested yet," he said at one point, "nothing we can think of that in any way alters my feeling that it can't be sold to the Senate. As of now, I see no compromise that I thought would be workable."

From the Republicans in the House of Representatives the Johnson administration received some strong support for the "open-housing" bill. A ranking member of the Judiciary Committee, Representative Charles McC. Mathias, of Maryland, proposed an important compromise on the housing section of the bill in an effort to help get the legislation approved. The House barely approved the Mathias amendment, 180 to 179. Dirksen did not appreciate this maneuver by Mathias. Indeed, Dirksen treated Mathias as though he had committed a personal affront to him, an act of *lèse majesté*. Dirksen publicly excoriated Mathias, a fellow Republican, for offering his amendment. "I thought it was a majestic piece of opportunism," Dirksen said. "What tortures those souls have gone through to come up with that." Dirksen acted as though he believed Mathias had improperly intruded on a jurisdiction that Dirksen had marked for his own. Mathias was not the only Republican to feel the lash of Dirksen's scorn for taking a stance Dirksen did not approve. The words of contempt for Mathias were a mistake. Not only did Mathias resent them, and he was elected to the Senate in 1968, but other Republicans regarded them as mere malice by Dirksen. They seemed the act of an aging man, jealous of his power.

The House of Representatives passed the civil-rights bill on August 9, 1966, by a vote of 259 to 157, and for more than a month thereafter the Senate fitfully debated the measure. The real question remained: would Dirksen finally endorse it? Repeatedly he refused.

President Johnson tried his wiles on his old friend. At a news conference, September 12, Johnson stated that the bill's fate rested with Dirksen. "I would hope," the President said, "that we could find some way to get his support, because I think whether it passes or fails will depend upon what the minority leader does about it." Johnson invited Dirksen to the White House, and there with Katzenbach and Senator Mansfield he made a final attempt to induce Dirksen to support the legislation. "Mr. President," Dirksen said, by his own account, "I do not intend to retreat one step, because this is a package of mischief for this country if I ever saw one." The next day the Senate voted on Mansfield's motion to invoke cloture on the filibuster against this bill, and with Dirksen voting "no," the motion failed 54 to 42. Five days later Mansfield tried again, and again the Senate refused to halt the filibuster. Mansfield was thus forced to abandon the legislation for that year. On the first cloture vote on this bill, only twelve Republican senators voted "aye," and on the second only ten. In 1964 twenty-seven Republicans had voted to halt the filibuster on that year's civil-rights bill, and in 1965 twenty-three Republicans so voted. The difference suggested the extent of Dirksen's command of his Republican colleagues on such questions and why he held a veto over these bills in the Senate.

"Somebody had to kill cock robin," Dirksen said after the vote, "and it might as well be me."

If he could control the Congressional decision on civil-rights legislation, Dirksen still could not force the Senate to adopt the constitutional amendments he wanted to rewrite decisions of the

Supreme Court. These were issues that divided the Democrats in Congress, and President Johnson cautiously kept himself aloof from Dirksen's campaign to adopt them. On March 22, 1966, Dirksen finally introduced his joint resolution to adopt an amendment to overturn the Supreme Court's school-prayer decisions. "I do not intend," he said, "to let nine men tell one hundred and ninety million Americans, including children, where and when they can say their prayers." Dirksen evoked intense emotionalism in his appeal for this amendment. Many of the leaders of the American clergy were opposed to Dirksen's amendment, but this did not trouble him. He knew who did support his amendment. "Not the professionals in the church hierarchy," he said, "not the cocktail-party, luncheon-circuit bunch. I'm talking about the church members, the rank and file, and they're in favor." Within the Senate the members knew from their mail how strong ran the popular indignation against the Supreme Court. Senator Birch Bayh of Indiana, chairman of the judiciary subcommittee to which Dirksen's resolution was referred, opposed the measure, and he let Dirksen know he did not intend to hurry it to the Senate floor. "I will not see this session end," Dirksen announced, "without getting a vote. That's for sure." Bayh eventually did hold hearings on Dirksen's amendment, but his subcommittee took no further action. In a tactical maneuver, Senator Bayh tried to vitiate Dirksen's proposal by offering a substitute for it, to permit "silent voluntary prayer and meditation." Dirksen mocked the idea. "Imagine school kids going in for silent meditation," Dirksen said scornfully. "Kids have no capacity for silent meditation. I'm interested in what it does for the kids." As Dirksen had done before when a proposal of his had been blocked in committee, he brought this one to the Senate floor by offering it as a substitute for a pending measure. He thus did force a vote on it in the Senate on September 21, and the Senate approved it 49 to 37. This, however, was less than the two-thirds margin required for approval of a constitutional amendment, and Dirksen had failed.

Earlier that year he had lost as well an attempt to force through Congress a constitutional amendment to overturn the Supreme Court's rulings on the apportionment of state legislatures, but he had not yet given up. "So long as I am a member of Congress," he pledged, "this issue is not going to die and it is not going to fade away." He concentrated thereafter on trying to convene a constitutional convention and abandoned his efforts to force Congress to act directly. Through the lobbying organization he had helped create, the Committee for Government of the People, Dirksen and his associates worked behind the scenes to persuade enough state legislatures to petition Congress for such a convention. Dirksen himself lobbied state legislators to make his case, and by the spring of 1967 thirty-two state legislatures had approved such petitions. In May, 1967, Dirksen and Senator Roman Hruska of Nebraska, his ally in this struggle, opened a debate in the Senate on the question to dramatize the issue and thereby to encourage other state legislatures to petition for a constitutional convention. "This," Dirksen said, "is perhaps the foremost constitutional issue to face our nation in a century or more." Dirksen's case, however, was not as strong as he tried to make it appear. "Let the people decide," Dirksen repeatedly had argued. His opponents bitterly accused him of trying to protect the inherent unfairness of the existing system. "Here is a deadly serious attempt," Senator Joseph Tydings of Maryland said, "to perpetuate the minority stranglehold, which special-interest groups now exert over all too many of our state legislatures." Beyond the rhetoric, other opponents of Dirksen's plan made ready to challenge the validity of the petitions approved by the state legislatures to call a constitutional convention. Senator William Proxmire of Wisconsin claimed evidence that all but six of the thirty-two legislatures so petitioning were "illegally constituted." Then not all the petitions agreed in language or purpose. Clearly the opponents had grounds to prevent the automatic calling of a constitutional convention by Congress even if the necessary state legislatures petitioned. In a further difficulty for Dirksen, the other state legislatures did not respond as he had hoped they would. More and more of the state legislatures were reshaped as the Supreme Court directed, and gradually the issue faded away.

On questions like the Supreme Court's school-prayer and apportionment decisions, Dirksen carried with him all the Republican senators except two or three of the party's outspoken liberals. Among the party's political activists and younger members, however, Dirksen's influence was beginning to wane. These senators increasingly realized that they approached political, economic, and social questions, as well as the Vietnam War, from points of perspective different from Dirksen's. The senators entering the Senate in the 1960's were mostly men a full generation younger than Dirksen, and they reflected the America of World War II and its aftermath, not the World War I world that Dirksen had known. Their minds and instincts were more urbane and sophisticated than Dirksen's, and the differences were more marked than their ages suggested. The new senators were of a different stamp and breed. In 1966 Dirksen turned seventy, and most of the new senators were in their forties. Indeed, one of them was Dirksen's own son-in-law, Howard Baker, Jr., of Tennessee, who was elected to the Senate in 1966 at forty-one years of age. They normally treated Dirksen with affection and respect, and they could be amused and charmed by Dirksen's extolling the virtues of the marigold. More importantly, they could be impressed by Dirksen's formidable parliamentary talents, but all the same they reacted differently than Dirksen to the world in which they lived, and they knew that they did. As significant as this inherent estrangement between Dirksen and the younger generation of senators was the increasing distaste among the more senior senators for Dirksen's cordiality with President Johnson. Particularly galling to these senators was Dirksen's total support of Johnson's conduct of the war in Vietnam.

As American casualties increased, with no obvious gains in the fighting, the American people more and more questioned the wisdom of Johnson's decisions in Vietnam. Among Republicans in Congress the growing unpopularity of the war was a plain political fact, and they grew restless for their party to adopt a stand on the war that could clearly differentiate them from the Johnson administration. Dirksen resisted their efforts in almost every instance. Representative Ford, the leader of the House Republicans, repeatedly criticized the President and his war policies, and as often Dirksen came to Johnson's defense. In April, 1966, Ford accused the Johnson administration of "shocking mismanagement" of the war. Dirksen made it plain that he did not agree. In a city where public statements tend to the vapid, Dirksen's caustic rebuke of Ford was stunning. "He went pretty far, didn't he?" Dirksen asked at an on-the-record news conference. "In what respect is it 'shockingly mismanaged'? Who is doing the shocking?" Dirksen went so far as to suggest that Ford was uninformed about the war. "I just don't deliver a hard judgment like that," Dirksen said, "unless I have some hard facts. I just wouldn't do it." He did not like Ford's attack on the President. "You don't demean the chief magistrate of your country," Dirksen said, "at a time when a war is on." Ford later attacked Defense Secretary Robert McNamara for his lack of "credibility," and again Dirksen disagreed. When President Johnson flew to the Philippines in October, 1966, in the cause of peace, Ford pronounced the trip "a political gimmick." Dirksen sharply reproved him for it. Dirksen did not want the Republican Party to make the Vietnam War a political issue. "You have to be circumspect," he said. "You don't denounce the commander in chief before the whole, wide world." Dirksen's constant undercutting of Ford caused considerable distress within the Republican Party hierarchy. Republican National Chairman Ray Bliss maneuvered behind the scenes to lessen this divisiveness, arguing with Ford against retaliating against Dirksen, and with Dirksen to restrain his public rebukes of Ford. Dirksen resented Ford, almost two decades younger than himself. Ford had ousted Dirksen's friend Charles Halleck from the Republican leadership of the House. On his part, Ford did what he could to alleviate Dirksen's hostility. Ford arranged never to take Dirksen by surprise on any of his statements about the war, and he went so far as to call on Dirksen when he planned to make a speech to inform Dirksen in advance of precisely what he intended to say. Ford had learned by experience that if he merely sent copies of his speeches to Dirksen, the senator would not bother to read them, nor would he stay his criticism. Ford carefully never showed anger at Dirksen's contradictions and contrariness. "We have had to learn to live with it," Ford said.

By the summer of 1966 there was a growing sense among Republican leaders that their statement on the war of the previous December was no longer adequate to the party's political needs. In that statement they had urged a more aggressive prosecution of the war through increased use of air and naval power. As the war became ever more unpopular, some of the party's leaders believed they needed to emphasize their interest in finding a peaceful settlement. Senator Thruston Morton of Kentucky, a talented political strategist, especially was concerned, and he believed he had found the tactic needed for the party in a fortuitous suggestion by Charles Percy, forty-six, then campaigning in Illinois for the Senate. On July 2 Percy had called for an "all-Asian peace conference" to try to settle the Vietnam War. Almost immediately Morton began to argue with other Republican leaders to endorse Percy's proposal. The idea for such a peace conference was not new with Percy, but, to Morton, Percy's sponsorship of it had the inherent political advantage of making it appear a Republican peace plan. Morton knew that persuading Dirksen to accept the Percy plan would be doubly hard. Not only did the proposal smack of criticism of the Johnson administration, but Dirksen personally disliked Percy. He would not willingly follow Percy's leadership. In private Dirksen mocked Percy's proposal. "It's not going to amount to a god-damn," he said. "It's like being against sin. . . ." Morton was not discouraged; he made the rounds of his colleagues, soliciting support for the Percy plan, and he maneuvered to bring it before a meeting of the Republican Coordinating Committee in August, 1966. Morton by then had rallied major support for the idea, even persuading Richard Nixon, who attended the meeting, to endorse it. Until then Nixon had been urging that American forces in Vietnam be increased to 750,000 men. Representative Ford and the other House leaders favored the Percy peace plan; so did many of the senior senators, and at the party conference the party's leaders formally endorsed it. By a considerable irony, Dirksen was the senior Republican officeholder at the conference, and, as such, he was automatically designated to announce the decision. In doing so, however, Dirksen took care to credit the idea of the all-Asian peace conference to the foreign minister of Thailand, not Percy. Among his colleagues, this was not missed.

In this party council, Dirksen had been outmaneuvered by Senator Morton, and he acquiesced in the group's decision only reluctantly. Morton, impatient with Dirksen's leadership, moved against Dirksen the following January. Pending before the Senate was a treaty negotiated by the Johnson administration with Russia to establish consulates in the two countries. The treaty had been signed in 1964, but President Johnson hesitated to ask the Senate's approval of it while the Vietnam War was under way. Dirksen opposed its ratification, and he reiterated his opposition to it on January 23, 1967. Senator Mansfield stated the obvious when he said that approving the treaty without Dirksen's support would be "extremely difficult." Morton was annoyed at Dirksen's opposition to this treaty, and he did not accept Mansfield's judgment either. Discreetly Morton approached the President's advisers, and he found them unwilling to try to pass the treaty with Dirksen opposed. "I can straighten him out," Morton told them. "If you guys will go, I'll go." On January 31, just eight days after Dirksen had restated his opposition, Morton took the Senate floor to advocate immediate approval of the treaty. He argued that adoption of the treaty would advance the cause of peace and that it should not be rejected because "hysterical voices of fear and hatred" had been raised against it. Morton urged President Johnson to take the lead in persuading the Senate to approve it, and thus goaded, Johnson did. Dirksen remained adamant, but Morton already had made inroads among his Republican colleagues in the Senate. Morton knew that this treaty had first been proposed by the Eisenhower administration, and he quickly received Eisenhower's endorsement of it when he called on the former President. Eisenhower gave Morton a statement that ratification of the treaty was "in our national interest." Within ten days after his Senate speech, Morton had wrung commitments for the treaty from twenty-two of the thirty-six Republican senators. The implications were plain: on this issue Morton had seized the leadership of the Senate's Republicans from Dirksen. Dirksen, a practiced cloakroom operator, learned soon enough what Morton was about, and he did not like it. He inadvertently revealed his anxiety in an overreaction to Senator Clifford Case of New Jersey. Case stated publicly that there was a "very definite possibility" that moderate Republicans in the Senate, like himself, might revolt against Dirksen's leadership in foreign affairs. Dirksen testily retorted that Case really belonged in the Democratic Party because he "never" voted with his fellow Republicans. Dirksen quickly regretted his remark, and he telephoned Case to apologize. "I got a little sensitive," he told Case, "and said things I didn't mean." A few days later Dirksen began to give way on the consular treaty. He first said he was not unalterably opposed to the idea of such a treaty, if appropriate safeguards were added; the fear among the opponents was that the Russians would use their consulates in the United States as espionage bases. Then Dirksen hinted that he might even vote for the treaty. He said he had corrected certain "misconceptions and misinterpretations" he had had about the treaty. By February 13 he was defending the treaty to his constituents in Illinois, and two weeks after that he publicly pledged his support for the treaty. Morton's maneuvers had worked. He had drawn a full majority of the Republican senators away from Dirksen on the question, and Dirksen, alive to the hazards in this to his own leadership, had followed them. Privately he had a special explanation for his change, and he went no further publicly than to hint at it and say he could not talk about it. To a few of his trusted colleagues, including Barry Goldwater, he told the details. "Top secret," Goldwater called it, and added that if he were still a senator he would vote for the treaty because of it. What had happened was that Walt Rostow, President Johnson's special aide for international matters, had privately briefed Dirksen on the real meaning of the consular treaty: it would give the United States far greater access to Russian secrets than it would give Russian spies to American secrets. The United States would gain far more than Russia. On March 16, by a vote of 66 to 28, the Senate approved the treaty.

Morton's success against Dirksen, in this intraparty intrigue, suggested that Dirksen's command of his own party in the Senate no longer was as complete as it had been. Morton himself publicly denied that he intended any specific challenge to Dirksen as party leader. Rather, he explained, his intentions were to give the Republicans in the Senate a more progressive and moderate image in international affairs. He was calculating also on the party's future, and he tried to use the consular treaty as a means to position the Republican Party for election year 1968. Morton wanted to deny control of the 1968 Platform Committee to the party's anticommunist hard-liners. Privately Morton talked to his colleagues and associates of the ease he had in outmaneuvering Dirksen in this struggle. "He's a chameleon," Morton said. "Ev rolls with the punch." Where Morton had succeeded, others could try, and by the end of 1967 Dirksen had been defeated on two other questions by freshman Republican senators.

The first of these challenges came from Senator Baker, Dirksen's son-in-law, and it came on a subject of personal commitment by Dirksen, the question of reapportionment. Because of their family relationship, Dirksen and Baker had worked out a private arrangement to avoid as much as possible any professional unpleasantness arising between them. Dirksen had never hesitated to appeal to any senator of either party for political help on a pending question, but he made an exception of Baker. "I wouldn't think of asking him for a vote," Dirksen said. "He's got a different situation." Baker, who normally called his father-in-law "Mr. D.," had a similar sensitivity about making personal requests of Dirksen. "I've never asked him for anything," he explained. When they had to disagree, they agreed to disagree without animus, and they took precautions not to embarrass each other unnecessarily. On the question of apportionment, Baker did disagree with his father-in-law, and when the question came before the Senate in late spring, 1967, in the form of a House bill dealing with Congressional apportionment, Baker called on Dirksen in his Capitol office.

"Senator," he said to Dirksen, "I'm going to be against you on this thing. I owe you the courtesy of telling you. I feel deeply on this."

Dirksen eyed his son-in-law for a moment.

"Howard," he said, "my only advice to you is this: if you are going to fight, try to win."

Baker formed an alliance in this struggle with Senator Edward Kennedy of Massachusetts, and the two young senators campaigned hard to carry the Senate against Dirksen. Kennedy concentrated on the Democratic senators, Baker on the Republicans. The bill as it came to the Senate floor would have allowed variations in the constituencies of Congressional districts up to thirty-five percent. Kennedy and Baker proposed an amendment to reduce that allowable percentage to ten. "We worked for it," Baker said. Dirksen worked against it and with all his persuasive wiles. In the end the Senate approved the Kennedy-Baker amendment, 44 to 39. Baker had wrenched away from Dirksen enough of the Republicans to make the difference, and Dirksen was left to read the wry headline in *The Washington Daily News*: "Senate's Young Pup Lames Old Growler."

Later in 1967 Dirksen was again defeated by a freshman Republican senator, this time on an amendment Dirksen tried to add to a bill authorizing 14.6 billion dollars in federal aid to primary and secondary schools. Dirksen touched off a lively debate in the Senate when he proposed to prohibit use of any of the bill's funds for busing students or teachers to correct racial imbalances in local school systems. "This," he said, "is the time to settle this vexing matter." Dirksen had struck a sensitive emotional nerve in the body politic, for the question of school busing had grown to angry controversy in many parts of the country. At his back-row desk, Senator Robert Griffin of Michigan, forty-four, sat listening to the Senate debate. He was distressed by Dirksen's proposal; the amendment catered to the whites' resistance of school integration, and Griffin believed it would tarnish the Republican Party's progressive record on civil rights. He scribbled an amendment to Dirksen's amendment, the effect of which would nullify what Dirksen proposed. "What the Senator from Michigan is proposing to do," Dirksen protested, "is to gut the amendment that I have offered today." Dirksen thought he had the votes to defeat Griffin's amendment, and he let it go to a vote. The Senate voted 38 to 38 on it, and Griffin's allies in this struggle moved quickly to try to carry his amendment. Among Griffin's supporters were most of the new Republican senators, including Charles Percy of Illinois, Mark Hatfield of Oregon, and Edward Brooke of Massachusetts; in a series of parliamentary maneuvers they stayed with Griffin. The unfinished struggle was put off a day, and Griffin and his young Republican allies worked hard to muster enough votes to carry the Griffin amendment. Dirksen likewise tried to bring into town his missing supporters, and neither side pressed immediately for another vote to break the tie. Finally Dirksen gave up, and he withdrew his own amendment, acknowledging thereby that Griffin's amendment would carry if the Senate voted. "The reason was extremely simple," Dirksen explained of his withdrawal. "All day long we were stalling each other to see who would increase his side. One member would arrive, and another would leave. At no point could you be sure to win." Rather than lose directly, Dirksen backed away from the contest to take his chances that the Senate's climate would improve for his proposal at a later date. "When they go home," he said of his colleagues, "they'll find out what the people feel, and we'll be in better shape."

These defeats to Dirksen on domestic matters, if embarrassing politically, were of minor consequence, especially against the foreboding implications of the Vietnam War. President Johnson kept sending more troops to Vietnam, and within Congress his decisions were attacked and defended with ever-increasing political venom. The danger that the war might abruptly expand beyond Vietnam immensely increased the tension, and on either side of the debate respected senators even talked of the possibility that their disagreements might yet lead to irresponsible charges of treason. In May, 1967, an inadvertent incident illustrated the strain under which political Washington was operating. The staff of the Senate Republican Policy Committee had prepared a report on the Vietnam War. Senator Hickenlooper, chairman of the Policy Committee, feared that the report had been leaked to the press, and he released it to the public, unread by any Republican senators. Hickenlooper claimed the document was merely factual, but the correspondents found such provocative passages as this: "Does the Republican Party serve America best by saying that politics stops at the water's edge? That we must rally behind the President? Does bipartisanship mean that Democratic mistakes are Republican responsibilities?" The report did not answer those questions, but the correspondents interpreted them as criticizing Johnson's policies. Those opposed to the war immediately hailed the report, while those who wanted a more aggressive assault on the Vietnamese Communists spoke their anger at it. Dirksen learned of the report on a late-evening television news program he heard in his room at a Washington hospital where he was recovering from pneumonia. He could not sleep, worrying about it, and he got up from bed in the middle of the night to draft a policy statement of his own. The next morning Dirksen left the hospital for the Senate to read his statement. It was a total endorsement of Johnson and Johnson's policies in Vietnam.

"Preserving wholly the right of full and fair inquiry and criticism," Dirksen said, in his capacity as the Republican leader, "we reiterate our wholehearted support of the commander in chief of our armed forces. We reaffirm our position of standing four-square behind him. . . ."

Dirksen's dramatic intervention prevented the exploitation of the committee's report by those in the party anxious to criticize President Johnson and his war policies. With a mixture of pleasure and pride Dirksen acknowledged his intentions of smothering that Republican criticism. "When I put on the silencer," he said, laughing, "they are silent!" He received a telephone call from President Johnson. "Thanks," the President said.

Despite Dirksen's attempt to make it appear that the Republicans stood behind Johnson in the war, many of the Republicans were moving away from the President. Dirksen did not intend to tolerate a Republican repudiation of the President on Vietnam; that would have been a repudiation of Dirksen's leadership too. He worked now to stem the growing tendency among Republicans to make the war a political issue, but he could not silence the senators voicing their distress. "As time passes," Senator Aiken of Vermont said in a Senate speech, "I come more and more to believe that the present administration cannot achieve an honorable peace in Vietnam. This administration is too bound by its own vague criterion, its own predictions . . . to see the interest of the nation except in terms of its own survival as the government in power." Other senior Republican senators voiced similar doubts. Senator John Sherman Cooper of Kentucky, Morton's ally, suggested that the President reduce the level of U.S. bombing of North Vietnam lest Communist China be prompted to enter the war. Plainly some of the most influential of the Republican senators were now close to Senator Fulbright and Senator Mansfield, the Democratic leaders, in their opposition to the war.

By late summer, 1967, the principal leaders of the Republican Party other than Dirksen were maneuvering, as Gerald Ford phrased it privately, "to disengage ourselves from the Johnson policies." Ford and the other House Republican leaders were increasing their political attacks on President Johnson, and they were receiving help from Republican senators. Ford and Melvin Laird, chairman of the House Republican caucus, wanted to position the Republicans as "the peace party" for the 1968 elections. What they were attempting was an unusually delicate political maneuver, liable to turn sour. For one thing, they did not wish to break too suddenly or obviously with Johnson because they did not want to be challenged on what alternatives they, as a party, suggested to Johnson's policies. They had no agreed-upon alternatives. For another, the maneuver, in effect, was intended to reverse Dirksen's long commitment to Johnson on the Vietnam War. They had been briefing Dirksen in advance on the public speeches they were making, if not the inner strategy they were pursuing, and they did so to try to neutralize him in their attack on President Johnson. Ford, Laird, and Senator Morton had been reading private polls, and, as one of them put it, they knew "what the people want." The people wanted an end to this stalemated war, and these Republican leaders proposed to seize the political initiative against the unpopular war. By election time, 1968, they planned to offer a Republican "solution" to the war. "We are the peace party," Laird said, and he and the others had to find a way to prove it.

In mapping this party strategy, Laird anxiously sought to avoid labeling the Democrats as the war party. "I think we should be more positive and not get into that," Laird said privately. "We're the party of peace. Positive! We don't want a negative charge. You have to spend your time defending that kind of thing. They'd accuse us of demagoguery. You don't want to be on the defensive. You want to be on the offensive."

Dirksen grumbled at these maneuvers by Ford and Laird, aware of their implications for Johnson and himself. In private he struck at them at the point where they acknowledged they were weakest. "They offer no alternative," Dirksen said. "There has to be an alternative. You don't declare a holiday in war unless both sides are willing to go to the table." Dirksen weighed his own position in this struggle and gave thought to what he should do.

By now, in September, 1967, angry speeches were being shouted in Congress in a cacophony of opposition to the war, and in private the voices were even more strident. Senator Case, normally a softspoken man, bitterly assailed Johnson for his "reckless tampering" with Congress in his dealings on the war. Senator Morton charged that the President had been "brainwashed" into making his military commitment to Vietnam. Morton acknowledged that he had supported the initial commitment. "I was wrong," he said.

Dirksen was troubled by the crumbling support for the war among his Republican colleagues, and he knew their bitterness at his continuing friendship with Lyndon Johnson. "I thought it was a good idea," Dirksen said privately, "to know the commander in chief and the President of the United States." He did not understand the trouble with his colleagues except to blame it on their reflection of the fatigue and frustration over the war at large in the country. "They're all getting 'iffy,' " he said. "I don't know what the hell's wrong with them."

Dirksen chose to reply to Morton's speech, and on October 3 he rose at his front-row desk in the Senate to speak his views of this abrasive treatment of President Johnson. "The President is not our ruler," Dirksen said, pounding his desk with his fist, "but you do not demean him in the eyes of people abroad, for when you do, you demean the prestige of this Republic." It was a historic irony, but Dirksen as the opposition leader proposed in this gathering crisis to defend the President from the members of the opposition party.

For Dirksen, his speech defending President Johnson was only a tactical skirmish in a larger strategy to defend himself within the Republican Party and to maintain his own influence on the party's decisions. In the previous summer the political admirers of Senator Percy proposed making him the "favorite-son" Presidential candidate from Illinois. Percy had ambitions for the Presidency,* and those familiar with Dirksen assumed that he would block his junior colleague even from being their state's favorite son. "Chuck has about as much chance of being the favorite son as I have of being

* In a private meeting with President Kennedy at the White House in 1962, Kennedy asked Dirksen, "What does Percy want?" "You ought to know," Dirksen replied. "I don't know," Kennedy said. "He wants to sit in that very seat that you're sitting in," Dirksen said.

the Queen of the Ziegfeld Follies," one Illinois Republican leader said. "If there's going to be a favorite son, it's going to be Dirksen." Dirksen evaded the question when pressed by reporters, and in doing so he left the appearance that he might seek the designation himself. He had, however, no such plans, and he used the speculation about it to conceal his own maneuvers. He already had figured out the roles he wanted to play at the convention, and they precluded the meaningless token honor of being designated as a favorite-son candidate for President. He wanted to be in the thick of the action at the convention, and he wanted to hold a position of power and influence there. First, he wanted to be chairman of the Illinois delegation to the convention. "That," he told an intimate, "I know I shall have." Second, he wanted to be Illinois' man on the Platform Committee, and he assumed his delegation would so designate him. Finally, he wanted to be chairman of that Platform Committee, a major officer of the convention. "That's a different dish," he said. "That's got some clout in it! When you sit at the head of the table, you've got clout!" He knew there would be major opposition to his becoming platform chairman, and he therefore maneuvered with considerable caution. He wanted no premature disclosure of his plans to jeopardize his chances for success. He approached Representative Laird, who had held the position at the 1964 convention. "I've been through it," Laird said. "I want to stay away from it." With Laird out of the running, Dirksen entered negotiations with Representative Ford. They worked out a private arrangement that Dirksen would support Ford for permanent chairman of the convention in return for Ford's support of Dirksen as platform chairman. There were others in the negotiations. They agreed, for example, that Laird would be temporary chairman of the convention. Senator Morton approved the arrangement too, and Dirksen had what he wanted, a position of great influence in drafting the Republican Party's statement of principles and commitment for the election of 1968.

When it became clear that Dirksen wanted the platform chairmanship, Republican moderates in and out of Congress took alarm.

The Republican state governors were especially upset, and they attempted to wrest the chairmanship from Dirksen. It was already too late: Dirksen had won the pledges of too many of the party's Congressional members to be denied. What troubled the Republican moderates most was Dirksen's friendship with Lyndon Johnson, presumably the 1968 Democratic nominee for President, and his support of Johnson's Vietnam policies. One Republican senator went so far as to say that if the Republican Party ever died, "Ev Dirksen will have killed it." The Republican senators were no longer amused at their leader's intimacy with the leader of the Democratic Party. "They're fed up," a Republican senator said privately. "They're fit to be tied."

Dirksen, however, would not equivocate on his friendship with Johnson. Privately, when pressed by colleagues, he snapped: "I won't do anything to embarrass the President of the United States!" Publicly he was scarcely less adamant. "I have known him," Dirksen said of Johnson, "since he was a doorkeeper on the third floor of the House. . . . All the years of acquaintanceship have ripened into friendship. Because I wear a Republican label, am I supposed to throw friendship in the rain barrel?"

On his part, President Johnson was not always given to praising Dirksen, especially in private. "Dirksen's good sometimes," Johnson told one private group, "and sometimes he's not. He will cut your guts out and leave them on the floor, and then smile as he walks away." Johnson had felt the sting of Dirksen's opposition on his domestic legislation.

Dirksen's friendship with President Johnson had cost him a large measure of his power over the Republicans in the Senate, and his maneuver to gain the party post to draft the Republican platform, including its Vietnam plank, had lost him more. Among some of the Republican senators the bitterness against Dirksen had grown so intense that there was talk that they might attempt a revolt against him to take from him the party's leadership in the Senate. Dirksen felt confident that they would not even try, for they could turn to no other leader in the Senate.

Only one Republican senator, Thurston Morton, seemed to have the appropriate political and personal credentials. For many months there had been gossip in the Senate's cloakrooms and corridors that Senator Morton was the obvious man to replace Dirksen. He had fought Dirksen on Vietnam and the party's stance on foreign policy and won. Among his colleagues he was liked and respected. Morton knew the resentments among his colleagues against Dirksen, but he also knew the nature of the job that Dirksen held. "It's a lousy job," Morton said, when approached about trying for it. "It's a drudgery job. He works like hell at it." Morton believed that there was not a senator in the party who really wanted Dirksen's job.

"I don't want it," Morton said. "I'm too lazy to do the work he does. I've told him that if he has a contest for the leadership, I'll be his campaign chairman. . . . There's no choice."

# Chapter 13

# An Uncertain Trumpet

*I've had a pretty long political career,*
*and you don't teach a fellow like me new tricks.*

Senator Morton's distaste for the punishing physical labors of the job removed any possibility that Dirksen might be challenged for the Republican floor leadership of the Senate. By his various maneuvers Morton had assumed a quasi-leadership over the younger and more progressive Republican senators, but whether he could have translated that support into a successful coup against Dirksen as party leader would never be answered. In fact, when next the Republican senators met in organizational caucus, Morton had retired from the Senate. All the Republican traditions in the Senate ran against the removal of party leaders once chosen. In the House of Representatives no such tradition existed, as demonstrated by the deposing as floor leader of Joseph Martin in 1959 and Charles Halleck in 1965. Dirksen, however, had more ways than an appeal to the party's traditions in the Senate to protect himself from intra-party attack. Whatever the sense of estrangement for him among some of his colleagues, Dirksen remained a formidable antagonist. He had the wiles and cunning of a practiced and skilled parliamentarian, the personal warmth of an instinctive politician, and the debts callable from countless favors extended to his colleagues over many years. He had no compunctions at all in simply demanding repayment for those favors, and he himself in Senate debate once described how he went about it: "Did I go to your state and campaign for you?" "Yes, you did." "Now, pay me back. Pay me back with a vote." He was a hard man to refuse when he put his pleas on such intensely personal terms. He knew the value and techniques of surprise.* He knew the importance of careful preparation and planning in any controversy. In the years he had spent in Congress he had tutored himself to the hurly-burly of legislative collisions. He had mastered the art of cut-and-thrust debate and, more significantly, the ingenious ways of persuading colleagues to his cause in the privacy of the Senate's cloakrooms. Dirksen did have increasing trouble with his party members, and a part of this trouble came from his own waning stamina for the daily contests in the Senate.

On his seventieth birthday, in 1966, Dirksen claimed he had the vigor of a man of fifty. A year later, at seventy-one, he claimed the strength of a man of forty-five. "I haven't become reconciled to the calendar," he said, "because I try to keep up with the times." The years, however, were telling on him, and he was harassed as well by constant sieges of debilitating ailments. He suffered from chronic emphysema, potentially a dangerous respiratory disease, but he ignored his doctors' warnings and smoked as many cigarettes as ever. "I'm going to have to quit one of these days," he said of his cigarette smoking. Even more dangerous to his physical safety was the condition of his heart. Sometime in the late 1950's, and without Dirksen's awareness of it, he had suffered a heart attack; his doctors discovered this on a routine cardiograph in 1959. In the years after, his heart not only grew dangerously large but also developed a leaky valve. To the end of his life he suffered chronic heart failure; his heart did not pump sufficiently to maintain his body at

---

* Dirksen, a precisionist in language, had a favorite anecdote about the word "surprise." As Dirksen told it, Noah Webster's wife caught the famed lexicographer in the kitchen kissing the maid. "Why, Noah," she said, "I'm surprised!" "Oh, no, my dear," Webster corrected her, "I'm surprised. You're astonished."

full strength. Dirksen refused to take afternoon naps as recommended by his physicians. "My doctor calls me a damn fool," he said. Repeatedly Dirksen had to undergo diuretic treatments to draw off the edema fluids that built up in his liver, lungs, and legs because of his weak heart. For extended periods he suffered from such difficulties as abdominal upsets, gastrointestinal spasms, and a bleeding ulcer. "They thought maybe tension was the reason," Dirksen said of his doctors' diagnoses of these ailments. For many months he wore an uncomfortable steel brace for his back to correct a wrenched veterbra. He became such a regular patient at Walter Reed Army Hospital in Washington that finally, for a while, he simply checked into the hospital and lived there, driving to the Senate in the morning and returning to the hospital each night. A man of great nervous energy and drive, Dirksen refused to let these illnesses interfere with his work unless absolutely necessary. Occasionally he would complain of his work load. "I've been trying for four years to get a vacation," he said in 1967. "If I don't get one pretty soon, something is going to happen to me." Yet he declined to slacken his own pace, and he refused to surrender any part of the political roles he had so hardly won. In his seventies, after a long day at the Senate, he would fly as far as St. Louis or Dallas to make a political speech and then fly back to Washington that same night. The next morning he would be at his chores in the Senate as usual, although he had not reached home until three o'clock that morning. At one time, when he was scheduled to make a nationally televised speech as the Republican leader of the Senate, he was confined to Walter Reed Army Hospital with a hemorrhaging bladder. "You've got to let me out of here," he told the doctors. He forced them to release him, and he made the speech, returning to the hospital from the television studio. In February, 1967, he was brought to the hospital suffering from "extreme fatigue." A month later he was back at the hospital, this time with "acute exhaustion." A month later, again he was back at the hospital, this time with infectious pneumonia so severe he almost died. At this period he looked like a dying man, his body wasted, his face cadaverous, and there were false reports that he had cancer. Privately he worried about his health, and he fed himself pills like a convinced hypochondriac. All the same he mocked his own debilities, and he laughed at his failing "old carcass," as he called it. Yes, he said in 1966, he would be out campaigning that fall, "if I quit falling apart so they don't have to be nailing me together." In the spring of that year, while undergoing a physical checkup at Walter Reed Hospital, he slipped from his bed and broke his right thigh bone. He had to undergo painful surgery to reset the bone, and after that, when he stayed at the hospital, the officials made sure he had a three-quarters bed instead of the single bed he had used previously. The injury forced him to cancel weeks of scheduled speaking engagements and gave him a rest he would not otherwise have had. He returned to the Senate in high spirits, brandishing his crutches, and he offered to let the photographers take pictures of his thirty-two stitches. "Like the cannibal said," Dirksen joked, "you can't keep a good man down." He did not allow the sicknesses and physical disabilities to dampen his good spirits or his zest for work. Returning from an earlier stay at the hospital, he voiced his joy at being back in the Senate. "I got copiously shot in this arm, that arm, and in the buttocks," he laughed, indicating in turn on his body the targets of the needle-wielding nurse.

The fatigue, however, did tell on him, and at the end of trying weeks he tended to become grouchy in private. He was too much the practiced politician to let this show in public. His personal secretary, Glee Gomien, one of his most trusted assistants for many years, did what she could to relieve his burdens. Mrs. Gomien ran Dirksen's leadership office in the Capitol, where he spent most of his time, and she tried to schedule his appointments in such a way that he would have some time each day to relax. The senator frequently baffled her plans, however. He was so intensely involved in his work that he would himself extend a scheduled two-minute appointment or five-minute appointment to a full half-hour. Oliver Dompierre, another trusted aide in Dirksen's office, did what he could to ease Dirksen's chores, with like results. Dirksen did give John Gomien, Mrs. Gomien's husband and his administrative assistant, a free hand in running his senatorial office in the old Senate Office Building, and a like freedom to Harold Rainville, who ran his Chicago office.

A part of Dirksen's growing difficulties within the Senate stemmed from his relations with the press. His regular Tuesday news conference in the Senate press gallery brought him continuing notoriety, but not without cost. Those news conferences he conducted with studied informality. He sat on a workaday wooden table, swept clean of the press releases, his left foot propped against a nearby chair and his right leg thrown across the table. "Who's got a cigarette?" he normally began. He would sip gingerly at the hot black coffee the press gallery staff had ready for him, and then launch into his spiel of the day. He twisted his hulking body as he talked, waved his arms, clenched his fists, grimaced, and shook his curly hair, to give the photographers a choice of a dozen poses. He stayed as long as the reporters plied him with questions, often more than an hour. And amid the stories he told and the cracked jokes, he reported on the substantive questions and quarrels of the hour. He even had a Tuesday story that he told now and then to illustrate that time was flying. "That reminds me of the fellow in the penitentiary who wrote to the governor," Dirksen said, in one version of this story. "He was to be hanged on Friday. His letter was delivered promptly: 'Dear Governor, they are fixing to hang me on Friday, and here it is Tuesday.' "

He tried to keep his news conferences on a friendly basis, and he was most charming when he mocked himself, a personal specialty in his showman's repertoire. On one such occasion he was asked the reason for a dinner scheduled in his honor. "Let me turn around and blush," he sighed, feigning embarrassment. He peeked around his hulking shoulder at the reporters. " 'The Senator of the Century,' " he said, coyly quoting how he was billed at the dinner. He turned away again in mock modesty. "I weep again," he said.

He could be engagingly candid and frank with reporters. In

changing his mind about the rent-supplement program, for example, he was blunt in telling reporters that he reversed himself because the real-estate industry now supported the plan. Asked why he had attacked President Truman during the Korean War, Dirksen tried to hide nothing in his reply. "At that time," he said of 1950, "I wasn't thinking of the Good Samaritan. At that time I was wondering where I was going to get the votes to get elected to the U.S. Senate, a quite pragmatic matter." Asked why he opposed the use of a tactical parliamentary procedure he had himself used, he answered: "I'll tell you: when I use it, it's a good device. When someone else uses it, I have to examine it on its merits." Questioned why he was moving cautiously on a controversial matter, he said, "I don't like the sidewalk to come up and hit me in the face." On another occasion Dirksen made a Senate speech extravagantly praising a colleague, and he was asked why. "Confidentially," he said, "if you want to do a little persuading on a fellow, do you hit him over the head with a baseball bat, or do you give him a piece of cake? I try to do him a favor. I was just using sweet appeal to my friend, and we understood each other perfectly." He was not always garrulous. "I had to look around and keep my mouth shut," he explained of one sudden change of affairs, "until I could find out something." He could laugh at his own abrupt reversals on pending questions. "I've often said," he joked, "that I should have been a woman; I'm so easy to persuade." Periodically he conceded his willingness to change his views. "My mind is as open as a forty-acre field," he once said, "but that doesn't mean I'm going to change it." In his normal talk he mixed biblical pieties ("One man clothed in righteousness is a match for all the host of error") with categoric pragmatisms ("In the pinches, I always have a strategy"). Whatever the pieties, however, and however much he mouthed the homilies of mid-America, he knew where he stood with men and affairs, and he could be blunt in saying where.

With some of the Washington reporters Dirksen had continually skirmished. Reporters specializing in "exposés," like Drew Pearson, the syndicated columnist, and Clark Mollenhoff of *The Des Moines*

*Register*, believed Dirksen a dishonest man in his financial affairs. They cited his association with a Peoria law firm and, by innuendo, suggested that he was receiving substantial payments for taking care of the firm's clients in their dealings in Washington. Among at least some of these reporters there was a visceral personal antagonism to Dirksen. "I get annoyed," one of these said, "at the adulation he gets for his antics." These reporters, however, did not state plainly in print what they believed privately of Dirksen's financial affairs. "If they dared, they would do it," Dirksen said privately. "Truth is an answer to libel. They haven't dared." Dirksen had his own explanation of their motives. "There are people born nasty," he said, "and they never get over it." Other correspondents believed Dirksen was an unprincipled charlatan, and they frequently jibed at him at his news conferences, asking questions that presumed his culpability or lack of principles. Dirksen normally ignored such provocations. He did occasionally jest at them. "You know what Daniel said when he went into the lion's den," he once told a news conference: " 'Whoever is going to make the after-dinner speech, it won't be me.' That's the way I am with you." Occasionally, however, his anger flared. "Why," he asked John Averell of *The Los Angeles Times*, "do you have to ask such inane, insipid, and stupid questions?" Usually, however, he controlled his anger, for to Dirksen anger was an emotion to be employed only when there was a point to be gained, and he did not want to show it with reporters. "I try to be what I am," he said once. "They think there's got to be guile. They assume mischief."

For other reporters Dirksen's weekly news conferences were useful and sometimes valuable sessions. Frequently as many as sixty reporters turned up for them. They came not so much for the amusing show Dirksen usually put on, but for the information he normally disclosed. When he chose, he could be an invaluable news source, for he not only had access to the privacies of all political Washington, including the White House, but he often did not hesitate to reveal the inmost details of the controversies of the moment. "I could keep this all to myself," he once told a news conference, and then he compared his approach to that of his predecessor as Republican leader of the Senate, William Knowland. "I could come up and do just what Bill Knowland used to do. You ask him a question, and he'd say, 'No comment.' You ask him another, and he'd give you a grunt."

Dirksen's news conferences were unique in Washington, for no other leader of Congress held such open-ended sessions with the correspondents. Senator Mike Mansfield, the Democratic leader, submitted patiently to reporters' questions when broached, but he shrank from public notoriety and he rarely volunteered information. Dirksen deliberately sought out the press, and he continued the news conferences for his own purposes, despite the occasional sniping by reporters.

Interestingly, Dirksen's very availability and his willingness to talk had a curious, subconscious effect on the reporters. They often tended to treat him as though he were actually the majority leader of the Senate, not the minority leader; as though he were in charge of the Senate's legislative agenda, a matter normally decided by the majority leader. In response to questions Dirksen frequently informed the reporters of coming Senate activities, and he did not hesitate to give his judgment ("I think that's very satisfactory progress") on the Senate's performance in meeting its legislative responsibility. At such times, he all but acted as though the Senate were *his* Senate and performing to his encouragements and instructions. The reporters discovered quickly enough that he, the Senate's Republican leader, was the best source for the thinking of the Democratic President, Lyndon Johnson. Senator Mansfield and other Democratic senators had a natural diffidence about revealing Johnson's private conversations, and frequently they did not know his real views as well as Dirksen. "I have had several discussions with the President of the United States on this matter," Dirksen told the Senate in 1967 in debate. "He would like to see this bill passed." Asked whether he had discussed the bill with the President, Mansfield replied, "No, I haven't heard from the President in this." Dirksen could not always answer every question about Johnson's thinking. "I know nearly everything," he joked at a news conference in 1967, "but not everything." "Was there something the President forgot to tell you?" one of the reporters asked. "Hush your mouth," Dirksen laughed back. That, Dirksen said, reminded him of a story. A Harvard professor was staying at a hotel, and he needed some information late at night. He went downstairs to the hotel clerk. "Have you a *Britannica*?" he asked. "No," the clerk said, "but what would you like to know?" At his news conferences the reporters sometimes questioned him as though he could answer not only for the President, but for his entire administration. Without blinking, Dirksen would do just that.

It was heady stuff for Dirksen, this capacity to sit at the President's elbow and all but make the decisions of state with him. Dirksen relished it. In the fall of 1967 the Johnson administration confronted a series of fiscal crises, and the Congressional conservatives threatened to block Johnson's bill to raise taxes unless he cut his budget. "Fowler called me up," Dirksen said, speaking of Secretary of the Treasury Henry ("Joe") Fowler. "He said, 'I want to come up and talk with you about a tax-spending package.' I said, 'Joe, I've talked to the President about that.'" Dirksen was prepared to tell the President's Secretary of the Treasury what the President really thought about the Secretary's primary field of responsibility, fiscal affairs.

In one area, that of his own finances, Dirksen declined to speak openly. With reporters and with the Senate itself Dirksen consistently took the position that his financial affairs and those of any senator were private matters. "I'm not the greatest success," he once said in an interview, "but not the greatest failure. And I'm neither rich nor poor." He refused, however, to state the amount of his outside income or the fees he received from the Peoria law firm Davis, Morgan & Witherell. "It's between fifty cents and five million," he once replied hotly when asked at a news conference about his legal fees from the firm. "That's exactly none of your business. You're prying into my personal business. . . ." Dirksen did not practice law; he was technically "of counsel" to the firm, not a partner. "Our agreement with the Senator," said Arleigh Davis, the senior partner, "prohibits him from taking part in any federal case. We pay him fairly nominal sums only in those cases to which he makes a contribution via consultations. We do not use the Senator to appear in court or prepare briefs. He is more of a consultant than anything." Dirksen described the relationship the same way. "If they have a sticky case," he said, "I might be able to advise them. They call me by telephone. If there's no federal aspect, I participate." Dirksen said he received "damn infrequently" fees that he described as "so modest that they would surprise people." The repeated charges by such journalists as Drew Pearson that he used his Washington office to help the law firm's clients in their business with the federal government, he categorically denied. "I have never talked to those companies," he said once. "I know a few of their officials, but just who the law firm has for clients I don't know."

In a real sense, the reporters seeking to expose his financial skul-duggeries, assuming his venality, missed the substance of Dirksen's ambitions. He sought power and influence, not money, and he was a rough-and-tumble player in the game of power politics, not always circumspect in the tactics he used. "It belies Everett Dirksen's ambition," Milton Viorst wrote in an article on the Senator in the October, 1966, issue of *Esquire*, "that he has behaved throughout his life as if he were indifferent not only to money but to the political wonders it often achieves. To be sure, he, like any candidate, puts the arm on political debtors at campaign time. He admits accepting a thousand or two from 'friends' when expenses pile up between campaigns. But, despite allegations, no shred of evidence has ever been produced that he is on the take from any of the industries whose interest he serves in the performance of his sena-torial duties. . . . Dirksen collects his Senate salary, an annuity from his old law firm in Peoria, and an occasional fat speaking fee. But if he's rich, he's managed to conceal it. And if he has money available to augment his power, he's not doing very much about it."

On the Senate floor Dirksen opposed all efforts to adopt rules requiring the disclosure by senators of their assets and income. The demand for such disclosures was prompted primarily by two institutional embarrassments to the Senate. The first of these was the forced resignation of Robert Baker, the secretary of the Senate's Democrats, for his financial dealings. The second was the disclosure, by Drew Pearson and his associate, Jack Anderson, of improprieties in the financial affairs of Senator Thomas Dodd of Connecticut. Baker was indicted, brought to trial, and convicted. Dodd underwent a long Senate investigation and then was censured by the Senate for the misuse of political funds contributed to him. Dirksen maintained a discreet silence throughout the Dodd investigation, and Senator Dodd and his associates had hopes that, in the end, they might receive Dirksen's support. He had been sympathetic to other politicians caught in the moils of campaign contributions. In a celebrated instance, in 1965, Dirksen had testified as a character witness for William Stratton, a Republican governor of Illinois, who was indicted for his misuse of campaign contributions. "I went out to testify," Dirksen bragged, "and I got him off the hook." With Senator Dodd, Dirksen saw the matter differently, and he voted to censure Dodd. "Do not forget that the Senate of the United States is on trial too," Dirksen said in a Senate speech. "I am proud of this institution, and . . . I want to be sure its name is not sullied and tarnished." If he voted to censure Dodd, Dirksen did not believe that the misdeeds of his colleague should be visited on all senators in the form of stringent financial controls. "I believe we have demeaned ourselves long enough," Dirksen said, "all over one fallen angel, and I think it is about time to stop." Dirksen believed that by submitting himself to the voters, a senator received a kind of endorsement of his integrity. "After all," he argued in the Senate, "does not character count for something in this body? Have we reached the point where, when we are elected by the people in an entire state, they have not had an opportunity to assess one's integrity and one's devotion to public service?" In thus opposing the adoption of a code of ethics for the Senate, Dirksen ignored the facts of the Dodd case.

Dodd had not been accused by any group of his Connecticut constituents; his integrity had been challenged and found wanting by two journalists and a select investigating committee of the Senate. Dirksen argued that requiring a senator to disclose his assets was "demeaning" to the Senate and that he himself did not become a "Class B citizen" with his election to the Senate. "The day you nail your income-tax return to the door," Dirksen told one group of badgering reporters, "I'll think about doing the same."

By his vigorous defense of his own right of privacy, and that of his fellow senators, Dirksen set himself apart from even those senators who agreed with him. On the ticklish subject of campaign funds, as well as their responsiveness to lobbyists, most senators traditionally maintained a discreet silence. Dirksen felt no such compulsion. Dodd had been brought to book for applying to his personal use funds raised at testimonials given for him. In the midst of the Dodd investigation in 1967, Dirksen blandly announced that his political allies and friends in Illinois would shortly hold a one-hundred-dollar-a-plate testimonial dinner for him. This was how he had always financed his political campaigns, and he saw no reason to change because of Dodd's embarrassment. He claimed, however, that he always scrupulously segregated these campaign funds into a separate account, preventing any commingling with his personal funds. "Keep a careful ledger," he said of campaign funds, something Dodd had not done. That way he calculated to avoid difficulties with the voters and the Internal Revenue Service. "Everybody," he said of his fellow senators, "finally is the judge of his own conduct."

Dirksen, by a perverse idiosyncrasy bred of his self-confidence and sense of humor, seemed to enjoy the impression he deliberately gave in public and among his colleagues that he was something of a political rascal. He was outspoken about his right of privacy on his finances. He openly championed the interests of private industry and business, where others of his colleagues tended to conceal such activities as much as they could. He made no secret of his defense of the drug industry when it came under investigation. When President Johnson asked Congress for an increase in postal rates, Dirksen told a group of protesting third-class-mail users in Chicago that he was a personal friend of the President and Postmaster General Lawrence O'Brien and that he would wring concessions from them. Back in Washington, curiously, Dirksen made no such demand, even though the Johnson administration would have had to grant him some concessions. Neither Johnson nor O'Brien wanted to risk Dirksen's categoric opposition to the legislation. Although he did make demands on the Johnson administration, he did not always make the demands he said he would make. At a correspondents' party given for O'Brien after Johnson named him Postmaster General, Dirksen mocked himself in the attentions he claimed he now would pay to O'Brien. "I'm going to coddle O'Brien," Dirksen said, to laughter. "I'm going to love O'Brien. I'm going to feast O'Brien. I'm going to genuflect . . . because, frankly, I need a lot of brick and mortar back in Illinois." Whenever he met O'Brien later, Dirksen went through a charade of rummaging through his pockets to find some notice of what he should ask O'Brien for in the way of new post offices for his state. He teased O'Brien with these antics. "Lawrence," he said in one such instance, "just a minute, I must have something here I have to talk with you about. I can't miss this opportunity." In a more serious vein and on the urging of industry leaders, Dirksen in 1967 personally led a drive in Congress to apply quotas on imports of steel and other commodities. In this campaign Dirksen was thwarted. Senator Morton, who opposed restricting international trade, telephoned the president of International Harvester, an important export company based in Illinois, and organized a countercampaign of business pressure on Dirksen. "He backed away from it," Morton said. "He said: 'I think we better put this over to next year.' I knew damn well what was happening." In these incidents and others, Dirksen seemed to lend credence, sometimes in jest, sometimes in earnest, to the popular cynicism about professional politicians, that he was a creature of "the interests." From this image of himself came the assumption among skeptics that he was appropriately rewarded.

In personal terms Dirksen did not live lavishly. On the contrary, he seemed indifferent to many of the material things that money could buy. He cared little for fine foods, and he ate, as he said, just "to keep alive." He did like a stiff drink of bourbon whiskey—"the usual," he called it—at the end of a working day. His clothes tended to be nondescript, although on occasion he was handsomely dressed. In 1959 he had the distinction of being named one of the ten "worst-dressed" men in the United States. The idea amused Dirksen. "They say I look like an unmade bed," he said. He had cut more than fifty pounds from his weight the year before, and he had not bothered to replenish his wardrobe. As a result, his clothes hung off him, and he actually liked the rumpled appearance that gave him. His wife finally persuaded him to buy some new clothes. "Mrs. Dirksen said it's about time I got some new suits," Dirksen said, "that I look like a bag of rags." Dirksen did sport a large diamond ring on the small finger of his right hand, but it was one of his few physical vanities. Once he became the Republican leader of the Senate, a limousine and chauffeur were provided him by the Senate. Not until his late sixties did he own his own home. On the land he and his wife bought near Leesburg, Virginia, they built a two-bedroom house that was handsome and comfortable, but hardly extravagant. Until then he had lived in Washington in hotels or apartment buildings. He did buy a vacation place in Florida with a fifteen-thousand-dollar mortgage, but his legal residence in Illinois was the home of his aged mother-in-law. His preoccupation with his legislative work all but precluded his taking part in the activities of social Washington. He spent most of his free evenings at home. "I work like a dog," he once said. His principal interest other than politics and Congress was his garden at his home near Leesburg. Whatever outside income he received, he gave no signs of spending substantial amounts of money, nor did he accumulate great wealth. When he died, his estate was worth between $150,000 and $200,000. His home in Leesburg and his vacation place in Florida were in the name of his wife. Through his career, he seemed primarily interested in the power political office offered him rather than the pelf or other spoils of personal aggrandizement.

Even as his control of the Senate appeared to be slipping, through the defections among the younger Republican senators and his own flagging energies, Dirksen's popularity in the world outside the Senate reached new heights. He received instant recognition wherever he went. So many tourists wandered into his office just off the Senate floor that he had to give orders to remove the "Mr. Dirksen" sign from the door. Invitations to speak poured into his office at the rate of from 200 to 250 a month. "It's a job sorting them out," he said. His personal popularity had reached such proportions that a year before his reelection campaign of 1968 the Democrats in Illinois all but despaired of any chance to defeat him. "He's become a sort of folk hero," said Representative Sidney Yates, who had been Dirksen's Democratic opponent in 1962. "He's more formidable now than he was in 1962." The only real chance the Democrats gave themselves depended on Dirksen's health failing to the point that he would have to retire.

He was in constant demand. A recording company, for example, persuaded him to record to music an album of patriotic readings. The result, titled *Gallant Men,* caused considerable excitement in the show-business world. The title song, with Dirksen's deeply resonant reading (*"Down through the years, there have been men, brave, gallant men . . ."*), became a popular favorite with radio disc jockeys. One critic compared Dirksen's voice in the reading to "rich plum jam" and said the "banality" of the record's scenario was "masked by Dirksen's gift for investing every word with overwhelming sincerity." *The Washington Star* editorially congratulated the record company for preserving for posterity "that great polemical voice" of Dirksen as a "part of our national heritage." "I feel it is an answer to the beatniks, draft-card burners, and those who are opposed to our efforts in Vietnam," Dirksen said. The recording was so successful that he made two more, one a collection of Bible readings for Easter and the other of Christmas hymns.

Later he published under his name a children's book of stories about American heroes. Under repeated pleas from the manager of a newspaper syndicate Dirksen in early 1968 began writing a weekly column he called "A Senator's Notebook." He did not write the book, but he took pride that he did write each week's newspaper column. Curiously, his written work had none of the flair of his spoken words. He was named Grand Marshal of the 1968 Tournament of Roses, and later that year he appeared in a mock debate at the National Press Club, where he was awarded a plaque inscribed "The High Order of the Open Mouth." He received star billing when he appeared on the television show of Red Skelton, a popular comedian. He relished his national popularity, but that popularity did not please everyone. "There he is, the fair-haired boy of the Senate," one Democrat said in 1967, "and we Democrats gave him that image!"

If the Democrats were dismayed at Dirksen's national popularity, they were even more dismayed at his political stance in the Senate against President Johnson's proposal to enact an open-housing law. Dirksen had slipped in his control within the Senate, but he still held a veto on civil-rights bills. The administration had no hope of breaking a Southern filibuster without Dirksen's active help. It was not an idle matter, for the President and the other advocates of the bill believed that its enactment would help relieve the racial tensions mounting in the nation's cities. President Johnson renewed his request for this legislation when Congress convened in January, 1968, but its prospects of passage were poor indeed. Pending before the Senate then was a stripped-down civil-rights bill that did not deal with open housing. Two of the Senate's most outspoken civil-rights advocates, Walter Mondale of Minnesota and Edward Brooke of Massachusetts, decided to offer the open-housing proposal as an amendment to that bill. Inevitably, and for weeks, the Southern senators filibustered against the entire measure, and there seemed no hope of passing the bill in the face of Dirksen's continuing hostility to it. Dirksen repeatedly stated that he would like to enact "a" civil-rights bill that year, but the proposals for open housing he would not abide. Dirksen, in effect, was applying "the Dirksen veto" on this legislation. Finally, on February 18, Senator Mansfield forced a vote on cloture on the filibuster with no hope that the Senate would approve it. Dirksen took the Senate floor to speak against Mansfield's motion. Three times in the 1960's the Senate had invoked cloture, and in each instance Dirksen had been the instrument of each success. Now, however, he equated cloture with "gagging" the Senate.

"I fervently hope, Mr. President," Dirksen addressed the chair, "that the Senate will not gag itself. I do not want to go home and say, 'I gagged myself by my vote.' What a confession of weakness that would be. . . ."

Mansfield's motion failed, 55 to 37, not the two-thirds margin needed. Senator Philip Hart of Michigan, the Democratic floor manager of the bill, could not conceal his despair over the bill. President Johnson had sent Hart a letter to read to the Senate— "The issue is whether we will continue to move toward equality as a fact, as well as an ideal, in America"—but the letter had no effect on the Senate. Johnson had not bothered to try to persuade Dirksen. "We're at our maximum," Hart said. "We need about a half-dozen Republicans." Hart had no expectation of persuading them.

On the cloture vote, the Republicans had divided equally, eighteen for it, eighteen against. Those for it were the traditional party liberals like Jacob Javits of New York and Thomas Kuchel of California and the younger, progressive senators led by Senator Morton. Those opposed were the senior conservatives and most of the Midwesterners. Senator Baker, whom Dirksen described as "not kin to me but he does have a legal relation to the family," voted with his father-in-law against cloture. Baker, however, was not opposed to all federal action on open housing. Like the other new senators, Hatfield of Oregon, Percy of Illinois, and Griffin of Michigan, he was concerned about the modern image of the Republican Party. Dirksen, indeed, was receiving from these senators many private pleas that he change his mind, that he consider the damage he was doing the party in this election year. Dirksen himself was up for reelection, but he had not been impressed favorably by the treatment he had received six years before by the Negro leaders in Chicago and the Negro voters. Baker, privately, was urging Dirksen to seek some compromise. Dirksen had worries of his own. He had been assured the chairmanship of his party's Platform Committee, and he was giving thought to the political campaign ahead. Predictions were everywhere that in the summer ahead racial riots would again break out in the Negro ghettos of the nation's cities. Although the passage of no legislation would likely stay the violence, it took little imagination to forecast how Dirksen and his party could be blamed for it if he blocked this bill.

The day after his unsuccessful cloture motion, February 21, Mansfield moved to kill the Mondale-Brooke amendment for open housing. It was a test vote to assay the sense of the Senate, but Mansfield also could not let the Senate's legislative agenda be stalled indefinitely by the continuing filibuster. The Senate voted 58 to 34 against Mansfield's motion. This was a considerably larger margin in favor of open housing than even the civil-rights advocates had dared expect. Dirksen, of course, took note of it, as he had noted that the Senate's Republicans had exactly divided on the question of cloture. The figures suggested room for Dirksen to maneuver. Later that same afternoon, at his own invitation, Attorney General Ramsey Clark called on Dirksen at his office in the Capitol. Clark was startled by what Dirksen said to him. In his earlier sessions with Dirksen there had been no signs that the Senator might change his position on open housing. "Well, Ramsey," Dirksen greeted him, "it's right here before me." Dirksen gestured toward a stack of civil-rights materials on his desk. "I'm trying to plow through on some compromise that will be fair to you and everybody else." There was no mistaking Dirksen. He no longer opposed open-housing legislation under all conditions. He was seeking a compromise. The implications of that, politically and legislatively, were staggering, and Clark knew it. Dirksen began to detail his terms to the Attorney General, the spokesman in the field for the Johnson administration. "It depends," Dirksen said, "on how all-inclusive you make it, on what you excluded. For instance, if it did not apply to an individual. I have a house, and you want to buy it, and I don't want to sell it to you. That's one situation. When it's handled with brokers and agents—they operate under a license of the state. It's a different picture." Dirksen did more than indicate he would support such a compromise. He also pledged he would try to persuade his Senate colleagues to go along with him. That was crucial, for more than Dirksen's vote was needed.

"This is in the lap of the gods," Dirksen said, "until we can get some kind of an understanding. I know where the bodies are buried. If we can get a specific package, I can then say: 'All right, we have a salable piece of property, and you ought to take it.' "

That Dirksen had changed position, that he was now willing to negotiate, was a closely guarded secret. Those few civil-rights senators who were informed agreed among themselves to say nothing about his change to anyone outside their immediate group. They feared that premature publication might jar Dirksen from his new course. Thus it was that two days after Clark's interview with Dirksen, Vice-President Hubert Humphrey telephoned Dirksen. He had not heard about Dirksen's altered position, and he called Dirksen to urge him to change. Humphrey told Dirksen that he was nearing the end of his public life, that he should consider his place in history, and that he should regard passage of this legislation a capstone to a great career. Dirksen let Humphrey talk on, not indicating that he had already changed. Rather he let Humphrey persuade him all over again, and Humphrey afterward excitedly told friends that he believed he had convinced Dirksen. This was not merely Dirksen's wry sense of humor at work. After all, Humphrey was the presiding officer of the Senate and thus in a position to repay Dirksen later on with a variety of courtesies of his own.

Meanwhile, Dirksen met almost constantly in private with senators interested in this legislation. He broached the subject himself with his son-in-law, Senator Baker. He asked Baker for suggestions on how the legislation might be modified in such a way that he could support it.

"I have some ideas," Baker said.

"Do you have them on paper?" Dirksen asked.

"No," Baker said, "but I can get them on paper."

Baker went right to work, and the draft he produced became the working model of the bill that was eventually fashioned. Not until February 26 did Dirksen announce publicly his changed position, and then he treated his shift with equanimity. "One would be a strange creature indeed in this world of mutation," he said, "if in the face of reality he did not change his mind."

Until then the civil-rights bill had appeared moribund, and Dirksen's announcement astonished political Washington. The two principal candidates for the Republican Presidential nomination, Richard Nixon and Governor Nelson Rockefeller of New York, each telephoned Dirksen to be briefed on what he was doing. "I think," Dirksen told a crowded news conference, "that we have a very substantial area of agreement. That's why I say to you, there will be a bill." For another two days the negotiations went on, with Senator Baker playing the central role of finding legislative language his father-in-law would accept. There was a sense among the bill's advocates of divine intervention on behalf of their flagging cause. "It's a miracle," Senator Mondale said of Dirksen's conversion. Clarence Mitchell, the chief lobbyist for the NAACP, could hardly restrain his tears. "In these things," he said, "when you put in it as much as we do, there just has to be a force greater than any of us. I'm not ashamed to say I did some praying myself." At the White House and within the Johnson administration, a different view of Dirksen's decision was taken. "Dirksen," said Larry O'Brien, remembering the predictions for race riots, "is just taking a little insurance for this summer." Dirksen explained himself similarly, if not so cynically. "I was looking down the road," he said, "and at the impact of this on the party. I was thinking of the party's future."

On February 28 Dirksen formally introduced "the Dirksen substitute" for the open-housing bill, a patchwork of old bills, odd amendments, and new language pasted together at the negotiating sessions. "I do not apologize for my conduct," he said. He told the Senate that the country had changed since his opposition to open housing in 1966, and he repeated again his now familiar argument that the only persons who did not change their minds were in insane asylums or cemeteries. Under questioning by reporters, Dirksen denied that he had been prompted by any fear that his position as party floor leader might be in jeopardy if he did not yield in this to the party progressives. A week before, Dirksen had stated that any senator voting to cut off the Senate's debate voted to "gag" the Senate. Now he himself offered a motion for cloture. He had made a complete about-face, and now, as he said, he would go "begging and crawling" to the party's conservatives to persuade them to vote for cloture.

Dirksen's reversal brought the instant assumption that the Senate would immediately approve the compromise bill he sponsored. All that was needed was for Dirksen to speak to his hitherto reluctant colleagues. "They are his buddies," one Senate intimate explained of the conservative Republicans, "and they go along with him. He's the leader. They go with him because he's the leader." That was how it had been on the civil-rights bills of 1964 and 1965. Now, however, Dirksen found resistance to his overtures to these senators. He spent an hour trying, unsuccessfully, to persuade Clifford Hansen of Wyoming. He talked at length with Karl Mundt of South Dakota, and Mundt hedged. He called on Jack Miller of Iowa, who insisted that he would have to consult with his senior colleague, Bourke Hickenlooper. Hickenlooper proved adamant, and both the Iowa senators were thus lost to Dirksen. His friend Wallace Bennett of Utah refused Dirksen as well, but the most grievous shock to Dirksen came from Roman Hruska of Nebraska, his closest friend in the Senate. Hruska had participated in the drafting of the new bill, and Dirksen had assumed his support. "Will you give me a vote?" Dirksen asked him, almost belatedly. Hruska shook his head. "No," he said. "But, Roman," Dirksen said, "if I have to have your vote?" "I can't," Hruska told him. The conservative senators were angry and annoyed at Dirksen. They had made commitments against the bill; politically they could not reverse themselves as abruptly as Dirksen now demanded. Plainly Dirksen had overestimated his influence with the very senators who were his principal supporters as party leader.

Despite his difficulties, Dirksen did not think he could be defeated. Norris Cotton of New Hampshire had changed; so had Len Jordan of Idaho. Senator Baker was openly working for cloture. Dirksen called on George Murphy of California. "I want your vote," he said, "and I need your vote." Murphy demurred at first. "Will you pray over it, George?" Dirksen pleaded. "And I'll pray over you." Dirksen left with what he regarded as a commitment from Murphy. Dirksen had an agonizing session with Frank Carlson of Kansas. Carlson was reluctant. He finally agreed to vote for cloture if his vote made the difference between approving or disapproving Dirksen's motion. With Carlson's pledge, Dirksen had precisely enough commitments to carry his motion. He had not calculated, however, the counterassault of the real-estate lobby, whose agents signaled their far-flung membership to telegraph a blizzard of protests on the Senate. Such telegrams as this arrived at senators' offices: "Dirksen-administration forced housing bill ludicrous. Stand firm in opposition." Senator Murphy slipped away from Dirksen. "Somebody fingered the poor bastard," a senator said. Dirksen had other problems. His previous allies among the Southern senators were furious at him. In private talks they called him "turncoat." Moreover, the administration Democrats overestimated Dirksen's capacity to deliver the Republican senators. Two Western Democrats, Frank Church of Idaho and Gale McGee of Wyoming, were in their home states and did not bother to return to Washington for the vote. The Senate on March 1 voted for the motion 59 to 35, not two-thirds.

Dirksen had been defeated, but neither he nor the other advocates of open housing were willing to quit. Senator Mansfield moved to force still another vote on cloture three days later. Dirksen went back to Senator Mundt and almost persuaded him. Carlson wanted to renege on his commitment, and Dirksen heard about it. "Frank, I need you," he pleaded. Carlson agreed again to vote for cloture if his vote made the difference. Miller told Dirksen that he would vote for cloture if Dirksen would pledge his support to an amendment Miller wanted to add to the bill. Dirksen could not agree, for he feared Miller's amendment would cost him the votes of other senators. "Jack, I can't do it," Dirksen told him. "What you'll do is unhinge the bill. I can't give you that commitment." Up to the hour of voting, the negotiations went on for the votes of Miller and Mundt. Meanwhile, the Democratic leadership canvassed their own ranks. Church and McGee were summoned back to Washington. Bob Bartlett of Alaska agreed, like Carlson, to vote for cloture if his vote made the difference. Howard Cannon of Nevada bargained for a weakening amendment to the bill as the price of his vote. The President's liaison man with the Senate, Michael Manatos, approached Cannon. "Would you like a call from the President?" he asked. "That won't be necessary," Cannon replied. He had received the commitment he wanted. Mundt finally agreed to vote for cloture, but even as the clerk of the Senate started to read the names of the senators on the roll-call vote Mundt changed his mind. Senator Brooke of Massachusetts went to look for him in the cloakroom and met Miller of Iowa. Miller, at that late moment, offered to vote for cloture if only Brooke would pledge his support for Miller's amendment. Brooke agreed and swiftly informed Dirksen. It was a tense moment. Dirksen walked back to Senator Carlson and signaled him that his vote was needed. Carlson voted "aye." Bartlett had been hiding in the Democratic cloakroom, and he hurried out at the last moment to confer with Mansfield in whispers. He voted "aye," and cloture was imposed by the barest margin, 65 to 32.

Dirksen had succeeded, but his success had been less than the personal triumph expected. When he had reversed himself on open housing there had been a general presumption that he would be able to deliver the votes of not less than thirty of his thirty-five

Republican colleagues, enough to assure cloture. On the first cloture vote on his bill, only twenty-one Republican senators voted with him. On the second, there were only twenty-three Republicans with him. They had provided the needed votes, but clearly Dirksen no longer had the command of the Senate Republicans that he had demonstrated in the past. His colleagues were displeased with his unquestioning support of President Johnson's Vietnam policies. The younger, progressive senators had balked at his leadership on such other questions as the consular treaty and import quotas. Now the older, conservative senators shrank away from his leadership too, refusing to follow where he directed on civil rights. He had worked without letup to persuade them, and the strain told on him. For years he had cadged what cigarettes he smoked from his colleagues and friends, but under the tension of this struggle he resumed carrying his own cigarettes in his pocket. The open-housing bill could not have been approved without him, and he had dictated the terms of its legislative substance. He could take satisfaction in that, but he had only narrowly averted defeat.

Even as Dirksen was trying to muster votes for cloture on his version of the open-housing bill, he received a prize from his party that he had sought and won. In February he was formally designated chairman of the Republican Platform Committee. The party's delegates would not convene in Miami Beach, Florida, until July, and in the meantime the nation was shaken by a series of convulsive shocks in national politics. On March 31 President Johnson announced that he would not seek reelection. "I could hardly believe it," Dirksen said, although Johnson had many times hinted to him that he might do precisely that. Dirksen's sympathies were with Johnson now as they had been all along, and he felt Johnson so acted because he could no longer tolerate the bitter invective he had so long endured as President. "How long do you take it?" Dirksen asked rhetorically. "After all, the President of the United States is a human being. You may laugh at this, and I don't give a damn, but Lyndon B. Johnson is one of the most sensitive men I ever knew." For Dirksen, the departure of President Johnson from office was of significant personal consequence. Not only did Johnson's retirement lessen Dirksen's compulsion to defend Johnson's policies, a matter of importance to him as Platform Committee chairman, but it would require him to reshape his own political stance within the Senate to accommodate the new reality of another President-to-be.

There were other shocks of this spring that forced on Dirksen other changes. None was more dramatic and terrible than the murders of Martin Luther King, Jr., the Negro leader, on April 4, and then of Senator Robert Kennedy of New York as he campaigned for the Presidency, on June 5. Dirksen had been an active defender of the gun lobby's opposition to federal controls on firearms. "Don't call it trickery," Dirksen laughed at one successful maneuver he had executed against a stringent gun-control bill; "call it parliamentary skill." The murders, however, caused a national horror at the rampant violence in the country, and Dirksen was among the many in Congress who quickly took a more somber view of the unrestricted sales of pistols, rifles, and shotguns. Dirksen announced that he now supported strong federal law restricting the sale of long guns as well as pistols. "If there is a demand for it," he said, "why should I resist it?" Dirksen, in fact, was willing to go far beyond the pending legislation. He was willing not only to require the registration of all guns, but also to consider licenses for those who possessed guns. "You have to admit," Dirksen said, "that a gun is a lethal weapon." He wanted the state governments given the chance to solve the problem before a federal solution was imposed. "I don't think anybody kicks about registering his gun," he said.

As his party's platform chairman, Dirksen knew well in advance what he intended to accomplish at the party's national convention. Publicly he stated that he wanted a platform that would be "brief, pungent, and in language the nation's voters can quickly understand." He wanted the platform acceptable to the party's Presidential candidate, whoever he was, and to be, as he called it, "the highway to victory." Dirksen privately had no naïve illusions that any party platform received more than a casual glance from the Presidential nominee or from the public at large. He had seen the divisiveness that the party platform caused at the 1964 convention, and he knew that if the platform could not greatly benefit the party in electioneering terms, it could damage the party's cohesiveness and unity. In personal terms, he had sought the chairmanship as a way of playing a substantive role at the 1968 national convention, but in party terms he had sought the post to help blunt the party's inner antagonisms. Dirksen wanted to draft a platform that would quiet the inherent controversies between the liberal and conservative wings of the Republican Party, and he maneuvered to accomplish just that. "We know," he said privately, "that you can't have divisiveness in the party and have a unified, hard-hitting army with which to go to the people." He arranged that the committee's subcommittee chairmen brought an ideological and geographic balance to the platform leadership. He consulted privately with the three leading candidates for the party's nomination, former Vice-President Richard Nixon, Governor Rockefeller of New York, and Governor Ronald Reagan of California. He had carefully avoided supporting any of them prior to the convention, and in private he told them that he wanted their help in creating a unifed party. His idea, he told each of them, was to produce a platform on which each of them could stand. "He was very persuasive," one of his confidants said. Rockefeller instructed his political lieutenants to avoid controversy on the platform. Nixon did the same. "It would be rather presumptuous of me," Reagan said, "to offer specific planks."

Before arriving at Miami Beach, Dirksen prepared a draft of the platform. "I could do it on my portable," he joked, and the word spread through the 106-member committee that Dirksen was writing the platform himself. "My goddamn waggish tongue wouldn't stop wagging," he said. "Then the hellfire started. After that I behaved myself." In reality, Dirksen had used four talented writers and lawyers to shape the platform draft, and he was not committed to the thirty-five-hundred-word document he and they had fashioned. At the committee's meetings, the platform grew to eight thousand words, and finally to almost twelve thousand words. It was neither brief nor pungent, but it did escape the bitter controversies. Dirksen yielded time and time again to amendments offered by the committee members. By so doing he blunted the ideological quarrels within the party, even on Vietnam. The original Dirksen draft offended those on the committee who wanted less than a full commitment to President Johnson's war policies, and Dirksen went so far to mollify them that he himself offered the amendment they drafted as a substitute. Only once did Dirksen come under open assault, and that was on a procedural question, not a matter of substance. Dirksen tried to speed up the committee's work, anxious to meet the necessary convention deadline, and Silvio Conte of Massachusetts, a fiery Congressman, objected. Both men were fatigued by the lateness of the hour. Dirksen upbraided Conte for his "stupidity," as he called it, and Conte retorted that Dirksen was "the worst chairman" the Platform Committee had ever had. The next morning they exchanged apologies.

Dirksen produced a platform that was unanimously endorsed by the Platform Committee. Belatedly, Governor George Romney of Michigan demanded the inclusion of an amendment dealing with labor unions and their elected leaders. Dirksen, more than accommodating, reconvened the Platform Committee for Romney, but Romney had great difficulty trying to fashion in words what he wanted his amendment to say. Dirksen had no objections to its inclusion; that fit his overall strategy of obviating controversy by accepting amendments to the platform. He became annoyed, however, when it became patent that Romney, still hopeful for a place on the party's national ticket, really wanted to use his proposed amendment as a means to address the party convention. "If there is any individual," Dirksen said angrily of Romney, "who is so anxious for public attention that he will disregard the unanimous action of this committee and take his action to the floor, let him do it." In the end Romney agreed not to offer his amendment in return for five minutes to address the convention.

Presenting the platform to the convention proper, Dirksen faced a vast crowd that had shown but little interest in the previous orators. Dirksen, a student of audiences, did not propose to be ignored. He tried his normal tactic of standing mute at the rostrum, attempting thus to silence the crowded floor. Finally he roared into the loudspeaker system: "Quiet!" He won a burst of applause and then silence. "I accept the nomination!" he shouted, to laughter. Then, still jesting, he threw from the rostrum a thick volume he claimed was the party platform, to renewed laughter. Finally he read his speech. *The New York Times* had sent another drama critic, Clive Barnes, to this convention, and he treated Dirksen less kindly than did his predecessor at the 1964 convention. "He would be a cornball actor, I suspect," Barnes wrote of Dirksen, "even in cornball roles."

A full month before the Republican National Convention, Dirksen had made a decision in private conversation with President Johnson that he shortly came to regret. Earl Warren had submitted his resignation as Chief Justice of the United States Supreme Court to the President. Before Johnson could appoint a successor, Robert Griffin of Michigan and a group of other Republican senators, including Senator Baker, resolved to block any such nomination. They circulated among their Republican colleagues a round-robin statement declaring that the new Chief Justice should be selected by the President taking office in January, 1969. By the time Johnson nominated Associate Justice Abe Fortas for Chief Justice on June 26, nineteen Republican senators had signed the formal statement. Before submitting the nomination, President Johnson repeatedly had consulted Senator Dirksen. This was normal procedure, for Dirksen not only was Johnson's personal friend and the leader of the Republican Party in the Senate, but he was also the ranking Republican on the Senate's Judiciary Committee. Dirksen would necessarily play an important role in the Senate's confirmation of anyone Johnson appointed to the high office. Johnson telephoned Dirksen shortly after he received Warren's letter of resignation and asked Dirksen to come to the White House. Johnson wanted to talk over whom to appoint.

"You got any suggestions?" he asked Dirksen.

"You ought to have suggestions," Dirksen replied.

The President asked Dirksen what he thought of Cyrus Vance, then one of the American negotiators at the Vietnam peace talks in Paris, for the post of Chief Justice.

"A top-flight fellow," Dirksen said.

Johnson worried at the possible diplomatic repercussions of naming Vance to the post. It might be interpreted as a token that the Americans were discouraged about the Paris negotiations. He asked Dirksen about Secretary of the Treasury Henry Fowler for the post.

"Hell," Dirksen said to the President, "you owe Fowler."

Secretary Fowler had been working tirelessly to resolve the administration's fiscal crises, and Dirksen believed the Chief Justice-ship would be an appropriate reward. President Johnson, however, feared that Fowler could not be spared from the important work he had undertaken in the fiscal field.

Dirksen, on his part, suggested for the post William Campbell, a federal judge who as senior district judge in Chicago had admin-istrative responsibilities not dissimilar to those of the Chief Justice. Only toward the end of the hour-and-one-half talk did President Johnson suggest the name of Associate Justice Fortas. Dirksen, a friend of Fortas through Johnson, readily agreed. He pointed out to the President that since Fortas already served on the Supreme Court his confirmation would be easier than the others. "It mini-mized the chores all around," Dirksen said.

In 1965, when Johnson had first appointed Fortas to the Supreme Court, the Senate had routinely confirmed the nomination. Dirksen dismissed the maneuvers by Griffin and the other Republi-can senators. "There will be a little ruckus," he said. Dirksen had no doubt about the Senate's coming judgment on Fortas. "He'll be confirmed, period," Dirksen said.

Griffin, a political activist, intended more than a protest against Johnson's choice of a Chief Justice: he planned to defeat the nomination. From the start Griffin talked privately of conducting "extended discussions" in the Senate against the nomination, the traditional euphemism used by senators when they mean to filibuster. With but routine support from those Democratic senators who traditionally opposed cloture, Griffin had enough commitments from Republican senators to conduct a successful filibuster. Justice Fortas himself inadvertently helped Griffin's campaign, for he miscalculated in agreeing to testify before the Senate's Judiciary Committee. There, under questioning, Fortas acknowledged that he had acted as an adviser to President Johnson while a member of the Supreme Court. Even more damaging to Fortas, the committee testimony disclosed that Fortas had given a series of seminars at the American University for which he was paid fifteen thousand dollars solicited from five prominent businessmen.

Early in the struggle Dirksen described Griffin's attack on President Johnson for naming Fortas as "improper and offensive," but the Griffin campaign had a telling effect on the Senate. In the first week in July, Griffin's "hard count" of the Senate showed twenty-two senators ready to vote against cloture on a filibuster against the Fortas nomination, with an additional seventeen senators "leaning" to that position. By mid-September Griffin's hard count showed forty-one senators opposed to cloture and another four tending that way. Griffin had thus in effect already defeated the Fortas nomination.

By early September Dirksen knew that Griffin and the other Republicans had far more strength than he had earlier anticipated. The prospects for approving Fortas, Dirksen said on September 5, were "not roseate." He could see that the expected filibuster could not be stopped. For himself, Dirksen said, he regarded voting for cloture as "a duty." Dirksen by now had to have regrets that he had not checked more carefully with his Republican colleagues before committing himself so totally to President Johnson on the nomination of Fortas. On his hard-count tally of the Senate, Griffin had the names of twenty-four Republican senators supporting him against the Fortas nomination, with four other Republican senators not decided finally. On this issue Griffin had taken most of the Republican senators away from Dirksen, not an insignificant thing for a party leader on so great a question. Dirksen had already retreated somewhat from his first support of the nomination by stating he would vote for cloture and the nomination, if it came to a vote; he plainly indicated that he would not himself try to persuade others to take that course. When the Judiciary Committee approved the Fortas nomination on September 17, Dirksen voted "aye." However, he was already considering reversing course. In submitting his resignation, Chief Justice Warren stated that he would remain on the Supreme Court until his successor was approved. Dirksen now considered proposing a Senate resolution declaring that since Warren remained on the court there actually was no vacancy to fill. On September 27, two days after Griffin began the formal filibuster against the nomination, Dirksen publicly stated that he was "neutral" in the struggle. Actually he had abandoned Fortas and was seeking a way to escape from his earlier commitment to Fortas as gracefully as he could. He invited Griffin to his office and there proposed the no-vacancy resolution to him. Griffin, with his victory as good as won, was wary. In the end he decided against accepting Dirksen's ploy to obviate a direct vote on the nomination itself. The Democratic senators supporting Fortas knew about Dirksen's maneuvers. "Hell," one of them said privately, "Dirksen is not a reliable ally in any fight. He can turn himself around, and no one can ever lay a glove on him." Frustrated by Griffin's unwillingness to join his stratagem of the no-vacancy resolution, Dirksen decided he had no choice but to join Griffin's group against Fortas. He announced that he would vote against cloture. Obviously embarrassed as he confronted reporters, an extraordinary circumstance for Dirksen, he groped for reasons to justify his decision. This was not really a filibuster, he argued; the Senate had scarcely debated the nomination twenty-five hours in all. He said also that a recent adverse decision by the Supreme Court on an Illinois case had just been called to his attention. Because of it, he said, he would have to oppose the Fortas nomination. Dirksen's flimsy attempts to rationalize his change did not persuade his listeners. They were convinced he acted solely to detach himself from a losing cause.

The miscalculation by Dirksen on the Fortas nomination damaged anew his standing in the Senate as the Republican floor leader. Again he had been driven to reverse himself by activist Republican senators presumably under his leadership. No one in the party was prepared to challenge him for the party leadership, but Dirksen knew as well as any of his colleagues the politician's adage that no one ever won by losing. His immense power in the Senate was eroding, slipping away under these repeated challenges by the new generation of senators. He himself was up for reelection, but he did not worry unduly about that. The Democrats in Illinois had nominated a relatively unknown candidate to run against him.

In the final days of the 1968 session of Congress Dirksen made one bold move to try to recoup somewhat his influence as Republican leader. Pending before the Senate was a bill to permit television debates between the Republican and Democratic Presidential nominees, Richard Nixon and Hubert Humphrey. Nixon had lost the 1960 Presidential election to John Kennedy in their televised debates; he had no desire to repeat the experience with Humphrey. Responding to his wish, the Republicans in the House of Representatives had tried, unsuccessfully, to block the bill. Humphrey himself came to the House to lobby for it. In the Senate Dirksen resolved to defeat the bill at any cost. He announced that he would use "every weapon at the command of the minority leader" to prevent a vote on the bill. He mocked the Democrats in their anxiety to pass the bill and cruelly reminded them that they had defeated a similar bill four years earlier, in 1964, when President Johnson did not wish to debate Senator Goldwater, then the Republican Presidential nominee. "If it was fish then, it ought to be fish now," Dirksen taunted. "And if it was fowl then, it ought to be fowl now."

Dirksen demanded the presence of a quorum of the Senate, without which technically the Senate could not legally function. He had, however, already instructed the doorkeepers and pageboys to inform all Republican senators approaching the Senate chamber not to enter. Thus they could not be counted as part of the quorum. This was October 10, and many senators were absent campaigning for reelection. Senator Mansfield, the majority leader, tried to produce a quorum anyway, but he found himself stymied by Dirksen's tactics. Dirksen had Mansfield and the majority Democrats neatly trapped: if they did not surrender the debate bill, he would not permit the Senate to function at all. "After some conversation with the distinguished minority leader," Mansfield said at last, "it appears to be in the best interests of all concerned that the pending legislation be set aside." Mansfield had had to yield to Dirksen's threat. For Dirksen this was a parliamentary victory, but of small recompense for his embarrassment on the Fortas nomination. All the same it was a token demonstration that he still was a force to be reckoned with in the Senate, that he knew the rules and dared to use them for his political purposes.

If he had endeared himself to his Republican partisans by defeating the TV-debate bill, Dirksen had not halted the erosion of his power and influence in the Senate and political Washington. His failing health, his flagging authority over his Republican senators, and such miscalculations as he had made on the open-housing bill and the Fortas nomination, all of these tended to weaken his position. The retirement of Lyndon Johnson as President, however, deprived Dirksen of his most unique influence of all, and he returned to Illinois to seek reelection to the Senate, knowing that if he won, as expected, he would have to make terms with a new administration in Washington operating under new management.

# Chapter 14

# A Different Mandate

*Don't you know me well enough to know I never
close any doors? There are no absolutes in this world.*

In Illinois the Democratic hierarchy had difficulty selecting an
appropriate candidate to run against Senator Dirksen in 1968. The
process was complicated by the Vietnam War, the dictatorial
powers over the state party of Mayor Richard E. Daley of Chicago,
and the doubts whether President Johnson really wanted Dirksen
defeated. The state's two most prominent Democrats eligible for
the Senate seemed to be Sargent Shriver,* the American ambassador to France, and Adlai E. Stevenson, III, the Illinois state
treasurer. Shriver had married President Kennedy's sister, and he
had served with distinction as the administrator of the Peace Corps.
Stevenson, son of the late Democratic candidate for President,
evoked a similar nostalgic popularity with Democrats as did Shriver.
Neither Shriver nor Stevenson, however, had any great desire to
run against Dirksen. In preliminary negotiations within the Demo-

---

* When Shriver was first mentioned as his possible opponent, Dirksen deftly
evaded commenting about him by saying his relationship with Shriver reminded
him of a story. A man came home to find his wife sitting outside their house
on a log with a stranger. "Sally," the husband said, "tell that man to get his
arm from around your waist." "You tell him," Sally said; "he's a stranger to me."

cratic Party, each indicated that he preferred to run for governor of Illinois, a presumably easier office to win than Dirksen's seat in the Senate. Both men, however, were vetoed by Mayor Daley as candidates for either job, for Daley resented their opposition to President Johnson's policies in Vietnam. To run against Dirksen, Daley and his political henchmen chose the state's attorney general, William G. Clark, a Democratic politician little known even in Illinois. On its face, the selection of Clark smacked of a deliberate attempt by the Democratic-party bosses in Illinois to let Dirksen win reelection to his fourth term in the Senate without undue difficulty.

There were widespread reports that President Johnson had intervened and that Mayor Daley, an admirer of Johnson, had chosen this unlikely opponent for Dirksen as a result. "There have been rumors," *The New York Times* said editorially, "that the President would just as soon see the senator reelected in light of the support he has given the administration as the Republican leader." Clark himself, in his campaign, accused President Johnson of making a "deal" with his "crony" Dirksen in return for Dirksen's support of the President's nomination of Abe Fortas as Chief Justice. Six months earlier there had been charges, equally untrue, that Johnson had made a similar deal with Dirksen in return for Dirksen's support of the fair-housing legislation. Mayor Daley, however, needed no such prompting from President Johnson to reject Shriver and Stevenson. An Irish-Catholic machine politician with a strong anticommunist disposition, Daley supported the war in Vietnam totally. He would not willingly tolerate an antiwar Democratic candidate for the Senate. Ironically, the candidate he chose, Attorney General Clark, who had been equivocal about Vietnam when Daley questioned him, proved to be even more outspoken against the war than either Shriver or Stevenson. Clark campaigned against Dirksen with the charge that the Senator was "a super hawk" completely supporting the war. Daley, embittered, denied Clark the usual financial support that the Chicago Democratic machine normally provided its statewide party candidates. Similarly, the AFL-CIO's

Committee on Political Education also curtailed the traditional campaign contributions this group usually gave Democratic candidates. Newspaper columnists Rowland Evans and Robert Novak reported that the sudden turn of affairs amounted to "a conspiracy" against Clark engineered by President Johnson, Mayor Daley, and organized labor. The obvious effect was to make more certain Dirksen's reelection.

In the campaign, Clark in effect blamed Dirksen for responsibility for the Vietnam War. He also accused Dirksen of misusing his Congressional franking privilege, and he condemned his voting record on domestic issues. "Dirksen talks in great rolling rhetoric about the *public* interest," Clark said, "but he votes with the *corporate* interests. . . ." Clark conceded, however, that he had been hurt by the rumors that President Johnson favored Dirksen. Clark had substantial support for his candidacy, including a letter of endorsement from Senator Edward Kennedy, the last of the Kennedy brothers. *The Chicago Sun-Times* wrote approvingly of Clark's "political prescience" on the Vietnam War. *The Chicago Daily News* saluted Clark for his courage in defying Mayor Daley and heaped abuse on Dirksen. "If he has political principles," the newspaper editorialized about Dirksen, "they are invisible to the researcher's eye." Ironically, *The Daily News* had planned to endorse Dirksen for reelection, but in a private interview with the newspaper's managers Dirksen had so offended them by his obstreperous statements and imperious claims that they resolved to support Clark instead. *The New York Times*, which occasionally had praised Dirksen in the past, denounced him in a savage editorial. "The tone of the Senate would be vastly improved by the repudiation of Senator Everett Dirksen by the voters of Illinois," *The Times* stated. "Through methods more proper to the entertainment industry than to serious civic life, Mr. Dirksen has become a kind of burlesque senator, parodying his own excesses. But his political behavior is no laughing matter. He remains a cynical opportunist and a servant of the drug industry, the steel industry, and other special interests."

Such verbal venom as distilled by *The New York Times* against Dirksen had little effect on Illinois voters, but he resented the abuse he received from the Chicago newspapers. Even so, he did not campaign with the vigor of a nervous candidate. He remained in Washington at his post at the Senate until Congress adjourned for the year in mid-October. With his Democratic opponent politically crippled by the defections of Mayor Daley and organized labor, Dirksen had little to fear. The political polls showed him far ahead of Clark. On election night, however, Clark polled far more votes against Dirksen than expected. Dirksen had been presumed an easy winner. At ten o'clock that night, Clark had a lead, from the early returns of the cities, of more than a half-million votes over Dirksen. At that hour, Dirksen appeared on television and somewhat nervously joked about his plight. He told the television interviewer that his situation reminded him of "the Irishman who fell off the fourteen-story building. When he went by the tenth floor, his friend Pat stuck his head out and said, 'Mike, so far you're all right!' " Dirksen won the election, 2,181,218 votes against 1,936,484 votes for Clark. He received fifty-three percent of the vote instead of the sixty-two percent the polls had predicted. He had won, but by a far smaller margin than he expected.

On that same election day, Richard Nixon was elected President, and Dirksen knew that he had a doubly difficult problem when he returned to the Senate in 1969. Not only did he confront a new administration, but one directed by his own Republican Party. The election had radically altered the political realities of Senator Dirksen's public life. For the previous eight years Dirksen had flourished in the Senate and Congress as the preeminent Republican in national politics primarily because the national administration was operated by Democrats. In those years he had grown to enormous political power and personal prominence. Across the whole course of national affairs, domestic and foreign, he had often worked a pervasive influence. His vote was the crucial vote on civil-rights legislation. His decision on such questions as repealing the "right-to-work" section of the national labor law decided the issue. His commitment to the Vietnam War for long controlled that of his party. In those years he had come to dominate the Senate as the leader of a minority party whose members did not, at times, make up one-third of the Senate's membership. The antique rules of the Senate, which allowed unlimited debate and therefore the filibuster, contributed greatly to his power and personal influence. So did the selfless leadership of the majority party by Senator Mike Mansfield. Dirksen dealt directly and intimately with the two Democratic Presidents of those years, John Kennedy and Lyndon Johnson. They in turn treated him with the greatest delicacy and consideration, as though he were a foreign power in his own right. Under their administrations Dirksen fashioned for himself a unique position in American politics. In a real sense, however, the power he wielded as a leader of Congress depended on his position as the leader of the opposition party. He could not have the independence he enjoyed under their Presidencies with a Republican in the White House. Indeed, Dirksen's own power and influence so much depended on the fact of a Democratic President that there was even the view that Dirksen, consciously or unconsciously, conspired to maintain that status quo. David S. Broder, for example, writing in *The Atlantic* in 1966, went so far as to suggest that Dirksen's performance in the Senate and in national politics might well be predicated on preventing the Republican Party from ever winning control of the White House. "A deliberate no-win policy?" Broder asked. "I do not know. But it is, I think, unarguable that Dirksen's political influence has risen steadily as the position of the Republican Party has declined. . . . Is it his deepest desire to see another Republican in the Presidency?"

On election day, 1968, seven Republican challengers won seats in the Senate that had been held by Democrats, and when the new Congress convened the following January, the Republicans had more members of the Senate than their party had had in a decade. That, on its face, would appear to make Dirksen more powerful and influential than he had ever been in the Senate. The appearances, however, were illusory, for the very structure of Dirksen's political world had been altered. The younger members of the Senate even earlier had begun to shift away from Dirksen's leadership on both foreign and domestic questions, and even the senior Republican senators had grown reluctant to follow Dirksen on civil rights and the Vietnam War. More than this, however, the election of a Republican as President demoted Dirksen from his position as the principal Republican leader in national office. The Republican members of the Senate, including Dirksen himself, would be looking to President Nixon for leadership on national questions. No one knew better than Dirksen the difference between the power of the President and members of Congress and that of a leader of Congress. Talking privately, Dirksen once explained the dilemma of a Congressional leader competing with an activist President for the votes of senators. "You have to always remember," he said, "that the only thing I can get across is on the basis of the facts, of loyalty, and of persuasion. I have nothing to offer. Odds and ends. . . . You have no patronage. The only patronage is the pages, the cloakroom attendants, and the doormen. It's so trivial it's hardly worth mentioning. We have no weapons. With the administration it's different. They have patronage and projects: postmasterships, the juicy ones, the first and second class; and the federal judges. That's at their disposal. It's a tremendous weapon. It develops a certain fidelity on the part of the recipient. He's going to be in that corner. When the chips are down, he's going to be there." Dirksen had no idea of competing with Nixon for the leadership of the Senate's Republican members. On the contrary, he was among the most forward when the Nixon administration handed out the loaves and fishes of political appointments. He had to build for himself a new posture in politics, one that took into account that Richard Nixon had become the preeminent Republican in the nation as well as the President.

Not until mid-December, 1968, did President-elect Nixon confer with Senator Dirksen, and then the occasion was an announced meeting between Nixon and all the Republican leaders of Congress. It was significant that the only member of Congress with whom

Nixon conferred in private prior to taking the oath as President was a Democrat, Wilbur Mills of Arkansas, chairman of the House Ways and Means Committee. Mills, through his enormous influence in the House of Representatives, had effective control of economic questions in Congress. Nixon assumed the cooperation of the Republican leaders of Congress, but from Mills he had no such warranty. It was significant as well that with Mills President-elect Nixon discussed substantive questions of tax policy and fiscal affairs. Nixon's meeting with Mills, two weeks before he met the Republican leaders, betokened a basic fact: this Republican President confronted a Democratic Congress. Nixon wished to avoid, if he could, a political stalemate with that Congress, and his meeting with Mills amounted to the opening of negotiations to that end. With the Republican leaders of Congress Nixon had no such problem, and the meeting with them in mid-December was scarcely more than ritual politeness. Substantive questions were not discussed, and those Republicans who had expected an unveiling of Nixon's legislative program left the two-hour session disappointed. "There was nothing of what we're going to do," one of them said. "We've got to mark time for a while." "We couldn't get down to the nuts and bolts," another said. "How could we? We don't even know what the budget is going to be. On international affairs, it's the same thing. We can't say anything." Nixon was cordial enough to the Republican leaders, but he showed them little more than that he intended to move with great caution on legislation. "You remember," Nixon told the Republican leaders, "we've got a Democratic Congress, and we want to get along with them."

At the meeting Dirksen had the place of honor at the President-elect's immediate right, but the lack of definition on forthcoming legislation indicated that Dirksen and the other leaders would have less to do in the coming Congress than they had expected. In the early weeks of his administration, President Nixon was preoccupied with the chore of choosing his chief associates in the government and then with the burgeoning concerns of international affairs. Not until after the Easter recess of Congress in April did Nixon begin to lay down a legislative program, and that program singularly reflected the caution and restraint that he had earlier indicated.

Even before the new Congress convened in January, Dirksen had faced an oblique challenge to his leadership of the Republicans in the Senate. Senator Kuchel, who had been Dirksen's assistant leader since 1959, had been defeated for renomination to the Senate in a Republican primary. Senator Hruska of Nebraska, Dirksen's closest ally in the Senate, announced that he was a candidate to succeed Kuchel in the party leadership. Hruska, eight years younger than Dirksen, had long been assumed the candidate of the Midwestern conservatives to replace Dirksen against the day Dirksen left his post. His election as assistant leader, or party whip, would make easier that succession. Dirksen, of course, supported Hruska's candidacy, and he was annoyed when Senator Hugh Scott of Pennsylvania announced that he too was a candidate for the position. Dirksen tried to dissuade Scott, arguing not only that he wished to avoid an intraparty controversy over the leadership positions but also that he felt he should be allowed to have a senator of his choice as the assistant leader. Dirksen tried to talk Scott into accepting a different party post, that of chairman of the party Policy Committee, but Scott declined the offer. "I do have the votes," he told Dirksen. Supporting Scott were the young progressives and the Eastern moderates of the party. Working for Hruska's election as party whip, besides Dirksen, were such conservative senators as John Tower of Texas and George Murphy of California. The night before the caucus, Dirksen told associates that Scott would be "lucky" to get as many as fifteen votes from the forty-three Republican senators. The next day, however, Scott received twenty-three votes and won the election as assistant leader. Trying to lessen the blow, Dirksen argued that Scott's victory was not a victory "for the liberals," that his election would make "no great changes" in Republican policy in the Senate. For Dirksen, however, the defeat of his candidate was still another token of his reduced status in the Senate. Scott's presence in the party leadership rankled Dirksen. Dirksen knew Scott to be ambitious, and before long Scott was preparing to challenge Dirksen for the actual leadership of the party in the Senate.

If Dirksen's stature had been reduced in the national government, still he received special deference from the Congress and the President-elect in a variety of ways. For one, he was named chairman of the Congressional Inaugural Committee. As such he conducted the formal ceremonies of Nixon's inauguration at the Capitol, and it was he who gave the oath of office to Vice-President Agnew. For another, a fortnight before the inauguration, Nixon traveled out to Leesburg, Virginia, to Dirksen's home to attend a party celebrating the Senator's seventy-third birthday. Nixon brought with him the Vice-President-elect and the principal members of his cabinet-to-be. Shortly after he became President, Nixon lunched at the Capitol with Dirksen and other Senate leaders, and it was Dirksen who had the honor to escort the President onto the Senate floor. There Nixon made a brief, conciliatory speech expressing his hopes for the Senate's cooperation with him in conducting the national government. At the weekly meeting of the Republican Congressional leaders with the President, Dirksen always sat at the right hand of the President, and after these meetings he and Congressman Ford announced to the press and the world the decisions that had been made. He could take gratification from these marks of his continuing importance, but they were not the same as the premiums he had enjoyed in the preceding years.

His new circumstances brought changes as well in Dirksen's weekly operations. For one, he abandoned the taping of his regular televised reports to his constituents in Illinois. He explained privately that he wanted his weekends, when he prepared these programs, freer for his gardening, but it was obvious that he no longer needed to maintain as before his contact with Illinois' voters. Starting a new six-year term at his age, he would not be running for reelection again. He and Gerald Ford quietly canceled their weekly meetings at the Capitol with the other Republican Congressional leaders and the "Ev and Gerry Show" that had followed them. "There's no reason to continue them," Dirksen said. The President had preempted their function; he would speak for the party. Besides, Dirksen said, the meetings at the Capitol might lead to confusion. "At the slightest inadvertence," Dirksen said, "something might be said . . . which would be slightly modified sixteen blocks away." He and Ford did not want to find themselves contradicted on party policy by the President.

For all his difficulties in adjusting to the new political realities, Dirksen had lost none of boldness. In the early weeks of the Ninety-first Congress, the question of increasing the salaries of members of Congress came before the Senate. Dirksen showed no hesitation; he argued openly for the increase in pay. To many of his colleagues this was a personally delicate and politically dangerous question. It came before the Senate in three separate phases, each indirectly related to the others—a proposal to raise the President's salary to $200,000; another to raise the salaries of members of Congress to $42,500; and, finally, a resolution to increase the pay of the Vice-President and the Speaker of the House to $62,500. This last proposal also provided salaries of $55,000 to the party leaders of the Senate and the House of Representatives, including Dirksen. He was foremost in advocating all three measures.

In a Senate speech Dirksen recapitulated the long and agonizing troubles the members of Congress had had over the years about their own salaries since the First Congress, when they voted to pay themselves six dollars a day. The country at large had always a tendency to label each increase in Congressional pay as a "salary grab," and the members of Congress had long since grown to fear retaliation by the voters if they voted for such measures. Dirksen told of his own role, as a member of the House of Representatives, in pushing through the salary increase in 1946. Members came to him then, he said, to plead that the legislation be approved without a roll-call vote. " 'Please don't have a roll call,' " Dirksen quoted them. " 'I'd like that pay increase, but I don't want to expose myself.' " Dirksen had no such squeamishness. He argued that some professional football players, who had only "a good pair of legs and the capacity to catch a football," were paid more than Congressmen. He argued that the $42,500 salary actually was not enough. "I had hoped to get included $5,000 of tax-free expenses," Dirksen said, but President Johnson, who proposed the salary increase, had turned him down. Dirksen argued that his colleagues in the Senate should show the courage of their convictions. "Isn't it time," he said in Senate debate, "to be a little realistic and remember senators have to eat too?"

In private Dirksen had pressed hard for additional salary increases for the Vice-President, the Speaker of the House, and the leaders of Congress. It was in response to Dirksen's "constant urging," said Senator Gale McGee of Wyoming, the chairman of the sponsoring Senate committee, that the committee brought the legislation to the Senate floor. In his enthusiasm for the measure Dirksen went too far, and he found himself embarrassed by one of his arguments. He stated that Vice-President Agnew was "hurting financially" on his salary of forty-three thousand dollars. He said that Agnew's wife, Judy, could wear a fancy dress to official parties only about three times and then had to go out and buy another dress for five or six hundred dollars. He had made a similar argument when he testified at the trial of the former governor of Illinois, William Stratton, that the governor's wife had to be well dressed. He had persuaded the jury then, with that argument, but this time the result was far different. Mrs. Agnew quickly denied that she spent so much for her dresses, and Dirksen's mail was heavy with complaints.

"I don't know why I ever said that," Dirksen said later, somewhat chastened. "I have been catching hell for it. My mail is full of letters from women who say they don't pay six hundred dollars for a dress. I have written some of them that one reason is they are not the wife of the Vice-President. Judy has sort of denied she pays six hundred dollars for a dress. I wish I hadn't said it."

From the opening days of the Nixon administration, Dirksen

made plain his interest in the persons Nixon appointed to the chief offices of the executive and judicial branches of the government. He started by insisting that the carryover nominations from the Johnson administration, those which the Senate had not yet confirmed, be immediately withdrawn by President Nixon.

"I probably put more pressure on the White House than anyone on those nominations," Dirksen said. "I said, 'You get those nominations out of here, and get them out of here right now, and I don't mean maybe!' We want those for ourselves. We've come into authority, mister, and I think we should exercise it."

Nixon did withdraw the Johnson nominations, and Dirksen enmeshed himself in the intrigue and negotiations of the new appointments throughout the administration. He had, in starting, no doubts about the process, and he approached the business with genuine relish.

"I got a call this morning," he said on February 18. "The goose hangs high. The bacon is frying, and everything is all right."

At this time he reiterated a position he had long taken: "You have to go on the theory that the President of the United States should have his own official family." Dirksen had followed this theory with Presidents Kennedy and Johnson, normally deferring to their judgments on who should serve in an executive capacity in the administration. In May, 1967, a controversy arose over a minor nomination by President Johnson. "I follow a rule laid down by Bob Taft," Dirksen said then. "The President is entitled, within reason, to have his own [official] family. In the absence of any corruption, immorality, or conduct such as to disqualify, I'm inclined to give him the benefit of the doubt." Later that same year, he enlarged this theme. "If you find a man who is equal to the job," he asked, "what difference does it make if he is a Democrat or a Republican?" With a Republican in the White House, however, Dirksen changed this nonpartisan position. Before long he also changed his view on allowing President Nixon to select, unimpeded, his official associates in his administration. Dirksen, indeed, went so far in opposing Nixon nominations as to suggest a dramatic confrontation between himself and the President.

His opposition began slowly, but then swiftly increased. He and Senator Goldwater, now returned to the Senate after a four years' absence, joined to prevent any appointment for Theodore Roosevelt McKeldin, the one-time Republican governor of Maryland who had nominated Eisenhower for President at the 1952 party convention. McKeldin had supported Lyndon Johnson for President in 1964 against Goldwater. Robert Finch, Nixon's Secretary of Health, Education and Welfare, wanted to name Creed Black, the managing editor of *The Chicago Daily News*, as assistant secretary for Congressional relations. Dirksen had not forgotten that newspaper's bitter opposition to him in his 1968 reelection campaign. He passed the word that Black was "objectionable" to him and thereby temporarily blocked the appointment. Only after extensive negotiations and the private arguments of Senator Percy, Dirksen's Illinois colleague, did Dirksen relent and let Black be appointed.

On federal jobs in Illinois Dirksen and Percy had little difficulty. "We have a nonaggression pact," a Percy aide explained. "It works the following way: we don't criticize his public positions, and he doesn't pressure us. This is what keeps peace in the family." They agreed on most of the appointees in Illinois, and those on which they disagreed they allowed to be disagreements without personal recriminations. What difficulties Percy had came from Harold Rainville, Dirksen's political operative in Illinois, who tended to act on his own on party patronage without specific instructions from Dirksen.

In one instance Dirksen forced Melvin Laird, President Nixon's Secretary of Defense, to revise his proposed civilian high command at the Pentagon. As a matter of courtesy Laird submitted to Dirksen the names of the men he wanted as assistant secretaries. The list did not include the name of James D. Hittle, a former Marine Corps brigadier general whom Dirksen first knew as the Navy's liaison officer with Congress during the Eisenhower administration. "I told Mel Laird to send down another list," Dirksen confided to intimates, "and if this man's name wasn't on it, don't bother to send down *any* names." There was implicit in Dirksen's words a threat to block confirmation on all the department's assistant secretaries. Subsequently, Hittle was appointed assistant secretary of the Navy.

"It worked," a Republican insider said of Dirksen's maneuver on behalf of Hittle. "This is a tough politician. He's a senator who understands his prerogatives and executes them."

Another appointment Dirksen arranged was that of Otto F. Otepka, a controversial government security officer, as a member of the Subversive Activities Control Board. Otepka had been dismissed from his position in the State Department in 1963 for passing secret government documents to the Senate's internal-security subcommittee. Otepka said he regarded his appointment as a "complete vindication"; and Dirksen advised him to accept it in place of "an apology" from the State Department. For Dirksen, Otepka's appointment was also something of a personal vindication, for he had struggled hard to keep the Subversive Activities Control Board in being. In 1967, amid considerable official embarrassment, the board was shown as almost totally moribund, with no work to perform. An attempt was made in the Senate, led by Senator William Proxmire of Wisconsin, to abolish the board, and Dirksen had intervened to save it. He sponsored a bill to expand and define more clearly the board's functions, and he went to President Johnson to demand that the board be given some work to do. "I told him," Dirksen said of his conversation with Johnson, "to tell the Attorney General to lob some cases over there." Still there were difficulties. Proxmire had tried to deny operating funds to the board. Then Proxmire demanded that Dirksen get a letter from the Attorney General, Ramsey Clark, approving his bill. "I got the letter," Dirksen said. Then, in private negotiations with Dirksen, Proxmire asked that Clark testify before the Judiciary Committee on the bill.

"Don't kid me," Dirksen told him. "You are trying to kill this thing. You tried, through the appropriations route, to take away the money."

Dirksen forced his bill through the Senate, which approved it

67 to 10. "I have not been around here all these years for nothing," he said, "and I was not born yesterday. I know the game of the senator from Wisconsin." Still Dirksen did not rest until he received the personal assurances of the Attorney General. "At long last," Dirksen said, "the Attorney General wandered into my office and said, 'I'm going to send some cases to the board.' "

The battling over appointments was routine for Dirksen. He had been hustling for patronage appointments for all of his years in Congress, and he had met with more than his share of success. He had even persuaded President Johnson to appoint one of the senior partners of his law firm in Peoria, Robert D. Morgan, to the federal bench. He had placed, or had helped place, friends and allies in many federal agencies, and the persons so located became, in a way, part of the senator's personal network throughout the federal establishment. They were persons on whom he could call, and they provided him with a private apparatus of information and help.

"Golly," he said at one point, "if I didn't know people all over the government, I'd have wasted a third of a century in this city. Some of them I've sponsored. I can call them up and say, 'What about this?' I can get information. I don't get any favors. That would get me in dutch."

Under the Nixon administration, however, Dirksen and other Republican senators and Congressmen unexpectedly discovered that they did not have as much to do with the naming of federal officials as they had assumed they would. Without warning, the President and his Postmaster General, Winton M. Blount, announced that they were abolishing the patronage system in the Post Office Department. This was a painful blow to Republican Congressmen and to state party leaders. No longer would they be the ones to choose the local postmasters. "Hell hath no fury like that of a Congressman whose patronage is about to be taken away," said Representative John B. Anderson of Illinois. Dirksen understood perfectly the outrage within the party at Nixon's decision on Post Office patronage. "My God, don't you see?" he asked. "There's nothing left for these county chairmen." Within the Republican ranks in Congress resentment began to build against Nixon's appointments and his policy in making appointments. He left many Democratic officials in their posts, and he neglected to inform Republican senators in advance of the appointments being made in their own states, a peculiarly sensitive subject for the senators involved. As early as February 5 a group of Republican senators called in Bryce Harlow, Nixon's chief liaison officer with Congress, and complained bitterly against the patronage policy. Senators especially angered were Clifford Case of New Jersey, Roman Hruska of Nebraska, and Hiram Fong of Hawaii. "The White House has certain obligations to the Senate," Harlow was bluntly told. Hruska was especially annoyed that so many Democrats in federal office were not being removed. Dirksen did not attend the meeting with Harlow.

"I didn't go," he said at a news conference. "I don't bitch. Don't put down that word 'bitch.' It doesn't look good."

He knew about the meeting, of course, and more than that he knew the depth of the resentment within the party for the President's patronage policies. Senators and Congressmen were coming to him with their complaints, and they were asking him to use his influence to relieve what was becoming for them an intolerable situation. He was as well hearing from his allies within the federal agencies. Because of his unique position in the Congressional party, these informants were relaying to Dirksen whatever damaging evidence they had against men they opposed for federal appointments.

"We have been hearing from home, and some places closer," Dirksen said, "that the new administration hasn't been moving fast enough in the appointment of Republicans to replace Democrats."

Dirksen did what he could to persuade the President and his lieutenants to withdraw offensive nominations already made and to cancel such appointments as previously planned. Nixon had named Franklin Long, vice-president for research and advanced studies at Cornell University, to be director of the National Science Foundation. Representatives James Fulton of Pennsylvania came to Dirksen to protest that Long was an activist Democrat who had supported Senator Robert Kennedy of New York and then Senator

Eugene McCarthy of Minnesota in their campaigns for the Democratic Presidential nomination. Dirksen thereupon announced his opposition to Long, and Nixon withdrew the nomination.

A more involved case came to Dirksen from tips from allies within the Veterans Administration. At the request of Democratic Congressmen President Nixon had agreed to continue William J. Driver as administrator of that agency. The Democratic Congressmen assured the President that Driver was an able and nonpartisan administrator. Dirksen checked out the tips he had received, and through unofficial means he received photostats of V.A. vouchers and other evidence that Driver had permitted staff aides to use government equipment to organize and raise money for Democratic clubs in the 1968 Presidential election. He also had evidence that Driver had permitted the agency's automobiles to be used to transport Democratic leaders at the Democratic National Convention in Chicago.

Dirksen presented his case against Driver at a regular meeting of the Republican Congressional leaders with the President at the White House. "I've got the evidence," Dirksen said. The President listened, but then he replied that he was "committed" to the reappointment of Driver. Dirksen, who always sat at the President's right hand at these meetings, cupped a hand over his mouth and whispered to the President: "I'll uncommit you." The President cupped his hand over his mouth and whispered back, "I don't care."

Returning to the Senate, Dirksen announced that he opposed continuing Driver as chief of the Veterans Administration. Driver resigned on April 15, and Dirksen claimed credit for his resignation.

"I would have knocked Mr. Driver out of the box," Dirksen said, "and Mr. Driver knows it. And I would have done it under oath. Mr. Driver resigned because he knew what I had up my sleeve."

At a meeting of a Senate judiciary subcommittee on March 27, Dirksen touched off a furor by attacking Clifford L. Alexander, Jr., chairman of the Equal Employment Opportunity Commission. Alexander was testifying before the subcommittee, chaired by Senator Edward Kennedy, when Dirksen angrily accused him of "punitive harassment" of employers in the way he operated the commission. Dirksen had read hearings that Alexander had conducted on the employment policies of various companies. "If this isn't halted," Dirksen shouted, "I am going to the highest authority in this government and get somebody fired."

The next day a White House spokesman announced that Alexander would not be redesignated as the commission's chairman. Alexander therefore angrily resigned as chairman. Dirksen, however, had not finished with this commission, for pending before the Senate was the nomination of William H. Brown as a member. Brown, under a recess appointment from President Johnson, had sat through the hearings that Alexander had conducted, and Dirksen was annoyed that he had not objected to Alexander's line of questioning of the witnesses. Dirksen's objections raised delicate questions. Nixon had indicated that he intended to appoint Brown as Alexander's successor as chairman of the commission. A further complication was that Brown, a resident of Philadelphia, had the total support of Senator Scott, the new assistant Republican leader of the Senate. Nevertheless, utilizing his prerogatives as a senator, Dirksen placed a "hold" on Brown's nomination; that is, he asserted his right to delay a vote on his nomination. Scott was furious. He regarded Dirksen's action as a personal affront to him, for he had recommended Brown's appointment, and he was not prepared to tolerate Dirksen's threatened veto. "I've reached the limit of comity," Scott said privately. "He's brought us to the edge of confrontation." Scott served notice on Dirksen that he would fight for this nomination. In a real sense, Scott had become what Senator Morton had been before his retirement, the unofficial leader of the younger Republican progressives in the Senate, and that put an extra edge to this quarrel with Dirksen. In the end, Scott worked out an amicable settlement with Dirksen. He brought Brown to Dirksen's Capitol office, and there the three discussed Brown's approach to his work on the commission. "I am satisfied to see Mr. Brown go on the commission," Dirksen said after their conference.

On May 5, when the Senate approved Brown's appointment, Dirksen said in Senate debate that he had found the nominee "attractive and personable," and that Brown had answered his questions satisfactorily. "I'm going to be watching him," Dirksen added, however. This brought Dirksen into a new row, this time with Senator Edward Kennedy, who had not liked Dirksen's denunciation of Alexander before his subcommittee. Kennedy rose in the Senate to say that he did not want Brown intimidated by Republican senators stating they intended to watch him. Kennedy also said that Dirksen's charges against Alexander amounted to "demagoguery."

"If the senator from Massachusetts is implying that I am engaging in demagoguery," Dirksen retorted, "he doesn't know what he's talking about."

These struggles over appointments, especially as depicted in the news media, seemed to place Dirksen in growing opposition to the Nixon administration, but most controversial of all was Dirksen's decision to oppose the man Secretary Finch chose as his department's assistant secretary for health and scientific affairs. Finch passed the word that he wanted Dr. John H. Knowles, director of Massachusetts General Hospital, for the post. The conservative leaders of the American Medical Association immediately took alarm. To them Knowles's ideas on medical care smacked of social- ism. For example, Knowles described Medicare as "a monument to the failure of private medicine" to meet the health needs of the elderly. He had also said that adequate medical care had to be provided to poor urban neighborhoods if "confrontations" in these areas were to be avoided.

Dirksen took up the cause of the AMA conservatives. At a White House meeting he told Finch that he opposed Knowles. Later he telephoned Finch. "If you send up Knowles's name," Dirksen told him, "I would stop him. . . ." Then Dirksen recounted to reporters what he had said to Finch, thereby making this a public quarrel. Asked why he opposed Knowles, Dirksen said bluntly: "Because the doctors don't like him."

Dirksen's announced opposition to Knowles set off a national controversy. He appeared to be standing alone against Knowles in defiance of the President and Secretary Finch. The White House announced that Nixon would appoint to the post the man Finch wanted. Privately, however, the word was passed that Nixon asked Finch to obtain substantial support for Knowles in the Senate and medical profession before formally proposing him for the post.

The controversy dragged on for weeks, a hidden struggle between Dirksen and Finch. Dirksen, however, was not alone in Congress in opposing Knowles, but the other Republican conservatives did not broadcast their opposition to Knowles on television and in the newspapers. House Republican leader Gerald Ford fully supported Dirksen throughout the struggle. "I agree with him," Ford said privately, and by Ford's estimate, about three out of every four Republican Congressmen also agreed with him. "He wasn't alone," Ford said of Dirksen. "A lot of our members have gotten help in many ways from the local doctors." Dirksen's open opposition Finch had to take as a challenge to his control of his department. "He left Finch nothing to do but stand by his man," a Republican senator said of Dirksen's threatened veto of Knowles. Finch refused to yield. So did Dirksen. "I don't propose to withdraw my objections," he stated. The struggle went on from mid-April until early summer.

Dirksen's challenge to Finch brought on him a barrage of unfavorable publicity and even testier criticism in the political gossip of Capitol Hill. Combined with his public opposition to other Nixon-administration appointees, Dirksen's attempted veto of Knowles's nomination convinced at least some of his colleagues that he was striking at the President in retaliation for his own reduced status in political Washington. "Ev wants to play all the positions by himself," a Republican said. "He's playing high, wide, and handsome," another Republican said. "His ham-handedness is embarrassing the Senate's Republicans," still another Republican said. There were reports that Dirksen had deeply angered Nixon by his actions. but the official confusion was so general that there were also reports that Dirksen actually was doing "a dirty job" for the President that Nixon could not do for himself. "Ev is Ev," one Republican senator quoted the President, suggesting that Nixon was tolerant of Dirksen's foibles. The President continued to show special deference to Dirksen, inviting him, for example, to accompany him to the Kentucky Derby.

There was no question that Dirksen was having difficulties adjusting to his new and lesser role in Washington under President Nixon. "He had to find his niche," one sympathetic Republican senator said. Dirksen tried to give the impression that he had an even closer relationship with Nixon than he had had with Johnson. "I'm in contact with the White House and administration officials," Dirksen said in April, "probably half a dozen times more a day than I have been in any other administration." Dirksen, however, did not have the private access to President Nixon that he had had with Lyndon Johnson, nor did Nixon confide in Dirksen as Johnson had done. Asked at a news conference why Nixon had decided to visit Rumania on an overseas trip, Dirksen simply did not know. "Doggone if I know," he said. "Maybe it was a whim." Dirksen did not enjoy the personal rapport with Nixon, nor the casual informality, that he had had with Johnson. In the evenings, in his back room over drinks, Dirksen loved to regale his fellow senators with amusing anecdotes of his escapades at the White House when Johnson was President. He no longer had these tales to tell, and senators who drank with him noticed the change. He had continuing differences as well with the younger Republican senators, who were talking now among themselves as with others of their sense of "alienation" with Dirksen and President Nixon. One of these senators, Charles Goodell of New York, chose to quarrel publicly with Dirksen. At a news conference he testily called Dirksen "an obstructionist."

Dirksen was annoyed at Goodell's accusation, and he felt as well that he could not permit the growing doubts about his loyalty to

President Nixon to continue among his colleagues in the Senate. He resolved therefore to chasten Goodell, and he chose to do it at a private meeting of all Republican senators. "I have lived through the time when Bill Knowland was at cross purposes with Eisenhower," Dirksen said to a friend. He wanted it known that he did not intend to be such a Senate leader for President Nixon. "What's a leader for if it's for that?" he asked. "I don't want anyone to think my course has been shaped by a selfish purpose, because it isn't." At the meeting of Republican senators Dirksen took up Goodell's charge that he was an obstructionist. "I wasn't irate," he explained afterward. "If you're going to excoriate a fellow, you're not irate. You want your wits about you." He began by cataloguing Nixon's legislative program. "I'm for the missile program," he said. "Is that obstructionist? I'm for President Nixon's obscenity legislation. Is that obstructionist? I'm for the postal-rate increase. Does that make me obstructionist? I'm for the President's tax program. Is that obstructionist?" Thus he ran through Nixon's legislative requests, announcing his support of each. His colleagues knew that Goodell did not support all of the President's legislation, and Dirksen's point was not missed. To underscore his point, however, Dirksen told his colleagues that he was prepared to compare his support for the Nixon program with that of any other senator. "So much for legislation," Dirksen said. Then he took up his objections to the administration's appointments, and he dealt with them in order.

"Here's the Driver file," he said. "I don't kick people when they're down, but I could hang anyone with this. I've done my homework."

He discussed each of the others. "Alexander knew what I had," he said. "That's why he quit as chairman." He detailed his negotiations with Senator Scott over the Brown nomination, and he denied that in any of this he was opposing the President for the sake of opposition for its own sake.

"Is that doing my duty," he asked his colleagues, "or is that obstructionist? If I know something derogatory about a fellow, don't I have a duty to expose it?"

Plainly, Dirksen had felt the sting of the private and public criticism. He wanted it known in the Senate and elsewhere that he was not a vain old man, bitter at the world and his reduced role in it. "Of all the human weaknesses that are not in me," he said to a reporter privately, "vanity is at the top of the list. I have not a smidgin of vanity in me, or jealousy. I do the best I can." Asked why he was objecting to the nominations, he replied: "Why am I doing it? Golly, I thought it was so very obvious. The President of the United States lives essentially a rather isolated life. He has people around him. He has to depend on them to give advice, to see that he makes no untimely mistakes, to shield him from many things. I'd be an awfully poor Republican leader if I was not shielding the President of the United States from people I feel do him no good and could do him harm. When someone comes along who I feel is not good for morale or who advances a philosophy or idea that couldn't be in keeping with the administration, then I am willing to go through hell and high water, no matter how much embarrassment it might occasion for me. I would be a poor leader if I didn't stand up for the President. The President knows at all times what I'm up to. He knows that if there's anyone on this hilltop that he can count on, it's the fellow from Illinois."

Dirksen thus argued that the President, in effect, approved of what he was doing to oppose these nominations, including that of Knowles, as he had privately approved of Dirksen's actions against Driver. Senator Goodell was not silenced by Dirksen's rebuke. He made a speech in the Senate on June 18 to attack Dirksen for opposing Knowles. "I stand here now," Goodell said, "as a matter of conscience to oppose the leader of my party in the Senate. . . . No one man should be permitted to dictate or veto a Presidential appointment." Dirksen did not reply publicly. Before Goodell made his speech, however, Dirksen glowered at him in the Republican cloakroom. "I'm not going to be on the floor when you give your speech today," Dirksen said to him. "I may wait until next year to answer. I've got a lot of political clout." "I know you have, Ev," Goodell said. "I'll use it against you next year," Dirksen said. "I could hurt you." Goodell, who had been appointed to the Senate, had to run for election to the Senate that next year. Dirksen's threat was obvious. Privately Dirksen was amused at what had happened. "I rather think Charlie may be a little uneasy about what's going to happen ahead in New York," he said.

In the end, Finch appeared to have defeated Dirksen's campaign against Knowles. He had enlisted substantial support for Knowles throughout the country, and Dirksen knew, of course, what Finch had done. "Well," Dirksen said on June 24, all but acknowledging his defeat, "there will be another day and other issues." Pressed by reporters, Dirksen conceded that he could not win all his fights. "You try to win them all," he said. He tried to evade the reporters' questions, and he declined to speculate on what others had said and done. "I'm not responsible," he said to them, with a grin, "for what your sister didn't hear." Asked why he was not as talkative as usual, Dirksen smiled. "When you are about to slay me," he said, "would I be singing hosannas and paeans of joy, saying 'Come and cut my throat'?" He said he had given his word to "somebody" that he would not discuss the Knowles case. "I won't tell you to whom I gave my word," he said, but it was clear that he meant the President. At this point, just as Finch seemed to have won on Knowles, other party leaders suddenly intervened. Senator John Tower of Texas and Representative Bob Wilson of California both talked to the President. They were, respectively, the chairmen of the Republican campaign committees for the Senate and the House of Representatives. A principal chore for them was to raise campaign funds. "It's a whole new ball game now," Wilson said after their talk with Nixon. Congressman Ford sent his advice to the President to choose someone "less controversial" than Knowles. Thus advised, Nixon again discussed the nomination with Finch, and on June 27 Finch announced "reluctantly and regretfully" that Knowles would not be nominated.

Finch's defeat amounted to a national sensation, and there were reports that he would resign from the President's cabinet. For Dirksen, this was an extraordinary triumph, if one of somewhat dubious value. Vice-President Spiro Agnew described him, jokingly, as "Secretary of Health, Education and Welfare *ex-officio* Everett Dirksen." Dirksen maintained a discreet silence, but elsewhere Nixon's capitulation raised questions over who was actually running the federal government. Senator Edward Kennedy, increasingly critical of Dirksen, charged nothing less than a "conspiracy" against Knowles by Dirksen and his allies. From the liberal-moderate wing of the Republican Party came cries of incipient revolt against Dirksen and the President. Senator Scott warned publicly that such a revolt was near. "I'm simply serving notice," Scott said. Senator Charles Mathias went further: "It has begun."

The Republican liberals had more than the Knowles nomination to trouble them. The administration at this time appeared to be moving in a starkly conservative direction. The President had announced his opposition to a simple extension of the voting-rights bill, a matter of alarm to civil libertarians. The President's associates had also softened the government's guidelines for school desegregation. Senator Mark Hatfield of Oregon was among a dozen or more Republican senators who felt increasingly "alienated" from Dirksen and the Nixon administration. "Dirksen's a grand old guy," Hatfield said, "but so is Santa Claus. He is a symbol of the system of the past. . . ." Earlier Dirksen had talked of reestablishing in the Senate the once powerful conservative coalition of Republicans and Southern Democrats. "As we move along," he said then, "I think there will not be so much emphasis on party labels as there will be on the viewpoints of members of Congress. . . . Members in the South are, as we know, inclined to vote conservative. We are assured that the Nixon approach is a conservative approach." Dirksen read the 1968 election as marking a new conservative trend in the nation's course, and he moved to meet the new political realities as he understood them. He tended to dismiss the liberal wing of his party in the Senate. "To be sure," he said, "we have a sprinkling of liberals, but beyond that, I still think there are enough conservative-minded people in Congress to go along with that trend." He expected to form an easy working relationship with the Southern Democrats in the Senate. "I never have found any great difficulty in speaking with my brethren from the South when I had to," Dirksen said. "They still speak our language. We get along pretty well." Dirksen's strategy further alarmed the liberal-moderate Republicans in the Senate, because they saw the country's future and that of their party as necessarily heading in exactly the opposite direction. They began to talk among themselves about strengthening their own coalition with the Democratic liberals across the center aisle. By early summer Senator Scott had entered negotiations with Democratic Senator Philip Hart of Michigan to join forces in opposition to the Nixon administration's voting-rights bill. Dirksen had couched his support of that bill in terms of working with the Southern Democrats. The civil-rights advocates wanted only a simple extension of the existing law, which applied only to Southern states, not a broadening of the law to cover all states. "What am I going to say to Jim Eastland," Dirksen said to President Nixon about the Senator from Mississippi, who was chairman of the Senate Judiciary Committee, "if I come in with a straight extension? He's going to say, 'You're punishing Mississippi for a situation as bad as the one in Illinois.' " Dirksen's catering to the Southern Democrats and the President's presumed "Southern strategy" convinced the liberal-moderate Republicans that they had no choice but to break with Dirksen and the President. Dirksen, however, was not upset by these portents of party revolt. "When you drop a cat from a tree," he said laconically, "he always lands on his feet." Within the Republican ranks, however, the talk went beyond opposing Dirksen and the administration on specific legislative measures. There was talk as well among the liberal-moderate senators of ousting Dirksen as the party leader. "His views seem to be reverting to a conservative mold," John W. Finney wrote in *The New York Times,* "and he is considered by insiders to be fast losing some of the rapport he has established with his fellow Republicans. A newer generation isn't swayed by golden oratory, nor can flamboyant style any longer be equated with senatorial worth. If the rest of the young Turks of the Republican Party grow even more restless than they now are, Senator Dirksen could be deposed as Republican leader."

Harassed as he was by the liberal-moderates of his own party, Dirksen came under a more personal and painful assault from the press in the spring and summer of 1969. Three separate news organizations conducted their own investigations of Dirksen's finances with a view to proving, if they could, that he had acted improperly over the years in this usually ambiguous and shadowy field of public life. The impulses for this sudden attention to Dirksen's fiscal affairs were two. The first was the publication by *Life* magazine of an article disclosing that Supreme Court Justice Abe Fortas had accepted a retainer of twenty thousand dollars from the private foundation of a financier, Louis Wolfson, who was later indicted and convicted of violations of federal law. Although Fortas had returned the retainer to the foundation, the sensation created by the article eventually forced him to resign from the Supreme Court. The significance of the magazine's startling success was not missed by other journalists anxious to achieve similar notoriety. The second impulse to investigate Dirksen's finances came from the disclosure, required of all senators, including Dirksen, by new Senate rules, of the outside income of members of the Senate. For the latter six months of 1968, the required period for reporting, Dirksen listed a total of $18,158.50 in outside income. Of this, $5,000 was for a professional television performance and $5,158.50 was remuneration for his weekly news column. He had also listed $3,500 for a speech to the U.S. Savings and Loan League, a $1,000 honorarium from the First Federal Savings and Loan, a $1,000 honorarium from the Illinois State Medical Society, a $1,000 honorarium from the Electrolux Company, $1,000 for an article he had written, and $500 for another article. Publication of these figures provided an extra incentive to the press to explore the finances of public men.

On the Fortas matter, Dirksen from the start declined to take a public or private position. "It is far better that I make no judgment at the moment," he said. In the House of Representatives, the chairman of the Judiciary Committee, Emanuel Celler, began the initial steps toward impeaching the justice, and Dirksen argued that he might, as a member of the Senate, have to sit in judgment on any charges against Fortas. He did not wish to prejudge Fortas. He did speak publicly of his distaste for the impeachment process. He had participated in those processes as a member of the House of Representatives in the 1930's, and he had then been convinced that the Senate proved an inadequate jury. During one such impeachment trial before the Senate, he said, there were as few as six senators in the Senate chamber listening to the presentation of the evidence against the accused. "Damned if I'd want to put my life in their hands," he said of his fellow senators. He did not wish to be so casual a juror as many senators had proved to be on such questions. "I want to be awfully careful that I don't overstep the line of propriety," Dirksen said. The embarrassment to Fortas, which forced him to resign from the court, also embarrassed Dirksen. Less than a year before, Dirksen had readily approved Fortas to be Chief Justice of the United States.

*The Chicago Daily News,* with a special antagonism for Dirksen, carefully checked out the details of his financial report to the Senate. The newspaper's reporters discovered that two of the items were incorrectly listed. The $500 fee turned out to be his pay not for an article, as listed, but for a brief appearance in a science-fiction motion picture. The $1,000 fee listed from the First Federal Savings and Loan turned out to be a mistake; Dirksen had been paid no such fee. The newspaper did not stop there; its reporters reexamined Dirksen's relationship with his law firm in Peoria and closely checked his campaign expenditures and those making contributions to his campaign. "Repeated investigations by newsmen," *The Chicago Daily News* reported in its July 11 issue, "have failed to show any link so far between the known clients of the Peoria firm and Dirksen's efforts in behalf of companies before federal regulatory bodies." The newspaper's reporters discovered inaccuracies due to carelessness rather than any desire to conceal. All the same, they continued to investigate Dirksen's finances.

A similar investigation of Dirksen was undertaken by the Washington staff of the Hearst newspapers. One of the Hearst reporters, Leslie Whitten, Jr., did find that Dirksen's Chicago political agent, Harold Rainville, had intervened with a federal judge on behalf of a Chicago bank on whose board Rainville had sat as a director. Rainville, however, conceded that he had acted without Dirksen's specific knowledge in sending the judge a telegram he signed with Dirksen's name. "I have authority," Rainville said, "to sign telegrams in the Senator's name." The Hearst reporters conceded privately that their investigation failed to show that Dirksen had an avaricious desire for money acquired by either proper or improper means. Rather they found that Dirksen lusted after political power and that he was not always discreet about the way he achieved his ends.

The most ambitious of the journalistic investigations of Dirksen's finances was conducted by Charles Roberts of *Newsweek*, whose report was published in that magazine's issue of June 16, 1969. Roberts ranged across Dirksen's varied activities, his Senate performance, the Peoria law firm, his relations with the regulatory agencies, and his style of living. Roberts quoted an unnamed person describing Dirksen as "the most venal man in American politics today," but Roberts himself was unable to sustain the accusation. "These counts against Dirksen," Roberts conceded, in summing up, "form only a web of circumstantial evidence. They do not prove that he has profited as a lawmaker, or even that he has any conflict of interest." Roberts conceded as well that there were no circumstantial evidences of Dirksen's receiving money beyond his known income. "Given all his sources of income," Roberts wrote, "Dirksen does not appear to live beyond his means."

The reporters conducting the investigations had failed to produce the damaging evidence they sought, and Dirksen took a mixed view of their efforts. With the article in *Newsweek*, he was sardonically amused. "Do you think they did a good, workmanlike hatchet job on me?" he asked a news conference. "If they didn't, I didn't get what I paid for, because I told them where to look." With the Chicago newspaper he was annoyed, doubtless because of his many bitter quarrels over the years with all of the Chicago newspapers. Periodically he had lashed out at one or another of them, and he did so again at *The Daily News*. At his regular Tuesday news conference on August 5, a reporter for that newspaper, William McGaffin, asked Dirksen a routine question on a measure then before the Senate. Dirksen refused to answer it. He stepped away from the desk on which he normally sat, obviously angry. "I have no stories for your paper," he said. "I know what you . . . have been writing about me. I read your newspaper, and then I throw it in the wastebasket where it belongs."

Not all of Dirksen's problems came from the press and his own rank-and-file Republicans in the Senate. In the early months of 1969 the Democrats, who held clear majorities in both the Senate and the House of Representatives, stayed whatever tendencies they had for partisan criticism and complaint against the Nixon administration. Indeed, both Senator Mansfield, the Democratic leader of the Senate, and John McCormack of Massachusetts, the Speaker of the House of Representatives, volunteered their cooperation to the new President in the running of the divided government. As they read the mood of the country, the Democrats believed the American people wanted to give Nixon a chance to adjust to the enormous responsibilities of the Presidency and to find his way on those responsibilities without the impediment of carping criticism. In deferring thus to the President, however, the majority Democrats slackened their own legislative efforts, and by the Easter recess there began a growing alarm at the pervasive inactivity of both political branches of the government. Speaker McCormack, coming under fire himself, blamed the President for the Congressional inaction. "It is exceedingly difficult," McCormack said publicly, "for the leadership in Congress to formulate a legislative program and timetable until it has before it the recommendations which the President has to submit to the Congress." Dirksen felt impelled to defend the administration publicly, although privately he was worried by the failures of the President's lieutenants to act. "Contrast this administration with the man who builds his house upon the rock with the man who builds on shifting sands," Dirksen said in late March. "This is not an administration which rushes in with the roof and with ready-made walls before the foundation is in place."

Among the younger and more activist Democrats in Congress there was far less patience with the new President than their party leaders offered. They began to plot their own stratagems to assume the legislative initiative in Congress. Among these, none was more prominent than Senator Edward Kennedy of Massachusetts. In January, after a bruising party quarrel, Kennedy had won the post of Senate Democratic whip. More than that secondary leadership post, however, Kennedy was regarded widely as his party's likely nominee for President in 1972. The liberal senators rallied around him, prepared to follow his leadership in the months ahead. For Dirksen, Kennedy's sudden emergence as his party's preeminent man created a double challenge. Kennedy not only appeared as the single most obvious threat to the Nixon administration, but he also was taking from Dirksen his supremacy in the Senate. This had given an added significance to the scraps they had had over Nixon's appointees. Kennedy took the lead among Democratic senators questioning the proposed expenditures for the military, and the group resolved to defeat, if they could, President Nixon's decision to build an antiballistic-missile defense in the United States. Kennedy was also active among those questioning military policy in the Vietnam War. In mid-May Kennedy made a Senate speech criticizing as "senseless and irresponsible" a military decision to defend a mountain in Vietnam nicknamed "Hamburger Hill." American losses had been heavy and after the battle was won the American troops were withdrawn. "American lives are too valuable," Kennedy said, "to be sacrificed for military pride." Dirksen resolved not to let Kennedy's criticism pass unnoticed. He took special precautions with his reply; he wrote it out in advance, something he rarely did. He said in that reply, which he delivered June 2, that Kennedy's speech was "something of a shock" to him. "It did not dislocate my affection for him," he said, "but it did jolt my estimate of his wisdom and judgment." Dirksen suggested in his speech that Kennedy had undermined troop morale in Vietnam. The next day, somewhat to Kennedy's embarrassment, Kennedy's mother telephoned Dirksen. "Now I'm calling to thank you," she told Dirksen, "for the gracious and temperate tone of your speech yesterday. You made your points without resorting to personalities." Dirksen told Kennedy about the call, and they had a laugh over it. Privately Dirksen denied any personal animosity toward Kennedy. "You can have these things," he said, "and never affect your personal relations. He's a nice guy. He and I get along very well." All the same, Kennedy was the rising man in the Senate, and Dirksen knew it. Instinctively he resisted Kennedy's surge. Yet Dirksen had seen enough of national politics to know how unpredictable and fickle human affairs could be. He had had his own Presidential ambitions frustrated. He had had his own ups and downs. "That's all obviously speculative," Dirksen said privately of Kennedy's presumed political future. "Who knows what destiny has in store for any of us? We can nurse our hopes. You plan, and you hope, and you see how it comes out."

There was in Dirksen, as in other politicians who had suffered the buffets of changing political fortunes, this pervasive sense of fatalism. He accepted without complaint, and almost with indifference, the altered circumstances of his own political career. Like a professional gambler, he played the cards he was dealt and did what he could with them. There was no point to whining or to protesting that he had been cheated out of his just deserts. He was caught up in events he could not control; they were beyond the immediate control of any man. He knew, however, that with energy and zest and his own talents he could influence them. He could make a place for himself. There was nothing new in this to Dirksen, for his entire political career had been played out under similar terms. He had, at times, achieved great prominence and power, and at others he had been reduced to political impotence and frustration. He had been hailed as a statesman and savaged as a charlatan. He was used to both. The election of Richard Nixon as President had shrunk Dirksen's political command in national affairs, and Nixon in office had treated him, if warily, with a cool independence that Dirksen had not known from either John Kennedy or Lyndon Johnson. That did not unnerve Dirksen or even upset him unduly. He played the game of politics as he always had, insistent that he not be dealt out, no matter the new rules of the game. It was the only game he really knew and the only game he wanted to play. A less compulsive player might have withdrawn and sulked. Dirksen, however, could not do that, and he managed, despite all the inherent disadvantages of his reduced status, to impose himself once again as a man to be reckoned with in the conduct of the national government. Weakened as he was, and under assault from so many quarters, it was of itself a remarkable feat.

# Chapter 15

# The Last Roll Call

*I don't know if we've added to the gaiety of nations*
*or the sum total of human understanding. . . .*

For Senator Dirksen, the summer of 1969 was a long, enervating, and frustrating travail. The defection of his own Republican senators from his leadership made matters difficult for him, and he was harassed as well by having to try to work at times with inexperienced and ineffective allies in the Nixon administration. Despite the public disputes with the administration, he did wish to serve the President, act as his spokesman in the Senate, and defend there the President's administration and legislative program. He had not expected the Knowles nomination to become such a national controversy, and among those closest to him there was the belief that he actually regretted the incident. "He was riding on the tiger's back," one sympathetic senator said of Dirksen. Once he had committed himself against Knowles, according to this thesis, he had no way to undo that commitment when it became a matter of embarrassment to the administration. As early as March, Dirksen had made a carefully drafted speech in the Senate to praise the new President and his administration. "This administration is building on solid rock," Dirksen said then, "and it works, and will therefore withstand the wind and the waves. This administration understands that it is better to do ten things well and get them done than to do one hundred things poorly which will later need redoing." Shortly thereafter, former Vice-President Hubert Humphrey suggested that the Democrats in Congress give President Nixon one hundred days before they raised any criticism of his administration. Dirksen promptly took Humphrey to task. "In terms of one hundred days," Dirksen said sarcastically, "anyone who thinks the festering sores of crime, violence, civil disobedience, inflation, and poverty inherited by this administration can be healed overnight is just as mistaken as one who expects the Vietnam War to be brought to an end in a few short days. Would Mr. Humphrey really have us believe that he would have resolved all these problems within this time, had he been elected?"

One legislative by-product of the Vietnam War deeply annoyed Dirksen. It was a resolution, with no actual authority of law, that had been reported by the Senate Foreign Relations Committee declaring it to be "the sense of the Senate" that only affirmative action by Congress could produce a "national commitment . . . to a foreign power." The resolution, sponsored by Senator Fulbright, amounted to a rebuke of the manner in which President Johnson had led the United States militarily into Vietnam, and it suggested as well that no similar action should be taken by any President in the future. "It didn't satisfy me worth a damn," Dirksen said privately of Fulbright's resolution.

Dirksen resolved to try to defeat this resolution, although he knew from the start that it reflected the growing antiwar sentiment in the country, and that it had overwhelming support in the Senate. "You couldn't very well argue with it," Dirksen conceded. All the same, the resolution seemed a hostile measure against not only President Johnson but President Nixon too. Dirksen raised the question with Nixon at a meeting of the Republican Congressional leaders with the President at the White House, and Nixon stated that he disapproved the resolution. Dirksen advised Nixon not to take a public position against the resolution, for he could see little chance of defeating it. The resolution had been approved by the Foreign Relations Committee by almost a unanimous vote, and Dirksen calculated that if the measure were passed by the Senate, the less involvement by the President in the matter the better.

"I didn't want the White House to come into the picture in any manner," Dirksen explained privately. "I strictly forbade it: 'No intervention! No arm-twisting!' We'll just make the record."

Dirksen sensed that he could not defeat the Fulbright resolution in a straight confrontation, and so he maneuvered to offer a substitute that would draw from the original resolution its thrust and purpose. In drafting that substitute resolution, he did get help from the Nixon administration. Then he approached Senator Karl Mundt, a member of the Foreign Relations Committee, and asked Mundt to become the formal sponsor of this substitute. Mundt agreed. Dirksen wanted bipartisan sponsorship of his proposal, and so he approached Senator John Sparkman of Alabama, the ranking Democrat to Chairman Fulbright on the Foreign Relations Committee. Sparkman also agreed, but only on condition that Dirksen persuade John Sherman Cooper, a Republican senator deeply respected, to co-sponsor the substitute resolution. Dirksen calculated that Sparkman might be able to pull the other Southern Democratic senators away from Fulbright, but he ran into difficulty when he asked Cooper if he could see his way clear to joining the group of sponsors for the substitute resolution. Cooper, in fact, was not satisfied with the Fulbright resolution, but Fulbright kept Cooper from joining Dirksen by agreeing to accept Cooper's suggested amendment to the resolution. It was a complex intrigue, this private negotiation, and Dirksen saw his own stratagems collapse for want of Cooper's support. Without Cooper, he could not persuade Sparkman. Dirksen and a few of his conservative allies went through the forms of making Senate speeches against the Fulbright resolution, but by the time it came to a vote, he had no hope of defeating it. "Obviously," Dirksen said, "it can't bind the President's hand. The President is the sole conductor of our foreign relations." This defeat was something more than frustrating for Dirksen, because in a real sense that resolution implicitly criticized the position he himself had taken in total support of the Vietnam War.

In a different field, generated by a similar antiwar motivation as the national-commitments resolution, Dirksen found a different frustration. Week after week in this summer, the Senate debated President Nixon's plan to build a limited antiballistic-missile defense system within the United States. This plan the liberals of both political parties resolved to defeat if they could. Dirksen himself pretended to no technical competence in the military field, and he played but a small role in this struggle. Repeatedly he predicted that the Senate would approve the antiballistic-missile system (ABM) by what he called a "comfortable" margin, and as often he said that the President would offer no compromise on the measure. "I'm confident we'll win the battle," he said in June. Even earlier he had made his own firm commitment to the ABM's approval and volunteered to help where he could.

"Let me simplify it," he said. "I know what I think. I know what I believe. If I believe it hard enough, then I will go out and get a few converts to my cause. I am for ABM, period. If I can talk somebody else into it who has some voting power, that will be all right, too, because I will just ask them to share my convictions, period."

Dirksen, however, on this question had not done his homework, and he did not possess the sophisticated knowledge of the complex weapons system to allow him to make a persuasive argument in its favor. Moreover, the senators of his own party who were opposing the ABM were the very senators who had lost confidence in him, the young liberals and moderates who saw him now as something of a relic of a passing political era. He could not easily go to them. He therefore left the arguments to others. When the Senate finally voted on August 6, the ABM system was barely approved. The Senate voted 50 to 50 on the measure, and Vice-President Agnew broke the tie by voting for it. The Senate had approved the ABM, as Dirksen had predicted, but scarcely by a comfortable margin.

In another field of great political moment, Dirksen did play a major role. This came on President Nixon's reluctant decision to continue the ten-percent income-tax surcharge enacted a year before at President Johnson's request. Nixon decided that the surcharge had to be continued as an anti-inflationary measure, and the House of Representatives approved the extension as part of an omnibus tax-reform bill. By the time the House acted on that bill, the existing surcharge had already lapsed, and it was obvious that the Senate would take many months more to approve the full tax-reform bill. The Nixon administration resolved on a strategy of persuading the Senate to separate the tax surcharge from the omnibus bill and thus get swift approval of it. Dirksen tried to execute that strategy. "I'll take what I can get to get a surtax on the books," he said. In a Senate speech on July 15, Dirksen tried to persuade Senator Mansfield to interrupt the pending debate on the ABM to take up the tax surcharge. He recited a long list of economic and fiscal troubles that otherwise would confront the country and the government. "Delay could be dangerous," Dirksen said. Mansfield was not to be thus swayed. He had earlier met with other Democratic leaders of the Senate, and they had decided not to divide the tax surcharge from the omnibus tax-reform bill. In blunt terms, they feared that President Nixon might eventually veto that tax-reform bill, and they wanted to hold the tax surcharge as a hostage for his approval of the omnibus bill.

"Our thought," Mansfield responded to Dirksen's plea, "is we should stick with the bill until it is finished."

"Mr. President," Dirksen replied, addressing the presiding officer of the Senate, "I know the sound of the death knell when I hear it."

Dirksen had no doubt that on this issue Mansfield had clear command of the Senate. The tax surcharge itself was unpopular, and Mansfield was not acting alone. Mansfield saw himself as the agent of the Democratic Policy Committee. In private talks with Mansfield, Dirksen acknowledged Mansfield's control. "I can count votes," Dirksen said to him. After a fortnight of negotiation, the members of the Democratic Policy Committee relented somewhat;

they decided to extend the tax surcharge for three months, the time they expected it would take to approve the tax-reform bill. Mansfield met privately with Dirksen and told him that decision.

"Can you make it six?" Dirksen asked him, arguing that an extension for merely one quarter of the year would complicate the Treasury's problems in administering any such law.

"I can do my best," Mansfield said.

He returned to the Policy Committee, and the Democratic senators reluctantly agreed to a five-month extension for the tax surcharge. Again Dirksen argued with Mansfield, citing the "administrative difficulties" of such a provision. He wanted six months. While these negotiations were underway, President Nixon had left the country on a trip to the Far East, and Vice-President Agnew stepped in to take command of the administration's cause. Agnew had the support of Secretary of the Treasury David Kennedy, and they resolved to insist on the full twelve-month extension immediately. They both started lobbying the Republican senators to stand with the Nixon administration. Both were inexperienced in Senate maneuver and naïve about how the Senate worked, and out of their inexperience and naïveté they refused any talk of compromise. They regarded Dirksen's negotiations as merely an attempt to sabotage the Nixon administration, and Dirksen was angered by Agnew's clumsy intrusion into this struggle. "He was playing 'President' while Nixon was overseas," one Democrat said testily of Agnew. Mansfield was even harsher; he stated that Agnew and Secretary Kennedy did not even understand what the Senate Democrats were trying to do. "They thought we were going to kill the surtax at the end of the year," Mansfield said. On the contrary, the Democrats intended to give the Nixon administration part of the tax surcharge immediately and the rest of the year's extension as part of the tax-reform bill. Dirksen knew what neither Agnew nor Secretary Kennedy knew: Mansfield had the votes to win in the Senate on whatever decision the Democratic Policy Committee made. This was no time for ruffling the Democrats, by Dirksen's calculations, nor was it a time for taking belligerent and adamant public stances. "It is necessary," Dirksen explained, "if you can't get a whole loaf, sometimes to take half." He himself took a conciliatory position with Mansfield, and he talked Mansfield into trying to persuade the Democratic Policy Committee to approve a six-month extension, instead of five. Mansfield did persuade the committee Democrats to do that, using Dirksen's arguments, and Dirksen pledged his vote for that compromise. Mansfield knew how Agnew was undercutting Dirksen's efforts, and he had nothing but admiration for Dirksen. "He got as much as he could, the limit, which was six months," Mansfield said later of Dirksen, "and nobody else on that side of the aisle could have gotten it." Mansfield obviously wanted to accommodate Dirksen as much as he could, especially because Dirksen was under attack from Vice-President Agnew. Mansfield thought that no Vice-President had any business intruding on the Senate's decisions. "The Vice-President should not interfere in Senate affairs," Mansfield said privately. "He is not a member of the Senate."

Dirksen tried to persuade the administration people to accept the six-month extension, with the Democrats' implicit pledge to grant the remaining six-month extension later. For the administration, Agnew and Secretary Kennedy refused; they insisted that an effort had to be made to win the full year's extension. Dirksen also tried to persuade his fellow Republican senators to accept the compromise, but he found most of them hostile to the idea. Some of them wanted now openly to show their independence of Dirksen, and others among them were angry at what they regarded as Mansfield's ultimatum. When the question came to a vote in the Senate on July 31, the Nixon administration forced a vote on a twelve-month extension. The Senate rejected it, 41 to 59. Then the Senate approved the Mansfield-Dirksen compromise 51 to 48. Voting with Dirksen for that compromise were only five Republican senators.

Dirksen could take satisfaction in his victory, such as it was. Vice-President Agnew had been publicly rebuffed, but that was not his only embarrassment. He had offended many of the Republican

senators whom he had approached. The Republican senators were
particularly upset by Agnew's lobbying them in the Senate chamber. The annoyance was so general that Agnew apologized for his
behavior in a note that he asked to be read at the next meeting of
the Senate Republican Policy Committee. That did not suffice. One
Republican senator, Len Jordan of Idaho, announced to the Policy
Committee what he called "The Jordan Rule . . . that whenever I
am lobbied by the Vice-President to vote one way, I will automatically vote the opposite way, no matter what the issue." Thus
rebuked, Agnew abandoned the role he had tried to assume, that
of the administration's chief lobbyist in the Senate.

Whatever satisfaction Dirksen found in his victory, he had to be
distressed by the overall performance of this Congress. As the
leader of his party in the Senate, he had to feel disquiet at its
remarkably lethargic pace. He had his own responsibilities to meet.
To many of the Democratic proposals for legislation Dirksen was
indifferent, for they were measures that he would oppose. There
were other measures, however, whose failure to move through
Congress with dispatch caused him alarm. Earlier in the year the
House of Representatives and the Senate had agreed to take a
summer recess in mid-August, and by that time Congress had not
passed a single one of the regular appropriations bills for 1969.
This made operation of the federal establishment increasingly difficult; it left many government departments and agencies uncertain
on how to proceed with their responsibilities. Moreover, the President himself had not moved expeditiously either in offering his
own legislative program or in urging its enactment. At his regular
Tuesday news conference on August 12, just before the summer
recess, Dirksen broached the problem. "I have talked to the White
House," he said, "about setting up some priorities and in addition
a 'must' list." Congress had done nothing about mail rates and a
pay increase for postal employees, Dirksen said, and there were
other measures equally important. "The clock and the calendar
are already running out," he said. The tax-reform bill would take
many weeks of work; so would the appropriations bills. "You can't

walk out on a tax bill," he said. "You can't walk out on the appropriations. Other things you can handle next session, but these are absolute musts."

The news conference was like hundreds of others Dirksen had held. When the reporters finished asking questions, he stayed awhile, as he usually did, chatting amiably with them. One reporter introduced his two young daughters to Dirksen, and the senator shook their hands with great formality and deference. He volunteered to give each of the girls his autograph. Then he left the press gallery. Thus he ended this news conference, and this was the last news conference he ever held. It proved to be the end of his public life.

Earlier that afternoon Dirksen had addressed the Senate on behalf of an amendment he had offered that day to the legislation then pending, the emergency student-loan bill. The sponsoring Senate committee had added 275 million dollars to the requested authorization, and Dirksen proposed to delete that extra money. He argued that the committee's increase in the authorization for student loans breached the very appropriations ceiling that Congress had approved earlier in the year as a limit on that year's government spending. "Why, in the name of all that is good and holy," Dirksen argued, "should a committee of Congress, or of either body, undertake to up this matter and kick off the very ceiling that we imposed? If that is not a piece of hypocrisy, I have never seen it, but that's what this bill does." Dirksen argued to no avail, for the Senate rejected his amendment on a vote of 38 to 56. In considering this bill, the Senate operated on a unanimously agreed limitation of debate. At the conclusion of Dirksen's speech, a Senate colleague asked him to yield. Dirksen begged off. "My time has expired," he said. Ironically, those were the last words he ever spoke in Senate debate.

On the previous Saturday, August 9, Dirksen had gone to Walter Reed Army Hospital for a routine checkup. Although he appeared outwardly as well as he had ever been in these later years, he was having physical difficulties. He suffered from shortness of breath if he so much as walked a city block without resting. He was sleeping with two pillows, and every morning his ankles bothered him, swollen as they were with edema fluid. He could not rid himself of a chronic cough. The Army doctors gave Dirksen a full examination, in the course of which, on X-rays of the chest, they discovered a small shadow on the upper lobe of his right lung that they had not noticed before. The doctors immediately suspected cancer. The spot had not been there in similar X-rays taken in May and June. Dirksen himself feared the worst. Those closest to him noticed that he seemed somewhat agitated in his final day at the Senate. He had kept the cause of this to himself, confiding only to his wife. After his last appointment on Tuesday, August 12, which was with the Greek Ambassador, Dirksen took his secretary, Mrs. Gomien, aside and told her that he believed that he would have to undergo surgery on his lung.

On August 14, Dirksen returned to the hospital, and new X-rays showed that the tumor on his lung was growing rapidly. The very rapidity of the tumor's growth increased the doctors' suspicions of cancer, but in the absence of positive evidence they could not act on the assumption that the growth was malignant. The tumor was so located as to make physical examination of it impossible without surgery. The Army physicians, however, put Dirksen through a series of collateral tests, trying to identify the exact nature of the tumor. Among other tests, they examined his saliva and his throat culture, but none of these indicated whether the tumor was malignant or benign. Thus frustrated, they recommended surgery, but their hope was that the surgery might be relatively minor in nature. They saw no other acceptable alternative. They dared not risk treating the growth with massive doses of radiation, because, not knowing the exact nature of the tumor, that might cause more harm than good. They could not risk doing nothing. That risked not only excruciating pain for Dirksen, but also the possibility, if the growth were malignant, that the cancer would spread, quite possibly to the brain. The doctors knew, in recommending surgery, that Dirksen's health was good. His chances of surviving even major surgery were excellent. He had suffered a case of influenza in the spring, but otherwise he had been in relatively good health all year. What did worry the doctors was Dirksen's heart and its ability to sustain him in the postoperative period. As they had known for several years, his heart was dangerously large, double the normal size. For more than a decade he had been suffering chronic heart failure. His heart had not been pumping adequate blood through his system to sustain him at full strength. It was this chronic heart failure, by his doctors' diagnosis, rather than his emphysema, that had caused the Senator to speak in a somewhat breathless manner over these years. He had, as well, hardening of the arteries and a leaky heart valve, as well as a chronically irregular heart rhythm that made his heart less effective than it otherwise would have been. Complicating matters further was his continued negligence of his health. He smoked cigarettes excessively and he still worked himself to the point of exhaustion. This added extra burdens for his heart.

"His heart should have gone out years ago," one of his doctors said.

The doctors, however, recognized that there was more to Dirksen's physical makeup than a mechanistic diagnosis of his ailments would suggest. "He could stay up twenty-four hours," one of his doctors said. "He could do things I'm not sure I could do." Despite all his ailments, Dirksen had "the will to keep going," as the doctor put it. "That's the secret of his living as long as he did. I don't think Ev let his worries angry up his blood." Yet his carelessness with his own physical condition kept his doctors on edge.

"He scared me all the time," one of his doctors said. "You thought it was going to happen all the time, but his tremendous emotional drive kept him alive."

Dirksen accepted the doctors' recommendation for surgery, and although he was a little tense in the days before the operation, he accepted it with equanimity. Years before, when other doctors recommended the removal of one of his eyes, he had refused their advice. It was different now. Then he was enormously vigorous, scarcely past fifty years old, and he could not face blindness as his lot. Now his physical strength was largely spent. For years he had known that he had been living on borrowed time. "He had no choice but to get rid of this tumor," one of those closest to him said. "He couldn't face becoming an invalid and deteriorating. . . . He had a beautiful attitude. He wasn't feeling sorry for himself. He just committed himself to God's mercy."

Dirksen had long since become easy with the idea of death. In a way he had prepared himself for death, for he had, as he said, purged "the acids of anger from my soul." He had as well expunged from his mind, as he also said, the arrogance of personal vanity. Occasionally, with friends or associates, he discussed his own death, and he did so with no outward indications that he feared it. "Every individual thinks of the day of his own physical dissolution," he said in one such private talk, "and a very pointed philosophy has built up in me which is based on the admonition carried in the book of Matthew. There the Gospel points out that it's not your sins of commission, but your sins of omission that will be the basis of the final judgment. He says, 'Ye did it not.' You take that to heart a little. You hope you haven't overlooked too many things . . . when that day comes."

His colleagues were quite aware of his private views. "He's got no more political worlds to conquer," a senator said of him in 1965, as quoted by Ben Bagdikian in *The New York Times*. "He's felt the winds of mortality. I think he doesn't want to be remembered as the man who played politics while the world burned. He knows the big issues, and he's got his conscience working on them." The senator smiled. "Of course," he added, "he's a wise old rat, and he can still take you through a lot of back alleys before you find yourself where his conscience wants you."

Through Dirksen's speeches in his later years, the idea of death was a recurring theme: "One of my age thinks about his destiny a little. . . ." In a way, he was beguiled by death and the idea of death, and for years the theme of death flowed through his jokes and anecdotes. "People like me don't fade away," he once said. "We just drop dead." He had a favorite story to tell whenever he was extravagantly introduced to an audience. It reminded him, he said in one such use of this story, of a widow in a church pew listening to the preacher eulogize her late husband. The preacher said he "was being gathered up into the bosom of Abraham," Dirksen said. "That was a courteous way of saying he died. After five minutes of such testimony, the widow turned to her young son sitting next to her and said, 'Johnny, go up and look in the casket and see if that is your pa.' " In his later years, when asked how he was feeling, Dirksen sometimes replied with what he called his "McGinnis story." An Irishman by the name of McGinnis, so went the story, asked his friends not to take him to the funeral parlor and put him in a box when he died. Instead, he wanted them to hire the biggest black limousine they could find, prop his body up in the back seat, and drive him around the old neighborhood. When he died, that is what his friends did, and as the limousine drove by, one of his old friends standing on the street corner nudged another friend. "That's livin', ain't it?" he said. Dirksen seemed to take an almost morbid delight in such stories. His long ill health had frequently touched him with intimations of his own mortality. He had, as he described it, his own favorite epitaph: "Here lies Peter Bacon, born a man and died a grocer." He found it amusing, yet beneath the dry humor he found in death, he held a calm and confident faith in an afterlife, a willingness to accept his lot, whatever it was, with undoubted courage. Occasionally this would creep into his speeches, as when, in 1963, he quoted Shakespeare's *Hamlet*: "There's a destiny that shapes our ends, rough-hew them how we will." In his later years he was not a regular churchgoer, but on his desk in his Capitol office when he left it for the last time there was a bronze tablet engraved with these words: "O, God, thy sea is so great and my boat is so small." Dirksen liked that prayer for itself and because it had been a favorite of President Kennedy.

On Sunday, August 31, Dirksen entered Walter Reed Hospital to prepare for the operation two days later. He had spent the time since the beginning of the Congressional summer recess at his home outside Leesburg. He had planned to visit his daughter, Joy, her husband, Senator Baker, and his grandchildren at their home in Tennessee, but this trip he had canceled, excusing himself on the grounds that he had to undergo some tests at the hospital. He was not more specific because he did not wish to cause them unnecessary alarm. In the interval, and between trips to the hospital, Dirksen busied himself with a variety of chores. He prepared some outlines for speeches he wanted to make, and he also drafted a preliminary summary of the accomplishments of the first session of the Ninety-first Congress. More importantly to him, he finished a memoir he had been writing about his own early years. He had made an abortive attempt to interest a publisher in the project the previous summer with an outline of what he planned to write. After the 1968 session of Congress and his own reelection to the Senate, he had taken on the writing of his memoir in earnest, dictating a rough first draft of the manuscript at his vacation home in Florida. Then, at odd moments during 1969, he had polished and refined that draft, usually dictating his revisions to one of his stenographers. He had named the book *So You Want to Be a Senator*, and in informal style it dealt with his life up to the point he himself had become a senator in 1951. One of his purposes in writing the memoir was to encourage young people to take an interest in entering politics as a profession. He finished his revision of the work on August 29, two days before he entered the hospital.

Mrs. Dirksen telephoned her daughter, Joy, in Tennessee on Friday to tell her that her father was entering the hospital that following Sunday and that there was a possibility of surgery. The Bakers flew to Washington Saturday night and went to visit Dirksen at the hospital Sunday afternoon. First Dirksen's doctors briefed them on the plan for the operation. Then, with Mrs. Dirksen, they visited Dirksen in his hospital room. They found him sitting on the edge of his bed, smoking a cigarette, and drinking Jack Daniels bourbon and soda out of a paper cup. Senator Baker thought Dirksen seemed "a little overbusy and animated." Dirksen had no desire to talk about his coming operation, and it was not discussed. The decision had been made, and Dirksen seemed to take the view that there was nothing further to be said about it. They chatted therefore about odds and ends. Dirksen handed Baker two scribbled corrections on his memoir and asked him to get them to Mrs. Gomien, his secretary. One restructured a paragraph in the book; the other asked Mrs. Gomien to check the accuracy of a quotation he had used in the manuscript. The Bakers and Mrs. Dirksen left, almost casually, when a nurse arrived to give Dirksen a sedative.

The next day Dirksen underwent treatment to draw off more of the edema fluids that had built up in his system, reducing his weight of 196 pounds thereby by eight pounds. President Nixon telephoned Dirksen to wish him well. On Tuesday morning, at 8:45, the operation began. It was performed by Colonel Alan R. Hopeman and a team of Army surgeons. The spot on Dirksen's lung was so located that it could not be readily examined without surgery, but in surgical terms it was in an almost ideal position, close to the periphery of his chest, so that the surgeons could cut cleanly and neatly into his chest and remove it with only a small incision. This they did without difficulty, removing the tumor, which by then had grown to almost an inch in diameter. The tumor was instantly frozen and examined under a microscope, and the doctors found what they feared, cancer cells. Then, as they had previously planned in such an eventuality, they proceeded to remove the entire upper lobe of his right lung. The operation had thus become major surgery, not the relatively simple operation they had planned if the tumor had proved benign. In all, the operation took a little over three hours. The doctors found no evidence that the cancer had spread.

In the days after the operation, Dirksen recuperated even more swiftly than his doctors had hoped. On Wednesday, when they were first able to visit him, Mrs. Dirksen and Senator Baker found

Dirksen "real alert," as Baker phrased it. Dirksen was obviously in pain and great discomfort. He had a tube running down his nose into his lung, a Bird respirator, to help his breathing, and he was wired in a half-dozen ways to keep a constant check on his temperature, pulse, heartbeat, urine output, blood pressure, and breathing rate. "We carried on a brief conversation, with him nodding," Baker said. His breathing improved enough that day that he no longer needed the assistance of the respirator, and the nose tube was removed. His doctors feared that he might develop pneumonia, which would be dangerous to his safety. His recovery seemed so rapid, however, that his doctors estimated that he would be able to leave the hospital in about six weeks. His voice had begun to return to normal.

On Thursday, Dirksen suffered severe confusion and restlessness, the cause of which was uncertain but which could have been the result of a minor stroke, an insufficiency of oxygen, or even withdrawal symptoms from liquor and cigarettes. He had used both as stimulants for many years. The next day, Friday, his mental status had improved and he was more himself. He was moved from the intensive care room to his own private room. One thing he wanted that he could not have was a cigarette. "They've taken my cigarettes away," he protested to one of his doctors. He tried to get a cigarette from his son-in-law when he visited him, but Baker, who had recently quit smoking, did not have one. Even with a major segment of his lung removed and despite the pain he suffered in breathing, Dirksen would not quit smoking if he could help it. Baker asked him how he felt. Dirksen was in obvious pain, which not even the heavy sedation completely blunted, but he looked at Baker with a glint of mischievousness. "Well," he said, "altogether, not very well."

That night, Dirksen underwent a new crisis. At 3:30 in the early morning, he suddenly became extremely agitated and without warning he wrenched out of his chest the tube that the doctors had inserted to drain the cavity of his removed lung. "It was a bad situation," one of his doctors said. The right lung collapsed. Army doctors took immediate action. Under local anesthesia, they redrained his chest and replaced the tube. For hours they worked on him, putting him under heavy sedation and replacing the respirator to help his breathing. Not until 8 o'clock Saturday morning did they have him back to a stable condition. X-rays showed that the doctors had successfully cleared his respiratory system. His whole body, however, had suffered a major shock, and this episode probably caused the bronchopneumonia which shortly developed.

Despite this ordeal, Dirksen by Saturday afternoon was able to sit up in bed to eat his meals. He began demanding that he be allowed to get up. He had recovered sufficiently to want to go to the bathroom on his own and thus avoid the indignity and humiliation of performing such natural functions in his bed. "He looked great," Baker said.

He spent a good night, needing only one dose of demerol to relieve the pain. Sunday morning, September 7, his condition remained stable, and he ate a good breakfast. He appeared to be past the immediate crisis of a postoperation heart failure. His doctors were more than pleased with his recovery, and, assured by them, Baker felt free to proceed with a planned trip to California, where he was to join President Nixon. Dirksen ate a good lunch at noon, and when his doctors visited him about 2 o'clock that afternoon, his spirits were up and he seemed fine. He was still under constant medical surveillance.

Abruptly, at 2:51 that afternoon, Dirksen turned suddenly pale and then collapsed. He stopped breathing, and his pulse all but disappeared.

"His heart stopped," one of his doctors said, snapping his fingers, "just like that."

Army doctors were at his side in a moment, and they immediately began massaging his chest, trying to restart his heart. They gave him sodium bicarbonate, calcium, and other medicinals. Repeatedly they applied electric shocks with a defibrillator to try to stimulate his heart into action. The doctors worked with desperation to revive him, massaging his chest so rigorously that they cracked five of his ribs, a minor matter in this emergency. Dirksen did not respond. The electrocardiograph showed no heart beat at all. The pupils of his eyes became fixed. Only then, at 4:52, did the doctors pronounce him dead. Dirksen's wife and daughter had been summoned, and they were with him at the end.

Word of Dirksen's death was flashed to the nation. The television networks interrupted their afternoon programs to announce that he had died, and that evening he received the ultimate accolade of contemporary America: the television networks carried special programs about Dirksen, a form of obituary of his life. The nation's newspapers headlined his death on page one, and many carried extensive stories recapitulating his remarkable political career. At the time he died, his political power had been fading, eroded in many ways, and he was beset with difficulties from many quarters, but still he died at the height of his national fame and in the full throes of his political career. The realities of his lessened political influence had not yet tarnished his national image as a politician of immense importance. His death was treated as a national event.

Despite Dirksen's age and his many ailments, his sudden death took even his colleagues in the Senate by surprise. "Those of us who knew him," said Senator James Pearson of Kansas, "knew that he was wired together, that he had a bad heart, a bad stomach, and that he didn't take care of himself. Yet I was shocked. We'd built a sort of myth about him, almost a cliché among us: he'll get up again; he always has."

On September 8 Senator Mansfield formally announced Dirksen's death to the Senate. "In the first shock of his passing," Mansfield said, "the words do not come. It is too soon. The void has opened too suddenly. The emptiness is too complete. It is possible, now, only to sense the loss, to sense in it the profound sorrow which his death brings to us."

In death, Dirksen was honored as only three senators before him had been. Under the great dome of the Capitol, on the same black catafalque that here had once borne the body of Abraham Lincoln,

Dirksen's body lay in state. "He was a big enough man for it," Mansfield said. His casket was sheathed in a blanket of scarlet roses, and atop the casket lay the seal of the United States Senate. The coffin was borne into the Rotunda and placed upon the catafalque by an honor guard of military pallbearers shortly after noon, Tuesday, September 9. Gathered to honor him there were the ranking members of the federal government: the President and Vice-President, the members of the Senate and the House of Representatives, the President's cabinet, the Chief Justice, the Joint Chiefs of Staff, and the diplomatic corps.

President Nixon spoke his eulogy:

Everett Dirksen was a politician in the finest sense of that much-abused word. If he were here, I think, he might put it this way: A politician knows that more important than the bill that is proposed is the law that is passed. A politician knows that his friends are not always his allies and that his adversaries are not his enemies. A politician knows how to make the process of democracy work, and loves the intricate workings of the democratic system. A politician knows not only how to count votes but how to make his vote count. A politician knows that his words are his weapons, but that his word is his bond. A politician knows that only if he leaves room for discussion and room for concession can he gain room for maneuver. A politician knows that the best way to be a winner is to make the other side feel it does not have to be a loser. A politician knows both the name of the game and the rules of the game, and he seeks his ends through the time-honored democratic means.

By being that kind of politician, this man of the minority earned the respect and affection of the majority, and by the special way he gave leadership to legislation, he added grace, elegance, and court-liness to the word "politican." That is how he became the leader of the minority, one of the leaders of our nation. That is why, when the Senate worked its way, Everett Dirksen so often worked his way. That is why, while he never became President, his impact and influence on the nation was greater than that of most Presidents in our history. . . .

As he could persuade, he could be persuaded. His respect for other points of view lent weight to his own point of view. He was not afraid to change his position if he were persuaded that he had been wrong. That tolerance and sympathy were elements of his character; and that character gained him the affection and esteem of millions of his fellow Americans.

We shall always remember Everett Dirksen in the terms he used to describe his beloved marigolds: hardy, vivid, exuberant, colorful, and uniquely American.

Senator Baker responded on behalf of the Dirksen family. He described his father-in-law as "a man of imposing presence and bearing . . . a man of eminent wit, humor, and perspective, who kept himself and others constantly on guard against taking themselves too seriously."

"He was an idealist," Baker said, "but he was a realist as well, and in the end he chose calmly to risk his life, electing uncertain surgery in order to gain the opportunity to live and serve further; and he lost. But in losing he fixed with permanence the image of a noble man of the people."

Dirksen's body lay in state for twenty-four hours. On his desk in the Senate chamber, to mark his passing, Senator Margaret Chase Smith placed a single marigold.

On Wednesday, Dirksen's body was carried to the National Presbyterian Church for a formal funeral service, conducted by the Senate's chaplain, the Reverend Edward Elson. President Nixon, Vice-President Agnew, and many of Dirksen's associates in the Senate and House of Representatives attended this service, as well as many of Dirksen's other long-time friends. The only person invited to the funeral service who did not attend was Lyndon Johnson, and his absence surprised those who knew how close he and Dirksen had been. After receiving the invitation, Johnson asked how he would travel from Texas to Washington, and President Nixon offered him the use of *Air Force 1*, the President's personal airplane. Then Johnson inquired, through an aide, where he would sit at the church. He was informed that he would sit next to President Nixon. Only after making these inquiries did Johnson decline the invitation. He did, however, send a warm letter of condolence to Mrs. Dirksen.

The next morning, Thursday, September 11, aboard *Air Force 1*, Dirksen's body and the funeral party were flown to Pekin, Illinois, Dirksen's home, and there, in a simple ceremony, he was buried. Chaplain Elson spoke briefly at the grave.

"The last march has ended," Elson said. "A mighty man of God has answered his last roll call. His battles are all fought. His victories are all won."

An honor guard fired three volleys in salute, and then a solitary bugler sounded taps.

# Index